Praise for Andrew Dornenburg and Karen Page's

Becoming a Chef

One of the best books ever written about the back-of-the-house side of the
restaurant business . . . Entertaining and enlightening . . . A must-read.

Restaurant Hospitality

Check out *Becoming a Chef* for a thorough
(read: celebrity) chef.

Time Out: New York

Its insight into the philosophy of chefdom t

ALISON ARNETT, The Boston Globe

Quite possibly the only book of its kind . . .
successful chefs got their start.

LOIS BLINKHORN, The Milwaukee Journal Sen

One of the most unique and engrossing bo

JOAN BRETT, The Minneapolis Star Tribune

Offers excellent advice and wisdom.

JEANMARIE BROWNSON, The Chicago Tribu

A serious, unromantic look at the restaurar
of success and early failure are often as fu
and informative.

ROD COCKSHUTT, The Raleigh News & Obse

Illuminating.

There aren't enough superlatives to describe *Becoming a Chef* . . . This book
is a treasure.

Filled with dishy details about the highs—and woes—of a business most of us see only
from tableside.

One of the top three food-related books of the year . . . . This fascinating book paints
an up-close, behind-the-scenes picture of the world of food.

Fascinating . . . Reveals the inner workings of stellar restaurant kitchens and the
culinary talents who do their creating there.

This insightful book has all the right ingredients.

Superb . . . A book rich with anecdote, insight and passion . . . In all, a completely
absorbing book.

Fascinating . . . Readers of *Becoming a Chef* are left with a genuinely rich impression
of the serious chef's intention.

becoming a **Chef**

REVISED

becoming a **Chef**

REVISED

Andrew Dornenburg and Karen Page

FOREWORD BY Madeleine Kamman

PHOTOGRAPHS BY Michael Donnelly

WILEY

JOHN WILEY & SONS, INC.

Authors' Note

Although this book is the result of a complete collaboration between the two authors, it is written in the first person singular voice of Andrew Dornenburg, so as to spare the reader confusion of identities.—A.D. & K.P.

This book is printed on acid-free paper. ♾

Copyright © 2003 by Andrew Dornenburg and Karen Page. All rights reserved.

Published by John Wiley & Sons, Inc., Hoboken, New Jersey

Published simultaneously in Canada

For general information on our other products and services or for technical support, please contact our Customer Care Department within the United States at (800) 762-2974, outside the United States at (317) 572-3993 or fax (317) 572-4002.

Wiley also publishes its books in a variety of electronic formats. Some content that appears in print may not be available in electronic books. For more information about Wiley products, visit our web site at www.wiley.com.

Library of Congress Cataloging-in-Publication Data

Dornenburg, Andrew.

Becoming a chef / Andrew Dornenburg, Karen Page.—Rev.

p. cm.

ISBN 0-471-15209-9 (Cloth)

1. Food service—Vocational guidance—United States.

2. Cookery—Vocational guidance—United States.

3. Cooks—Training of—United States. I. Page, Karen. II. Title.

TX911.3.V62D67 2003

641.5'023'73—dc21

2003007732

Printed in the United States of America

10 9 8 7 6 5 4 3 2 1

Design by Vertigo Design, NYC

www.vertigodesignnyc.com

Dedication

To all those who make their living working with food who do so with a spirit of professionalism, pride, and passion

K.P.

and especially

To Chris Schlesinger, who has been both a role model and a mentor to me and whose spirit of cooking continues to inspire me, and to Cary Wheaton, who originally hired me into the East Coast Grill;

To Lydia Shire and Susan Regis, who managed to convince me that putting my arm in a 600-degree tandoori oven was a good idea, for their liveliness and generosity;

To Anne Rosenzweig, who was a tireless teacher, whether at the restaurant or at special events where I had the privilege of assisting her;

To Madeleine Kamman, for being the guiding light and inspiration that she is to me and to countless other American cooks and chefs; and

To Bobby Delbove, Paul O'Connell, Paula Danilowicz, Rebecca Charles, and Tony Bonner—my sous chefs over the years—who were responsible for a lot of my on-the-job learning and are surely the leading chefs of tomorrow

A.D.

Contents

List of Recipes

The authors requested of every chef interviewed for *Becoming a Chef* a recipe which held special meaning to his or her development as a chef. The recipes contributed range from old family recipes to original creations of which the chefs are most proud, and their special meanings typically underscore some aspect of the subject of the particular chapter. As much as possible, the recipes remain as the chefs intended them, with minimal editing of abbreviations, terminology, length, or other aspects of style. This provides further illustration of the personality and unique "point of view" of each individual chef.

Acknowledgments

We never could have written this book without the generous help of many people. First and foremost, it is impossible to express our deep gratitude to the chefs we interviewed, who were overwhelmingly generous in sharing with us their time—which we know all too well is their most precious commodity—as well as their insights, their advice, their recipes and, quite often, their hospitality, their food, and even their homes. The experience of getting to know them is one we will cherish all our lives.

Nor can we thank Madeleine Kamman enough: for making the time to review and critique (ouch!) our original manuscript and staying up all night in order to do so, for making suggestions of ways to improve it, for contributing her beautiful Foreword and, most of all, for her friendship. (We love you, Madeleine!) Our sincere thanks, too, to Mark Miller and Jimmy Schmidt for reviewing our manuscript and offering specific comments and encouragement, and to Mark for praising it so loudly to the food press that it made our phone ring!

We'd like to thank those at Van Nostrand Reinhold and John Wiley & Sons who shared our passion for seeing this book and its second edition come to life. *Becoming a Chef* was blessed with three godmothers, each of whom ably adopted this book as her own: from acquiring editor Pam Chirls to Caroline Schleifer to Melissa Rosati. To Pam, we owe our eternal gratitude for recognizing the need for this book and giving us—two first-time authors—the opportunity to write it. Our thanks to the rest of the VNR team, especially Paul Costello, Louise Kurtz, Jackie Martin, Amy Shipper, Mike Suh, Veronica Welsh, Linda Wetmore, and Craig Wolynez, and to the team at Wiley: Andrea Johnson and Edwin Kuo. Thanks, too, to James Peterson, Gary Holleman, and others who took time to read and critique various drafts of our original manuscript, and to this edition's copy editor, Virginia McRae. Our gratitude to the talented folks at Vertigo Design (especially Alison Lew and Renata De Oliveira) for giving this edition a fresh, contemporary look.

Thanks to Kitchen Arts & Letters for existing, and to Nach Waxman for doing what he does so well—the bookstore was an invaluable resource for gathering information. Our thanks to Chris Hussey, Sumi Luth, and others who shared with us their experiences abroad as stagiaires, and to Rori Spinelli, for her comments as a former chef.

Special thanks are due to our very talented and dear friends, photographers Michael Donnelly, whose photographs for this revised edition breathed new elegance into the book, and to Jamie Columbus, whose beautiful photographs adorned the pages of the first edition.

We join Mike in thanking the following establishments in New York City for allowing him to photograph there: Alain Ducasse, Amy's Bread, Artisanal, Babbo, Blue Hill, Etats-Unis, Hampton Chutney, Inside, Institute of Culinary Education, Jean Georges, Kitchen Arts & Letters, Ouest, Patio Dining, Pearl Oyster Bar, and San Domenico, as well as Matt Baumgardener and Heather Evans, and Lisa Wood and George Richardson, for opening their homes to us.

Other friends were supportive in ways too numerous to detail, but we'd like to give special thanks to Cynthia Penney, an exceptional writer who was an invaluable sounding board, and Cynthia Gushue and Leo Russell, for their 1993 loan of a computer at a critical time. Andrew would like to thank chefs Ed Brown and Jamie Bergin for all he's learned from them. Karen would like to thank those people who played an important role in developing her own love for food, including her family, with whom she has enjoyed many wonderful food memories (from Yates apple cider to White Castle hamburgers!); the late Eleanor Van Alstyne, whose enormous backyard garden was a child's paradise; Larry Popelka, who introduced her to Chicago's food scene; and Tracy McDonald, with whom she first explored Manhattan's. She also thanks her National Endowment for the Humanities research subjects (especially Susan Davis) as well as her former career and admissions advisory clients over the years, from whose candid stories she developed an ear for the rhythm of chronicling others' careers and lives.

We'd like to thank all our friends and family members who offered their encouragement, who never tired of asking, "How's the book coming?" (even after we'd long tired of answering), and who stood by with patience and understanding while we traveled or secluded ourselves, weekend after weekend, in order to research and write it. It's done! We've missed you, and we can't wait to see you again.

And, finally, we'd like to thank each other again, for persevering through the many challenging moments of this collaboration. Then again, our nearly eighteen-year relationship has survived other tough challenges: after eating our way through Quebec City and Montreal, we both ran the Montreal International Marathon on the last day of our honeymoon in 1990. Here's to crossing yet another finish line together!

Andrew Dornenburg and Karen Page

Foreword

On June 9th of 1940, my mother and I took the last train leaving Paris for the Loire Valley before the Germans invaded our native city of Paris. It took us two full days to reach the small market town of Château La Vallière where we were to find refuge in the home of my great-aunt Claire. Claire was the owner-chef of her small Michelin-starred hotel and restaurant.

Exhausted as a nine-year-old would be after forty-eight hours of travel to cover only 170 miles, I was not too aware of much as I entered the hotel, except that the house was extremely busy, that there were many people in the dining room, and that something smelled so good that my stomach positively started to convulse. Having been recognized as a possible casualty of my own hunger, I received a plate of sweetbreads in Madeira cream sauce; I nearly swooned over it, it was so good. . . . My double career as an inveterate eater and cook had started. We are now in 1995, it is still lasting, and probably will last in one way or another until I finally bow out of this world.

In between the many vacations spent working in the kitchen and serving in the dining room of my aunt or washing thousands of plates in her scullery, I acquired the strenuous education given to all French children by the government of their Republic. I relished learning several modern languages and Latin. I delved into French, English, and German literatures, geography, world history, and geology with glee; tolerated mathematics; loved chemistry, biology, and botany. It was hard work, with many nights spent studying long, unreasonable hours, but it was well worth it, for much later, when I finally became a chef and restaurateur, I realized how much I was using all the culture acquired on the school benches.

I met Alan, my Philadelphia-born husband, in Paris while I was directing the reservation office of Swissair and he was conducting a tour of American engineers across Europe. We worked together for a very short time and liked each other so much that, four months later, we married. Marriage between two persons of different nationalities is always interesting and at the same time difficult, for each must get accustomed to very different traditions. After the birth of my first son, I had such a strong bout of homesickness that I countered it by immediately looking for something to keep my brain occupied with a challenge. Since America speaks mostly English, there was no question for me to use my knowledge of foreign languages, so I started to cook for fun. Of course, cooking meant my native French cooking and the challenge consisted in making French food taste really French with the American ingredients of the early sixties. There was not a shallot in sight, not a leek. Fresh herbs were not to be found anywhere except in a few gardens

well surrounded by high fences; herbs came only dried in small glass jars; the bread was English-style white bread, mushy and pasty to my teeth used to the crunch of French baguettes. Ah . . . what to do? Simply show people that nothing is impossible to the adventurous. Having received a catalog of the adult education classes offered at the Greater Philadelphia Cheltenham High School, I reached for the telephone and asked the director of the school whether, per chance, she could use a French cooking teacher. I passed her test of proficiency, which consisted of cooking a serious, professional-style meal for her, and I started teaching classes in the basics of French cuisine at night, after enjoying raising my children during the day.

The classes were so popular that besides teaching at the Adult School, I started also giving classes in my own kitchen. My second son, born in between, complied with my timetable by sleeping just long enough for the lessons to be over and then have his little French lunch. He loved, it too: Mommy's nice meat mashed with fresh potatoes and a dab of sauce mixed in pleased him much more than the cans of Gerber baby food.

When I started writing my first cookbook, I gave him three percolators of three different sizes all jumbled up, and one hour later, after I had peacefully written a few pages, he had reconstructed all three percolators and we celebrated with Oreos and milk. With time forging ahead, both boys went to full-time school and we moved to Boston, where it all happened.

Boston in 1969 was still a very colonial American city. But there was also wonderful, intellectual Cambridge on the other side of the Charles, with its universities and their wonderful collections of food chemistry books. I decided to start investigating food chemistry after several of my students repeatedly asked me why I chose to execute a dish with one technique rather than another. At first I answered as plainly as I could, thinking the answer out myself, but soon I realized that there was something more behind my explanations.

In 1971 I took the school out of my house to make it a legitimate business. With it came all the worries of legitimate businesses: advertising properly, coping with the ever-increasing number of students, insuring the business, paying taxes, training assistants and teachers, etc. . . . It was the training of the assistants which revealed the crux of the true problem: My school was a drop in the bucket of the enormous amount of education that was needed to bring the United States into a league able to compete with Europe and its wonderful technical schools for cooking and restaurant procedures. Boston at the time had no really modern professional program, so I decided to offer one. It took me three years to have it run as smoothly as I wished and I shall be forever grateful to Dr. Rachel K. Winer of the Massachusetts Board of Education for her guidance through this very important project.

A year after the opening of the professional program, some rather interesting circumstances brought on the opening of our restaurant, which I called Chez La Mère Madeleine, but which everyone called Modern Gourmet, which was the name of the school. Two years after the opening of the restaurant, the Mobil guide gave us a four-star rating, and three years after the opening, Anthony Spinazzola, then restaurant reviewer for *The Boston Globe,* gave us a five-star rating. Using all the knowledge I had brought from France, long hours of studying and reading American technical texts, the latest French culinary publications, and cookery books from all over the world, I had become, with Alice Waters (of Chez Panisse) and Leslie Revsin (of Restaurant Leslie and later the Waldorf-Astoria), one of the first three "visible" women chefs in the United States.

The dictionary defines the substantive chef as "a cook, especially the chief cook of a large kitchen staff." The word came from the Latin *caput,* meaning the head and by derivation, the chief of any social, military, or political body. In old French, the "chef" meant the physical head; the medieval French word for kitchen chef was *queux,* which is related to the English cook; chef had slowly acquired its meaning of kitchen chef by the end of the seventeenth century.

Up until the last two decades, the title of chef applied only to the highly visible and widely recognized men whose names you will find in the historical review starting on page 8. But there were also other chefs, called *cuisinières,* accomplished and often very distinguished women, whose great talents remained, up to the 1930s, hidden in large, upper-class, forever entertaining households. One purposely never spoke of one's cuisinière for fear of losing her to a wealthier house. Claire had started her career as one of those cuisinières. Modern times, with the arrival of the automobile and the development of popular tourism, have changed all that, as the cuisinières slowly acquired small restaurants of their own. Even if the progress is not as fast as one would wish it, chefs now come in the masculine and the feminine, all working under the pressures of producing elegant fare for an ever more demanding public. It has become so prestigious an occupation to be a chef—a welcome change that is due mostly to the large amount of public relations work done by French chef Paul Bocuse in the 1960s and 1970s—that by now the title tends to be given to untrained home cooks or backyard barbecuers who, although lovely cooks, have not undergone the grueling baptism by fire true chefs receive.

Andrew and Karen have written this interesting book on how to become one of those men or women whose profession it is or has been to prepare and serve large numbers of meals per day to larger numbers of people. Their book is interesting because it brings you into personal contact with many younger women and men who, in our days of stringent labor laws and often less-than-understanding investors, have worked to bring their restaurants to national notoriety, with often nothing more than tiny assets and an inspired and dedicated skeleton crew. Their words will reveal the passion and knowledge that is required to be a chef. More than one of the chefs you will read about will give you the impression that he or she "fell into the work"; indeed quite a few did, but any one of them will tell you that their profession is their passion in spite of the many dilemmas and choices it brings into their lives.

This book is also about some of these choices. The first choice is usually made between schooling or apprenticeship. Each of them, as you will see, presents advantages and disadvantages. A school puts a seal of approval on a graduate, but so does a good master. After teaching two generations of American chefs, both in the classroom and at the stove, I remain a great advocate of the European system, which combines schooling in the daytime and restaurant work at night, for it is a fitting and demanding preparation to practice a profession, which I believe to be the most demanding existing.

Whichever way you choose to become a chef, be sure that it spells enrichment for that sort of "holy trinity" that is the foundation of your future profession: your mind, your heart, and your hands. Challenges will come to you daily at such speed that, more than once, you will feel like throwing your hands up in the air and your apron in the hamper, and want to yell: "Enough is enough, I quit!" . . . while in the back of your mind, that lovely voice will say, "Oh no, you don't, you know you can do it, don't quit." This will be the moment to stop right then and there for one minute, void your mind altogether, take a deep breath, and simply continue working. This will be the time when you realize that your chef, the woman or man you entrusted with a phase of your professional development, is caught in the same dilemma as you. For your chef there is not only you; there are also your colleagues who make their own mistakes, there is that bottom line at the end of the month and the end-of-the-year statement to greet the New Year and there are growing family responsibilities, so important and to which it feels like one can never devote all the time one would like to.

Aim high in your choices of masters and of restaurants in which to train. Be persistent, until you find the master who can teach you nothing but the best, whether she or he has the reputation of being mean. What will count in the long run is what you will learn. In my many years of helping young people find the right corner in the best possible kitchens, I have had some striking successes and a few disappointments, the latter coming in 99 percent of the cases from a lack of maturity and patience on the part of the student/apprentice. It takes a nice and long number of years to become a full-fledged chef, one who has the vision and the sensitivity not only of an artist but also of a great businessperson.

Prepare yourself for following orders for a number of years. Oh, I know, you are in a great hurry to acquire your own restaurant and to be your own master. Well . . . slow down, take your time, and think about it for a while. A restaurant, any restaurant, is not to be started on half the amount of knowledge needed, especially in the modern economic climate, and yet another choice is facing you.

Will you start your own very small restaurant, very humbly and gradually building your business and improving your house year after year all the while you are honing your business acumen? Or will you precipitate yourself into a partnership or even end up on "sweat equity," while an entrepreneur puts up financing for you? Reflect and think hard before you make any decision, for momentous consequences can result from being overenthusiastic. Whereas sweat equity may work out very well, it may also bring on frustration, lack of creative personal freedom, and resentment between business partners, especially if a reviewer visits your dining room precisely on the night you were sent out to the antipodes to "do an event."

Remember always, it is your choice; you can concentrate on becoming the absolute master of your work, let your plates speak for themselves and display your work at its best, or you can let your sponsor put his publicity agent to work. It depends entirely on what you want most: the inner certitude that your work reflects you fully or a quicker success and better income faster.

Either way, you will know that you have achieved something special when copies of your work start appearing here and there on colleagues' tables, and when minor food writers paraphrase and imitate your culinary conceptions. Remain unflapped and peaceful, for what you created can only be brought from concept to reality by yourself; imitations will remain imitations, which brings to mind the concept of competition. I cannot remember the number of times I asked by newspaper reporters who my competition was. From the start, set your mind to the fact that success evolves from having only one competition: yourself and your will to become always better. Unless this principle becomes a religion to you, you will be heading for troubles, for worrying about what the others do is a loss of time, energy, and concentration. Be "an athlete of the plate"; give your best performance at all times. Know yourself, be yourself, and give of yourself; this principle is the only road to total success.

Brace yourself for the day when a review of your work will appear in a newspaper. Think of it this way: Since we all have to eat, we are all food experts. That includes, of course, the reviewer who, unlike you, did not necessarily spend years studying the techniques of the masters, reading *Gray's Anatomy* at 3 A.M. to understand the structure of meats, nor poring over food history and food chemistry books. A reviewer is just another human being who has to eat, and consequently is a food expert, and will remain forever incapable of perceiving tastes and textures exactly the same way you or any of your sous chefs or cooks ever will. So, forget all about reviewers, taste your food productions carefully, and watch your plates both as they go out to the dining room and when they come back from it, for if they are not "licked clean" and empty, beware . . . something may not be right.

And then, as you work like a Roman (a euphemism for the probably more accurate "slave"), you will have to try to keep in good physical shape if you want to be able to pursue your passion for food preparation until you reach the pinnacle of your career. It will mean eating and drinking wisely, sleeping enough, exercising a bit each and every day (or at least every second day), and learning to leave all work irritations at the kitchen door so that your time at home with family is a relaxing one.

Also have another passion. Travel as much as you can, ride a bike, run, climb mountains, swim, read mysteries or history, collect old porcelains or whatever, make wine or beer, be a Buddhist or a philosopher, but do something that will replenish your font of creativity, for since you will be giving a lot of yourself to many, it is essential that you never forget to give your soul a little nourishment. If you do not, you will slowly become overtired and put yourself in danger of becoming less efficient and creative.

Go ahead, enjoy your kitchen career and do not ever suffer those prophets of doom who will try to tell you that after all, if you become a chef, you will be practicing "just another craft." If you learn well, practice, and persevere, you will live to become a true culinary artist whose plates will be models of good taste, in both senses of the term, for a new generation of cooks. I can guarantee you that you will acquire the most amazing sense of humor and become a social success, if only for all the stories that you will have to tell at dinner parties. If I ever meet you, just ask me for the story of the gentleman who spread his butter on my tablecloth because he did not like the size of my porcelain plate; we shall have a good giggle together. Good-bye. Meet you in your restaurant.

Madeleine Kamman

Woman, wife, mother, grandmother, culinary educator, chef, former restaurateur, author, TV personality, and winner of The James Beard Foundation's 1998 Lifetime Achievement Award

Chez La Mère Madeleine

(Madeleine's menus have a certain timeless quality to them—this menu sounds as fresh and inviting today as we're sure it did in 1976!)

Menu for Friday and Saturday nights from June 1 to July 15, 1976

Due to the difficulty of finding some ingredients and the irregularity of arrival of quality meats and fish in Boston, we may have to change a few of the items on our menu each week. We apologize for any possible change. We thank our guests for understanding that all changes are made for the sake of always fresh looking and fresh tasting dishes.

First Courses

Cream of red peppers with a garnish of saffron butter and a fine julienne of zucchini 2.75

Salad of large shrimp with watercress dressing and a small garnish of red radishes and zucchini salad 6.00

Soft shell crab sautéed in lightly curried butter with warm slices of avocado and papaya 6.00

Terrine of veal sweetbread with green herbs and carrots served with a tiny garnish of etuveed yellow squash and dill 5.50

Lukewarm rabbit salad with toasted hazelnuts, bitter greens, carrots, baby peas, and cucumbers in sherry vinegar dressing with a dash of Armagnac 5.50

Main Courses

Braised squab pigeon with cooked garlic and honey sauce garnished with cooked garlic cloves, pignoli, and chopped parsley 18.00

Saddle of lamb with mustard and gremolata sauce 18.00

Mousse of chicken with a puree of artichokes sauce and a garnish of diced ham and baby peas 18.00

Tenderloin steak with button mushrooms, wild "marasmius oreades" mushrooms, pancetta, and persillade garnish 18.00

Mousse of salmon with a rhubarb and citrus rind sauce 18.00

Vegetables

Spinach, baby tomatoes, Jerusalem artichokes with scallions, jardiniere of carrots, white radishes, and asparagus or fresh pickles when the asparagus is out of season, small green salad with a very light blue cheese dressing

All vegetables as well as the salad are included in the cost of the main course

Desserts

French cheeses as available on the market 4.50

Fresh strawberry sherbet and coconut and Kirsch sherbet 4.00

Frozen velvet ice cream flavored with coffee and 2 liquors 4.00

Tartlet with strawberries and raspberry puree 4.00

Galliano succes cake 4.00

BECOMING
a Chef

WITH RECIPES AND REFLECTIONS
FROM AMERICA'S LEADING CHEFS

Preface to the Revised Edition

Who knew that eight years after its publication we'd be writing a preface to the second edition of this book? Not us. *Since Becoming a Chef*'s publication in the summer of 1995, we've received a tremendous response to it—from readers as well as from the chefs featured in its pages. In fact, we thought we'd share some of their letters in response to receiving their copies of *Becoming a Chef* as a way of summarizing the kind of impact it seems to have had on people:

> *Becoming a Chef* gives you a wonderful feeling about our world and the passion it takes to succeed.
>
> DANIEL BOULUD

> Andrew and Karen are the first to capture the real inside look of becoming a chef because they got their information from the ultimate source. This book not only chronicles what has made many success stories, but should be required reading for aspiring professionals and foodophiles alike!
>
> ED BROWN

> The next best thing to working in the kitchen and experiencing life as a chef.
>
> TODD ENGLISH

> The book cultivates self-evaluation, to identify strengths and weaknesses of our trade. It motivates the reader to chase their passion from within and establish a personal mission statement.
>
> VICTOR GIELISSE

> For those considering entering the profession, reading *Becoming a Chef* will take the place of twenty informational interviews. The book presents diverse points of view and illustrates that with perseverance and passion, one can attain the goal of becoming a chef.
>
> JOYCE GOLDSTEIN

I have given this book to several of our sous chefs and enjoyed their reactions, from immediately sitting down and beginning to read it cover to cover to staying up all night. . . . I am hearing a *lot* of quotes from the book in our kitchens!

CINDY PAWCLYN

Kudos on an amazing book. I am so impressed, moved, and genuinely excited about what you have done.

SUSAN REGIS

This book serves as an almanac for chefs and a must-read for everyone who wants to become a chef, as well as those people in love with food and culinary arts.

DIETER SCHORNER

Once I started reading *Becoming a Chef,* I couldn't stop until I finished it. Really, FORMIDABLE!!!

ANDRÉ SOLTNER

I am thoroughly enjoying the book and have ordered additional copies for my staff.

JEREMIAH TOWER

One night shortly after *Becoming a Chef* was published, during the middle of service, a phone call came in from someone who was reading the book and had a question about something I said. I decided that if the person was brave enough to call, I would make his day and answer—which shocked him! I realized that, as a chef, it is important to be there for young cooks and, as a cook, you need to have the courage to ask for advice! Though I *don't* recommend calling chefs during service, it reminded me of a line from a speech at my high school graduation ceremony: "The door to opportunity is marked 'Push'!"

NORMAN VAN AKEN

I just got my copy of *Becoming a Chef.* My work is suffering for it. It's been a real struggle to put it down. Any time I pick up the book, I can open it anywhere and be immediately absorbed. You have woven together a totally seamless narrative that flows from one chef and topic to the next effortlessly and entirely logically. I am in awe of the job you have done putting together so many thought-provoking and inspiring insights. I have already learned more than I could have hoped. I don't remember the last time I was this enthused over a book. For a chef, your book provides a tremendous sense of community. As I read through all the shared experiences we've had, I have a heightened sense of camaraderie and belonging. We have all been through a similar crucible, making it very thought-provoking to see how perspectives vary. This book will be by my bed for a long time. I am ordering a number of copies for my staff and friends. Congratulations!

JANOS WILDER

We also started receiving letters and e-mails from readers themselves, and *we* were moved by how moved *they* seemed to be by our book. The very first letter we received was:

I would like to say that your book was fantastic!!!! My name is Robert Hansen and I am an inspiring [sic] chef. I am fourteen and have been helping in the kitchen at the Beard House and other restaurants for about a year now. I was looking at cookbooks when I saw your book. After reading the front flap, I bought it in the blink of an eye. I was just about to go on vacation in Montreal. I started reading the Introduction in the car on the way home from the bookstore. The next day on the way up to Montreal, I spent the whole day reading your book. That night, once I arrived at the hotel, I went straight up to my room and refused to leave until I finished your book. Even when my father offered to take me out to dinner, I asked him to order room service. That night I stayed up until four A.M. when I finished your book. I think that your book was one of the best I've ever read. Your book didn't just show the good and bad, but what really happens from a chef's point of view. Not only did I enjoy reading your book, but I found it a real inspiration. I would recommend your book to anybody and have already recommended it to many people. Sincerely yours,

ROBERT HANSEN, Bay Shore, New York

Others were no less passionate:

I have never written a letter like this in my life. Not because I am timid, but because I have never been so truly grateful for the impact a book brought to my life. I am no longer frightened—I am inspired! Thank you so very much for your inspiration and your beautiful book. I will reread *Becoming a Chef* the same way I have reread few other beloved books. Congratulations, continued success, and God's blessing on your gifts you share so passionately. Gratefully yours,

TONIANN BEATTIE

Thank you so much for the inspiration that your book has provided me. As a young cook, I really enjoyed reading about the trials and tribulations of my idols who have made it. It made me realize my passion was not strange but that it was something I shared with a lot of other people. It also helped my wife understand my passion. She would have loved it if I had given up on this business and gotten a "normal" job like everyone else. After reading *Becoming a Chef,* she realized that I would be miserable without the long hours and the headaches, and is encouraging me to get formal education and to pursue my dreams.

RICHARD COUNTRYMAN, Des Moines, Iowa

I'm a twenty-three-year-old who has been working in kitchens for as long as I can remember. In September, I was run over by a truck and haven't been able to work very much with my broken leg. One day I was hobbling through Barnes & Noble looking for a new book to pass the time with when I saw your book. I bought it, and read it in about two days (which for me is blindingly fast), and it has changed my life. My thirst for knowledge has grown enormously, and I was encouraged to learn that I am going through the business the same way a lot of other successful chefs did. I gave the book to my chef and he loves it (enough to go out and buy it for himself). Well, it's not every day that a book does to me what your book did, so I guess I just wanted to say "thank you."

ANTHONY DEGIULIO

I'm sure you've heard all manner of praise, richly deserved, for such a wonderful book. I just want to add that it has been a great success in my course on Culture and Cuisine here at Wesleyan. I've used it at several junctures in the course, but most prominently in a week we devoted to professionalism and culinary education. Best wishes,

JOHN FINN, Wesleyan University

Put simply, your books have done nothing less than change my life. I read *Becoming a Chef* and *Culinary Artistry* in three days (I could barely sleep). These two books are my new bibles. The only thing to slow my reading of them was the need to stop, go to the kitchen, and test the inspirations that your books provide. Your books have proven to me that cooking is my passion, and that I really belong in the kitchen. You've lighted a fire in my belly that is never going away. Thank you for the massive knowledge and inspirations that have sent me down the right path. You've shown me the light! Thank you both,

TOR WESTGARD

We count ourselves lucky indeed to have the pleasure of interviewing many of the most talented people in the world whose mission it is to create and celebrate great food, and of distilling their wisdom into words that can inspire the next generation.

Little did we ever dream, when we first set out to write this book, that we—a restaurant cook and a magazine publishing executive with a Harvard MBA—were starting down the path of becoming full-time authors. But, just as Norman Van Aken has said of his line of work in these pages, "This is not a profession that you choose; *it* chooses *you*."

It has been the privilege of a lifetime that *this* profession chose *us!*

Andrew Dornenburg & Karen Page
Summer 2003

Preface to the First Edition

Through six years in the kitchen as a full-time professional cook, the only thing that becomes clearer each day as I discover a great technique I've never seen used before or a wonderful ingredient I've never tasted before, is that I know absolutely nothing about cooking. Often my realization of how much there is to know is overwhelming, and that's exactly the feeling that drives me into the cookbook sections of bookstores or prompts me to set my alarm clock early to squeeze in time for reading before I leave for work.

It's also the feeling that drove me to undertake a task as daunting as co-authoring this book. In combing through bookstores, I noticed a void: While there were many books *by* chefs, I could find none strictly *about* chefs. I clearly knew that becoming a good cook had infinitely more to do with cooking than with reading, but I was looking for some additional guidance and inspiration on how to get the most out of all the time I did spend in the kitchen. As a cook just starting out in my career, I always wanted to know more.

I wanted to know about their first jobs and whether they started out with a cooking school diploma, or started at the bottom and worked their way up through the ranks. How did they get noticed? Was it a straight and steady path, or did they face setbacks along the way? How did they turn things around? Did they know, through years of low pay and back-breaking work, that they would eventually succeed? What helped them keep pushing?

Part of the reason I wanted to know was to see whether I was on the right track. What I've since learned is that there is no single "right track." Sure, some European-born chefs started in the kitchens of three-star restaurants at the age of thirteen. But other leading American chefs actually got their start in their later teens at the local Carvel or Friendly's. This was a relief to me, because my first restaurant job—like that of millions of other American teenagers—was at the local McDonald's.

I grew up in a San Francisco Bay Area neighborhood transitioning from farmland to suburb; our backyard had five fruit trees and three walnut trees. My earliest memories were of gathering walnuts and getting to crack them for winter pies. Three days out of high school, my love of the outdoors led me to a job fighting fires for the Northern California Division of Forestry during one of the worst summers for forest fires in the state's history. As an eighteen-year-old, I found myself spending twelve- to fifteen-hour days for six weeks straight battling a single fire. But once the blaze had been extinguished and the last K-ration eaten, I took on the responsibility of cooking for the guys in the firehouse one day a week. It was the best day. I would read cookbooks and reproduce large-quantity versions of the dishes I knew, from creamed tuna on biscuits to spaghetti with meat sauce.

The next summer, my two best friends and I decided to move to Wyoming, hoping to make our fortunes working on an oil rig. After none of us could find a job on a rig and we were down to our last twenty dollars, I fortunately landed a job as a cook—at the Holiday Inn in Cody. I discovered that cooks can learn something anywhere. Wyoming is cattle country, and I learned the importance of a sharp knife and how to butcher meats. I knew I was making progress when they let me trim the filet mignon.

The following summer I trekked to Alaska, and ended up working in a salmon processing plant. I loved getting to work with fish at its source, instead of out of the freezer. I gorged myself on fresh 100-pound halibut and grilled salmon, and learned how to tell salmon apart by the width of their tails. I processed salmon roe to be consumed in Japan, and I learned a new respect for food from the Japanese technicians. While I found the Japanese to be stern taskmasters when it came to salting and packing the roe, they were all smiles when they made and shared their sushi with the crew.

All the while, I found my on-again-off-again college education less and less fulfilling. After I moved to Boston in 1985, I took a job as a waiter and soon realized that I loved the restaurant business more than anything I was studying in college. While working at the East Coast Grill in Cambridge, Massachusetts, I asked chef-owner Chris Schlesinger about cooking schools. Instead, Chris handed me a knife and a case of cabbage, along with a chance to work part-time in his kitchen.

My apprenticeship there gave me one successful chef's insights. Chris taught me a lot about how to run a restaurant—ordering, receiving, storing, rotating foods, and other day-to-day tasks that are a core part of running a kitchen—as well as the amount of dedication it takes. There's no such thing as "good enough" when receiving ingredients or plating a dish. I learned to respect my fellow cooks, our equipment, even the floor of the kitchen itself—that a floor deserves as much attention and respect as the edge of your knife blade, because it's a part of the machinery that makes up a well-functioning kitchen. I also learned a respect for the history of cuisine and the sense of community among chefs through two gifts from Chris: a copy of Escoffier's *Le Guide Culinaire* and a membership in the American Institute of Wine and Food.

I left the East Coast Grill in 1989, with Chris's blessing, to cook at Lydia Shire's brand-new restaurant, Biba, in Boston. Every day in Biba's kitchen reminded me that there do not have to be culinary boundaries in a restaurant—the world is Lydia's pantry. Seeing her love for various foods, even for the simplest dishes like spaghetti with bread crumbs, was an inspiration to expand my own food horizons.

Along the way, I always asked my chefs and sous chefs for advice on books to read or classes to take, particularly since I never attended a full-time cooking school program. I made an effort to attend the demonstration or presentation of any leading food authority passing through Boston to promote a restaurant or book, and I was lucky enough to see Julia Child, Lorenza de' Medici, Diana Kennedy, Jacques Pépin, Julie Sahni, and Anne Willan, among others.

When my wife, Karen, and I moved to New York City, I was lucky enough to land a job cooking at Arcadia. Anne Rosenzweig underscored the importance of understanding your clientele and respecting them and their preferences. In contrast to the wild, spicy dishes at East Coast Grill, and the bold, eclectic ones at Biba, Arcadia's food—while equally creative—is classic and elegant. It involved a daily refinement of my technique.

The most inspirational episode in my cooking career to date was the two-week period I spent in 1992 with Madeleine Kamman at the School for American Chefs at Beringer Vineyards in California's Napa Valley. The other chefs in my class—Mark Gould of Atwater's (Portland, OR), Alan Harding of Nosmo King (NYC), and Chuck Wiley of The Boulders (Carefree, AZ)—and I lived an idyllic life of cooking, eating, talking, and breathing food and wine with the most knowledgeable and passionate person about food I've ever known—Madeleine.

My outside-of-work education continues. While it doesn't yet rival the size of seasoned chefs', my home library continues to grow at the rate of about two or three cookbooks a month. Karen and I love to visit used book stores for unusual or out-of-print cookbooks. And during the time we spent working on this book, we had an opportunity to travel widely throughout the United States on the weekends, eating at some of the country's best restaurants. Each meal was an education in itself. Each conversation we had with the leading chefs featured in this book was a graduate-level seminar.

In selecting chefs to be interviewed for the book, we aimed to tap a diverse range of opinions and experiences. After surveying cooks across the country through our publisher, we chose chefs among those they considered to be at the top of the profession. We also strove (often, with difficulty) to represent chefs from different parts of the country, of different backgrounds, cooking different styles of food. (The chefs are typically referred to throughout the text by their names only; for additional biographical information, including their restaurants and locations, see Appendix D, which begins on page 339.) We also aimed to transcend popular "glamorized" media images of chefs to portray what it's really like to work in a kitchen. While consumers flipping through a cooking magazine might be enchanted by a chef holding a beautifully styled plate of food in an elegant-looking dining room, what they don't see is that the chef's smile may be fleeting—and that, as soon as the camera crew leaves, there's a clogged drain, a malfunctioning air conditioner, a late meat delivery, and a sick sous chef to deal with.

This profession requires a tremendous amount of hard work. There is more to being a chef than creativity, just as there is more than creativity to being an artist. As in any other craft, chefs must practice,

practice, practice. Perfection is the only acceptable benchmark. Chefs must continue to learn and must rise to the challenges that will allow them to grow. They must be open to criticism. Work hot. Work cold. Work hurt. Work under intense pressure. And be willing to destroy a canvas or two.

What does it take to become a truly good chef in America? This is the central question we explored, for the sake of other aspiring chefs or the otherwise interested reader. Wherever one might practice this profession—from a four-star kitchen to one more modest—any cook can learn a great deal from the experiences of the leading chefs we interviewed. First, we tried to understand the experiences that were most formative to the chefs' lives and early careers; these experiences are addressed in the first half of the book. Second, we hoped to gain a sense of the practices that keep leading chefs at the top, which are addressed in the second half.

The paths to the top are as varied as the chefs who have made their way along them. We met introverted chefs whose strength was in creating quiet and elegant spaces in which to serve their refined food, and extroverts whose colorful and loud decor matched both their flavors and personalities—as well as everything in between. The most successful have succeeded in creating restaurants that represent both figurative and literal extensions of themselves, their personalities, and their preferences.

As a cook, I'm overwhelmed by how fortunate I am to have been personally guided and inspired by the thousand years' collective experience of the leading chefs you'll meet in these pages. The depth of their knowledge, passion, and generosity—as well as the breadth of their diversity—represent what I love most about this profession.

Despite the immense benefit of having had this experience, every day I'm in the kitchen I realize how much I still have to master. However, through the course of writing this book, I've come to recognize that everything I don't know about cooking—the techniques I've yet to learn, the ingredients I've yet to discover, the dishes I've yet to taste—represents not a deficiency, but a syllabus for a lifetime of learning and experiencing and enjoying that will not only contribute to my development as a chef, but continue to enrich my life every step of the way. I can't imagine a better way to spend a career, or a lifetime.

Andrew Dornenburg
Spring 1995

becoming a Chef

REVISED

1. Chefs
YESTERDAY AND TODAY

"A country without a past has no future." In a culinary sense, we have to reaffirm our past because we have one. And if we have any future, it is our past. We have to understand who we are and where we are.

MARK MILLER

Rick Bayless's life is not atypical of the lives of America's other foremost chefs who, like Rick, alternately wear the hats of chef, restaurateur, businessperson, author, television host, activist, and/or sometimes even celebrity. Bayless runs two successful restaurants—Frontera Grill and Topolobampo—in Chicago, but he crisscrosses the United States to participate in various benefits with other chefs, and regularly travels the globe for business and pleasure. He's an active leader of the Chefs Collaborative, a not-for-profit organization of chefs concerned about the quality of food in America. Rick is also a spouse and a parent—and, even more impressive in this demanding profession, he has found a way to balance all of these professional and personal roles admirably.

Before even having a shot at reaching this level of success, however, working cooks—as I was for ten years—are known to experience "rites of passage" not unlike those one might encounter in boot camp. Our hours are long, the work is physically demanding, and the conditions are, well, hot. Our "uniforms" are anything but—while most kitchens require cooks to wear the traditional white chef's jacket, these days the pants worn could be anything from the traditional black-and-white houndstooth check to a brightly colored print of red chile peppers. Headgear ranges from a traditional toque (the classic tall white hat) to a baseball cap. Footwear might be tennis shoes or clogs, which are particularly popular among cooks who've worked in French kitchens. Kitchen work during lunch or dinner service is always intense, but the atmosphere may range from a tense calm to loud and frenzied screaming and yelling.

Those able to stand the heat are finding that the growth of the foodservice industry today is opening up greater opportunities for cooks and chefs in the profession. These opportunities carry with them an important responsibility, as the choices made by the next generation of chefs will transform the food of tomorrow. I believe aspiring chefs should recognize this influence and use it responsibly, striving to master their profession. This process starts with an understanding of its history.

Looking Backward

Why is it important to understand culinary history? It is the rich tradition of the culinary field that allows this profession to be so much more than standing at a cutting board or a hot stove all day. I have worked with fellow cooks who didn't understand my own interest in the subject. They would ask, "Who cares who James Beard or Escoffier were? Why should I care what anyone did twenty years ago, let alone two hundred years ago? I'd rather hear about what's new."

In fact, the media's emphasis on the latest culinary trends adds to the pressure chefs feel to come out with something new and different to attract attention, to define their style, or to satisfy our American desire for innovation. However, how much is ever truly new? André Soltner provides an interesting perspective of history's importance: "We've had the same food for two hundred to three hundred years—everything we do today was already done before." Could he possibly be right? Think about the wide variety of ethnic and regional cuisines we eat today, the modern demands for convenience and sophistication placed on today's cook, and our concerns about healthful food. Consider these cooking magazine articles: "Foods of the Rio Grande Valley and Northern Mexico," "Italian Cooking," "Russian Recipes," "Fifteen-

Minute Meals," "Lentils: A Meat Substitute," "When Unexpected Company Comes," "World-Famous Recipes by the World's Most Noted Chefs," "Creole Cooking," "Delicious Cooking in a Small Space," "Making Gnocchi," "Homemade Timbales," "Making and Serving Curry." Could such variety and such specific needs even have been imagined more than a few years ago? Well, yes. Each article listed appeared in a United States publication between the years of 1895 and 1910!

> **Understanding the history of the dish you are preparing will allow you to put a little more of your heart and soul into what you're cooking. I think that's what it's all about.**
>
> JIMMY SCHMIDT

In addition, how many people are aware that architecturally structured food, covered extensively in the food press in the 1990s as a "new" trend toward "tall" food, was prepared by chefs in the nineteenth century? As one might imagine, the chefs who pushed food in new directions were real pioneers in their day and thus, not surprisingly, fascinating human beings. Ralph Waldo Emerson wrote, "There is properly no history; only biography." History is simply compelling stories about compelling people, and the people who played a role in culinary history particularly so.

Until recently, the chef's profession was not particularly prestigious. Only in the last twenty-five to thirty years have chefs begun to gain the respect and recognition they deserve. Much of the media coverage today stems from their participation in various high-profile charity benefits. But turn to history and you'll see that chefs have long contributed to their communities through food. One example described in the pages that follow includes a chef who fed more than a million people over three months during the Irish potato famine.

As a not-unimportant bonus, an historical perspective allows cooks to give their food greater depth. At the School for American Chefs, Madeleine Kamman would have us think about where and when a dish originated and what the local people might have used to season it in centuries past. In preparing a particular Mediterranean dish, we saw the value of that thinking when we substituted anchovy for salt, and the dish took on a deeper richness and complexity. Understanding the profession's history will make you a better cook—in more ways than one.

Today's cook has a rich and impressive lineage dating back thousands of years, and understanding one's place as a link in a chain to the past—as well as to the future—can help a cook see the profession in a more balanced perspective. The timeline that follows doesn't pretend to be comprehensive—it merely highlights some interesting people, books, and events we hoped might help stimulate the reader's appetite to learn more and feel a stronger connection to the past.

Great Moments in Culinary History

5th Century B.C.

Chefs play an important role in society from this time forward.

4th Century A.D.

Apicius reputedly writes *De re conquinaria libri decem* ("Cuisine in Ten Books"), considered to be the very first cookbook, in which sauces are prepared in much the same manner followed by the French up to 1955.

Middle Ages

Guilds are formed, with chefs beginning their long tradition of community.

1380

Guillaume Tirel Taillevent (1312-95) writes *Le Viandier*, one of the oldest cookbooks written in French, which provides a complete synthesis of all aspects of cookery in the fourteenth century. Its main contribution is considered to be its emphasis on spiced foods and sauces (predominantly saffron, ginger, pepper, and cinnamon), soups, and ragouts, which include the preparation of meat, poultry, game, and fish. (The heavy seasoning served the useful purpose of disguising the taste of stale or rotten food.) He served as the cook of Charles VII of France.

1390

Richard II of England's cooks write *The Forme of Cury* ("The Art of Cookery"), which emphasizes heavily seasoned dishes and recommends the liberal use of almond milk in cooking.

A fourteenth-century European guild manual described the early master chef this way: "He is a professional craftsman. He is a cook. He takes fowl from the air; fish from the waters; fruits, vegetables, and grain from the land; and animals that walk the earth, and through his skills and art transforms the raw product to edible food. He serves to sustain life in man, woman, and child. He has the sacred duty through his efforts and art to sustain and maintain the healthy bodies that God has given us to house our souls."

1475

De Honesta Voluptate ac Valetudine ("Honest Pleasure and Health"), the first printed cookbook, is published in Italy by **Bartolomeo Sacchi Platina** (1421-81).

1533

Italian princess **Caterina de Medici** marries the Duc d'Orleans (later Henri II) of France and arrives in France with her Florentine chefs in tow. They collectively give rise to Florentine influences on the classic French fare, including simplicity, elegance, more delicate spicing, and the addition of new ingredients, most notably spinach.

1651

Pierre François de la Varenne (1615-78) publishes the first cookbook to give an insight into the new cooking practices of the French: *Le Cuisinier François*. It is important as the first book to record the advances of French cooking through the Renaissance era, and represents the turning point when medieval cuisine ends and haute cuisine begins. Notable is the use of mushrooms and truffles, imparting more delicate flavors, and the use of butter in pastries and sauces instead of oil. La Varenne may also have written *Le Pastissier François*, the first exhaustive French volume on pastry making.

1671

The Prince de Condé's cook **Vatel** (1635-71) commits suicide by falling on his sword when the fish he ordered for a banquet honoring Louis XIV fails to arrive. (The fish is delivered fifteen minutes later.)

1765

The first restaurant (or eating establishment serving restorative broths, known then as "restaurants") opens its doors in Paris, with proprietor **M. Boulanger** hanging out a sign: "Boulanger sells restoratives fit for the gods."

1774

Antoine Augustin Parmentier (1737-1813), an agronomist, begins his campaign to promote the potato, at the time regarded as food fit only for cattle or the destitute. A highlight of his efforts includes serving an entire meal—from appetizer and entree to bread and dessert—made from potatoes! Hard evidence that history repeats itself: The night of our first visit to Charlie Trotter's, the dinner menu featured a "potato study" of eight courses using potatoes.

1782

The first restaurant as we know it today, with regular hours and featuring a menu listing available dishes served at private tables, is opened by **Antoine Beauvilliers** (1754-1817) in Paris. Its very French name? The "Grande Taverne de Londres (London!)."

1789-99

The French Revolution spurs many French chefs, previously employees of the monarchy or nobility, to flee the country, and many go on to open their own restaurants elsewhere.

1796

Amelia Simmons publishes *American Cookery,* the first cookbook written by an American for an American audience, giving voice to an "American mode of cooking" and providing the first printed instructions for the cooking of colonial produce such as corn, and specialties such as Indian pudding and johnnycake. One hundred and ninety-three years later, another New Englander, Jasper White, will publish a cookbook with his own recipes for the same.

1800

Count von Rumford, a scientist born **Benjamin Thompson** (1753-1814) in his native United States, develops the stove. Prior to this, cooking was done over open hearths.

1801

When **Thomas Jefferson** (1743-1836), a gourmand and wine connoisseur, becomes president of the United States, he hires the first French White House chef, Chef Julien, and stresses the utmost freshness and quality in produce and other ingredients. His garden features broccoli, endive, peas, and tomatoes (still considered poisonous by some Americans of the day), as well as fresh herbs. He is credited with introducing ice cream, pasta, and new fruits and vegetables to America.

1803-14

The first restaurant guides are published, sparked by the growing popularity of restaurants in Paris.

1820s

Chefs begin to wear the now traditional large white hats known as toques (a white version of the black hats of Greek Orthodox priests).

1825

Seventy-year-old gastronomy philosopher **Jean Anthelm Brillat-Savarin** (1755-1826) anonymously self-publishes *Physiologie du Gout,* in which he challenges, "Tell me what you eat, and I shall tell you what you are."

1833

Marie-Antoine Carême (1783-1833), the most celebrated culinarian of his time, known as the "chef of kings, king of chefs," dies. In 1856, his *La Cuisine Classique* is posthumously published, thanks to the help of his student Plumery. As a young cook, Carême copies architectural drawings, upon which he bases his patisserie creations, which are greatly admired and gain him favor. Through his apprenticeships with the best chefs and pastry chefs of the time—in addition to assisting other leading chefs with special events—he develops in twelve years into their superior. Carême uses his sense of what is in vogue and whimsical to prepare both dramatically presented and elegant dishes, and his work as a philosopher, saucier, pastry chef, craftsman, and author of recipes raises him to the top of his profession. He is credited as the originator of grande cuisine.

Carême believed that "of the five fine arts, the fifth is architecture, whose main branch is confectionary." He saw the ideal cook as having a "discerning and sensitive palate, perfect and exquisite taste, a strong and industrious character; he should be skillful and hardworking and unite delicacy, order, and economy."

1846

Alexis Soyer (1810-58), a French cook, publishes his first book, *The Gastronomic Regenerator.* While contemporary chefs like Jimmy Schmidt and Wolfgang Puck later popularize the wearing of baseball caps (instead of the traditional toque) as headgear in certain American kitchens, Soyer is known for characteristic headgear of his own: his trademark red velvet cap. Even contemporary chefs who donate their time to charitable events on a regular basis would be impressed with Soyer's contributions to the less fortunate: In 1847, Soyer starts a large soup kitchen in London, which feeds thousands of people a day, and during the potato famine the following year, he does the same in Ireland, where he feeds over a million mouths in three months. In 1855, he publishes *A Shilling Cookery for the People,* establishing himself as the "Frugal

Gourmet" of his time. Long before the creation of American Spoon Foods by Larry Forgione and other contemporary businesses started by today's chefs to sell their prepared products to consumers for home use, Soyer markets his own bottled sauces (and so will Escoffier!).

Publicity is like the air we breathe; if we have it not, we die.
ALEXIS SOYER

1850s

Traditional French service, in which all the dishes of a meal are arranged artfully at the start of a meal, resulting in cold food, gives way to Russian service (service à la Russe), in which the courses are portioned in the kitchen and served on platters in sequence, resulting in hot food.

1863

Charles Ranhofer (1836-99) begins his thirty-four-year reign as chef of Delmonico's in New York City, becoming the first internationally renowned chef of an American restaurant. He publishes his cookbook, *The Epicurean,* in 1893.

1889

The opening of the Savoy Hotel in London in 1889, under the leadership of the lengendary hotelier **César Ritz** (1850-1918) and celebrated chef **Auguste Escoffier** (1846-1935) transfers grande cuisine, the culinary movement founded by Carême, from the upper-class household to the hotel deluxe kitchen. This marks the age when chefs went from working as servants to becoming entrepreneurs with their own restaurants.

1896

Fannie Merritt Farmer (1857-1915), principal of the Boston Cooking School, publishes *The Boston Cooking-School Cook Book,* which has since sold almost 4 million copies. Hardly slowed, though confined to a wheelchair, Farmer makes a major impact through her school, speeches, and writings on cooks' use of measured ingredients in recipes.

1900

The first *Guide Michelin* (restaurant guide) is published.

1902

Escoffier publishes the culinary classic *Le Guide Culinaire.* He establishes his place as one of the most influential forces on the foodservice industry by creating the French brigade system, which improves the organization and speed of kitchen operations. In contrast with the stereotypical

The Wisdom of Escoffier

"Society had little regard for the culinary profession. This should not have been so, since cuisine is a science and an art and he who devotes his talent to its service deserves full respect and consideration."

"Not for me is it to point out to what acts of plagiarism the chef must submit. A painter can sign his work, and a sculptor can carve his name upon his, but a dish—how can the chef, its inventor, place his mark upon it?"

"The life of a chef is no idle one, apart from the labor of actual preparation and serving of diverse dishes. His brain must ever be on the alert, and his inventive powers always acute. But there is actual and lasting satisfaction . . . in accomplishing the very best that can be accomplished."

The Wisdom of Fernand Point

"Every morning one must start from scratch, with nothing on the stoves. That is cuisine."

"As far as cuisine is concerned, one must read everything, see everything, hear everything, try everything, observe everything, in order to retain in the end, just a little bit."

"A good meal must be as harmonious as a symphony and as well constructed as a cathedral."

"A man is not a machine and a chef gets tired—but the clientele must never know it."

"The duty of a good cuisinier is to transmit to the next generation everything he has learned and experienced."

screaming that goes on in kitchens of his day (as well as before and since!), Escoffier's style as a chef is to walk away from a situation rather than lose his temper, and he forbids both profanity and brutality in his kitchen.

1924

Fernand Point
(1897-1955), who inherited the restaurant his father had opened two years earlier in Vienne, France, renames it La Pyramide. Point is the first chef to leave the kitchen in order to speak with his customers in the dining room. He is considered a great teacher, and many leading contemporary chefs of France, including Paul Bocuse, Alain Chapel, the Troisgros brothers, François Bise, Louis Outhier, and Raymond Thuilier study with him.

1938

Prosper Montagné (1864-1948) publishes *Larousse Gastronomique*—to this day, a culinary bible—with the intention of providing a single reference for the history of gastronomy through the ages, and the spectrum of cooking in the twentieth century. The son of a hotelier, he worked his way up through the ranks of the kitchens of some of the most famous restaurants of his day.

1941

Gourmet begins publication, elevating food to a serious topic meriting its own journal of record.

1941

Henri Soulé (1903-66) opens Le Pavillon in New York City, the first United States restaurant dedicated to French haute cuisine, which later spawns other great French restaurants (including La Côte Basque, La Grenouille, Le Cygne, Le Périgord) and chefs (including Pierre Franey and Jacques Pépin).

1946

During the beginning of the rise of the television era, **James Beard** (1903-85), one of the most esteemed and respected food writers in America and considered the "dean" of American cooking, is tapped for his own cooking show on television because of his experience as both an actor and a cook.

1947

To a Queen's Taste, one of the first televised instructional cooking shows in the United States, featuring **Dione Lucas,** debuts.

1948

Two women, **Frances Roth** and **Katharine Angell,** open the New Haven (CT) Restaurant Institute, which in 1951 becomes known as The Culinary Institute of America (CIA), the first serious cooking school in the country.

1957

Craig Claiborne is named food editor at *The New York Times,* subsequently raising restaurant reviewing from a form of promotional advertising to honest critique.

The 1960s

With new discoveries in science and technology came change, resulting in the advent of fast food, the decline of regional distinctions in food, and the homogenization of the American palate. The 1960s helped usher in a new emphasis on healthy, natural, and organic foods. As more Americans traveled abroad, and as the United States' own ethnic population composition began to shift, there came greater emphasis on the foods and cuisines of other countries. Still, interest in French food was reinvigorated as the "nouvelle cuisine" movement of the young French chefs (including Paul Bocuse and his "band" of chefs) made headlines. Julia Child's presence on TV, with her widely watched series *The French Chef,* exposed Americans to her version of this popular foreign cuisine.

> When I started out in the early 1960s, there were no celebrity chefs. Escoffier and Brillat-Savarin had passed away long ago. Our heroes were our instructors.
>
> MARCEL DESAULINIERS

The 1960s decline of classic cuisine was the result of it having become slowly apparent that the complicated concoctions involving technique built upon technique (Beef Wellington, souffléd crepes topped with egg custard, en croute preparations of all sorts) were too expensive to produce and also too heavy for the modern human machine with its worry about a youthful and slim appearance.

MADELEINE KAMMAN

1961

First Lady Jacqueline Kennedy nearly single-handedly revamps White House dining by hiring French-born chef **René Verdon.**

Julia Child, with co-authors Simone Beck and Louisette Bertholle, publishes her first book, *Mastering the Art of French Cooking,* still cited as an important reference to today's chef.

1963

The French Chef, hosted by Julia Child, makes its television debut.

1969

Fernand Point: Ma Gastronomie is published posthumously.

The 1970s

In the 1970s when Jasper White attended The Culinary Institute of America, "the school wasn't anything like it is today, back then. It was attracting a different crowd, more working-class kids who really wanted to become chefs because they thought it would be a great way to make a living. There was no glamour. There were no famous chefs in America in 1975. Not one."

The American restaurant scene was forever changed, however, in 1971 when Alice Waters opened her Berkeley, CA, restaurant Chez Panisse, which emphasized seasonality and freshness in ingredients whose natural taste became the star on the plate. In the years that followed, when Waters received national acclaim, she inspired countless American chefs to follow suit, while attracting a new breed of thoughtful, well-educated men and, notably, women into her kitchen and into the profession. The number of leading American chefs who have worked at Chez Panisse is a testimony to its—and Waters's—influence (see page 104).

The news media responded to the newly burgeoning restaurant scene by hiring food critics and covering food more extensively, spurred on by competition from the new food magazines such as *Bon Appétit* and *Food & Wine,* which chronicled the new generation of young American chefs.

André Soltner recalls, "Suddenly, when the star chefs appeared in magazines, the level of respect for chefs became much, much higher. Young Americans were interested because suddenly the chefs were in the limelight. Before, which American wanted to become a cook? But suddenly, they started to go to

The 1970s saw an explosion of nouvelle cuisine, but is that cuisine really completely new? Some of it—the use of exotic ingredients and spices, the shorter cooking times for better texture and nutrition, for example—is new; some is not and is definitely borrowed from the font of ancient cooking. For example, the sauces based on reduction echo the food of Apicius and all the women who for centuries thickened by reduction because they had to keep flour to make bread. It reflects the shrinking of our world through the interpenetrations of diverse cultures, thanks to air travel.

MADELEINE KAMMAN

school and became chefs. I remember the change—the publicity, the people like Bocuse and a few others who were suddenly on the cover of *Newsweek*. Customers—doctors and lawyers—said to me, 'My son wants to become a chef, he goes to The Culinary Institute of America.' Some went to France to train, some came to our restaurant, some went to La Côte Basque, La Grenouille . . . and some became very good. The level of chefs in America changed dramatically."

This decade is also when American cooking started coming into its own, as American chefs and customers rediscovered pride in the cuisine and ingredients of their own country and its regions.

1971	1972	1973
Alice Waters opens Chez Panisse in Berkeley, CA. **Madeleine Kamman** publishes *The Making of a Cook,* the first cookbook in the United States to attempt to explain cooking with why's instead of only how's. It is still cited by contemporary chefs as an important reference.	**Leslie Revsin** is the first woman chef to take the helm of a major hotel kitchen when she is named chef of the Waldorf-Astoria Hotel in New York City, making the headlines of Manhattan newspapers. **Calvin Trillin** writes in *Playboy,* only half tongue-in-cheek, that "the best restaurants . . . are in Kansas City," sparking new attention to and pride in hometown cuisines across the country. The Culinary Institute of America opens in its Hyde Park, NY, location.	**Madeleine Kamman** opens Chez la Mère Madeleine at Modern Gourmet in Newton Centre, Massachusetts—one of the first, if not the first, French nouvelle cuisine restaurants in the United States. French chef Paul Bocuse proclaims it "the greatest in the U.S.A."

1975

French chef **Paul Bocuse** is named to the Legion d'Honneur by President Giscard d'Estaing—the first chef to be so honored. Six months later, he is featured on the cover of *Newsweek* for an article entitled "Food: The New Wave."

Every morning I go to the market and stroll among the displays. Sometimes I do not even know what dish I will make for the noon meal. It is the market that decides. This, I think, is what makes good cooking.

PAUL BOCUSE

The more one travels, the more one realizes that other cooks are not standing still; they are progressing. Today anyone who wants to progress must go around the world. Each time that I go to another country, I come back with many ideas.

PAUL BOCUSE

1976

Jeremiah Tower, then of Chez Panisse, is inspired by *The Epicurean—A Franco-American Culinary Encyclopedia,* and features the first California menu at the restaurant, with dishes ranging from "Monterey Bay Prawns" to "Walnuts, Almonds, and Mountain Pears from the San Francisco Farmers' Market."

1977

Jane and Michael Stern write the first edition of *Roadfood,* celebrating old-fashioned American restaurants.

1979

Paul Prudhomme opens K-Paul's in New Orleans' French Quarter, launching the national craze for Cajun food and "blackened" fish.

I must include Larry Forgione with such people as Alice Waters, Jeremiah Tower, Mark Miller, and a few other brilliant young chefs who are making the effort to create a cuisine that is distinctly American and capable of rivaling any other in the Western world.

JAMES BEARD

Selected American Restaurant Openings: 1960-1994

Year	Chef	Restaurant	Location
1961	André Soltner	Lutèce	New York City
1970	Georges Perrier	Le Bec-Fin	Philadelphia
1971	Alice Waters	Chez Panisse	Berkeley, CA
1973	Jean Banchet	Le Français	Wheeling, IL
1978	Patrick O'Connell	The Inn at Little Washington	Washington, VA
1979	Jean-Louis Palladin	Jean-Louis at the Watergate Hotel	Washington, DC
	Paul Prudhomme	K-Paul's	New Orleans
	Barry Wine	The Quilted Giraffe	New York City
1980	George Germon and Johanne Killeen	Al Forno	Providence, RI
	Elizabeth Terry	Elizabeth on 37th	Savannah, GA
	Wolfgang Puck	Spago	Los Angeles
1983	Larry Forgione	An American Place	New York City
	Cindy Pawlcyn	Mustards Grill	Napa Valley, CA
	Jasper White	Jasper's	Boston
	Janos Wilder	Janos	Tucson
1984	Joyce Goldstein	Square One	San Francisco
	Anne Rosenzweig	Arcadia	New York City
	Jeremiah Tower	Stars	San Francisco
1985	Jimmy Schmidt	The Rattlesnake Club	Denver
	Chris Schlesinger	East Coast Grill	Cambridge, MA
	Allen Susser	Chef Allen's	Miami
	Barbara Tropp	China Moon Cafe	San Francisco

Year	Chef	Restaurant	Location
1987	Rick Bayless	Frontera Grill	Chicago
	Susanna Foo	Susanna Foo	Philadelphia
	Gordon Hamersley	Hamersley's Bistro	Boston
	Zarela Martinez	Zarela	New York City
	Nobu Matsuhisa	Matsuhisa	Los Angeles
	Mark Miller	Coyote Cafe	Santa Fe, NM
	Michel Richard	Citrus	Los Angeles
	Charlie Trotter	Charlie Trotter's	Chicago
	Jimmy Schmidt	The Rattlesnake Club	Detroit
1989	Todd English	Olives	Boston
	Bradley Ogden	Lark Creek Inn	Larkspur, CA
	Lydia Shire	Biba	Boston
	Nancy Silverton and Mark Peel	Campanile	Los Angeles
1990	Emeril Lagasse	Emeril's	New Orleans
	Susan Spicer	Bayona	New Orleans
	Jean-Georges Vongerichten	Jo Jo	New York City
1992	Rick Bayless	Topolobampo	Chicago
1993	Daniel Boulud	Daniel	New York City
1994	Nobu Matsuhisa	Nobu	New York City

The 1980s

In the 1980s, the French cuisine craze hit America full force, spurred by chefs like Jean Banchet, founder of Le Français (Chicago); Jean-Louis Palladin of Jean Louis at the Watergate (Washington, DC); and Georges Perrier of Le Bec-Fin (Philadelphia). There was a melding of French technique and American ingredients that helped give rise to the California cuisine movement pioneered by Alice Waters, Jeremiah Tower, Mark Miller, and Wolfgang Puck. Puck is credited with developing a prototype of a successful restaurant through opening Spago in Los Angeles in 1982, with its emphasis on stylish design, informal service, and memorable food. The dining-out phenomenon of the 1980s created celebrity chef groupies, who came to be known as "foodies," as well as the immensely popular *Zagat Surveys* published nationally by Tim and Nina Zagat.

> **Right around the 1980s, there was a major change where everybody got back to their roots. Across the country—from New Orleans to California people started accepting their grandmother's meatloaf as a meaningful food experience, and America started to define its own standards for what a dining experience was.**
>
> CHRIS SCHLESINGER

The 1990s

The 1990s generated creative responses to such trends as growing interest both in healthier food and in melding the cuisines of multiple cultures. Jean-Georges Vongerichten, with the publication of his cookbook *Simple Cuisine: The Easy, New Approach to Four-Star Cooking,* illustrated the strides he'd been making at the four-star Manhattan restaurant Lafayette to provide maximum flavor with minimum fats through an array of juices, flavored oils, and infusions—techniques going back to the Egyptians.

Norman Van Aken is credited with coining the term "fusion cuisine," referring to a harmonious combination of foods of various origins, popularized at restaurants ranging from Lydia Shire's restaurant Biba (Boston) to Susan Feniger and Mary Sue Milliken's City Restaurant (Los Angeles). The era of "political correctness" has pushed chefs to participate in a wide range of charitable events, many benefiting such organizations as Meals on Wheels, City Harvest, and Share Our Strength, which also help keep chefs and food in the media spotlight.

Letter to President Clinton, on Behalf of Chefs' Coalition for Chefs Helping to Enhance Food Safety

December 8, 1992

Dear President-elect Clinton:

We, chefs from across the country, believe that good food, pure and wholesome, should be not just a privilege for the few, but a right for everyone. Good food nourishes not just the body, but the entire community. It increases our awareness of the sources of life and of our responsibility to pre-serve all life-sustaining resources. Chefs know this, farmers know this, and with your leadership, the whole nation can be reminded of it. Good food is about seasonality, ripeness, and simplicity. Where there is good food—food that is delicious, wholesome, and responsibly produced—good health readily follows. The broader health of our nation is in peril. By your example at the White House, our hopes for the restoration of the nation's health will be nourished.

By promoting the value of organically grown fruits and vegetables, your table would reaffirm Thomas Jefferson's ideas of a nation of small farmers—caring custodians of the land whose work would greatly benefit from your endorsement. Similarly, a discriminating quest for fish and meat of quality would herald the need to care for our waters, pastures, and the areas surrounding them.

We urge you to select a White House chef who embraces this philosophy. The President's own table would then be a singular expression of long-absent values. Set with honesty and integrity, it would speak profoundly to the American people.

The coalition would welcome any opportunity to work with your office on this appointment and the important issues it addresses.

Respectfully,
Alice Waters for the Chefs' Coalition

President Clinton's White House also added high visibility to the American food movement, as Alice Waters and others lobbied for an end to French menus with French ingredients served with French wines (the menus written, of course, in French) at White House state dinners. In a letter to the President, Waters and dozens of other cosigning chefs urged him to appoint a White House chef who would promote American cooking, emphasizing local ingredients and organic food. Even celebrated French chef

Larry Forgione on American Food

I think absolutely, without any stretch of the imagination, the chef in the White House should be American. I think his influence or training should be American food. His fondness should be for American food. His knowledge should be of American food. And I think when dignitaries and heads of state come to this country, they should only be served American food. I think it has been absurd over the years. The reason that I got involved and agreed to continue to be involved with the White House is that it's about time the head of our country serves the cuisine of our country. When our head of state or dignitaries travel to different countries, and they go to Germany, they get German food. If they go to Japan, they get Japanese food. I mean, dignitaries from other countries come to this country and get what? French food? It doesn't make any sense. It's like the White House is years behind what's going on. Again, this isn't a put-down of French chefs or French food—it's just out of place. It shouldn't be there.

Those two stories in the *New York Times* [on Forgione's participation in the Clinton White House's Kitchen Cabinet of American chefs] got more of a reaction than anything I've ever done in my life. I was called by every television station and interviewed by media from every European country. It was interesting that the rest of the world didn't know that we had American cuisine.

I always turn around and say, "You define French cooking to me, and I'll tell you what American cooking is." What's French cooking? A series of dishes that have French names? It's so hard to describe. What is Japanese cuisine? After being in Japan last summer, I realized that what I thought was Japanese food was a very small portion of what is Japanese food. So it's one of those things that we'd have to accept—that our country is made up of many, many influences, from almost every country in the world. When those settlers arrived in the Americas, they brought with them little parts of their country and heritage, maybe seeds of some of their favorite things, and were met by natives or the people there before them who had left a little bit of their country there.

Paul Bocuse admitted that it was "ridiculous" for the White House not to have an American chef. In response, First Lady Hillary Rodham Clinton named her "Kitchen Cabinet" of American chef-advisors, including Larry Forgione of An American Place (NYC), Anne Rosenzweig of Arcadia (NYC), and John Snedden of Rocklands—Washington's Barbeque and Grilling Company (DC) before the Clinton administration's first official dinner. In March 1994, French-born White House executive chef Pierre Chambrin's

You look at New England and you say, "What's New England cooking?" Well, the Portuguese seaports that cook food that is sort of Portuguese-Italian is as much New England cooking as anything else. Portuguese seafood stew from Port Judith in Rhode Island is as much New England cooking as a clam chowder. There is the influence of English cuisine, which is boiled dinners, creamed stews, and then you have the influence of the Portuguese settlers. You obviously have the influence of Native Americans. You have the influence of the French settling the area through Canada. You even have the influence of the Tropics, because of the trade triangle that existed. The Boston port would receive rum and spices from the East or West Indies. That's why when you go through old historic cookbooks, you'll find out that powdered ginger is an ingredient in old, old recipes for codcakes. The dish that we do at An American Place—one of our most popular desserts—is called the Banana Betty. That's a combination of two very old New England desserts that incorporates gingersnaps and bananas and rum. Well, all those things came up on the trade ships. You find pineapple in a lot of old-fashioned dishes, like pineapple upside-down cake. That's New England. Where did it come from? The pineapples came from the coast, the brown sugar and rum from the Islands.

If you look at the old Junior League cookbooks—well, the Junior League of Richmond, Virginia, could only get the ingredients that were in Richmond, Virginia. Nobody would ever think that curry has anything to do with American cooking. Curry is a very intricate part of Georgia, because Savannah was the port to which the ships that came from the Indies would return. And a dish called "Country Captain Chicken" is a classic dish from Savannah. When the sailors would bring back their pouches of curry powder, their wives would prepare for them this curried chicken dish upon their arrival back in port. So here we have chicken curry during the 1800s in America. So is that part of American cuisine? Or does the [imported] curry not make it American cuisine?

resignation was accepted. Less than two months later, California-born Walter Scheib, a graduate of The Culinary Institute of America and executive chef of The Greenbrier, had taken over the position.

The influence of leading chefs cannot be underestimated. While they themselves can personally feed only a tiny fraction of the United States population, they train and inspire countless other chefs and cooks who spread their lessons through their own cooking across the country and around the world. Some chefs have branched out into their own business ventures—such as Wolfgang Puck's (frozen) Spago Original California Pizza and Rick Bayless's Frontera salsas to make their products available to a wider audience. In a growing trend, major food and foodservice corporations, from American Airlines to Kraft General Foods, consult with leading chefs on improving and expanding their own offerings. In addition, the chefs' writing and political activism touch people who might not ever have eaten their food.

A Profession Growing by Leaps and Bounds

The restaurant industry employs more than 6 million people, making it the country's largest retail employer. Chefs, cooks, and other kitchen workers hold about 3 million jobs in the United States. Job openings are expected to be strong, reaching a projected total of 13 million people, through 2010. Unlike many industries, the restaurant industry has had steady growth for more than twenty years—with 2001 posting a 7½ percent growth rate. The aging population is creating more demand for sit-down restaurants, which in turn is leading to a need for more qualified cooks. "Culinary professionals are very fortunate, because there are still plenty of good and interesting jobs out there," says Patrick O'Connell of The Inn at Little Washington.

While workers under twenty-five have traditionally filled a significant proportion of these jobs, the pool of young workers is expected to continue shrinking. Thus, older career-changers will likely help fill the gap. For example, upward of 45 percent of the students at the California Culinary Academy come from nonfoodservice backgrounds, and their average age is twenty-eight. "We are seeing a lot of career changing taking place that was not a legitimate option ten years ago," O'Connell observes. "Now that there is some glamour and a certain respectability attached to the culinary field, people who have been locked into mundane jobs dream about cooking at a restaurant or having a bakery."

Cuisines of the World Find Their Way to the United States

The following list indicates the decade each type of cuisine first received its own heading in the *Readers' Guide to Periodical Literature,* along with characteristic (not comprehensive!) ingredients and/or flavor combinations represented in the recipes included. All names of the types of cuisine are indicated as originally published, however politically incorrect or inaccurate they may be now—further underscoring the fact that times change!

Decade	Type of Cuisine	Characteristic Ingredients
1920s	Chinese	garlic, ginger, mushrooms, rice, rice wine, scallion, soy sauce
	French	butter, cheese, cream, eggs, garlic, herbs, olive oil, stock, wine
	Italian	basil, garlic, olive oil, oregano, red wine vinegar, rosemary, tomato (Italian cuisine is influenced by Greek, which is influenced by Oriental cuisine)
	Japanese	garlic, ginger, rice, sake, scallion, sesame oil, soy sauce, sugar
	Jewish	chicken fat, onion
	Mexican	chile, chocolate, cilantro, corn, garlic, lime, rice, scallion, tomato (Mexican cuisine is influenced by Indian and Spanish cuisines)
1930s	Armenian	parsley, yogurt
	Czechoslovak	caraway seeds, sour cream
	Danish	butter, chives, cream, dill, potatoes, tarragon
	English	bacon, dill, mustard, oats, potatoes, Worcestershire (British cuisine is influenced by medieval cuisine)
	Finnish	berries, game (e.g. reindeer), milk, mushrooms
	French-Canadian	maple, salmon, seafood, wild game, wild rice
	German	caraway seeds, dill, mustard, vinegar
	Hungarian	caraway seeds, dill, onion, paprika, sour cream (Hungarian cuisine is influenced by ancient Magyar nomad origins)
	Norwegian	potatoes, smoked and cured fish, sour cream
	Russian	beets, cabbage, dill, mushrooms, potatoes, sour cream
	Swedish	dill, gravlax, herring, lingonberries, potatoes

Decade	Type of Cuisine	Characteristic Ingredients
	Swiss	charcuterie (bacon, meats, sausages; Swiss cuisine is influenced by French, German, Austrian, and Italian cuisines)
1940s	Brazilian	beans, chile, lime, rice
	Greek	cinnamon, garlic, goat cheeses, lemon, mint, olive oil, oregano, tomato
	Hawaiian	coconut, pineapple, sugar
	Irish	cabbage, oats, oysters, potatoes, rye
	Latin American	chile, corn, garlic, plantains, potatoes, red beans, rice
1950s	Korean	brown sugar, chile, sesame, soy sauce
1960s	Argentinian	beef, corn, peppers
	Austrian	cream cheeses, onion, paprika, poppy seeds (Austrian cuisine is influenced by German, Italian, and Hungarian cuisines)
	Basque	garlic, peppers, tomatoes
	Chilean	meat, onions, pimentos, seafood
	Dutch	fish, seafood (Dutch cuisine is influenced by Indonesian cuisine)
	East Indian	aromatics, coconut, coriander, curry, mint, saffron, turmeric
	Middle Eastern	cinnamon, dill, garlic, lemon, mint, olive oil, parsley, tomato, yogurt
	Polish	dill, mushrooms, potatoes, sour cream
	Portuguese	cabbage, chile, chorizo, cod, eggs, garlic, olive oil, potato, rice
	Scottish	fish, oats, potatoes
	South Seas	coconut, ginger, red curry
	Spanish	garlic, nuts, olive oil, onion, seafood, sweet peppers, tomato
	Thai	basil, chile, cilantro, coconut, curry, fish sauce, garlic, mint, peanut, sugar (Thai cuisine is influenced by Chinese and Indian cuisines)
	Ukranian	dill, sour cream
1970s	Belgian	beer, mussels, potatoes
	Jamaican	beans, fish, jerk (herbs, peppers, spices)

Decade	Type of Cuisine	Characteristic Ingredients
	Lebanese	bulgar, sesame oil (Lebanese cuisine is influenced by European, Arabian, and Oriental cuisines)
	Moroccan	cinnamon, coriander, cumin, dried lemon, fruit, ginger, onion, saffron, tomato
	North African	cumin, garlic, mint (North African cuisine is influenced by imperial Roman, Turkish, and Jewish cuisines)
	Pakistani	fruit, pulses, rice, spices
	Puerto Rican	ginger, lime, plantains
	Turkish	allspice, bulgar, lemon, olive oil, onion, parsley, walnuts, yogurt (Turkish cuisine is influenced by Muslim, Jewish, Orthodox, and Christian cuisines)
1980s	African	chile, peanut, tomato
	Black	cornmeal, greens, pork (bacon, chitterlings, ham, ribs)
	Cajun	chile, game, seafood, strong seasonings, tomato
	Caribbean	chile, cinnamon, jerk seasoning, nutmeg, okra, rum, seafood
	Creole	alcohol, banana, chile, okra, pineapple, rum, seafood, spices, tomato (Creole cuisine is influenced by African, Caribbean, French, Hindu, and Italian cuisines)
	Dominican	chile, chorizo, coconut, corn, meats
	Egyptian	fruit, pine nuts, turmeric
	Haitian	red pepper flakes, cumin
	Indian (U.S.)	beans, corn, peppers
	Indonesian	brown sugar, chile, curry, lemongrass, lime, peanut, rice, soy sauce (Indonesian cuisine is influenced by Indian and Chinese cuisines)
	Israeli	carbohydrates (baked goods, potatoes, etc.)
	Mediterranean	anchovy, garlic, olive oil, parsley, tomato
	Peruvian	chile, corn, lime, onion, tomato
	Philippine	garlic, soy sauce, vinegar

Decade	Type of Cuisine	Characteristic Ingredients
1990s	Australian	fish and shellfish, meat, tropical fruits and vegetables (Australian cuisine is influenced by British and Dutch cuisines)
	Balinese	banana and banana leaf, chile, lemongrass, palm sugar, turmeric
	Colombian	coconut, corn, onion, pimento, tomato
	Corsican	broccio cheese, citrus fruits, olives, tomato
	Cuban	black bean, cumin, garlic, lime, bitter orange, plantain, pork, pineapple, rice, yuca
	Iranian	almonds, aromatic spices and herbs, rice, saffron, yogurt
	Jordanian	marjoram, oregano, peanuts
	Laotian	basil, chile, eggplant, freshwater fish, ginger, lime, mint, rice
	New Zealand	apples, kiwi, lamb, mussels, pears, venison, wine
	Romanian	garlic, root vegetables, tomato
	Singaporean	chile, cinnamon, coconut, onion, scallion, turmeric
	Syrian	pine nuts, pistachios, pomegranate, red pepper paste
	Tex-Mex	beans, cheese, cilantro, rice
	Venezuelan	banana, beef, corn, red beans, rice
	Vietnamese	basil, chile, cilantro, fish sauce, garlic, ginger, lemon, lime, mint
Since 2000	Cambodian	basil, chile, citrus, eggplant, fish, fish sauce, ginger, lemongrass, rice
	Catalonian	garlic, nuts, orange, parika, rice, shellfish, saffron
	Ethiopian	allspice, beef, chicken, chile, cinnamon, garlic, ginger, honey, lentils, onion, turmeric
	Georgian	beets, cilantro, citrus, dill, dill pickles, garlic, herring, pickled foods, red beans, walnuts
	Malaysian	cardamom, chile, coconut, cumin, fish, ginger, lemongrass, lime, shrimp paste, tamarind
	Polynesian	banana, coconut, ginger, sweet potato, taro
	Serbian	sweet paprika, potatoes, veal

The New Millennium (2000 and Beyond)

Today, American palates have been honed, resulting in an enthusiastic market of diners patronizing restaurants who can recognize, and demand, the best ingredients and cooking—and who are passionate in their enjoyment of food and wine. "People talk about hitting America's top ten or twenty restaurants, as if they're collecting them," observes Patrick O'Connell. "This never happened before. People are developing American reference points, the way they used to try to hit all the Michelin three-stars in France."

The best American restaurants are considered world class, and the New American cuisine that is emerging through the melding of the best ingredients and techniques from throughout the world is influencing and even exciting chefs around the globe. In 2002, the Relais Gourmand organization had a celebration of American cuisine in Paris, at the suggestion of Patrick O'Connell of The Inn at Little Washington. Twelve American chefs were matched with Michelin three-star chefs and created a collaborative meal, marking the first time that American chefs had cooked in these restaurants.

According to Daniel Boulud, a native of France, "Many American chefs are definitely superior—in their cooking and in promoting themselves." He adds, "When many French chefs come to America, they get a real kick in the butt."

The torch has been passed. Restaurants in the rest of the world are not evolving as rapidly, while you'll find tremendous vitality, energy, and movement in America today.

PATRICK O'CONNELL

Baked Goat Cheese with Garden Salad

ALICE WATERS, Chez Panisse, Berkeley, CA

"Salad is something that I've been obsessed with since I encountered the classic mesclun mix when I visited a friend in Nice twenty-five years ago. I love all of the different tastes, textures, and colors that come together in this salad. We've had goat cheese with garden salad on the menu in the Café ever since it began fifteen years ago, and some people come here just to have it. It's adaptable enough to change with the seasons and is a great companion to serve with fresh figs, olives, walnuts, pears, and many other ingredients. I prefer it after a meal, although many people use it as a starter."

Three to four 2½–inch-diameter rounds of fresh goat cheese, each about ½ inch thick

½ cup olive oil

3 to 4 sprigs fresh thyme

1 bay leaf, crumbled

2 tablespoons balsamic vinegar

Dash red wine vinegar

Salt and pepper to taste

1 cup fine dry bread crumbs (toast the bread first, then grind)

About 4 handfuls garden lettuces (rocket, lamb's lettuce, small oak leaf and red leaf lettuces, chervil)

Marinate the goat cheese rounds in ¼ cup of the olive oil with the thyme and bay leaf for a day.

Prepare the vinaigrette by whisking the remaining ¼ cup of olive oil into the vinegars until the vinaigrette is balanced, and season with salt and pepper. Wash and dry the lettuces.

To bake the goat cheese, take the rounds out of the olive oil marinade and dip them in the bread crumbs. Put the cheese on a lightly oiled baking dish and bake in a preheated 450°F oven for 4 to 5 minutes, until the cheese is lightly bubbling and golden brown.

Meanwhile, toss the lettuces with enough vinaigrette to lightly coat them and arrange on round salad plates. Place the cheese in the centers of the plates with the browner side up.

Serves 4

Emeril's Portuguese Kale Soup

EMERIL LAGASSE, Emeril's and NOLA, New Orleans, LA

"When I think of my childhood in Fall River, Massachusetts, I remember a happy blur of Portuguese festivals, wonderful celebrations of music, dance, and food from the old country. The feast was known as *buon fester,* or 'good festival,' and the dish that stands out in my memory from the festivals is the *suppische kaldene,* or kale soup. This unusual soup was prepared many ways, often with chorizo, split peas, and mint accompanying the base of kale, potatoes, and stock. When I became chef at Commander's Palace, I made kale soup for the staff, substituting local andouille sausage for the Portuguese chorizo. The response was so enthusiastic, I began to run kale soup as a special on the menu in the spring and fall when the kale is in season in Louisiana. There's even a sweet little Portuguese song about *suppische kaldene*, but I'll spare you."

2 tablespoons olive oil

3 cups chorizo, sliced in ½-inch rounds

1 cup chopped onions

2 tablespoons minced fresh garlic

¼ cup coarsely chopped fresh parsley

3 cups diced peeled potatoes (about 2 large), cut in ¼-inch dice

4 quarts chicken stock

6 cups kale, rinsed, stemmed, and leaves torn into pieces

2 bay leaves

¼ teaspoon dried thyme leaves

1½ teaspoons salt

¼ teaspoon red pepper flakes

5 turns fresh ground black pepper

½ cup chopped fresh mint, optional

Heat the oil in a large pot over high heat. When the oil is hot, add the chorizo and the onions and sauté, stirring once or twice, about 2 minutes. Add the garlic, parsley, and potatoes and cook, stirring occasionally, about 2 minutes.

Add the stock and kale and bring to a boil. Stir in the bay leaves, thyme, salt, red pepper, and black pepper. Reduce the heat to medium and simmer until the potatoes are fork-tender, about 30 minutes. Remove from the heat and skim the fat from the top.

To serve, pour about 1¼ cups of the soup in each bowl and stir in ½ teaspoon of the mint, allowing it to infuse for a minute or two. Serve with a crusty Portuguese or French bread.

Serves 8

Spinach-Wrapped Sea Urchin Roe in Spicy Hollandaise

NOBU MATSUHISA, Matsuhisa, Los Angeles, CA, and Aspen, CO; Nobu, New York, NY

"Fifteen years ago, before the sushi boom, most Americans were hesitant to eat raw sea urchin. Therefore, I wanted them to open up their eyes and expand their palates to my favorite seafood. If I made the appearance enticing and heated the sea urchin in a way that did not ruin its delicate taste and texture, then I was confident in having my American customers at least take a bite. Once they took a bite, the rest was automatic, and eventually they were eating it raw."

3 ounces sea urchin roe

1 shiitake mushroom, finely diced

6 large pieces spinach leaves

1 fresh asparagus stalk, cut in half

Sauce

1 egg yolk

2 tablespoons melted butter

1 teaspoon lemon juice

1 tablespoon tobanjan (red chile paste)

2 tablespoons beluga caviar or salmon eggs

Preheat the oven to 450°F. To prepare the spinach balls, mix the sea urchin roe and mushroom together. Blanch the spinach in boiling water for 2 to 3 seconds, then rinse in cold water. Spread the spinach leaves out and fill with the roe mixture, then wrap the leaves around the mixture to form a ball. Bake for 10 minutes.

To prepare the sauce, beat the egg yolk until smooth; add the butter and continue beating until blended. Add the lemon juice and tobanjan.

To serve, cut the spinach ball in half and place in the center of a plate. Top each half with a generous portion of the caviar or salmon eggs. Pour sauce around the halves to cover the bottom of the plate. Garnish with asparagus.

Serves 1

2. Early Influences
DISCOVERING A PASSION FOR FOOD

This is not a profession that you choose. It chooses you.

NORMAN VAN AKEN

You would not be holding this book in your hands if there wasn't something about the idea of cooking that strikes a chord within you. What is the origin of that chord, of that instinctive urge to work with food? Are chefs born or made?

Some chefs are convinced that great chefs are born with that potential. Alice Waters believes that "most of it's in the genes. The really good cooks seem to just have a natural ability. They don't exactly learn it—it's just in them." Susanna Foo has found that "a good chef is born with a good palate, just as a good musician is born with good ears."

> A good cook who is born with an interest in gastronomy will naturally become, under favorable circumstances, a more accomplished artist than the individual to whom cooking is an unpleasant task.
>
> ESCOFFIER (1846–1935)

Other chefs feel that all influences are important. Jean-Louis Palladin felt lucky to have had a Spanish mother and an Italian father: "All that genetic influence was put together in my subconscious." On the other hand, he credited external influences, too, particularly his childhood in the south of France. Almost all of the chefs we interviewed brought up transformational events in their early lives that elevated food to a special level of importance.

This comes as no surprise to Mark Miller, a former college instructor, who notes, "Children reach consciousness between the ages of five and seven. Basic personality, taste, and aesthetic ability are formed that early. So it is very important to have a multitude of culinary experiences at an early age. I had those—I was lucky." Lydia Shire agrees, and counts herself as fortunate for having artists as parents, whom she credits with teaching her about aesthetics and design. Shire says, "To be good in this profession, you need to have something really special working for you. It could be how you were reared as a child, what your parents did, what kind of values they instilled in you. Some of this has to start when you're young." Jasper White is even more specific. "Most of the really good chefs that I've met have a connection that started in the embryonic stage," he says. "It has to be instilled—a love for food comes from your family."

In sharing the backgrounds of leading chefs, our purpose is to show that passion and greatness have a variety of origins. While some few were fortunate enough to have eaten in some of the world's finest restaurants as children, others were raised on good (and sometimes even bad) home cooking. The important thing was not always the food itself, but the meaning that was attached to it. "Even eating a hot dog can be a peak experience," points out Chris Schlesinger. Certainly, these chefs' early lives were filled with a wide variety of peak food experiences.

There is no single straight and narrow path to becoming a chef, and perhaps more than anything, the diversity of the lives of the chefs we interviewed illustrates this fact. The key that unites leading chefs is merely the fact that they absorbed and used what they learned about food, wherever they learned it—cooking at home, learning from relatives or neighbors, growing up on a farm, eating out in restaurants, being raised in a restaurant family, even watching cooking shows on TV.

Early influences establish an encyclopedia of tastes and ideas that becomes a foundation for future work. For example, cooking with raspberries recalls every experience a chef has ever had with a raspberry, which has been recorded in his or her memory bank. While other influences may shape and update a particular dish, the influence of the original raspberry is still there. Your own food history and food memory indirectly shape every dish you produce. It's important to be in touch with those memories and to understand how they are shaping the way you cook. Being in touch with the experiences involving food that made food important to you at a young age provides a context for all the ideas about food you will have later. While it's easy to overanalyze food, your experiences bring food back to a personal level, which helps takes your cooking beyond rote. It's also useful to be able to tap positive food memories, as your pleasurable associations with food are what can keep you going when long hours of hard work challenge your dedication.

Mark Miller of Coyote Cafe (Santa Fe) and recalls that as a child of four or five, at mealtime he would offer such comments on his mother's cooking as, "This sauce is too oily."

I still remember weekends spent harvesting walnuts from the four walnut trees at home. Dad would use a pole to knock the nuts off the trees and at the age of six, I would run around with a bucket, gathering them up. We'd pour them by the bucketful into burlap sacks, which we'd store in the cellar. The ones we cracked and ate on the spot weren't anything like the dried walnuts they'd become months later, which were slightly bitter. The fresh ones were sweet and moist, with a thin, tan skin. Even now, I particularly enjoy cooking with walnuts. This is not only because when they're featured on the menu it means they're around for me to snack on in the kitchen, but because my greater knowledge of ingredients and techniques now helps me to use their flavor and texture in particular dishes in ways that enhance my—and (I hope) others'—enjoyment of them. It's always more pleasurable to cook with ingredients you like rather than with those you don't. I find that when I cook with walnuts, for example, whether it's the first or the twenty-first such dish I've made that night, I can't wait to taste it when it's done and to send it out to the dining room. While I don't expect the customer to enjoy the dish in the same personal way I do, I hope that some of my passion for it comes through on their plate.

When speaking with *Death by Chocolate* author Marcel Desaulniers about the origins of his own love of chocolate, we weren't surprised to learn how deep the roots of his passion ran. "My father died in his early forties, when I was ten years old, and my mother was left with six kids ranging in age from an infant to a fourteen-year-old," Desaulniers recalls. "Those were some tough times and food meant a lot, because sometimes there wasn't much of it. There were nights when there might only be potato pancakes on the table for dinner.

"The one thing my mother had throughout her life was her passion for chocolate—and my positive memories of food are rooted in that. Despite how hard she worked and how little we sometimes had, she would always have a pot of fudge on the stove, or cookies in the oven. So, while we may have only had potato pancakes for dinner, we knew that there would also be some cookies to look forward to!

"It made a huge impact on me to realize how powerfully food can affect people in a positive way—and how happy you can make someone through food," he says, adding, "I think it's also significant that my mother never made us feel guilty about eating chocolate. She'd never say, 'Don't touch that!' If there was a plate of cookies out and you sat down to the table, you could always have one. She is still the same way today: At eighty-three, she is still making fudge and cookies (see page 60)—and making people happy."

Lydia Shire on Early Influences

Both my parents were artists, commercial fashion illustrators. I was surrounded by art and by a mother who told me that black was the absence of color. She never liked black, and to this day I don't like black. She got me so excited about things that I love to this day, like lots of color and things that uplift you. I'm happy that my parents started out by teaching me about painting, design, how to look at something, why something is of good quality, why it looks great, why you might put a bit of pepper on this side of the plate but not all over the plate because, as in all good art, it's not asymmetrical.

They were of middle class, of middle income. I would get one new outfit for school, but my mother would go to Best & Company or one of the other better stores, and I would have a real Scottish plaid skirt and that would be it. I would say, "Well, all my friends have seven new outfits," but they were all less expensive or they'd get them at Zayre or some[place] like that. I always say, "I taught my children the difference between cotton and polyester." At Christmastime, my kids never have to return my presents. Why? Because I know what quality is, because I've developed my aesthetic sensibility. Of course, when I was young I didn't understand why, but now I think, "Thank God my parents were the way they were and that I learned those little differences."

My father was Irish, and my mother's Yankee, as in English Yankee. My father was a great cook. He was very soft-spoken, very quiet. He was also an alcoholic, but a quiet alcoholic. He used to cut out recipes from *The New York Times* and, after he'd worked all day, he would come home and start cooking. He would make veal scallopine with marsala sauce—he would take fresh mushrooms and cut them up and sauté them in a pan with a little piece of veal. This was when I was eight years old, so this

Home Cooking

Cooking or baking at home is, naturally, often the first exposure many children have to cooking. Whether relatives provide role models, or whether experimentation alone teaches the basics, home is often a chef's first laboratory. Alfred Portale recalls following the recipe for Toll House Chocolate Chip Cookies on the back of the Nestlé Semi-Sweet Morsels bag, and being compelled to modify it to his liking. "For years, I would make them. I remember adjusting the recipe because I liked chewier ones, so I would reduce the amount

Gary Danko of Gary Danko (San Francisco) used to love to bake as a child: "My mother saw this tendency to cook, so I spent a lot of time with her, with cookbooks like the *Betty Crocker Boys and Girls Cookbook.*"

was back in 1956. If you consider the time, a man would have to be pretty dedicated to want to come home and do those things.

We would have rare flank steak on Saturday night, and spaghetti aglio olio, which is still to this day my favorite dinner in the world. He used to put newspapers on the floor and he would use an old cast-iron pancake griddle and really sear the flank steak. He would press it down a little so that it would stay flat and get really black. Then he would let it rest. I remember him saying, "We don't cut it right now"—he knew instinctively that you shouldn't cut hot meat right away, or else all the juices would come flying out. Then he would always put butter on the meat, so you'd get this great juice.

Because I was the youngest kid in the family, he would pour the meat juice for me into a little Chinese Canton cup. I would get to drink the juice, or what we'd call "the bottom of the bowl"—you know, when you make spaghetti aglio olio, some of the garlic kind of sinks to the bottom? I would eat all that garlic up. That's why to this day, garlic is my favorite thing in the world. It's what I crave.

My mother cooked, but she would take all day to make an apple pie. She's a very good cook, but I think because my father shined in the kitchen, he kind of ended up doing all the fancy things. When they would have dinner parties, they would have little linen cocktail napkins—I still have some of my mother's great cocktail napkins. They'd have a real martini pitcher and stirrers for your drinks—I still have some of those stirrers. It's of a day that's gone. That's why my dream now is to open a very fancy cocktail bar with great bar food and little linen napkins and things like that. I think it would be great. It will happen, someday.

George Germon of Al Forno (Providence, RI), recalls that his father did all the cooking at home. "He was a lunatic about fresh ingredients. We always had a garden—there were no canned goods, no frozen foods in our house." He can still recite the typical weekly menu: "Monday, chicken; Tuesday, some other type of meat; Wednesday, lamb stew; Thursday, fish; Friday, lentil soup and fish; and on Saturday, a soup of lamb's head. On Sunday, my mother cooked pasta."

of flour," he says. How did the young Portale know to do so? He reasoned, "The instructions read, 'If you want a more cakelike cookie, add flour' or something like that, so I just assumed if you took some of the flour out, they'd be chewier. And I was right."

French-born André Soltner recalls, "During the four years of war in Alsace, we were considered a part of Germany [by the Germans], so we couldn't go to the other part of France. But right after the war, as soon as we [were liberated], my mother went to visit an aunt in the south of France for about four weeks, because we'd had no contact with her [during the war]. I was about thirteen, and I took over cooking for my father and my brother, completely—you know, making dessert tartes, everything. I loved to cook, and my father and my brother loved what I cooked. They'd come home at noon from work and I had everything ready—more food than my mother had, because maybe she was more concerned about budget, and I was not concerned at all. I'm still not concerned! But when my mother came back, she thought I'd spent too much money."

Soltner confesses that at first he wanted to become a cabinetmaker, like his father. "But I had a brother four years older than I was, and at this time it was the eldest brother who was supposed to take over the parents' business. So he became a cabinetmaker, and when I was thinking, at the age of fourteen, that I wanted to be a cabinetmaker, too, my mother said, 'No way. Not two in the same business.' And because I was in the kitchen a lot with my mother, I said, 'No problem for me, I want to be a chef.' And then my parents looked for an apprenticeship for me. Otherwise, maybe, I would have become a cabinetmaker," Soltner says, causing the culinary world to shudder.

Families of Serious Cooks

Growing up surrounded by good cooks and, consequently, good food, awakened many chefs' taste buds at an early age. Leading chefs can recall their early food memories in remarkably vivid detail. Jasper White describes his grandmother as "insane" about food. "She was totally passionate," he says. As a child, before weekend trips with his family to visit his grandmother, White would call her to plan the weekend menu. His

Some Chefs' Best-Loved Childhood Foods*

Larry Forgione	His grandmother's chocolate layer cake
Mary Sue Milliken	Veal tongue
Bradley Ogden	Mom's pot roast, rhubarb pie
Chris Schlesinger	Barbecue
Lydia Shire	Spaghetti aglio olio, rare flank steak
Jasper White	His grandmother's apple fritters

*many have appeared on the chefs' menus

favorite dishes included apple fritters for breakfast. "My love for food was eating it, not working with it," White admits. "I never touched food, really, as a child. All the time I spent with my grandmother, I just sat there and watched her do the cooking. I never cooked. I just ate it, that's all. And still my great love is eating it, you know. That's still the bottom line for me."

Through his grandmother, White developed what he termed an "Italian respect" for good, fresh local ingredients. This included traveling to the "best" apple orchard where, at a young age, he learned to taste the difference in the quality of produce. White attributes his solid connection with food in part to his father, a farmer and hunter. "I don't really particularly like hunting, but I do like game and I do know how to hunt and fish, and it was all because of him. I think I had, clearly, a very solid connection to where food comes from and how it gets on the table. That's still the focus of what I do today. Really, the ingredients are everything to me."

When Sandy D'Amato was growing up, he would eat at his grandparents' house every day—where it was his grandfather, not his grandmother, who was the great cook of the family. "My grandparents owned an Italian deli and grocery store, and my grandfather would bring home the best vegetables for our meals," D'Amato recalls. "He was an incredible cook, while my grandmother was, bar none, the world's *worst* cook. Luckily, she only cooked once in a while. Still, our first question would always be, 'Who's cooking tonight?' If she was cooking, we would suddenly crave a sandwich from the grocery instead of dinner! But if my grandfather was cooking, we wouldn't want to miss it. I still remember his sautéed artichokes to this day.

"Many things I have made over the years have been influenced by him. He made great *spiedini* [skewered meats]. I took it as a real compliment when my sister told me that my *spiedini* were better than his, because she had never said that about anything else I'd ever made!

"His Sicilian burger was also amazing [see recipe on page 58]. It was his meatball recipe, only made with leaner beef. He would sauté the burger in olive oil and serve it with French fries also cooked in olive oil. It was so fabulous!" D'Amato raves. "My grandfather was not fond of kids at all, but when I started cooking, he took an interest in me because that was something he respected."

Edna Lewis recalls, "In Washington, D.C., even during slavery time, some of the diplomats would send their cooks to French cooking schools, and that would create a lot of good cooking around Washington. My aunt had cooked in Washington and came back and lived three towns away. I used to go and visit her, and her kitchen smelled divine. She was a great cook. I didn't cook at her house, but I just tasted her food and noted what she was doing. She had a dime on the table all the time for her baking soda, and a nickel for her cream of tartar. I think that was pretty common, using a dime and a nickel [to measure out the soda and tartar in a 1:2 ratio to make one's own baking powder].

"They killed hogs, and she would cook the head and the jaw and the liver, and she would boil it all together and add spices and cook it until it fell apart. Then, she would grind it all up and make sausage. It was the best sausage in the world. And she always had a pound cake ready in case anyone dropped in. It was absolutely delicious! So when I left home, I knew what good food tasted like."

Pastry chef Emily Luchetti remembers always seeing a copy of *Gourmet* around the house when she was growing up. "My parents were always into food and subscribed to *Gourmet* since 1952," she recalls. "When I was seven, I remember my dad cooking dishes like trout almondine, and making his own *pâté* from scratch and putting it into margarine tubs to give as gifts. This already had me curious about food, but then I got a copy of Julia Child's *Mastering the Art of French Cooking* for Christmas. I ended up cooking my way through it, from the first page through the last.

"When my father turned fifty, he gave up his career in publishing and moved to Florida to open a cookware store, which he ran for fifteen years," says Luchetti. "I worked there over the summers during college, and I always loved it."

On the Farm

Chefs who spent time as kids living near or on a farm had a jump on learning, often without realizing it. They learned about product seasonality through the types of vegetables grown and eaten at different times of year. They also learned how to tell when something was ripe, at the same age the rest of us were learning how to tie our shoelaces.

Daniel Boulud grew up in the French countryside, where he became attuned to the seasonal cycle. "There's a season, for example, in late February, early March for baby goat. For about a month and a half we would eat baby goat twice a week. Then after that, there is squab. Than after that, you start to have all the game, the birds. There was a peak for everything."

Seeing how hard his parents worked on their farm, from five in the morning until nine at night, made Boulud think he wanted a better life for himself. "What I liked was helping my grandmother in the kitchen. That was where I really liked to be. I could feel the warmth in the making of the food, because she was cooking for about twelve people every day, lunch and dinner. What I liked most was helping her peel potatoes and garlic, and tending to all the birds. And I used to love making the goat cheese. It all seemed like fun."

Larry Forgione says he had "the good fortune of growing up in a situation where my paternal grandmother had a completely self-sufficient farm on eastern Long Island. We would go out every other weekend and for summer vacations, so I grew up understanding what strawberries from vines tasted like, and apples off the trees, and corn picked two minutes before you ate it. On the other side, my maternal grandmother was one to get up in the morning, go to church, come back, put an apron on, and spend the entire day preparing lunch or dinner. Even a weekday dinner had to have at least two or three different desserts. Weekends had seven different desserts. So I grew up in one of these situations where everyone cared about food and took time to make it good."

His favorite dessert growing up? "Chocolate layer cake," he says without hesitation. "On our birthdays, we were allowed to pick what kind of cake we wanted. The chocolate layer cake was my birthday cake. It's the same cake that we served at An American Place. It's her recipe—minus about two pounds of sugar," he adds.

Johanne Killeen of Al Forno (Providence, RI) remembers having "lots of periodicals around—*Gourmet, House and Garden, House Beautiful, Vogue*—that featured food. For some reason, I always wanted to get my hands into the kitchen. I can even remember the first thing I ever cooked: It was a fried egg, and I forgot the butter. It was not quite a disaster, but I was probably about four at the time."

"My Italian grandmother was a great Italian cook, and a great canner and preserver," Forgione says. "I remember in August, when all the tomatoes [would] ripen at exactly the same time, her entire first floor—her couches, sofas, and carpets—were all covered with drop cloths. There may have been a thousand pounds of tomatoes all over the house. She had two large pots going all day, trying to get those stewed tomatoes into jars before they went bad. We'd help bring them down to the old-fashioned stone storage basement that was nice and cool all year round, and we'd put them on the shelves for her."

While his family didn't have a farm, self-described "country kid" Charles Palmer grew up in a farming town in upstate New York and spent time working on a dairy farm where his duties included slaughtering chickens. Palmer believes that "one of the advantages I have over a lot of chefs is that I grew vegetables, I worked on a dairy farm, I was exposed to slaughtering chickens and rabbits, and hunting and fishing, and that kind of thing. We had big vegetable gardens ourselves—everything from beets, carrots, [and] turnips, to Swiss chard, kale, spinach, green beans, and peas. I remember eating venison, partridge, and pheasant when I was ten years old because, you know, you went out and shot it and then you ate it. We used to eat beet greens while my friends were eating canned peas and Green Giant frozen vegetables. I'd have my friends over and they'd look at the beet greens and say, 'You gonna eat that?'"

Living Close to the Land

Given the day and age in which they were growing up, some chefs' early upbringings were unusual in their emphasis on living close to the land.

Growing up in Portsmouth, New Hampshire, as part of a large family with five kids, Odessa Piper recalls, "My parents were very 'Yankee' in that they believed it was cheaper to make everything ourselves rather than to buy it. We had a garden, and went clamming, and got our fish at the pier right off the boats. My mom baked her own bread, and we even made our own soda pop. It got to the point where, as kids, we cherished having store-bought food because it was so rare for us! But we grew up immersed in food, because every day involved making meals, eating them, and then planning and delegating responsibilities for the next one. In hindsight, what could be better training for a chef-restaurateur than that!"

Born in Ethiopia, Marcus Samuelsson was adopted at the age of three and grew up in Sweden eating the food of his seventy-year-old grandmother, whose cooking he felt reflected her wartime sensibilities. "When we had chicken, it would be chicken breast one day, chicken leg the next, and chicken soup the day after that. Her pantry was so well-stocked that if she always had six jars of jam on hand, she considered herself low at five jars! She was always growing something in her garden, from vegetables to fruit trees. Going out to pick wild mushrooms with her wasn't strange—it was just a part of life."

Samuelsson spent early summers in a fishing village where his father had been raised, and he credits the culture and work ethic of village life as having a strong effect on him. "We'd get up early to work hard cleaning the nets, and live our lives around the seasons. You could say I was raised with 'Old World' attitudes," he says. "It also meant that we got to eat every day what most people consider to be luxury food. If a neighbor had some extra seafood, they would walk it over and share it, whether it was fresh halibut, shrimp, crab, or lobster."

While Samuelsson wouldn't describe his mother as passionate about food, he found her passionate about his always making it home for dinner so everyone could eat together. "We ate every night at five, and no one would ever be late or miss it," he insists. "That instilled in me the importance of the table."

Zarela Martinez of Zarela (NYC) grew up on a cattle ranch, where every bite of food was used. "We fed the potato peels to the cowboys, we fed the other scraps to the animals. Nothing was wasted." There, the family produced most of what it would eat. "It was part of the fun of growing up."

Growing Up in a Restaurant

Kids who grew up in or around a restaurant got to learn at an early age about how a restaurant functions. While the rest of us might have perceived some mystery surrounding the inner workings of a restaurant (as a child, I always wondered what was behind the door with the little window where the food came from), restaurant kids knew there was no mystery—just long hours of hard work. In fact, this sometimes steered them away from going directly into the business in favor of first pursuing other interests.

Victor Gielisse grew up in a family of restaurateurs in the Netherlands. "My grandfather, my father, everybody was in the business. So although it was not automatically assumed that I would go into the business, the option was left open to me."

Gielisse originally tried to pursue another path. But during his first year at technical college for electronic engineering, "I'm sitting there and the teacher says to me, 'Hello, Mr. Gielisse? Maybe if you wake up you would like to join us? Would you mind telling us what you're doing?' And I said, 'I have no idea. I haven't got the faintest idea what I'm doing here.' I was at the wrong school, at the wrong time, and it was just totally wrong. I did not fit in there. So they said, 'What is it you like to do?' And I said, 'I like to cook.' They said, 'You are in the wrong school.' And I said, 'Yeah, I know that.'" After he began working at a restaurant where his father was at the time, "things started to fall into place."

Rick Bayless was always interested in cooking. While his brother always asked for sports equipment as gifts, eleven-year-old Bayless found himself asking his parents for a two-volume set of *Mastering the Art of French Cooking.* "I had watched every single episode [of Julia Child's TV show] since her first season in 1963. I still have all my notes from when I was nine years old, writing the recipes down."

Bayless spent a lot of time at his parents' restaurant—a family-style barbecue restaurant in Oklahoma. "I always worked there in some capacity, even if it was just prepping vegetables or something like that," Bayless recalls. "But I never had any sense of where things were coming from. The meat came in plastic bags, and that was the most we could say about its origins. My grandparents were definitely of the 'have your own garden' and 'can your own food' and 'freeze your own food' school, and I was really drawn to that. When I was seven, my parents had a catering business in conjunction with their

Lissa Doumani of Terra (St. Helena, CA) recalls when she was twelve, being asked by a friend of the family, "And what do you want to do when you grow up?" Having grown up as a self-described "restaurant brat," she never hesitated in answering, "I want to have a restaurant."

restaurant, and I would go out on catering parties and help them set up. I would fill drinks and pass out things like ice cream. I always loved it very much. But the older I got, the more I realized I didn't want to inherit my parents' restaurant, and I didn't want to live in Oklahoma City."

Bayless had other goals in mind. "At the time, I wanted to go out and explore the world," he says. By pursuing this early passion, Bayless eventually put his own stamp on Mexican cuisine. "I loved cultural things. From the time that I was in mid-high school, I knew that I wanted to study Spanish and Latin American culture. I had traveled to Mexico when I was fourteen, with the Spanish Club at school, and I just fell in love with it."

Judy Rodgers was an exchange student during her senior year of high school in 1973, and was strongly influenced by her surrogate family. "The family I was placed with was the Troisgros family [which

What They Thought They Wanted to Be When They Grew Up

Mario Batali	Pro football player
Marcel Desaulniers	Undertaker ("I liked the way they dressed.")
Larry Forgione	Physical education teacher
Joyce Goldstein	Painter
Emeril Lagasse	Musician
Emily Luchetti	Civic planner
Nobu Matsuhisa	Architect
Patrick O'Connell	Actor
Anne Rosenzweig	Ethnomusicologist
Chris Schlesinger	Plumber or electrician
Jimmy Schmidt	Electrical engineer
Craig Shelton	Neurosurgeon
Lydia Shire	Artist
André Soltner	Cabinetmaker
Jeremiah Tower	Architect
Jasper White	Piano tuner
Janos Wilder	Lawyer

owns a three-star restaurant in France]. It was an accident of fate," Rodgers says. "It was still a fairly modest kitchen, pretty old-fashioned, very friendly. It was in an out-of-the-way part of France and there had been hardly any Americans through there, so I was pretty much a curious beast, and they loved it. I spent as much time as I could in the kitchen, in the dining room, marketing with Jean, meeting all his purveyors. He was such a compelling personality, to begin with, and sort of infectious in his approach to his profession.

"It was made clear to me that it was one of the more desirable, pleasant kitchens to work in among the three-stars—they were not at all rough, terrible, screaming chefs. Jean especially took a great interest in teaching and explaining everything to me, because I would copy down every recipe and take notes on everything I saw. They would call me 'Mata Hari.' They all thought I'd become a food writer for sure," she remembers. But Rodgers says she gave no thought at the time to becoming a chef herself. "I figured you had to start as an apprentice when you were thirteen, plucking feathers off grouse, and that it was too late for me to be a cook. I'd had no relationship with the food industry in America, other than a summer job at a Dairy Queen."

Elizabeth Terry of Elizabeth on 37th (Savannah) remembers trying escargot for the first time at age sixteen at Tour d'Argent in Paris, as well as its most famous dish: "I had pressed duck, and I still have the little card with the duck's number on it," she recalls, referring to the restaurant's practice of numbering its ducks.

Eating Out

The experience of eating out in restaurants, whether for special occasions only or as a weekly ritual, also influenced many chefs.

Joyce Goldstein recalls hating the food she ate growing up. This was exacerbated by the mandate of the era, which instructed children to "clean their plates" and "drink a big glass of milk with every meal"—something that brought untold misery to the undiagnosed lactose-intolerant Goldstein. "I was a problem eater," is how Goldstein describes her early relationship with food. "Restaurants saved my life." Part of the pleasure of eating out, according to Goldstein, was being allowed to order whatever she liked—including a soft drink instead of milk!

Jean Joho of Everest (Chicago) still remembers a meal he had as a child at Auberge de l'Ill, after his father instructed him, "Order what you like." Nine-year-old Jean ordered a first course of foie gras, a second course of whole black truffle, and a third course of lobster. "It was a great food moment," he adds, unnecessarily.

Eating out in restaurants also provided some chefs with their first introductions to ethnic foods, even if not quite at the same level as the food the chefs would eventually come to cook themselves. The late Barbara Tropp, an authority on authentic Chinese cooking, grew up in New Jersey. "On Friday nights, we went out for Chinese food. If not Friday night, then Saturday night," she told us. "Instead of celebrating the Sabbath, we'd run away to chop suey."

Nobu Matsuhisa, who was born in Japan, first thought he wanted to become an architect like his father, partly because his father's career took him to faraway places. He remembers looking through his father's photo albums at buildings of different shapes and sizes in the cities his father had visited. But a trip to a restaurant when Matsuhisa was seven years old, where he saw sushi being prepared for the first time, changed all that. "That sushi experience, seeing the sushi man filleting the fresh fish and creating beautiful presentations, reminded me of the beautiful pictures in my father's photo album. I thought being a sushi man or a chef might also take me to different places," Matsuhisa says. (His career has since taken him from the Far East to South America and, finally, to the United States.)

It wasn't always the food that made the biggest impression when eating out, either. Michel Richard still remembers the first time he went to a restaurant and saw the chef wearing a toque. "That's the moment I knew I wanted to become a chef," he swears.

Coming to See a Job as a Career

While many chefs worked in and around food at a young age, it often took a "Eureka!" moment for them to make the transition from seeing restaurant work as something that allowed them to earn a dollar into something that could provide them with a career.

While still in high school, Marcel Desaulniers had worked for three years in a restaurant starting out as a dishwasher and working his way up to a cook's position. "The chef of the restaurant had read about the CIA [Culinary Institute of America] in a trade journal, and drove me down to New Haven [its

original location] to take a look at it. For me, it was like going to Oz! I saw chefs in those white coats and tall tocques, and can still remember the aroma of lamb roasting in the kitchen. It was all so new to me, and so exciting! Having worked part-time in a kitchen, it wasn't until that moment that I realized that this was something I could get excited about doing professionally."

Amy Scherber had gone to college to earn a degree in psychology and economics as preparation for a career in marketing. "But when I graduated, the job market was flat, so I went back to waitressing, becoming a head waitress and trainer for a year and a half. Then I got a job in marketing in New York City, where I started noticing all the ethnic markets and restaurants and felt compelled to explore them," she says. "Once I found out that a colleague of mine was going to cooking school, I found I just couldn't stay focused on marketing! After three years, I decided to quit to pursue my dream, starting out by taking classes in Italy and then returning to New York to attend cooking school."

Pastry chef Gina DePalma studied political science in college, with an eye on a career in law or government. "Since I'd grown up in a food-obsessed Italian-American family, I started cooking when I was eight. I worked in restaurants from the day I got out of college. Once the owner of a restaurant where I'd applied for a waitressing job found out I knew how to cook, he cut a deal with me: I would cook some lunch and brunch shifts in exchange for his giving me the most lucrative waitressing shifts on Friday or Saturday nights. So I did this while I was trying to decide between going to law school and earning a master's degree. Despite my subsequent jobs in a law office, and even the mayor's office, I always found an excuse to keep cooking. I eventually got to the fork in the road of having to decide between graduate school and

Chefs Who Changed Careers to Enter the Field

Chef	Prior Career
Rick Bayless	Linguist
Susanna Foo	Librarian
George Germon	Artist
Johanne Killeen	Photographer
Amy Scherber	Marketer
Alice Waters	Montessori teacher

cooking school, and after taking the LSAT [Law School Admissions Test] I had applications to graduate schools, law schools, *and* cooking schools on my desk! In the end, I went with my heart. While it enraged my family and made my mother cry, I ended up taking out every possible student loan, maxing out my credit cards, and going to Peter Kump's [now known as the Institute for Culinary Education]."

Learning from the Past

No matter what age you are now, you've already learned much about food that can serve you well, should you decide to make a career in this profession. Don't discount what you already know. Take the time to be conscious of it, understand it, and value it. Review your own personal food history, your earliest and most memorable experiences involving food. What was it that made these experiences stand out? The freshness of the flavors? The particular combination of flavors? The setting? Something else? You'll begin to understand what you value in food, as well as the elements other than food that are important in food experiences.

Art museums and galleries often post biographies of featured artists at the beginning of exhibits so that viewers have a sense of the artists' influences, which can enhance their understanding and appreciation of the artists' work. Similarly, understanding the influences and inspirations behind chefs' food can add another dimension to customers' enjoyment of it.

Thinking about food this way will put you in touch with your personal prejudices—the foods you love best, the foods you don't care for, a preference for spicy or rich foods, or foods of your ethnic heritage or American region. These seeds, planted in you years ago, may grow into your eventual direction as a chef.

Granny's Chocolate Cake

LARRY FORGIONE, An American Place, New York, NY

"For a long time, this was the only cake on our menu. We began serving it when we opened An American Place in 1983, and everyone loved it. When I was growing up, it was one of my favorites. We have modified the recipe from the days when my Irish grandmother made a similar cake on request for my birthday every year, but the spirit is the same. When Granny made the cake, she put an inch of fudge frosting between every inch-high layer, which made it a really big cake; eating it meant having as much fudge as cake. The cake should never be refrigerated but kept under a cake dome. If you refrigerate it, it will dry out."

Cake

2⅓ cups flour

1 teaspoon baking soda

½ teaspoon baking powder

½ teaspoon salt

1 teaspoon vanilla extract

1¼ cups buttermilk

11 tablespoons (1 stick plus 3 table-spoons) unsalted butter, at room temperature, plus some for preparing the pans

1½ cups sugar

3 large eggs

4 ounces unsweetened chocolate, melted

Fudge frosting

6 ounces semisweet chocolate

½ cup plus 2 tablespoons water

Pinch salt

1½ teaspoons vanilla extract

10 tablespoons (1 stick plus 2 table-spoons) unsalted butter, melted

7 large egg yolks, beaten

5 cups confectioners' sugar

Preheat the oven to 350°F. Butter three 9-inch round layer cake pans and line them with parchment paper. Lightly butter the paper. Dust the pans with flour and shake out the excess.

Sift together the flour, baking soda, baking powder, and salt. In a small bowl, combine the vanilla and buttermilk.

Using an electric mixer set at medium-high, cream the butter until soft. Slowly add the sugar and continue beating until well blended and light colored. Add the eggs, one a time, beating well after each addition. Add alternating amounts of the dry ingredients and the vanilla-buttermilk mixture to the batter, mixing well after each addition. When the batter is smooth, stir in the melted chocolate. Blend until the batter is smooth and even-colored.

Spoon the batter evenly into the prepared pans. Smooth the tops with a rubber spatula. Bake for 30 to 35 minutes or until a toothpick inserted in the center of a cake layer comes out clean. Let the cake layers cool in the pans set on wire racks for 10 minutes before removing them from the pan. Peel off the paper and let them cool completely on the racks.

To make the frosting, break the semisweet chocolate into squares and put them in the top of a double boiler with the water, salt, and vanilla extract. Stir the mixture over hot, not simmering, water until the chocolate is almost melted. Remove the top of the double boiler from the heat and stir in the melted butter until the mixture is smooth and blended. Let the mixture cool slightly.

Transfer the frosting to the large mixing bowl of an electric mixer and with the mixer set on the lowest speed, incorporate the egg yolks and then the sugar. Add both gradually and beat well after each addition.

Allow the frosting to cool to room temperature before spreading it on the cake. If you prefer, the mixing can be done by hand, but this must be done gently. Never beat the frosting at a high speed in the mixer or too quickly by hand.

Place a cooled cake layer on a cardboard round or flat serving plate. Use a metal spatula to spread about ½ cup of frosting on the layer. Position another layer on top and spread with another ½ cup of frosting. Place the last layer on top and smooth any filling that may have seeped from the sides. Refrigerate the filled cake for 15 to 20 minutes until the filling sets.

Remove the cake from the refrigerator and brush any crumbs from the sides and top. Frost the cake with half of the remaining frosting, beginning and ending with the top. Refrigerate the cake for another 15 to 20 minutes. Take it from the refrigerator and frost it with the remaining frosting. The chilled frosting acts as a "crumb coating" and makes the final application easy and smooth. For an extra silky finish, use a metal spatula warmed in hot water and wiped dry to smooth the frosting. Serve the cake at room temperature. Store it under a cake dome or upturned bowl. Do not keep it in the refrigerator.

Makes three 9-inch round layers

Apple Fritters

JASPER WHITE, Jasper White's Summer Shack, Cambridge, MA

"The smell of my grandmother's kitchen in the morning would wake the dead. An early riser, she would start baking and cooking as soon as the sun came up and within an hour, everyone else would be awake, not because of the noise but because of the intoxicating aromas that filled the house. Apple fritters were a special favorite of my brothers and me. We could eat them as fast as she could make them, but she would keep up with us until we could eat no more. My grandmother inspired me to be a chef, like her father was."

2 cups all-purpose flour

1 tablespoon baking powder

½ cup sugar

1 tablespoon salt

2 eggs

⅔ cup milk

4 large firm green or other tart apples, peeled, cored, and sliced ¼ inch thick

2 tablespoons unsalted butter, melted

Vegetable oil for deep-frying

Confectioners' sugar for dusting

Sift together the flour, baking powder, sugar, and salt in a bowl. Mix well.

Beat the eggs and milk together and add the flour mixture, stirring until smooth.

Fold in the sliced apples and melted butter. Allow the batter to stand at least 10 minutes before using.

Heat the oil to 375°F in a pot suitable for deep-frying. Drop large spoonfuls of batter, the size of walnuts, into the hot oil. Cook the fritters for a few minutes until they are golden brown or even a little darker. Drain on paper towels. Dust with confectioners' sugar and serve at once.

Serves 6 to 8 for breakfast or dessert

Kougelhopf

JEAN JOHO, Everest and Brasserie Jo,
Chicago, IL

"As a young man I always made kougelhopf on Saturday for Sunday morning's breakfast. This was for two reasons: Kougelhopf is always better the second day, and Sunday morning was the only morning my father had breakfast with the family."

Accompany with a Gewürztraminer or a Cremant d'Alsace.

1 ounce brewer's yeast
¾ pint milk, warmed
2¼ cups plain flour
½ ounce salt

3 eggs
10 ounces (2½ sticks) butter
5 ounces sugar
5 ounces pitless sultanas (can substitute raisins), steeped in kirsch or water
A small glass of kirsch, optional
2½ ounces almonds, peeled and wiped

Prepare the dough with the yeast, half of the milk, and sufficient flour to make a dough of average consistency; leave the dough in a warm place.

In a separate basin, mix the remaining flour with the salt, eggs, and the rest of the warm milk and knead energetically for about 15 minutes, lifting the mixture with the hands.

Add the butter and sugar, softening the mixture in your hands, and knead in the dough, which will have doubled in volume.

Continue to knead for a few minutes, cover the bowl with a cloth, and leave to settle in a warm place for about an hour.

Knead again, break open the dough, mix in the sultanas and then add a small glass of kirsch, if desired.

Grease thoroughly the bottom and ridges of a kougelhopf mold, decorate the bottom with almonds, and then place the dough into the mold.

Once more, leave the dough to rise until it reaches the top edge of the mold and then place in the oven on a medium heat.

If the kougelhopf browns too quickly, cover with a sheet of paper; bake for about 45 minutes.

Serves 4 to 5

Pearled Barley with Seared Foie Gras, Roasted Granny Apple, and Rhubarb Essence

CHARLIE TROTTER, Charlie Trotter's, Chicago, IL

"When I was growing up in the Midwest, fresh apples just off the tree were an everyday treat. My mom spent many hours in her kitchen making homemade applesauce, apple pies, and baked apples. The Midwest also has an abundance of fresh rhubarb—the scent of strawberry rhubarb pie used to be almost overwhelming. Being able to utilize these ingredients in my cooking keeps me close to my roots, close to my family."

> 1 cup cooked pearl barley (cooked in water)
>
> Five 1¾-ounce slices foie gras
>
> 1 Granny Smith apple, cut into ¼-inch slices
>
> ¼ cup Almata apple pieces, finely cubed, plus ¼ cup julienned Almata apples
>
> 1 tablespoon snipped parsley
>
> ⅛ cup julienned rhubarb, lightly blanched in a simple syrup
>
> 4 ounces rhubarb essence (recipe follows)

Heat the cooked barley over a double boiler. Sear the foie gras slices over medium heat, reserving the rendered fat. In a nonstick pan, sauce the Granny Smith apples on both sides in a table-spoon of rendered fat, then roast them at 350°F for 4 to 5 minutes. Remove from the oven and blot off excess fat. Sauté the cubed Almata apple pieces until just cooked in another tablespoon of the foie gras fat. Sauté the julienned apple in ½ tablespoon of the foie gras fat.

Cut one of the pieces of seared foie gras into a fine dice and fold the pieces into the barley, along with the cooked apple pieces and about half of the parsley. Season to taste with salt and pepper.

Place a piece of seared foie gras on each of four warm plates. Top with a timbale of barley and a slice of roasted Granny Smith apple. Place a little julienned apple around the top of each slice of apple. Strew some barley around the edges of the plate, along with the rest of the julienned Almata apple and the julienned rhubarb. Drizzle about a tablespoon of rhubarb essence onto each plate and sprinkle with the remaining parsley.

Rhubarb Essence

> 6 tablespoons raspberry vinegar
>
> 3 tablespoons sugar
>
> 6 ounces peeled and diced rhubarb
>
> 2 cups chicken stock

Make a gastrique out of the raspberry vinegar and the sugar by simmering over a medium heat until reduced to a syrup. Add the rhubarb and briefly stew in the gastrique. Add the chicken stock and slowly reduce down to ¾ cup; strain.

Serves 4

Lamb with Mint Sauce

CINDY PAWLCYN, Mustards Grill, Napa, CA

"This dish is what I always requested of my mom for birthdays and other special-occasion meals. I was lucky to have a mother who could roast meat and serve it medium rare to medium, not well done. I truly think that the only reason I liked lamb was for her mint sauce, which she made the same way her mother had made it. Mint was the only fresh herb she grew in her garden."

One 7 to 8 pound leg of lamb

3 to 4 garlic cloves, peeled and sliced

Salt and freshly ground black pepper

6 to 8 sprigs mint (big ones)

2 cups white wine

Mint Sauce (recipe follows)

Preheat the oven to 450°F. If your butcher hasn't already, trim the lamb leg of excess fat. Cut small slits in the leg and insert slices of garlic. Thoroughly season with salt and pepper. Put the white wine in the bottom of a roasting pan. Place the leg of lamb on mint sprigs in the roasting pan. Roast for 15 to 20 minutes until a golden brown. Reduce the heat to 350°F and continue roasting and basting with wine until an internal temperature of 125°F is reached. Allow to rest for 25 minutes before carving. Serve with mint sauce.

Mint Sauce

2 cups finely chopped fresh mint leaves

3 to 4 tablespoons sugar

4 tablespoons vinegar

4 to 6 tablespoons water

Combine all the ingredients. Let steep for 1 to 2 hours. Taste and add additional water if too intense.

Serves 10

Watermelon Salad

CHRIS BIANCO, Pizzeria Bianco, Phoenix, AZ

"Eating watermelon as a kid was always fun. This salad has only five ingredients, and really typifies the simplicity of my food. The recipe is made to eye and to one's own personal taste."

Watermelon, cut into cubes, with any watermelon juice reserved

Fennel, sliced thin

Italian parsley leaves

Lemon juice

Gray sea salt

Mix the watermelon, watermelon juice, fennel, and parsley together. Squeeze a little lemon on top, then season with a pinch of the sea salt.

My First Cheesecake

PATRICK CLARK (1955-1998)

"From the age of nine, I was always tinkering in the kitchen. I would spend all of my weekly allowance on cream cheese in search of the ultimate cheesecake. By the time I was seventeen, I found the almost-perfect recipe, which I still make for family and friends. But I always keep tinkering. Just recently, I decided to use vanilla beans instead of the extract, and found that it's so much better that way!"

3 pounds cream cheese, at room temperature

1½ cups sugar

Pinch salt

1 teaspoon vanilla extract or the seeds of 1 fresh vanilla bean

3 large eggs

1 cup sour cream or heavy (whipping) cream

Graham cracker crumbs and butter for crust

In the bowl of a mixer, place the cream cheese, sugar, salt, and vanilla bean seeds, if using (if using vanilla extract, add after creaming).

Cream the mixture at medium speed, until light, then add the vanilla extract (if using), and the eggs, one at a time, mixing for 2 minutes after each addition. Stir in the sour cream or heavy cream until well combined.

Butter a springform pan (10-inch diameter with 2½-inch sides) and sprinkle with graham cracker crumbs. Pour the batter into the pan and bake in a preheated 350°F oven for about an hour and 10 minutes, or until the cake tests done in the center.

Remove to a cake rack and cool completely. Remove the cake from the springform pan and refrigerate. Serve chilled plain, or with your favorite fruit or fruit compote.

Serves 16 to 20

Sicilian Burgers on Semolina Olive Buns

SANFORD D'AMATO, Sanford Restaurant, Milwaukee, WI

4 tablespoons extra-virgin olive oil

½ cup finely minced onion

¼ cup dry white wine

2 tablespoons sweet Marsala wine

1 small bay leaf

Freshly cracked pepper

½ teaspoon salt

1 pound ground beef (preferably chuck)

½ pound ground pork

1 large egg, lightly beaten

¼ cup dry white bread crumbs

½ cup grated imported Romano cheese

2 tablespoons chopped fresh parsley

1 tablespoon chopped fresh basil

Semolina Olive Buns (recipe follows)

Heat 2 tablespoons of the olive oil over medium-high heat. When hot, add the onion and cook until translucent, 3 to 4 minutes. Add the white wine, Marsala, bay leaf, 1 teaspoon pepper, and ½ teaspoon salt. Bring the mixture to a boil, bring down the heat, and simmer until most of the liquid has evaporated, about 10 minutes. Remove the bay leaf, transfer the mixture to a plate, and let it cool in the refrigerator.

In a large bowl, gently but thoroughly combine the beef, pork, cooked onion mixture, egg, bread crumbs, cheese, parsley, and basil.

Gently form four patties. They can be made in advance and held covered in the refrigerator until cooking.

Before cooking, season the patties with a little salt and a fresh crack of pepper. For medium-rare burgers, grill them over a medium fire or sauté them over medium-high heat for 6 to 7 minutes.

To serve, split the buns, brush with a little of the remaining olive oil, and toast them flat side down on the grill or in the pan until golden brown while the burgers rest.

Serves 4

Semolina Olive Buns

1½ cups warm water

2 tablespoons plus 1 teaspoon extra-virgin olive oil

1 tablespoon barley malt

1 teaspoon sugar

2 tablespoons active dry yeast

3 cups bread flour

1¼ cups semolina flour

2 teaspoons salt

½ cup pitted, chopped, oil-cured, ripe black olives

In the bowl of a mixer, place the warm water, one tablespoon of the olive oil, the barley malt, and sugar. Add the yeast and stir to dissolve. Allow the mixture to sit for 5 minutes, until it foams.

Fit the mixer with a dough hook. Add to the yeast mixture 2½ cups of the bread flour, the semolina flour, and salt. Mix on low speed for a minute. Stop and scrape down the bowl. Continue to mix at medium-low speed until the dough is smooth and elastic, about 5 minutes.

Place the dough on a lightly floured work surface, using the remaining bread flour as needed. Flatten the dough. Place the olives on top and fold from end to end and knead for 2 to 3 minutes.

Coat the inside of a stainless steel bowl with the teaspoon of olive oil. Place the dough in the bowl and wipe the bowl with the dough. Cover the bowl with plastic wrap. Allow the dough to rise in a warm place until it has doubled in size, about an hour.

Preheat the oven to 325°F.

Place the dough on a slightly floured work surface. Using a sharp knife, cut the dough into eight equal portions. Shape each portion into a ball. Place the balls on a baking sheet lined with parchment paper. Loosely cover the dough with plastic and allow to rise again in a warm location until doubled in size, about 30 minutes.

Using a dough cutter or the back side of a thin knife, press an X in each bun, being sure not to cut the buns. Let rise again for 10 minutes. Brush with the remaining olive oil.

Bake the buns for 35 to 40 minutes, until golden brown. Allow to cool before serving. The buns will keep for 2 to 3 days in a sealable bag at room temperature.

Makes 8 buns

My Dad's Best-Ever Roast Chicken and Our Family Rice

TRACI DES JARDINS, Jardinière, San Francisco, CA

"I grew up in the rural farmland of central California. My father and grandfather were rice and cotton farmers, descendants of Louisiana Cajuns. Our family has always been about food and gathering together as often as possible to share stories and good meals. It is because of this that I have become a chef. The following are a couple of my favorite dishes. I make this recipe for friends and when they inevitably ask for the recipe I have to sheepishly admit to the use of Campbell Soup. I still am delighted to have my dad cook these things when I come home exhausted from the restaurant world. I hope that you, too, will enjoy them."

1 large free-range organic chicken, whole

1 bunch basil, stems removed

2 garlic cloves, thinly sliced

1 lemon

1 tablespoon dried thyme

1 tablespoon dried oregano

1 teaspoon savory

1 teaspoon dried sage

1 teaspoon dried rosemary

4 tablespoons Dijon mustard

Salt and freshly ground pepper

Consommé Rice (recipe follows)

Preheat the oven to 450° to 500°F. Loosen the skin of the chicken by running your fingers up under the skin of the breast. Thread in between the meat and skin the basil leaves and sliced garlic, trying to distribute them evenly. Poke holes in the lemon with a fork and place in the cavity. Combine all of the dried herbs. Rub the Dijon mustard over the entire bird, then sprinkle the herbs over the entire skin of the bird. Finish by seasoning well the the cavity and the outside with salt and pepper.

Place the bird breast side up in the preheated oven and cook for about an hour. You may have to reduce the oven temperature after 15 to 20 minutes if you notice that the skin is getting dark too fast. Barbecue option: Cook over a kettle barbecue after allowing the coals to become completely white; spread to the outside of the barbecue. When the chicken is done, all of the juices coming from the cavity should be clear. Carve the chicken and place on a platter, remove the lemon from the cavity, and squeeze over the chicken. Serve with the consommé rice or any variety of accompaniments such as mashed potatoes, roasted heirloom potatoes, and corn or parsnip puree.

Consommé Rice

 2 cups California raw short-grain rice
 4 cups Campbell Soup Beef Consommé
 4 tablespoons butter

Place the butter in a heavy-bottomed saucepot and place over a medium-high burner. Add the rice and cook until nicely browned. Bring the consommé to a boil and add to the rice, bring all to a boil, cover; reduce the heat to the lowest possible setting, and cook for 20 minutes. Allow to sit covered for 10 minutes before serving.

Serves 4 to 6

Mrs. D's Chocolate Chip Cookies

MARCEL DESAULNIERS, The Trellis, Williamsburg, VA

"As a toddler, I teethed on this cookie (along with her fudge). As time passed, it greeted me after school and brought my family together around the kitchen table. When I was in the service, this cookie brought me joy in Viet Nam and put a smile on the faces of my Marine buddies desperate for a taste of home. With a cookie like this from Mom, I don't know why anyone needs apple pie."

 4 cups all-purpose flour
 1½ teaspoons baking soda
 ½ teaspoon salt
 ½ pound (2 sticks) unsalted butter, cut into 1-ounce pieces
 2 cups tightly packed dark brown sugar
 2 large eggs
 2 tablespoons dark rum
 1 teaspoon pure vanilla extract
 24 ounces chocolate chips

Preheat the oven to 300°F.

In a sifter combine the flour, baking soda, and salt. Sift onto a large piece of wax paper and set aside until needed.

Place the butter and sugar in the bowl of an electric mixer fitted with a paddle. (If a table-model electric mixer is not available, this dough may be mixed by hand using a stiff rubber spatula or a wooden spoon. Make sure the butter is at room temperature.) Beat on medium speed for 4 minutes, until soft.

Use a rubber spatula to scrape down the sides of the bowl, then add the eggs, dark rum, and vanilla and beat on medium speed for a minute until combined. Scrape down the bowl.

Operate the mixer on low speed while gradually adding the sifted dry ingredients until incorporated, about a minute.

Add the chocolate chips and mix on low speed for 30 seconds. Remove the bowl from the mixer and use a rubber spatula to finish mixing the dough until thoroughly combined. Using 2 large heaping tablespoons of dough for each cookie (just shy of 3 ounces); portion six cookies, evenly spaced, onto each of four nonstick baking sheets.

Place the baking sheets on the top and center racks of the oven and bake for 28 to 30 minutes, until the cookies are dry to the touch. Rotate the cookies from top to center about halfway through the baking time (at this time also turn each sheet 180 degrees). Remove the cookies from the oven and allow to cool at room temperature on the baking sheets for 30 minutes. Store the cookies in a tightly sealed plastic container until ready to serve.

Note: Mrs. D and her family love crisp cookies. If your preference is for a softer cookie, bake them for 20 minutes at 325°F. These cookies will keep forever, or close to it, when held at room temperature in a tightly sealed plastic container. For long-term storage, up to several weeks, the cookies may be frozen. Freeze in a tightly sealed plastic container to prevent dehydration and freezer odor.

Makes 2 dozen 4-inch cookies

3. Cooking Schools
LEARNING IN THE CLASSROOM

I would push for some way to figure out how much kids really like food before admitting them to cooking school. In the waiting room [for an admissions interview], have cookies around and see if they steal them. If they steal them, you let them in the school. If they don't steal them, then you don't take them. What's needed is some kind of test to find out—do they want to be in a magazine, or do they really want to work with food?

JASPER WHITE

No matter how strong a chef's inspirations, they are not enough to give rise to greatness. They must be carefully honed and refined through directed effort. The palate, which allowed a chef to first learn what he or she found most enjoyable, must be trained to discern subtleties in flavors and flavor combinations, and to critique as well as taste. Similarly, basic cooking techniques must be mastered, with speed and efficiency developed over repeated efforts, in order to be able to create desired effects. This is what leads chefs into professional kitchens and, increasingly, into professional cooking schools.

First of all, you must have a good, solid foundation of techniques, ideally classical. This builds your understanding of the available components that could be placed in a dish, so that you know all your options. It's kind of like having a road map—you may know how to get from Detroit to Chicago, but you have a choice with a very intricate map and a lot of knowledge of many different ways to go. You can take the more scenic route, the faster route—there are a million different directions you can go in. The more you know, the better off you are.

JIMMY SCHMIDT

Cooking is a profession that places extraordinary emphasis on continuous learning, and today a chef's first formal education often takes place in a cooking school classroom. There are hundreds of cooking schools in both the United States and abroad, offering opportunities to learn about specialties ranging from vegetarian to confectionery to microwave cooking. In fact, *The Guide to Cooking Schools* (ShawGuides) lists more than 1,100 programs in its 2003 edition. However, a much smaller number are considered to be primarily professional (degree, diploma, or certificate) programs, and are the primary emphasis of this chapter.

While many of the country's leading chefs reached the top of the profession without the benefit of a cooking school degree, an overwhelming majority of the chefs we interviewed recommend cooking school as the most expeditious start for an aspiring chef today. Cooking school offers an opportunity to gain exposure in a concentrated period of time to an immense amount of information, from cooking techniques (knife skills, sauté, grill) to theory (nutrition, sanitation), to international/regional cuisines (French, Italian, Asian).

A cooking school diploma can also be an important credential in opening doors and demonstrating commitment to the field. "I only hire cooking school graduates," says Patrick O'Connell, who himself doesn't hold a cooking school degree. "If I had to do it again at this point in history, I would probably go to culinary school." Alfred Portale is even more adamant. "I think that if you can go to cooking school, you should. I feel very strongly about it," he says. "It immediately legitimizes you as a professional and exposes you to a broad base of information, even though not much of it is practical. It certainly puts you at a greater advantage than someone who's self-taught or learns going up through the ranks."

While attending cooking school full-time represents a certain trade-off in terms of the opportunity cost of forgoing a full-time income while at school, the vast majority of chefs interviewed see it as an investment well made. In fact, the cooking school naysayers have little criticism for the cooking schools themselves; they reserve it for the popular misconception that merely attending cooking school can create a chef, which they believe often misleads people without a real passion for food and cooking into the profession. "Cooking schools do an important job," says Anne Rosenzweig, "but the final results depend a lot on the students." Victor Gielisse concurs: "Cooking school gives aspiring chefs a tremendous foundation. But school alone cannot give you a passion for food. It's impossible. Not even the best teacher can do that."

Amy Scherber says she's asked constantly by aspiring chefs whether she recommends cooking school. "I'm always quick to counsel them that there is only so much they're going to get out of school," she says. "It all depends on the school, the caliber of your teachers and classmates, how much your teachers make you compete and learn, and how good your classmates' questions are.

"But cooking school will provide you with a vocabulary for the profession, some experience working with other people in front of a hot stove, as well as some basic skills to be able to offer a prospective employer," Scherber adds.

Given the abundance of reputable cooking schools and programs, there is likely to be an option to suit everyone's specific budget, time frame, and other needs. From four-year bachelor's degree programs, to certificate programs that can be completed in a few brief months, to one-session cooking demonstrations by culinary experts, there are numerous opportunities to learn about cooking in a classroom. With the hundreds of cooking schools available, it is up to the prospective student to research various options to determine which offers the best fit. In this chapter, the entire scope of the cooking school experience is explored, with recommendations from leading chefs as to how to get the most out of your experience before, during, and after cooking school.

Choosing the Right Cooking School

The decision whether and where to attend is highly personal and dependent on many factors: How long a program best suits your needs? Is location a factor for you? What is your budget for school? Are you looking to attend full-time or part-time? During the day or in the evening? (Certain schools have offered classes twenty-four hours a day.) While it is not our intention to recommend specific schools, we hope that the insights of leading chefs and the brief information on cooking schools that is included will help guide your eventual decision.

"I first started cooking during the summer before college," says Sandy D'Amato. "I worked Friday night fish fries, which are a Midwest tradition. I would bread fish and onion rings all night long. During the rest of the week, I basically did short-order cooking.

"I started at the University of Wisconsin with the eventual goal of getting into hotel/restaurant school. While I was there, I looked for an apprenticeship program—and the only one I could find was a vocational program that turned out to be essentially a work release program for prisoners. I was the only one in the program who was not a former convict."

Brief Histories of Selected Cooking Schools

The Culinary Institute of America in Hyde Park, NY, is the country's oldest culinary academy. Originally founded by Frances Roth and Katharine Angell in Connecticut in 1946 as The New Haven Restaurant Institute, the school moved to its current location in 1972 and has produced more than 35,000 culinary graduates. Many are among the country's leading chefs (see page 68). The Institute bills itself as "the only residential college in the world devoted entirely to culinary education," and proudly quotes Paul Bocuse in the school's literature as saying, "[The Culinary Institute of America] is the best culinary school in the world."

Johnson & Wales University opened in Providence, RI, in 1973 with 141 students, and has expanded to other campuses in Charleston, SC, and Norfolk, VA. The school offers associate, bachelor, and graduate degrees in foodservice, hospitality, teaching, education, and technology.

The Restaurant School was founded in Philadelphia in 1974, and offers majors in culinary or pastry arts. It offers students an eight-day gastronomic tour of France.

Institute of Culinary Education (formerly known as Peter Kump's New York Cooking School) offers 26 to 39 week diploma programs in Culinary Arts, Pastry and Baking Arts, and Culinary Management. Founded in 1975 by Peter Kump, the founding president of The James Beard Foundation, the school is now headed by Rick Smilow. Nick Malgieri, the Institute's director of Pastry and Baking, was named one of the top ten pastry chefs in America by *Pastry Art and Design Magazine*.

L'Academie de Cuisine is a proprietary vocational school offering a 48 week Culinary Career Training Program, a 34 week part-time Pastry Arts program, part-time certificate courses, continuing education and nonprofessional courses, and a cultural and culinary program in Gascony, France. Established in 1976, it is based in Gaithersburg, MD, just outside Washington, DC.

"Fortunately, the chef-instructor asked if I had considered culinary school, and introduced me to the idea of going to the CIA," says D'Amato. "I got a bunch of student loans, and ended up attending the first year the CIA moved to Hyde Park [New York, from its original location in New Haven, Connecticut]."

Pastry chef Emily Luchetti had already earned a bachelor's degree in sociology when she found herself working in an executive dining room on Wall Street at a firm that paid for its employees' continuing education. "I studied French at the Alliance Française because I wanted to be a chef and thought that's what all chefs spoke," she now laughs. "I even studied with [Italian culinary expert] Giuliano Bugialli when

California Culinary Academy is a for-profit institution founded in San Francisco in 1977 to provide technical and professional chef training for individuals desiring an entry-level position or advancement as a cook, chef, or baker. Its sixteen-month program is modeled after the European system of closely monitored apprenticeships.

The New England Culinary Institute was founded in 1980 by Frances Voight and John Dranow in Montpelier (VT). The first class had 7 students. In 1989, the school expanded to a second campus at the Inn at Essex in Essex Junction, VT.

Academy of Culinary Arts—Atlantic Cape Community College is a two-year college offering two-year AAS degrees in Culinary Arts and Food Service Management, a one-year certificate in Baking and Pastry Arts, and a six-month certificate in Culinary Arts and Management. Established in 1981, it is the largest cooking school in New Jersey.

The Cooking and Hospitality Institute of Chicago is a private institution offering a two-year associate degree in the culinary arts and eight-month certificate programs in professional cooking, baking and pastry, and restaurant management. Established in 1983, the school has a total enrollment of about 750 students.

The French Culinary Institute was founded in 1984 in New York City, and offers a 600-hour day or evening program in classic French cuisine. The Institute's faculty includes Jacques Pépin as Dean of Special Programs and Alain Sailhac as Dean of Culinary Studies.

For information on other leading culinary schools, visit www.shawguides.com and www.culinaryschools.com.

Selected Culinary Institute of America Alumni

Class of	Chef	Restaurant	Location
1965	Marcel Desaulniers	The Trellis	Williamsburg, VA
1974	Sanford D'Amato	Sanford	Milwaukee, WI
	Larry Forgione	An American Place	New York, NY
1976	Jasper White	Jasper White's Summer Shack	Cambridge, MA
	Roy Yamaguchi	Roy's Restaurant	Honolulu, HI
1977	Gary Danko	Gary Danko	San Francisco, CA
	Susan Feniger	Border Grill	Santa Monica, CA
	Sara Moulton	Host, *Cooking Line*	New York, NY
	Bradley Ogden	Lark Creek Inn	Larkspur, CA
	Chris Schlesinger	East Coast Grill	Cambridge, MA
1978	Anthony Bourdain	Brasserie Les Halles	New York, NY
	Dean Fearing	The Mansion on Turtle Creek	Dallas, TX
	Rick Moonen	RM	New York, NY
1981	Alfred Portale	Gotham Bar and Grill	New York, NY
1982	Michael Chiarello	Tra Vigne	St. Helena, CA
	Todd English	Olives and Figs	Charlestown, MA
1983	George Morrone	Redwood Park	San Francisco, CA
1984	Caprial and John Pence	Caprial's Bistro	Portland, OR
	Jamie Shannon	Commander's Palace	New Orleans, LA
1986	Rocco DiSpirito	Union Pacific	New York, NY
1988	Melissa Kelly	Primo	Rockland, ME
1989	Ken Oringer	Clio	Boston, MA
1991	Sherry Yard	Spago	Beverly Hills, CA
1992	Scott Conant	L'Impero	New York, NY
1994	Grant Achatz	Trio	Evanston, IL

he was still in New York. But after making the decision to attend cooking school full-time and being accepted at the Culinary Institute of America, I realized that after four years of college I really didn't want to spend another two years in school." Instead, she opted to attend the New York Restaurant School as part of the school's third group of matriculating students.

If you know the kind of restaurants you'd like to work in after graduation, consider taking the time to ask some chefs at similar restaurants in your area to recommend cooking schools to you. Carefully read all of the literature available from each of the schools you're considering. This alone should address some of your most basic concerns, such as the range of course offerings and whether the program costs are within your reach. If you're able, plan to spend a day at each of the schools you're seriously considering.

When visiting schools, don't hesitate to ask a lot of questions of administrators, instructors, and even students. Find out whether they offer (or require) an externship program or an international study program. Ask what kind of placement assistance they provide to graduating students and alumni. Find out where some of their recent graduates are working and what the breadth of the school's network is. Who are some of their most successful alumni? Are typical alumni working in the kinds of places you'd like to work in someday? Spend time talking with other students, and decide if they're the type of people with whom you'd enjoy learning and spending time. You'll be happiest at a school that offers a "good fit."

> **As a woman, you should sit in on classes [at cooking schools]. Interview a professor or two about the philosophy of the school: Does it believe women can contribute, that women can reach the top?**
>
> ELIZABETH TERRY

Alma Maters of Leading Chefs

Chef	Restaurant	Alma Mater
Dan Barber	Blue Hill, New York, NY	The French Culinary Institute, New York, NY
Bobby Flay	Mesa Grill, Bolo, New York, NY	The French Culinary Institute, New York, NY
Mark Franz	Farallon, San Francisco, CA	California Culinary Academy, San Francisco, CA
Emeril Lagasse	Emeril's, New Orleans, LA	Johnson & Wales University, Providence, RI
Mary Sue Milliken	Border Grill, Los Angeles, CA	Washburne Culinary Institute, Chicago, IL
Michael Romano	Union Square Cafe, New York, NY	New York City Technical College, Brooklyn, NY
Jimmy Schmidt	The Rattlesnake Club, Detroit, MI	Modern Gourmet (Madeleine Kamman), Newton, MA
Lydia Shire	Locke-Ober Cafe, Boston, MA	Le Cordon Bleu, London, England
Hiroyoshi Sone	Terra, St. Helena, CA	Tsuji Cooking School, Osaka, Japan
Allen Susser	Chef Allen's, Miami, FL	New York City Technical College, Brooklyn, NY
Gina DePalma	Babbo, New York, NY	Institute of Culinary Education, New York, NY
Colin and Renee Alevras	The Tasting Room, New York, NY	Institute of Culinary Education, New York, NY

Certain schools, such as The Culinary Institute of America, Johnson & Wales University, the New England Culinary Institute, the California Culinary Academy, and the French Culinary Institute, attract a national (and even international) student body. Other schools, such as the Cooking and Hospitality Institute of Chicago, tend to attract a greater proportion of their students from their regions, and local chef alumni may show some preference to graduates of their alma maters over graduates of other programs. Still other schools tend to draw more closely from their immediate vicinities.

Schools also differ in their orientation to particular types of cuisine. The French Culinary Institute (NYC) specializes, obviously, in French technique. The Culinary Institute of America, which has traditionally offered training in classical French cuisine, has now added classes in Italian and other international cuisines. The Natural Gourmet Cooking School (NYC) emphasizes healthy, vegetarian cooking.

Even many outside the profession have at least heard of the venerable Culinary Institute of America, often by its double-entendre acronym, "the CIA" (as it is sometimes referred to). Founded in 1946, the oldest cooking school in the country has historically offered a twenty-one-month Associate Degree Program in Culinary Arts, in which students master basic culinary skills through hands-on instruction. Course work includes classes in American and international cuisines, seafood cookery, nutrition, sanitation, charcuterie, and service and hospitality management. All students must also complete an externship semester off campus and work in the Institute's four restaurants. The Institute also offers a twenty-one-month Associate Degree Program in Baking and Pastry Arts, in which students study culinary concepts and then take specialized course work in baking, pastry, patisserie, and breads and desserts.

The Culinary Institute of America also has two Bachelor of Professional Studies degree programs in Culinary Arts Management and in Baking and Pastry Arts Management. The new programs are designed to build upon the associate's degree programs and require two years of subsequent study, with courses in leadership and management, marketing, communications, finance, ethics, foreign languages, history and culture, and advanced cooking. Students are expected to research a senior thesis in food. The programs also include a six-week food and wine seminar at the Institute's Napa Valley (CA) campus.

Other leading schools include the College of Culinary Arts at Johnson & Wales University in Providence, Rhode Island. Like The Culinary Institute of America, it offers a four-year bachelor's degree program in addition to its two-year associate's degree program, which emphasizes progressive individualized development, environmental and nutritional awareness, sanitation and food safety, marketing and

> The schools have gotten better, or at least the generation of cooks that have come out in the last five years are more aware and more capable. Whether that actually came from the cooking schools or whether it came from an awareness within the society, I don't know. But it's different than it was ten years ago. The things you learn in cooking school are very important: how to clean up after yourself, how to care for and sharpen your knives. You have to have a certain familiarity with equipment, with protocol.
> **ALICE WATERS**

merchandising, financial controls, production, and a six-month cooperative education experience. The New England Culinary Institute (NECI) in Montpelier, Vermont, has its students spend 75 percent of their time—starting the first day of class—in a hands-on environment, cooking and managing The New England Culinary Institute's ten foodservice outlets, which are open to the public. The New England Culinary Institute students also spend two out of four semesters in a paid internship program, which allows them to work in any foodservice establishment in the world that meets the school's standards. The California Culinary Academy in San Francisco offers a sixteen-month career program emphasizing classic and modern techniques, which is modeled after the European system of closely supervised apprenticeships and features three student-staffed restaurants open to the public.

For those unable or unwilling to dedicate two to four years to their culinary education, another option is a school such as the Institute of Culinary Education in New York City (formerly known as Peter Kump's New York Cooking School), which offers 610-hour diploma programs in both Culinary Arts and Pastry Arts. Students must complete 400 hours of instructional time and 210 hours of externships in restaurant, hotel or catering kitchens or other culinary enterprises. The Institute will also arrange externships in Europe and Asia. In addition to these programs, career students may participate in the school's six-session Wine Essentials class and three single-session specialty classes, which typically feature a guest chef.

For those looking to specialize in baking, Amy Scherber advises, "Take a two-week seminar and learn basic skills. Follow that by an externship in a bakery, and then you can decide whether you want to go into a heavy-duty long-term program, or go into a great bakery and start working your way up.

"As for bakeries, there are several to choose from in New York City or the San Francisco Bay Area. In New York, I'd recommend either our bakery [Amy's Bread] or Balthazar, because they have great technique. In the Bay Area, you could spend time at Acme Bread in Berkeley or Artisan Bakers in Sonoma. So many of these bakeries are using organic ingredients and great technique—and they're all pretty open to sharing information.

"Regarding schools, there are many—although I don't think you necessarily need to go through a six- or eight-week course, since there are plenty of one- to two-week classes. At the San Francisco Baking Institute, they do a great job. The main reason to go there is Didier Rosada, who is an absolutely great baker and speaks French, English, and Spanish. He has all the technical skills that anyone could ever look for, and can work with professionals as well as with someone who's never baked," she marvels. "I could have learned more from him in one day than I learned in three months in France!"

Don't think that if you can't attend school full-time you can't receive a fine education. "If you don't have enough money, you can still attend part-time," emphasizes Dieter Schorner, a Certified Master Baker who currently teaches patisserie and pastry skills at The Culinary Institute of America. Schorner, along with other experienced chefs who cooked in restaurant kitchens by day, taught classes in the evening at New York City Technical College, a vocational college based in Brooklyn. "I found some of the most dedicated teachers at this little college," he says.

A brief word about programs in hospitality management: Such an education can certainly prove valuable to aspiring chefs, particularly to those who aim to become executive chefs or chef-owners. Cornell University in Ithaca, New York, offers both four-year bachelor's degree and two-year master's degree pro-

> **Going to school is only one of the first steps to growth and development in understanding what to do in a kitchen, and what to do with cuisine.**
>
> ALLEN SUSSER

grams in hospitality management. As the college's literature on its School of Hotel Administration has stated, "If your goal is to become one of America's great chefs, we can get you started, but we won't teach you to cook." While their course offerings have included selections such as Culinary Theory and Practice, such schools place most of their emphasis on the teaching of management skills through courses in such areas as communication, finance, food and beverage management, human resources, information technology, law, management, marketing, operations, real estate management, and tourism. Having some training in these subject areas becomes increasingly important as you move up the ladder in a kitchen, and an advanced degree is something to consider seriously if you see your ambitions as one day expanding beyond the kitchen walls.

Admissions Requirements and Process

If you're aiming for a competitive program, getting in presents the next hurdle. Some of the top schools aren't able to admit everyone who applies. At other less competitive programs, merely submitting an application and application fee is basically all it takes. Given the increasing demand for trained cooks and chefs, many cooking schools have been expanding their programs to accommodate more students.

The admissions process, depending on the school, may be simple and straightforward, or relatively more involved. The Culinary Institute of America, for example, requires a completed application form, an application fee, and a high school transcript, as well as transcripts from any postsecondary studies and at least two letters of reference from employers, foodservice instructors, or Culinary Institute alumni. In addition, applicants must submit an essay explaining why they wish to enter the foodservice field, what research on the industry they have done, details of their foodservice background, and why they're interested in attending The Culinary Institute of America.

The New England Culinary Institute requires applicants to submit a written personal statement on their background and experiences, why they have decided to seek a career in the culinary arts, and their reasons for applying to the New England Culinary Institute. Also required are letters of recommendation; copies of high school, vocational school, or college transcripts; and the application form and an application fee.

At the Institute of Culinary Education, a minimum of two years of college or two years of professional work experience—not necessarily in the food industry—is required. Applicants are asked to submit a completed application, verification of college attendance or work experience, and a 10 percent deposit of the total school fees (including tuition and materials). If students are not admitted to the program, the down payment will be refunded, minus a nonrefundable registration fee.

While some local cooking schools will have less rigorous application processes, most schools will require you to apply well in advance of your desired date of attendance, so plan ahead.

Before Attending Cooking School

Pastry chef Gina DePalma credits having worked for a few years in the restaurant business before attending cooking school as making a world of difference for her. "Simply having knife skills, as well as a sense of comfort in the kitchen, was such a help," she attests.

Some schools, such as the New England Culinary Institute, see prior work experience as a plus but not a prerequisite. Many cooking schools, however, require work experience in a kitchen as a condition of admission. The Culinary Institute of America requires a minimum of three to five months of food-service experience that includes exposure in a professional kitchen. This is for the prospective student's benefit as much as it is the cooking school's. Both parties have a vested interest in seeing that students who enter successfully complete the program, and not everyone who's attracted by the perceived "glamour" of the profession finds that the reality of the work is a good fit. When Emeril Lagasse offered high school students who had expressed an interest in cooking a chance to spend some time in his restaurants, he found that more than half of them changed their minds after they saw what kitchen work was really like. Is cooking something you could come to love as a profession? It's best for all concerned that a reality check be taken sooner rather than later.

Because of all the benefits that accrue to a student who works before attending school, this is something that should be considered seriously by everyone thinking about attending cooking school, whether the school requires it or not. Larry Forgione says, "I think people really ought to think about whether this is what they really want to do before they jump into it with both feet. I might suggest stepping in with one foot—working weekends at a place, hanging out at a restaurant to understand what the restaurant business is all about." While the glamorous image of the restaurant business might help to attract people to the profession, only those who have actually worked in a kitchen know the intense effort involved.

In addition to practical experience, other preparation can provide an edge at cooking school. If you can't work full-time in a kitchen, consider getting some part-time experience working for a caterer, at a gourmet store, or as a waiter or waitress. Spend as much time as you can reading about food and cooking, if you don't already. Charles Palmer recalls, "When I decided that I was going to go to The Culinary Institute of America, I read about food and cooking so that when I got there, I found that I was more knowledgeable than most. Every night, I would read *Larousse Gastronomique*. I read any cookbook that I could get my hands on. I especially liked the Time-Life series because it really explained things so that you could understand." In addition, restaurant experience before cooking school offers an opportunity to determine what area a student might want to specialize in—for example, cooking on the line, or pastry.

You may, in addition, have prior academic or work experience in a field unrelated to cooking. Prior experience can be a great help in preparing you for the rigors of a tough cooking school program and difficult first jobs. You are likely to have already developed study habits and writing skills. Also, food is so basic that few fields don't offer some degree of overlap—from art to science to history. Alfred Portale's work in jewelry design certainly hasn't hurt his reputation for artistic presentation, and Barbara Tropp's academic training helped her to succeed as both a chef and an author. If you have already invested time and energy in another field, you are likely to ask good questions and have a clear idea of what you are looking to get out of your education.

At Cooking School

While at cooking school, it's important to make the most of your opportunity. Several leading chefs noted the tendency of some students to put more effort into their social life at cooking school rather than into the important learning process that takes place both in and out of the classroom. This can be a tragic mistake. Alfred Portale, who graduated first in his class, recalls: "I started at The Culinary Institute of America a little older than most of the students there. I had good experience and was very, very serious. For a lot of the students, it's their first time away from home, and they can't really get over that part. They go crazy partying, and it takes them a whole year to calm down. And by then it's too late."

The Culinary Institute of America

Through illustrating various cooking school curricula, it's easier to discern the process of skill development. As in the mastery of any subject, you first learn the basics and work toward the complex. Starting with the mastery of basic knife skills and product and equipment knowledge, students move into more sophisticated applications. You don't start out baking ten-tiered wedding cakes. The same set of basic skills and knowledge is important to learn no matter where one attends cooking school.

As an example, we've outlined below the courses required for a two-year associate's degree in culinary arts at The Culinary Institute of America. The first semester includes Introduction to Gastronomy; Culinary Math; Nutrition; Sanitation; Meat Identification; Meat Fabrication; Product Identification and Food Purchasing; Culinary French; and Culinary Skill Development. The second semester includes Introduction to Hot Foods; Supervisory Development; Seafood Cookery; American Regional Cuisine; Oriental Cuisine; Charcuterie; Breakfast Cookery; Lunch Cookery; and Advanced Garde Manger. The third semester consists of a required eighteen-week externship. The fourth semester includes Baking Skills Development; Cost Control; Patisserie; Menus and Facilities Planning; Management of Wine and Spirits; Business Law; International Cookery; and Advanced Culinary Principles. The fifth semester includes Classical Banquet Cuisine; Introduction to Table Service; and Catering Seminars, as well as practical dining room and kitchen experience in the school's four restaurants: St. Andrew's Café, the Ristorante Caterina de' Medici, Escoffier Restaurant, and American Bounty Restaurant.

In contrast, the two-year associate's degree in baking and pastry arts requires a different curriculum. The first semester includes Introduction to Baking Science; Baking Math; Sanitation; Baking I, II, and III; and Pastry I. The second semester includes Pastry II and Pastry III; Patisserie I; Costing Examination; Baking Practical Examination; and Patisserie II and III. The third semester consists of a required eighteen-week externship. The fourth semester includes Nutrition; Ice Carving, Display Work, and Showpieces; Cost Control I; Supervisory Development; Cost Control II; Cooking Fundamentals for Bakers; Menus and Facilities Planning; Management of Wine and Spirits; Business Law; Product Identification and Food Purchasing; and Advanced Culinary Principles. The fifth semester includes Bread and Desserts in St. Andrew's Cafe, the Caterina de' Medici, and the American Bounty; Entrepreneurship; Costing Examination; Baking Practical Examination; and Advanced Patisserie.

In addition to using classroom time as an opportunity to ask questions and learn as much as possible, it's important to take advantage of extracurricular learning. Volunteer to assist professors and visiting chefs with special events, and make an effort to get to know them. Aside from the knowledge they can pass along, these interactions get you noticed, and may spawn leads on future jobs.

Some chefs found that the most important lessons they learned came outside the classroom. "I spent a lot of time in the library [at The Culinary Institute of America]," says Gary Danko. "And I came across this book called *The Making of a Cook* [by Madeleine Kamman], which made so much sense to me. It went into the how's and why's of cooking—like how to make a hollandaise sauce, and if it breaks, how to correct it—and that was something that I wasn't learning in the classroom at that point.

"When I went to another cooking school, before transferring to The Culinary Institute of America, the first thing I noticed was that every instructor was saying, 'Now this is how you make the best [blank],' and the next was saying, 'No, no, no, this is how you make the best [blank].' All of a sudden, the confusion starts. But as you learn cooking, and you do different things, and see different people's styles, that influence becomes part of your style. And eventually that style will become your cuisine."

Danko advises, "Be serious when you go to cooking school. Make sure you have some books to draw from, and that you spend some time and really pick the instructors' brains. Ask them every question you can. Spend extra time cooking with instructors. Volunteer for things. Because to me, that's where the real learning comes from, putting in the extra time. And, as Madeleine Kamman would always say, 'Get an education. Don't just go to cooking school.'"

Working While at Cooking School

Many chefs we interviewed emphasized how much their in-class learning was complemented by their outside work in a kitchen while attending school, and suggested that students maximize their learning by working while attending school. Allen Susser says, "I think you need to see the real side of the ideal things you're cooking in the school kitchen." Mary Sue Milliken goes so far as to recommend that students work full-time while they attend cooking school: "If the

Learn the basics. You must understand the products, the ingredients, how to season and taste, the actual cooking, the composition of dishes, and food presentation.

JEAN JOHO

schedule is too rigorous, this is probably not a good career choice."

Working while attending school can serve many purposes. It can reinforce what you are learning in the classroom and point out what you are not. Jasper White advises working during cooking school "because then you can start applying things every day and retain a lot more." It can give you extra practice on your knife and other skills, and allow you to pursue other interests in food, such as ethnic cuisine or catering, that may not be covered. White loved his work at the Waccabuc Country Club in Westchester County, New York. "We did buffets on Sundays— I got to use a lot from school that I wouldn't have had a chance to use otherwise."

Any experience is what you make of it— you don't have to work at a four-star restaurant in order to learn. Susan Feniger worked at a fish market in Poughkeepsie, New York, while attending The Culinary Institute of America. Boston chef Jim Becker worked at the sandwich counter at a wine and cheese store while attending cooking school, in order to educate himself about cheeses. I know another cooking school student who chose to work in catering instead of a restaurant because of the flexibility in scheduling, which allowed her to learn and practice her culinary skills without the intense pressure of daily service at a restaurant. She was also able to see a wide variety of food at the catering company—

> If there's one thing I wished I'd studied at school, it's mechanics. It's very hard to fix your stoves, your kettles, your dishwasher, and all that. Chef-restaurateurs need to be versed in the mechanical aspects of the machinery they work with—otherwise, it's fifty or a hundred dollars for a visit to hear "Well, you're going to need a new compressor, son . . . ." VICTOR GIELISSE

from two hundred wontons to an entire theme dinner centered around the early settlers in Boston. There is a price to pay for all of this—less sleep, not to mention less energy and time for other school activities. While the burden of such a workload might give pause to some, leading chefs seem to be in agreement with Nietzsche's principle: "That which does not kill me makes me stronger."

Externships

An externship is a period of time spent working in a restaurant for the purpose of gaining practical, on-the-job experience, and may be paid or nonpaid. Some schools mandate serving an externship as a requirement for graduation, while others offer it as an option to students. Certain schools even offer a chance to work abroad or at leading resorts. It's important to research the options available through the school you're interested in and, if there's a particular restaurant you'd like to serve an externship with, to take an active role in doing all you can to pursue it. Find out which faculty or administration members have the strongest ties to the restaurant and speak with them, write a letter to the chef, or possibly offer to work for free until the time your official externship commences.

Every experience is different. Some restaurants have students cook on the line, while others allow externs to do only basic prep work. André Soltner required that The Culinary Institute of America students he took into his kitchen at Lutèce (NYC) commit to a minimum one-year externship, which maximizes both the student's learning and his restaurant's ability to benefit from it. If an externship is offered or required, make the most of it. Work in the best kitchen you can get hired into. If you make a good impression, you may find yourself with an offer for permanent employment, and at worst you'll end up with a good reference for future jobs. At the New England Culinary Institute, about 70 percent of second-year internships turn into job offers.

One extern I know was passed over for a permanent pastry position because of his inexperience, yet he kept coming in on his own time to keep his skills sharp while looking for a job at another restaurant. When the pastry chef left unexpectedly, he was hired into the position. Another extern received an offer to join a restaurant as garde manger because of her excellent work habits and attitude (including coming in early, staying late, working fast, and taking direction well). While she had no experience, her work habits spoke volumes about her potential and she was given a chance to prove herself.

After Graduation

Chefs emphasize the importance of viewing graduation from cooking school as merely a starting point in one's education. André Soltner puts it this way: "I think cooking schools give students the basics they need. But they are not accomplished chefs. They are just coming out of school. A doctor, after his four years, goes to a hospital not as the chief surgeon but as an intern. We have to look at cooking school graduates as what they are." Schools and parents were thought to feed students' expectations. "Parents send their kids for two years at The Culinary Institute of America and then think they are André Soltner or Paul Bocuse," Soltner notes. "But they are not."

Emily Luchetti notes that there's a significant difference between culinary school graduates today versus when she graduated twenty years ago. "In my day, we didn't have such a clear vision of what our futures might hold, or what we might aspire to, so we were much more internally and intrinsically focused on the process of becoming skilled at our profession," she says. "Today, there are so many prominent chefs that students are more focused on things like getting their names on the door of a restaurant or winning the James Beard Award. They are not engrossed in the process of waking up every day, going to work, and getting excited by the thought of making the very best food they can make that day. I try to slow cooks down, and some 'get it' and others don't. I think part of becoming a great chef is living in the moment and not just in the future."

Cooking school graduates might find themselves tempted with offers to become full-fledged chefs upon graduation—welcomed by students, at least in part, because of the sometimes substantial debt incurred through financing cooking school. However, leading chefs speak discouragingly of the notion of accepting a job as a chef too soon. The late Patrick Clark always advised, "Don't look for glory right away. When you get there, it's harder."

Some chefs advise that after graduation you should work with your "idols," in order to continue your education. Upon graduating from The Culinary Institute of America, Alfred Portale answered an ad and was selected to work at the food shop that Michel Guérard was opening at Bloomingdale's. He recalls: "Here I'm just out of school, and I'm standing in a kitchen with Michel Guérard, the Troisgros brothers—all these huge French guys, all my idols. It was thrilling. I learned all the butchering and the charcuterie, the poaching and the smoking, and the stuffing and the sausage making, and all that kind of stuff that young cooks dream about. After putting in a year with these guys, they invited me to France. So I spent a year working first at Troisgros, and then with Guérard. I had a car and toured France, spending the last six weeks in Paris, going out every day and every night, going to every bookstore, every cooking store, just learning and submerging myself in everything."

After graduating from The Culinary Institute of America, Gary Danko began a dogged cross-country pursuit to track down Madeleine Kamman, to persuade her to let him study with her. While Danko says she expressed reservations about working with a newly minted culinary school graduate, he set out to change her mind. "I pulled up in my car the first day of class with all these local products that I'd been working with—goat cheese, guinea hens, ducks, geese, lamb, you name it. She saw that I was very serious about cooking and she sort of took me under her arm."

Continuing Education

Just because you graduate from cooking school doesn't mean the learning process ends. In this profession, it should never end. You don't have to earn a cooking school degree to benefit from time spent in a classroom learning how to cook. Patrick O'Connell attended a Chinese cooking school on Saturdays for six months. Susanna Foo, who entered the restaurant business mid-career, found the eight-week stint she spent at The Culinary Institute of America invaluable. "After The Culinary Institute of America, I decided I only wanted to use fresh vegetables that tasted fresh, the way they did when I was growing up," says Foo. "I went back to the restaurant determined to meld Chinese ingredients with French technique, and started to re-create my kung pao sauce, black bean sauce, curry sauce, and other sauces."

If your goal is not necessarily to earn a degree but to learn about cooking from chefs themselves, there are a growing number of venues available offering classes with, and demonstrations by, leading chefs and other food authorities. For example, De Gustibus is a popular program at Macy's (NYC) run by Arlene Feltman Sailhac, which has featured such chefs as Daniel Boulud, Anne Rosenzweig, and André Soltner. Other places such as Ramekins in Sonoma Valley (CA) and Sur La Table (with several locations, including Seattle and San Francisco) also offer demonstrations by culinary experts such as Hiroko Shimbo, author of *The Japanese Kitchen*.

While I was cooking during the lunch shift at Biba, I made it a point to attend Boston University's Seminars in the Culinary Arts in the evening, where I was able to take classes with local chefs such as Gordon Hamersley, and visiting luminaries such as Lorenza de' Medici, Julie Sahni, and Anne Willan. The Boston Public Library sponsored a Cooks in Print series which, in lecture format, offered wonderful

Patrick O'Connell speaking at The Culinary Institute of America

"I have brought this brand-new instrument that you may have seen before but perhaps never actually understood the significance of. If you can master this incredible tool, it will open new doors and allow you to do anything. This instrument will explain to you the essence of cooking."

A giant violin case was brought out. I opened it up, and inside was a broom. I showed them some real dirt I had brought with me, and I threw it on the floor and said: "I will now teach you something that you did not learn for your twenty-thousand-plus dollars in annual tuition: I will now teach you how to sweep.

"If you can allow yourself to become one with the broom, you will understand the basic foundation of how to become one with the food—and thus, how to cook. Unless you can do that, you will not understand cooking because you will always be separated from it. This way, you can practice creating this flow between your psyche and your body, and then transferring it into something else, into a tool."

I demonstrated two methods of how many students would sweep. I did the "macho" method, where the student sweeps it all over the wall, followed by the "timid" method, where they sweep it right into their shoes!

The first thing you learn coming into the kitchen at The Inn at Little Washington is how to sweep the floor. No one knows how to do that anymore. No one ever showed them, ever!

I explained how to let energy flow into the broom handle, and how pleasurable it was when *I was* the broom, and how efficient the sweeping became. I then suggested that they all go to their dorms and practice.

Every night, I still find myself telling my cooks, *"Get in the pan with the food!"* I want them to feel total focus and flow. It is exciting when you see them merge with the food! It is a true high for a chef.

opportunities to learn about food from leading authorities like Julia Child and Jasper White. The Schlesinger Library at Radcliffe College also offers panels of leading culinary experts on various issues, from food safety to customer service, which are open to the public. To find similar kinds of programs in your area, check with adult education and continuing education programs, with your local library, or with local chapters of national associations such as the International Association of Wine and Food.

Many cooking schools also sponsor continuing education programs for working chefs, where one can spend anywhere from a day to a month learning more about cooking. The Culinary Institute of America even offers courses on videotape.

Nancy Silverton took a break from her career to attend Lenôtre (the namesake school of noted French pastry chef Gaston Lenôtre), in France, to study pastry. "I was working at Michael's, which at the time was considered one of the top restaurants in Los Angeles, and my desserts were very well regarded. I went to Lenôtre and thought I might end up teaching them a few things." Silverton was surprised and humbled to find herself in classes with pastry chefs, some of whom owned their own pastry shops and who had been working in the field for thirty to forty years. Silverton admits, "That's when I first came to realize that you never learn it all."

If you do decide to pursue cooking school, as recommended by the majority of chefs we interviewed, the most important point to keep in mind is to stay focused on what you're hoping to get out of it. Work for at least a year before attending, in order to confirm your interest, before making such an important investment in your career. This will give you a more realistic view of the profession and also make you more focused once you're at school. If an externship is offered, take advantage of it. Work at the best restaurant you can get into, and learn and absorb everything you can. And, once you graduate, beware the paradox of "commencement": You're not a master chef yet—you've just taken the first important step in beginning to acquire an important base of knowledge on which to build. As Jimmy Schmidt says, "Remember: A building is only as strong as its foundation. If you don't have a strong foundation, you can never erect a skyscraper."

Recommended Reading

The Guide to Cooking Schools: Cooking Courses, Vacations, Apprenticeships and Wine Instruction Throughout the World. Coral Gables, FL: ShawGuides. New editions published annually.

Culinary Schools: The Complete Guide to U.S. and International Cooking Schools, Restaurant Management Programs, and Culinary Apprenticeships. Princeton, NJ: Peterson's. New editions published anually.

Chocolate Chip Cookies

NANCY SILVERTON, Campanile,
Los Angeles, CA

"All my life, I've waited for a recipe for the perfect chocolate chip cookie—crisp, buttery, with a cracked surface and a plump interior with hand-chopped high-quality chocolate. I wanted it to hold its shape all the way to the edges. Even when it cooled, I wanted it to have the rich, incredible aroma of a freshly baked cookie. The downside of this story is that I can't take credit for formulating this recipe—it belongs to Michelle Guyer, a pastry chef who worked at Campanile. The upside is that I get to eat them every day!"

8 ounces chocolate (bittersweet Valhrona is the best)

8 ounces (2 sticks) plus 2 tablespoons unsalted butter

1 cup granulated sugar

¾ cup brown sugar

1 egg

1 teaspoon vanilla extract

2½ cups all-purpose flour

½ teaspoon baking soda

¼ teaspoon baking powder

1 cup walnuts, chopped

Chop the chocolate coarsely and chill in the refrigerator for 2 to 3 hours. Using the paddle attachment of an electric mixer, beat the butter on medium speed until it whitens and holds peaks, 3 to 5 minutes. Add the granulated sugar and brown sugar, beating until well blended. Whisk the egg and vanilla extract together and beat them into the butter mixture, scraping down the sides of the bowl as necessary.

Sift together the flour, baking soda, and baking powder. Beat half the flour mixture into the butter mixture, scraping the sides of the bowl; then add the remaining flour mixture, mixing until just combined. Beat in the chopped walnuts and the chilled chopped chocolate. Wrap the dough in plastic wrap and chill until firm, about 2 hours.

Preheat the oven to 325°F. Roll the dough into 1½-inch balls and place on a paper-lined cookie sheet 2 inches apart. With the palm of your hand, lightly press down on the balls. Bake until the cookie has risen and cracked, 8 to 10 minutes. Do not overbake.

Makes about 2 dozen cookies

Swiss Onion Soup

SUSAN FENIGER (CIA '77), Border Grill,
Santa Monica, CA

"When I was a teenager, my boyfriend's mom used to make this dish. It was extremely comforting and the surroundings we often dined in were, too. In front of a big fire, we'd sit on the floor and talk and eat. I have to say that is how I see food and its importance—bringing people together to share and be comforted in many ways. Unlike some onion soups where the cheese forms a tough, stringy mass at the top, the cheese in this hearty soup grows softer and sweeter as it simmers in the milky broth. It may not look great, but the taste is superb. You can refrigerate this homey soup for as long as 6 days with no loss of quality. When gently reheating it, remember to keep stirring."

- 8 tablespoons (1 stick) unsalted butter
- 3 medium onions, thinly sliced
- 2 teaspoons salt
- ¼ teaspoon white pepper
- ½ day-old French bread or 6 slices white bread
- 1 teaspoon sugar
- ½ gallon milk
- 1 pound good-quality Swiss or Gruyère cheese, diced

Melt the butter over moderate heat in a large heavy stockpot or Dutch oven. Cook the onions with salt and pepper until soft but not colored, 15 minutes.

Cut the bread into medium dice and add to the pot along with the sugar. Stir constantly for about a minute, until the bread absorbs the butter.

Add the milk and bring to a boil. Add the cheese, stir, and reduce to a simmer. Cook, uncovered, stirring occasionally, for about 1 hour 15 minutes. Serve immediately.

Serves 8 to 10

Potato Gnocchi

TODD ENGLISH (CIA '82), Olives and Figs, Charlestown, MA, and nationwide

"My grandmother taught me how to make these potato gnocchi. She learned from her mother, and she from her mother. I distinctly remember her bent old fingers working ever so gently with the dough. She instructed me that when made properly, they should be as light and fluffy as a kiss from an angel."

- 2 russet potatoes, peeled and cut into chunks
- 3 egg yolks
- Salt
- Freshly ground black pepper
- 1½ cups all-purpose flour, plus extra for dusting work surface

Boil the potatoes in enough salted water to cover. Cook until soft, about 20 minutes. Drain well for 10 minutes or more in a colander.

Dust a clean work surface with flour. Mash the potatoes through a ricer onto the work surface to form a pile.

Add the egg yolks and salt and pepper to taste. Add the flour (small amounts at a time) and knead gently just to incorporate.

On a floured surface, form a strip of dough ½ inch wide and 2 to 3 feet long. Cut the strip into ½-inch pieces. Roll into balls.

Using two forks, roll the dough balls the full length of the fork prong, pressing at the end to create a pocket in the middle and a fork mark at the end.

Bring a pot of salted water to a boil. Drop in the gnocchi and cook approximately 8 minutes—they will float to the surface when done. Remove and toss with sauce.

Makes about 60 gnocchi

Note: It is best to work with ingredients when they are still warm. It is also very important not to overwork the dough—knead only to incorporate the ingredients. The dough can be prepared ahead of time and then frozen. Be sure to sprinkle with generous amounts of flour before freezing and do not stack.

4. Apprenticing
LEARNING IN THE KITCHEN

In any good cooking, you have to be humble in front of the ingredients and you have to be humble in front of the fire. You have to daily deal not with what you've learned but with what you don't know. If you're not a curious person, if you're not a humble cook, there's a lot you simply don't learn. **BARBARA TROPP**

It takes diamonds to cut diamonds. And the best training comes alongside the world's best chefs, both here and abroad. The previous chapter noted that many cooking schools offer or even require a period of practical work experience referred to as an externship, and apprenticing can be thought of as serving an extended externship. Both are valuable for the same reason: They offer opportunities for hands-on learning through practical experience, as there is only so much one can learn about professional cooking in a classroom. There is nothing like the pressure of paying customers in a dining room waiting for their food to teach speed and timing. In fact, some chefs decide to forgo cooking school altogether in order to work their way up through the ranks of a kitchen, learning as they go.

It can't be taught; it has to be caught.

PATRICK O'CONNELL

Apprenticing has its roots in a long European tradition that originated in France. For years, the young French cook learned by becoming an apprentice, sometimes at as young as thirteen years old. Apprenticed to a chef able to teach them the business of cooking, young cooks worked their way up from peeling vegetables to running a kitchen. The French system has remained virtually unchanged through the years, except that apprentices now start relatively later (at fourteen after earning a Certificat d'Etudes, or at sixteen after junior high), while keeping up with regular school a few days a week while they work. Also, the sometimes violent discipline characterized apprenticeships of years past has reportedly calmed into mostly good-natured hazing.

Ten to twenty years ago, many ambitious American chefs made their way to France to spend time in the kitchens of Michelin-starred restaurants as a sort of "finishing school" experience. Patrick Clark recalled, "If you didn't have European experience, restaurant owners wouldn't bother with you. There were no great American chefs back then." Today, given the proliferation of truly excellent restaurants in the United States, aspiring chefs need no longer look beyond domestic borders for the opportunity to work with world-class chefs.

While the American Culinary Federation administers a three-year national apprenticeship training program for culinary students, the United States does not have the same widespread apprenticeship arrangement on a par with the European system. André Soltner notes, "There are not enough restaurants here that can take the time, and the laws do not allow us to do apprenticeships the way we used to. You cannot hire young people—they have to be of a certain age." Larry Forgione adds, "I don't think, given the economics of restaurants, that we have the ability to have layers and layers of people to walk you through everything all the time. The way kitchens are structured today, I don't think that they can teach you completely." In the United States, then, such learning takes place informally, with cooks taking the initiative to volunteer to work inexpensively or even for free in a desired kitchen. As experience is gained and skills developed, apprentices may be able to work their way into regular, paid staff positions.

Traci Des Jardins is a contemporary American chef whose meteoric career has benefited from apprenticeships both in the United States and abroad. "I had no culinary training whatsoever when I started cooking with Joachim Splichal at his first restaurant when I was seventeen," she remembers. "I started in the pantry, and worked for him for two and a half years. When he recommended that I go to France, I landed an apprenticeship at Troisgros and spent a year there. After working at Montrachet in New York City, I went back to France to work at Lucas-Carton, Arpège, and Louis XV with Alain Ducasse [before returning to California at age twenty-three to open Patina as Splichal's chef de cuisine]."

Des Jardins describes the experience of learning the foundations of French cuisine in France in 1986 as both "challenging" [as the only American and the only female working in those kitchens] and "invaluable." "It was very important training for me from an historical standpoint if not from a practical one, in that in France you'd have a brigade of twenty-five people making dinner for a hundred guests versus in the United States, where you'd have far fewer cooks serving many more guests," she points out. "The apprenticeship system teaches you how to do everything for your station, because there are no prep cooks."

The guiding principle behind deciding where to work is timeless. "To become one of the best, you still want to work with the best," advises Daniel Boulud. "Everyone needs to have mentors to create a strong foundation. You should choose three or four chefs to learn from who will provide the foundation of who you will become as a chef. You need to believe in, and be patient with, that plan. I started cooking at fourteen, so at twenty-five I was ready to be an executive chef. Today, a kid who starts at twenty thinks that he or she is ready at twenty-five to be an executive chef—and that is scary.

"It is important to know yourself and what you want to do with your training. [Chefs] Riad Lasser and Will Hanson of Balthazar restaurant in New York City had previously cooked with people like Jean-Georges Vongerichten and myself. However, they didn't go into four-star dining with their own place. Instead, they opened Balthazar, which is a brasserie. It is great and they put their soul into the food. You don't think of their food as a cerebral experience: It is not about how fancy it is, but about how good it is. Their strong foundation is what has allowed them to achieve that."

The European Apprentice System

Learning about the historical tradition of apprenticing can help you understand more about a chef who is a product of it, as well as appreciate the apprenticing process in its current form. The European-born chefs we interviewed typically began their apprenticeships between the ages of fourteen and seventeen. They commonly spent six days a week, for ten or often more hours a day, in some of the world's leading kitchens, under the watchful eyes of some of the world's leading chefs. If you've ever wondered where some of these chefs got their drive and knowledge, imagine all that they were exposed to before they even turned twenty-one.

André Soltner got his start as an apprentice in the mid-1940s. He was fourteen when he started, at a salary of five hundred old francs—about a dollar—a month to work sixteen to eighteen hours a day.

Soltner recalls, "Chefs then were not stars. Nobody knew the chef, they knew the restaurant, they knew the owner, but they didn't know the chef. Looking back now, I know my chef was a very good chef. I still analyze what he taught me, what he said to me, over those three years. He always said, 'The dish needs what it needs.'

Jean Banchet worked with legendary French chef Fernand Point for a couple of years in his mid-teens. He recalls, "If you were late three times, you were fired. No excuses."

"I remember when my parents signed the contract," says Soltner. "The chef said to my parents, 'I own him—he's mine!' He was a little kidding, but he meant I was his. He did with us whatever. Today you cannot understand. Even kicking us—I mean, I got a few good ones. He almost knocked me out once or twice. My chef was a very good man. He had a big heart. But he was very tough, and he was very severe with us."

Soltner considered his chef a good man because he was kind after he punished his apprentices. "I was a small kid, and crying, and the next day I'd be a few hours late. He'd say, 'Bubbi'—he called me Bubbi–'Thursday, you'll have lunch at my house.' That meant I couldn't go home to my parents [as Soltner typically did on his day off] and he could make up."

Soltner also acknowledges that his chef was a good teacher and prepared him well for the *Certificat d'Aptitude Professionelle* exam, required of all apprentices after serving their three years. "I was first in the region, I think, because of how he taught me." After passing the exam, the young cook is considered a *commis,* a paid position. Soltner remembers that even thirty years after finishing his apprenticeship, he visited his chef whenever he went back to France. "That means I respect him very much."

A generation later in France, Daniel Boulud lived alone at the age of fourteen in a small place owned by his uncle, while serving his apprenticeship. The owner of the restaurant where he worked liked him, but the chef was frustrated not to have full control over the young Boulud. "They were very tough in France when they wanted to crush you. He once chased me around the stove with a ladle," recalls Boulud, with amusement.

Later, during his apprenticeship, Boulud would fill in for cooks at other restaurants (for example, when cooks injured themselves and were unable to work). He described the pranks the tightly-knit fraternity of French chefs would play on one another and on each other's young cooks: "They would send you with junk that was nicely wrapped, and tell you to take it to a certain restaurant. Once you were there, the restaurant would catch on and tell you that they'd love to keep it, but that they really thought it should go to another guy, so they'd send you on your way to the next chef. Or they'd send naive cooks around from restaurant to restaurant asking for a 'parsley curler' or another piece of [nonexistent] equipment."

The first time Boulud met legendary French chef Paul Bocuse, who was well known for his playful antics, Boulud was on his way to a catering job with his boss. While Boulud's boss was attending to other business, Bocuse gave Boulud a tall glass of blanc cassis (a strong, black currant liqueur) while he waited. Not wanting to offend Bocuse, and wanting to seem like one of the guys, Boulud drank up. However, by the time his boss returned, young Boulud was completely drunk and unable to work.

Antics aside, Boulud believes the apprenticeship system has many merits. "In the past [as an apprentice], you did your best to assist the chef or owner, and I think this is the best passport to life. They

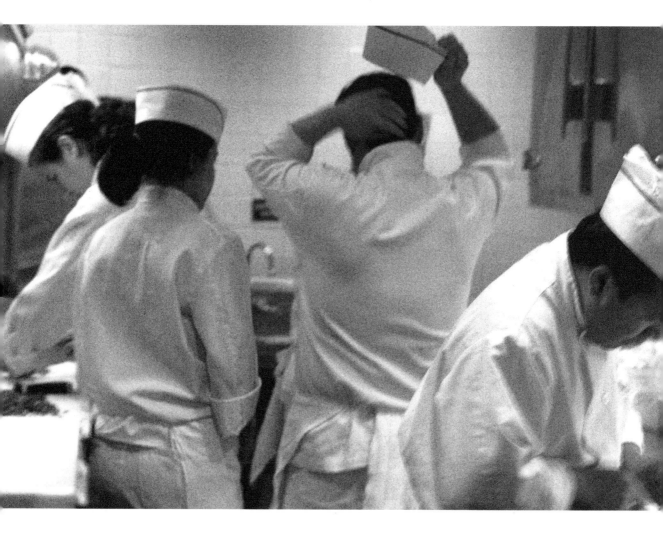

would open any door. What's important is to create a bridge between places you've worked and never to disconnect the bridge. My cooks come back to ask me for advice, or about looking for a job, or about what salary they should ask for in a new job. I think it's very good because these people worked very hard for me, and gave everything they had for me, and I think in return I owe them for that support."

Jean-Georges Vongerichten recalls of his apprenticeship in the early 1970s, "At first, I never saw the stove. I really learned about the products. We had all these wild animals coming in, like hare and pheasant. I was plucking pheasants, cutting chickens, and cleaning meats and fish. The first year I learned what a good carrot is like and what a bad carrot is like, and all the seasonal foods. I was trained like that, so when I see someone in the middle of August having pheasant or hare or venison, it doesn't sound right in my head.

"Some days you'd spend seventeen or eighteen hours in the kitchen. Two or three days in a row of that, before Christmas, with so much preparing and things, you'd say, 'Why am I doing this? My friends are running around chasing girls, and I'm at the stove.' It was tough.

"After my apprenticeship, I stopped for two months, just to think about whether it's what I wanted to do or whether I should move on to something else. I was just nineteen, and I had my whole life to do something else. But when I stopped for two months, I missed it so much—touching the food and working with the public every day.

Former White House pastry chef Albert Kumin started his three-year apprenticeship at the age of fifteen in a pastry shop in Switzerland. "It was a better type of pastry shop in a town called Wille. I started scrubbing pots and trays for two months, and then I would weigh and measure ingredients," he recalls. "After that, I got to make almond paste. You would cook the almonds in boiling water, and then you would peel them, fifty pounds of almonds. The first time I worked more than a day on it, peeling them one by one. But you get smarter with time—I got it down to an hour or so. You learn when the other people laugh at you, and then they show you how to put them in a bag and rub them up and brush them off. But first they have to make a joke out of you."

Kumin describes the Swiss apprenticeship system of his time (the 1930s) as not very different from the French system: "One day of school, and six days of work." Learning on the job required special traits. "You had to be very nosy so the chef would show you something. You learned a lot in school, but in many kitchens nobody knew the recipes but the boss. In my time, the secrecy of recipes was much, much greater than it is today. When somebody had something special, they didn't want to give it to you. Now, it's like an open book."

A French Culinary Family Tree and Selected American Branches

Chef/Teacher/Restaurant	Influenced/Restaurant	Who Influenced/Restaurant	Who Influenced/Restaurant

Fernand Point (1897-1955) **La Pyramide,** Vienne, France

Paul Bocuse **Paul Bocuse,** Collonges au-Mont-d'Or, France

Jean Banchet **Le Français,** Wheeling, IL

Vincent Guerithault, **Vincent's on Camelback**, Phoenix

Yoshi Katsumura **Yoshi's Café,** Chicago

Jackie Shen **Red Light,** Chicago

Hubert Keller **Fleur de Lys,** San Francisco

Georges Perrier **Le Bec-Fin,** Philadelphia

Jovan Trboyevic **Le Perroquet,** Chicago

Susan Feniger and Mary Sue Milliken both of **Border Grill,** Los Angeles

Jean-Georges Vongerichten **Jean Georges, JoJo, Vong,** NYC

Wylie Dufresne **WD-50,** NYC

Didier Virot **Aix,** NYC

Francois Bise **L'Auberge du Père Bise,** Talloires, France

Alain Chapel, **Alain Chapel,** Mionnay, France

Louis Outhier, **L'Oasis,** La Noupoule, France

Joachim Splichal **Patina, Pinot Bistro,** Los Angeles

Jean-Georges Vongerichten **Jean Georges, JoJo, Vong,** NYC

Jean and Pierre Troisgros **Les Frères Troisgros,** Roanne, France

Jean Banchet **Le Français,** Wheeling, IL

Alfred Portale **Gotham Bar and Grill,** NYC

Judy Rodgers **Zuni Café,** San Francisco

| Others | | | |

Georges Blanc
Georges Blanc
Vonnas, France
→ Daniel Boulud
Daniel, NYC
→
Jean Francois Bruel
DB Bistro Moderne, NYC

Andrew Carmellini
Café Boulud, NYC

Alex Lee, **Daniel**, NYC

Brad Thompson
Mary Elaine's, Phoenix

Michel Guérard
Les Prés d'Eugénie
→ Daniel Boulud, **Daniel,** NYC

Patrick Clark (1956-1998)
Tavern on the Green, NYC

Alfred Portale
Gotham Bar and Grill, NYC
→
Tom Colicchio, **Craft,**
Gramercy Tavern, NYC

Gale Gand and Rick
Tramonto, **Tru,** Chicago

Diane Forley
Verbena, NYC

Tom Valenti, **Ouest,** NYC

Paul Haeberlin
L'Auberge de l'Ill
Illhausen, France
→ Jean Joho, **Everest,** Chicago

Hubert Keller
Fleur de Lys, San Francisco

Jean-Georges Vongerichten
Jean Georges, JoJo, NYC

Gaston Lenôtre
Ecole Lenôtre
Plaisir Cedex, France
→ Michel Richard
Citronelle, DC

Nancy Silverton
Campanile, Los Angeles

Jacques Maximin
Hotel Negresco
Nice, France
→ Hubert Keller
Fleur de Lys, San Francisco

Alfred Portale
Gotham Bar and Grill, NYC

Joachim Splichal, **Patina,**
Pinot Bistro, Los Angeles
→
Traci Des Jardins
Jardinière, San Francisco

Jacques Torres, NYC

Joël Robuchon
formerly of **Jamin,** Paris
→ Craig Shelton
Ryland Inn, Whitehouse, NJ

Hiroyoshi Sone
Terra, St. Helena, CA

Roger Vergé
Le Moulin Mougins
Mougins, France
→ Daniel Boulud, **Daniel,** NYC

Hubert Keller
Fleur de Lys, San Francisco

Victor Gielisse trained in his native Holland, where the apprenticeship process was similar. "My chef was an animal in the sense that he was so passionate about what he did. I went in at ten [A.M.] and left at ten-thirty [P.M.]. We both rode the same bus in and out of work—God forbid if I should miss that bus, or if I wanted to go to a movie in the afternoon [during the standard break between lunch and dinner service]. The chef would do his stocks and sauces in the afternoon, in the time off. This is when I picked up most of his skills—what we use a strainer for, why some stocks are less gelatinous than others—all this, I picked up in the off-hours when he was on his own.

"He was a hard individual. This business makes you hard. It is tough. I can only look back and say, 'Why was he so hard?' Kitchens in those days were in the basement—no air conditioning. It was hot as hell."

When spending time cooking in Italy, Gielisse was instructed by another chef to wash his car. "I didn't say, 'Hey, I'm not washing your car.' I said, 'Well, chef, what do you mean?' He said, 'You wash my car. Otherwise, you work two lunch shifts for two days.' I washed his car. And then he took me to Milano, to the Italian pasta factories. I wanted to ask, 'Can I wash your car tomorrow so we can go somewhere else?'"

On the other side of the globe in Japan, things were not so different for Nobu Matsuhisa, who became an apprentice in his native Japan at the age of eighteen. "In my first three years as an apprentice, I washed a lot of dishes and sharpened a lot of knives—I wasn't even allowed to touch the fish." In the Japanese kitchen, mistakes were simply not tolerated and, as in France, physical punishment was not unheard of—"Some cooks got knocked in the head or chased after." In those days, the restaurant would board the sushi chefs, in some cases with ten guys sharing a single room. Matsuhisa says, "My early restaurant experience included everything from serving tea to washing the chefs' blankets and underwear."

In addition to his apprenticeship's giving him an opportunity to acquire practical skills, Matsuhisa credits it with imparting real knowledge—including how to cook from the heart. "You can have the same exact ingredients go into the same exact dish, and you can always tell which was made by the amateur and which was made by a professional," he says. "I learned so much just by watching, watching very closely."

"Apprenticing" in America

Before cooking schools became the more standard training ground, many contemporary American chefs started out by working in the kitchens of some of the leading restaurants in the United States. Certain restaurants seemed to spawn great chefs, such as Chez Panisse in Berkeley, California (see page 104).

In the United States, the reasons to apprentice are varied. The investment of time and money involved in attending cooking school may be prohibitive to some aspiring chefs. Others may find they prefer a more hands-on approach to learning. Still others are lucky enough to happen upon a chef willing to teach and to overlook an occasional mistake.

All of the above played a role in my own decision to forgo cooking school in order to keep working, as I made the transition from the front of the house to the kitchen. After I asked Chris Schlesinger, a

Chefs Without Cooking School Diplomas

Chef	Restaurant(s)	Location
Mario Batali	Babbo	New York, NY
Rick Bayless	Frontera Grill, Topolobampo	Chicago, IL
Gordon Hamersley	Hamersley's Bistro	Boston, MA
Zarela Martinez	Zarela	New York, NY
Mark Miller	Coyote Cafe	Santa Fe, NM
Patrick O'Connell	The Inn at Little Washington	Washington, VA
Susan Regis	Upstairs on the Park	Cambridge, MA
Anne Rosenzweig	Inside	New York, NY
Susan Spicer	Bayona	New Orleans, LA
Norman Van Aken	Norman's	Coral Gables, FL
Alice Waters	Chez Panisse	Berkeley, CA
Janos Wilder	Janos	Tucson, AZ

Culinary Institute of America alumnus, about cooking schools, I jumped at his offer to instead teach me what I needed to know. He let me work into the kitchen slowly, starting one or two days a week and gradually increasing my schedule until I was cooking full time.

I started from zero. I owned only one cookbook, *Joy of Cooking,* and only one knife. I heard the names "Escoffier" and "Madeleine Kamman" for the first time. Chris gave me a copy of Escoffier's *Le Guide Culinaire* and told me to go out and buy *The Making of a Cook.* I also learned that most chefs owned their own knives, which they kept stored in their own knife bags. As I heard the cooks around me come into work and discuss the food pages of *The Boston Globe* and *The New York Times,* I developed the habit of reading both papers over coffee first thing every Wednesday morning. I learned which chefs were the most respected and why, and I started my passionate search of what else successful cooks had ever read or done in their lives, so I could become inspired to incorporate some of the same habits into mine. I also learned to adapt the spirit of modesty exemplified by Chris, who used to tell me: "I've been cooking fifteen years, and I don't know shit about cooking." (Since that time, he has opened more restaurants and published numerous cookbooks, and I know he still has the same humble attitude.)

Passion and humility play integral roles in starting in a kitchen as an apprentice. You must have the passion to convince a chef to take you on, and that you—as an untrained cook—will be worth the chef's and staff's time and effort to teach you. The length of time you are willing to commit may also be a factor. You can demonstrate your humility by showing respect for the food and the entire staff. Even the dishwashers who have been working longer than you may know more.

Mario Batali takes a contrarian's approach to culinary education. "I dropped out of culinary school, and I don't happen to believe that it is a prerequisite for a cooking career," he asserts. "If two peo-

> **If you had anything to do with Chez Panisse from 1971 to 1980, you had a ticket. You had a certain amount of attention, especially in the Bay Area.**
>
> JUDY RODGERS

"The Alice Waters School of Cooking"

Selected Chefs Who Have Spent Time in the Kitchens of Chez Panisse

Alice Waters
Chef and Co-Owner
(1971-Present)

Lindsey Shere
Pastry Chef and Co-Owner
(1971-Present)

Jeremiah Tower
Chef (1972-78)
Retired chef-owner of Stars
and Stars Cafe

Mark Miller
Cook (1975-79)
Chef-owner of Coyote Cafe

Jonathan Waxman
Cook (1978)
Chef-owner of Washington
Park

Deborah Madison
Pastry Cook (1970s)
Founding chef of Greens

Steve Sullivan
Bus boy (1970s)
Owner of Acme Bread

Michel Troisgros
Cook (late 1970s)
Replaced father at the helm
of Troisgros

Judy Rodgers
Cook (late 1970s)
Chef-owner of Zuni Café

Mark Peel
Pastry Cook (1980-81)
Founding chef of Spago; chef
and co-owner of Campanile

Joyce Goldstein
Café Chef and Manager
(1981-83)
Retired chef-owner of
Square One

ple came to me and one had worked for a great restaurant in Europe for two years and the other had gone to cooking school, I would rather hire the person with real experience because I know that they really learned how to cook. The other person may know how to make a raft and clarify a consommé, but that is more about technique than about cooking.

"I think you can learn the technical stuff in your spare time, if you're dedicated," Batali continues. "You can read Harold McGee's books to understand certain things while you work at the heels of a great chef. And you can watch the Food Network and learn a ton. If you are a forty-year-old career changer, you have probably been cooking dinner for twenty-five years. Why do you need cooking school? You just need to get in a kitchen and cook." Batali cites as a perfect example the case of the literary editor of *The New Yorker*, who at the time we interviewed him was spending several weeks in his kitchen at Babbo while researching and writing a seventeen-page profile of Batali for the magazine. "Bill Buford is in our kitchen boning rabbits, chopping mire poix, and braising—just at a slower speed than the rest of the cooks," Batali points out. "But if he were here six months full time, he would not only be a lot faster, he could be working the line!"

Emily Luchetti credits her apprenticeship at a small French restaurant in New York City with teaching her not only skills, but shaping her management philosophy as a chef. "It was only the chef and myself, and he would have me do everything. He would throw me on the grill station one day and someplace else the next. I was in over my head, but I learned a tremendous amount.

"One night, my then-boyfriend/now-husband Peter called me at work to invite me to Lutèce, where he was being taken by clients. My chef heard me say, 'No, I have to work.' He then interrupted and said, 'If you have an opportunity to go to Lutèce, you can learn more there in a night than I can teach you. Go!' So I went home, changed my clothes, and went to have dinner at Lutèce—which was great!

"For me, it was an invaluable lesson as to how to manage people," Luchetti admits. "I have a strong sense of responsibility to give people opportunities to develop their skills. We all need to do it for the future of the industry.

"As the financial incentives are not high in this business in the kitchen, I will ask cooks what they want to learn in the next three months and will work it out so that they can. We'll discuss what they make, and then serve it at staff meal. Or I'll have them take the ten minutes or so to have the experience of baking a cake from *The Simple Art of Perfect Baking* by Flo Braker." Luchetti adds, "I tell them, 'If you do a good job for me, I'll be behind you 100 percent.' By supporting them that way, they will do anything you ask—just as I did for my chef."

Getting In

The best way to land an apprenticeship is to speak with the chefs at the restaurants you're interested in about your willingness to work for free while you learn the business. You may have to try many restaurants, and some more than once, but persevere. As Emeril Lagasse puts it, when he was seeking his own apprenticeship in France, "The wheel that squeaked was the one that usually got the oil. Sometimes I would go to places twice a day and knock on the door and try to explain to the chef how much I really wanted to work there."

While chefs certainly like the idea of free labor, recognize that it represents a significant commitment of time and energy to teach you. Demonstrate to a chef that you bring some basic skills to his or her kitchen, whether knife skills, baking experience, knowledge of cooking, or something else. For those interested in apprenticing in pastry, consider bringing in something you baked yourself as a sample of your capabilities. If a chef tells you that he or she is unable to take you on at the moment, use the opportunity to ask the chef what books they might recommend you read, what local classes you might take, or anything else you might do to increase your value to the restaurant.

Alice Waters accepts apprentices only on an extremely selective basis, which typically means a strong recommendation from another chef she knows and respects. "I do like to have people come in and help, and especially young kids," she says. "We had two extremely rewarding people come last summer, and I feel like we changed two lives. I think that they will forever go out and spread the good word, and that makes it all worthwhile."

If a chef agrees to take you on, sit down with him or her to assess your skills and goals. Realize that your development as a cook will take time, and express your willingness to start anywhere you're needed. Set a time frame to talk again about next steps, such as moving into a regular staff position down the line.

Meanwhile, do your best to demonstrate that you learn quickly, handle criticism constructively, and know enough to ask good questions. Working your way up means you also must be much more aggressive and structured about your education outside the kitchen. Although, starting at the bottom, you may learn very good technique and speed, you must seek out on your own the how's and why's of what you are doing. Chefs and co-workers do not always have the time to explain more than the minimum a cook needs to know in order to accomplish a particular task. Much of my own on-the-fly learning came with the caveat ". . . and I don't have time to tell you why it works best this way—just trust me that it does and do it that way." I learned the techniques, but I didn't learn the theory behind them until I went home and did some reading on my own.

In some cases, it was only upon having further discussions with the chef, time to reflect, and/or the opportunity to eat certain dishes in the dining room for myself that I was able to "get" what the essence of a

What you need at the outset is a taskmaster of a teacher who gives you a real foundation. After that, you can spend a year or so at five or six restaurants, providing you with five or six very different experiences, so that you can see what you like and what you don't like. Put ten thousand dollars away, and then be nomadic through Europe, going from restaurant to restaurant saying, "Hey, I'm looking for work—would you hire me?" In France, you'll see fifty or sixty different mentalities, or styles, of cooking—in Italy, you can find four hundred! Becoming a chef is a very, very long process. There's not a day that passes, even today, that I don't learn something. MADELEINE KAMMAN

dish was all about. Leading chefs see these developmental experiences not as "extra credit" but as central to the process of learning to cook. "What the educational process is unfortunately missing too often is knowledge," observes Patrick O'Connell. "I can show a cook how to make a dish, and they can duplicate it because they are used to following steps: one-two-three-four, one-two-three-four. What they often can't do is understand the meaning behind the dish or what the dish is intended to be. Some cooks are also not even used to having this explained to them, so doing so is like opening a new door for them. It is a great moment when you see a cook finally realize and understand what they have been making."

To help his staff achieve this, O'Connell will use language and examples already familiar to a particular cook. "In training cooks, it is important to employ different analogies so that they can look at food as an art form or as a vehicle of communication. I absolutely believe that even cooks who haven't thought about food that way before are capable of this. You just need to find a way in with them," says O'Connell.

"For example, if a cook is interested in music, I'll explain it in those terms. I'll tell them that the problem with a dish is that I can't tell who the lead singer is, because she is being drowned out by the bass and the drums. Then the cook will get it.

"I will even prepare a storyboard of the dish so that the cook can realize that the dish is communicating something. That whole level is missed in their training, so that they too often feel like they are doing something mechanical when in actuality it is far more than that. Once they see that, then they can participate in the concept of 'who the dish is pretending to be.' It's exciting that if you work with cooks enough, peeling the layers away of what they're doing and showing them other dimensions of it, they'll come to realize that they are not just robots."

In addition to developing depth as a cook, it is also important to develop breadth through seeking out opportunities to work with food you are unfamiliar with. While at cooking school there may be required classes covering diverse areas of food, from baking to Italian cuisine, a self-taught cook must take responsibility for this self-education. A cook who strives to become better educated may come in early to assist the pastry chef, or spend a day off working for free in a bakery learning the art of bread making, or volunteer to help at local cooking classes to broaden skills and knowledge. Other avenues for self-education are explored in Chapter 8.

Anne Rosenzweig got her start in a kitchen by working for free for nine months. She was the only woman there and did experience some hazing, yet she persevered and eventually worked her way into a paid position. She says, "My first chef became a mentor and schooled me, and I got a great education from him. I think I learned more than if I had gone to cooking school."

As mentioned previously, the American Culinary Federation's Educational Institute (ACFEI) also sponsors a formal National Apprenticeship Training Program for Cooks, through which more than eighteen thousand apprentices have passed since the program's founding in 1976. The three-year program allows aspiring chefs to 'learn as they earn,' by working forty hours a week and spending an average of fifteen to twenty hours a month in classroom instruction. For more information, contact the ACFEI in St. Augustine, Florida, at (800) 624-9458.

Apprenticing in Europe

Some Americans still find the idea of apprenticing in a European kitchen alluring and are motivated to find a stagiaire's (essentially, a French term for an apprentice) position. The initial contact can be made either through an intermediary or directly. Cooking schools with contacts abroad (such as the Institute of Culinary Education) can make these arrangements. Otherwise, prospective apprentices can contact chefs directly by letter.

Georges Blanc, for example, chef of the three-star restaurant in Vonnas, France, that bears his name, has brought in stagiaires for three- and six-month commitments. (At this writing, only about forty restaurants hold the Michelin Guide's highest three-star designation worldwide.) Several former stagiaires mentioned that they found the food quality between three-, two-, and one-star restaurants surprisingly close, so you shouldn't assume you won't learn anything unless you're accepted to work at a three-star restaurant.

After working in "all-American" kitchens, Emeril Lagasse decided that he needed to take a break and would go to Paris. "I wanted to understand more of the chemistry, and more of the religion, if you will, of fine cooking," says Lagasse. "I just went. I didn't speak the language. I didn't have any money. I just went over there and banged on doors, washed a few dishes, and just got my butt kicked. I did whatever I could do to work, making a little money where I could, for about two months." After a subsequent stint in Boston, Lagasse went back to France where he briefly served as a stagiaire at La Castrant and Tour d'Argent.

Janos Wilder landed a job in a Michelin-starred restaurant in France this way: "I bought a Michelin Guide and sent letters along with my resume to every single restaurant listed, asking for a chance to work in their kitchen. The following months brought me some of the most beautiful letters you've ever seen, on creamy engraved stationery with brightly colored stamps, all saying essentially, 'No way!' Finally, I received a letter from the chef at a tiny one-star restaurant in Bordeaux. It happened that he was visiting Los Angeles and was willing to visit me in Santa Fe. I cooked for two days, preparing his dinner. At the end of the meal, he said, 'Well, you need to come to France.' It was music to my ears."

Michelin Three-Star Restaurants—2003

France (25): Auberge de l'Eridan; Lameloise; Les Prés d'Eugénie; Auberge de l'Ill; Michel Bras; Paul Bocuse; Ferme de mon Père; Jardin des Sens; L'Ambroisie; Grand Vefour; Guy Savoy; Ledoyen; Lucas Carton; Pierre Gagnaire; Plaza Athénée; Taillevent; Boyer "Les Crayères"; Troisgros; Côte d'Or; Buerehiesel; L'Arnsbourg; Georges Blanc; Arpege; Le Cinq; Louis XV.

Benelux (4): De Karmeliet; Bruneau; Comme Chez Soi; Park Heuvel.

Spain (4): Martín Berasategui; El Bulli; El Racó de Can Fabes; Arzak.

Great Britain (2): Waterside Inn; Gordon Ramsay.

Germany (5): Residenz Heinz Winkler; Schwarzwaldstube; Dieter Müller; Im Schiffchen; Waldhotel Sonnora.

Italy (2): Dal Pescatore; Al Sorriso.

Switzerland (2): Hôtel de Ville; Le Pont de Brent.

After working at Bouley, Amy Scherber found that David Bouley was willing to provide introductions that helped her set up some stages in France so that she could learn more about bread baking. "I lived in my chef's basement and would work in his bakery through the middle of the night," she recalls. "Afterward, I would come home and write in my journal everything I'd learned that day, then get some sleep. Every day, the chef's wife would make us a beautiful Provençal lunch, after which I'd take a nap then get back to work.

"In some ways, now it is better to do an internship in the United States than to go to France. There is so much information here now, and people are willing to share it," she observes. "When I went to France, they were still trying to figure it out. Still, I was able to learn the realities of production, how to speak French, and what it was like to work in a bakery all night.

"From there, I went to Cannes and Paris. In Cannes, the baker was so happy to have some company that he let me do everything! In Paris, while they were very secretive about their baking formula, I was able to see the beautiful final results which taught me standards," Scherber recalls.

Allen Susser moved to Paris for a year to work at The Bristol Hotel after graduating from cooking school, and found his eyes were opened to a whole new level of appreciating food. He recalls, "I loved the way that foods were handled, the way they were treated as part of the culture, not just as a food product. It just changed the whole focus of food for me. It was a matter of respect for food, for the way chefs were treated, for the way restaurants, food, and wine were considered a significant part of the national culture. That's something that wasn't going on in the [United States] in 1976."

Special work permits are not needed to serve as a stagiaire in France in non-paid positions, and a regular passport and tourist visa are sufficient. For positions that pay a small salary, a special visa is required, which limits your working stay to a few months. Some restaurants may be able to recommend local housing or nearby youth hostels, and all typically provide meals to staff members.

The French Kitchen

In his earlier years as a cook, Larry Forgione wanted to work in France, so he wrote to a Parisian chef he'd read about. However, the chef had since moved to London to the Connaught Hotel. Forgione went anyway: "Once you got inside the hotel's kitchen, you wouldn't have known whether you were in London or Paris." Working as a stagiaire in a French kitchen—no matter where it's located—involves learning to adapt to this unique culture.

The first requirement for serving as a stagiaire is being able to subjugate all ego. "You've got to be willing to do whatever it takes," says Emeril Lagasse. "I knew that I was going to get kicked and screamed at, but I also had a vision and was very focused on why I was there, which was to learn. I think the biggest thing it accomplished for me was learning not to be intimidated because I wasn't European, and that Americans were just as good, or could be just as good, as anyone else in the craft. Because the thing that I figured out was that it's a craft. It's doesn't matter if you're white, black, male, female, green, purple—it's a craft. And what you can explore and learn and build on the foundation of that craft—that's what makes the difference."

Knowing at least basic kitchen French, and preferably more, is an asset. You should at the very least know the names of equipment and ingredients, be able to ask basic questions, and understand simple instructions. The better

your language skills, the easier the time you're likely to have. Janos Wilder admits, "My French during my apprenticeship was not very good—often we would communicate by writing in flour that had been sprinkled on the counter and then wiping it off." Luckily, most things can be demonstrated in a kitchen.

A stagiaire might start out cleaning and prepping vegetables, learning the perfectionism of a highly rated French kitchen. Of an entire head of lettuce, only four or five of the best leaves might be used. Stagiaires typically assist those in charge of a particular station, such as meat, fish, garde manger, and vegetables. Stagiaires might also be assigned a special project for the kitchen; one stagiaire recalls cleaning more kilos of cèpes (mushrooms) than he could stand, and plucking countless chickens and ducks.

The ratio of diners to cooks is far smaller than in the vast majority of American restaurants. At the height of the season, Georges Blanc might have as many as fifteen stagiaires in addition to his regular staff to put out perhaps a hundred dinners. In contrast, at a sixty-seat restaurant, for example, three cooks would produce as many, or more, dinners. With such a large kitchen staff, there is more labor and time available to ensure that everything is done perfectly.

Stagiaires are not assumed to know much, so it is essential to be assertive in communicating your knowledge and taking the initiative to help out. During dinner service, however, stagiaires reported simply observing, and taking it all in: the precision of the cooking, the artfulness of the plating. This is the time that you will probably learn the most.

The culture of the French kitchen is different from that of most American restaurants. There is typically little or no talking allowed during the day, and none at all during service. However, there is lively conversation when the staff sits down before service to eat dinner together, which likely includes wine, a cheese course, and even dessert.

Your glamorous image of working in a Michelin-starred kitchen for a few months should be tempered by a realistic sense of what to expect. Stagiaires are not likely to ever have the opportunity to cook, and your day will involve a minimum of twelve hours of peeling and plucking. No matter what the state of your linguistic skills, you may find that some of the lessons you learn, delivered at high decibels, may even transcend language. "I learned a lot from my French experiences, and more about what not to do," admits Alfred Portale. "This happens when you put up a plate on the line and the chef grabs it and says, 'This is [! *#?$!]' and 'You're a [! *#?$!]' and 'You'll never be a cook!' and all this other nonsense."

Any non-male and/or non-French stagiaire should not expect to be welcomed with open arms. Given the centuries-long all-male tradition in most French kitchens, women should not necessarily expect to work with enlightened colleagues. However, former women stagiaires have mentioned that they found it easier to work with younger cooks, or at somewhat less-competitive (e.g., one- or two-starred) restaurants. And "younger" is not merely a relative description; with French apprentices starting out so young, Americans can find themselves working side by side with seventeen-year-old colleagues. One former stagiaire commented, "It's not hard to stand out next to them, because at seventeen their immaturity is apparent. You're able to do better in part because you have more riding on what you're doing, and you've invested time and money to get this opportunity."

Still, most stagiaires say they'd do it again. The exposure to great French food and the experience of living and working in France are incredibly motivating, prompting one former stagiaire to remark, "Being in France, seeing the products, experiencing how they feel about their food and restaurants—you just can't read about it. You have to experience it."

Last Word on Apprenticing

Whether you apprentice in the United States or abroad, the key criteria in selecting a kitchen should be the quality and reputation of the restaurant. But, particularly when making the choice to apprentice abroad, choose a cuisine and culture that appeal to you. Many chefs have chosen to study the cuisines of countries other than France. For example, French-born chef Jean-Georges Vongerichten's time spent cooking in Thailand later contributed to his decision to open his French-Thai restaurant Vong (NYC). Whether you're interested in Italian, Mexican, Thai, or some other cuisine, do your research into the chefs who are best respected for cooking that type of food, and contact them to offer your services. Travel guides to other countries almost always list the best restaurants in a particular city, and these can be used as a guide to finding apprenticeship opportunities abroad. Within the United States, the *Zagat Survey* lists the best restaurants in major cities across the country, and using their food ratings (as opposed to popularity ratings) can help guide you to some of the best kitchens.

Once you get there, it's simple (if not necessarily easy). Watch. Listen. Absorb. Learn. And make a contribution, whenever you can. As Mario Batali points out, "If an apprentice is in your kitchen for only two weeks, all they're able to do is steal the ideas it took you a lifetime to acquire. Now, I am happy to share, but you've got to give me something back: I want to love *you*, too!"

Crustillant of Crab with Razorback Caviar and Blackberry Chutney

RAJI JALLEPALLI [1950-2002], formerly of Restaurant Raji, Memphis, TN

"This dish on my menu is one of my very favorites, which I refer back to like an old book of poems or a diary of fond memories. Shortly after Jean-Louis Palladin visited me in Memphis, he asked me to come and spend a few days in his kitchen. I still remember the joy and exhilaration I felt about the energy in his kitchen—to me, it is one of the last culinary temples of the world. It is there that I learned the importance of originality and respect for standards and quality, and I was delighted to go home with that precious inspiration. I remember assuring Jean-Louis that out of respect to him I would not copy anything that I had seen in his kitchen. But he got slightly hurt and said that for a French chef to have somebody copy his work was a form of flattery. He felt that with my imagination and creativity, it would take a completely new turn, and he was curious to see what it would be. I sent copies of the menus I developed, and he was very pleased with this dish and many others that I sent him. A couple of years later, when I found out that he had my lobster with coconut milk soup on his menu, I thought I had died and gone to heaven!"

Crustillant

¼ **pound goat cheese**

½ **pound small lump crabmeat**

A few fine fennel leaves

2 **cups crushed ultrafine vermicelli or shredded phyllo**

1 **cup melted clarified butter**

Chutney

3 **tablespoons peanut oil**

¼ **teaspoon mustard seeds**

¼ **teaspoon cumin seeds**

½ **cup blackberries**

Pinch turmeric

½ **teaspoon salt**

4 **fennel sprigs for garnish**

2 **teaspoons Arkansas razorback caviar for garnish**

Preheat the oven to 500°F. To make the crustillant, mix the goat cheese, crab, and fennel leaves thoroughly and shape into four balls. Roll them in vermicelli or shredded phyllo until totally covered. Drizzle with clarified butter until completely covered. Bake until golden, about 2 minutes.

To prepare the chutney, heat the oil, then add the mustard and cumin seeds. When they start to pop, add the blackberries, turmeric, and salt. Stir the berries gently, being careful not to break them, until soft. Set aside.

Plate the crustillant and top with a dab of caviar. Spoon the chutney on the side. Garnish with fennel sprigs.

Serves 4

Chocolate Crème Brûlée

JACQUES TORRES, Jacques Torres
Chocolate, Brooklyn, NY
www.mrchocolate.com

"Two weeks after I started my apprenticeship at age fifteen, my mom brought me to the doctor. I wasn't feeling well and had some unexplained discomfort in my stomach. After a long discussion, she deduced that I was eating too much chocolate! Valhrona chocolate was the first truly fine chocolate that I experienced, and I was instantly addicted. Since Le Cirque is famous for its crème brûlée, I was anxious to add my signature by combining the legendary recipe with my favorite chocolate. To me, a dessert is more interesting when it has contrasts. In the crème brûlée, I like the differences in the textures, creamy and crunchy, and the tastes, bitter and sweet. The lightness of the chocolate mousse complements the heaviness of the cream. I still have a sweet tooth and chocolate crème brûlée remains one of my favorites."

Crème brûlée

2 cups heavy cream
1 vanilla bean
1 egg
½ cup sugar
4 egg yolks
1 banana, diced

Preheat the oven to 200°F. Scald the heavy cream and vanilla bean. Mix the egg and sugar. When the cream is hot, slowly pour it into the egg mixture. Discard the vanilla bean and mix well with a rubber spatula. Pour into a mini muffin pan and sprinkle with the diced bananas. Bake for about 40 minutes, or until set. Let cool and put into the freezer.

Chocolate mousse

⅔ cup heavy cream, plus 2 cups, whipped
9 ounces semisweet chocolate, chopped in small pieces

Heat the ⅔ cup heavy cream to a boil. Slowly pour over the chopped chocolate. Mix well. Be sure all the chocolate is incorporated and melted. Fold in the whipped cream and be careful not to overmix. Place the mousse in a piping bag fitted with a large tip. Using a large muffin mold, fill each mold to half. Unmold the frozen crème brûlées and place one in the center of each large muffin mold. Fill the remainder of the mold with the remaining chocolate mousse. Top with a small round of sponge cake. Place in the freezer.

Garnish

4 sheets phyllo dough
5 tablespoons melted butter
¼ cup confectioners' sugar
5 tablespoons cocoa powder

Preheat the oven to 400°F. Line a standard-size half sheet pan with parchment paper. Place a sheet of phyllo dough on the pan and brush with melted butter. Sprinkle lightly with sugar and lightly dust with cocoa powder. Repeat the process with the phyllo dough, butter, sugar, and cocoa powder. Bake at 400°F for about 6 minutes.

Unmold the chocolate crème brûlée and reserve in the refrigerator to defrost, about an hour. When defrosted, center the dessert on the serving plate. Decorate with broken pieces of phyllo. Sprinkle the phyllo crumbs around the plate's edge. Dust lightly with confectioners' sugar and serve.

Serves 12

Warm Blue Cheese Soufflé in Phyllo Pastry

GARY DANKO, Gary Danko,
San Francisco, CA

"Early in my professional career, I had the opportunity to live and work in Napa Valley and Sonoma County. My challenge was to create and prepare menus for special winery events, formulating dishes that complement vineyard-designate and reserve bottling. Entertaining with winemakers often means a five- to seven-course menu to accommodate the succession of variously styled wines. As a result, I endeavored to repopularize the savory course. From English tradition, the savory—two small bites, usually with cheese—is served after the entree when guests linger over wine. Proper wine selection, to create a fitting comparison with each dish, is a hallmark of my time spent in the wine country."

4 sheets phyllo pastry
¼ cup walnut or hazelnut oil or clarified butter

Brush the phyllo with butter and stack; cut into 4-inch squares. Brush a small cupcake tin with butter and press the squares into the tin, making small cups. Flatten the corners to form petals. Chill.

Filling
4 ounces Blue Castello cheese or triple crème blue cheese
1 ounce cream cheese
1 egg
1 ounce heavy cream
1 medium basil leaf, chopped
Pinch rosemary leaves, chopped fine
Salt and pepper to taste

Mix well until smooth and blended. Pour into the formed cups. Bake at 350°F until the cups are golden and the mixture is lightly puffed. Serve with a small salad of mesclun, dressed with vinaigrette.

Serves 6

Carpaccio with Green Peppercorn Dressing and Summer Salad

VICTOR GIELISSE, The Culinary Institute of America, Hyde Park, NY

"Perhaps the picture that stands clearest in my mind, and made a lasting impression, was the food served at a small restaurant called Grotto in 1971 in northern Italy, en route to Lago Di Como, in a village called Chiavenna. The robust flavors, crisp and refined, cooked to perfection, served in rustic, simple, country surroundings, yet serene and comforting, displayed the innermost passionate skills of a craftsman who loves his trade. The carpaccio and the summer salad are intended to reflect these feelings—the simplest of foods expertly prepared."

Carpaccio

¾ cup olive oil
¼ cup red wine vinegar
2 tablespoons finely chopped parsley
½ teaspoon finely chopped garlic
1 tablespoon fresh chopped oregano
One 20-ounce sirloin strip steak

In a bowl, combine olive oil, vinegar, parsley, garlic, and oregano. Lay the sirloin in the marinade and turn until well coated. Marinate for 4 hours.

Preheat a grill to high heat. Remove the meat from the marinade and pat dry with a towel. Brown the strip very quickly on both sides, then set it on a rack and place in a 500°F oven for 3 minutes. Remove from the oven and refrigerate immediately.

Once the sirloin is thoroughly chilled, trim the outside brown crust completely and slice the sirloin into paper-thin slices.

Arrange the slices on chilled plates, spoon some green peppercorn dressing over each portion of beef, and serve with rye melba toast.

Green peppercorn dressing

¾ cup olive oil
½ cup chopped parsley
½ cup capers, drained
½ cup green olives, pitted
½ cup Dijon mustard
½ cup white vinegar
⅓ cup green Madagascar peppercorns
12 cornichons
2 garlic cloves, chopped

In a food processor, blend all ingredients until just combined, 5 to 10 seconds. Serve with the carpaccio.

Actuelle summer salad

2 pounds young green beans, washed
1 pound white mushrooms, julienned
1 ounce truffles
4 tomatoes, cut in wedges
16 artichoke hearts

Snap off the ends of the beans and string them. Cook in a large quantity of boiling water. Make sure that the beans remain crunchy. Once the beans are cooked, cool under cold water and drain at once. Pat dry.

Place the beans in a salad bowl. Top with the julienned mushrooms and truffles. Surround and alternate with the tomato wedges and artichoke hearts. Season with the vinaigrette and freshly minced chives.

Vinaigrette

½ cup walnut oil

¼ cup red wine vinegar

2 shallots, finely chopped

Salt and freshly ground pepper

2 tablespoons minced fresh chives

Whisk together all ingredients until fully combined.

Serves 4 to 6

Aïoli

JEREMIAH TOWER, formerly of Stars, San Francisco, CA

"The most dramatic difference between hand- and machine-made mayonnaise can be tasted in aïoli (garlic mayonnaise) made in a mortar and pestle (not the smooth chemist's variety but one of semi-rough marble). The texture is like velvet, the flavors are subtle, and the result is more digestible. It was Richard Olney who showed me the best way to make aïoli. Later I made the red pepper version, rouille, for Julia Child in her house at Plascassier in the south of France in 1978, when a group including the English novelist Sybille Bedford, Richard Olney, and other friends gathered, and Julia let me cook. Put in a fish soup, the rouille was a sensation. Yet another version of aïoli can be made by adding sea urchin puree—the result is transcendental."

4 cloves garlic

2 egg yolks

¼ cup fresh white bread crumbs

½ teaspoon salt

4 tablespoons fish or chicken stock (depending on whether aïoli is to be used for fish soup or chicken dish)

2 cups olive oil

Work to a paste the garlic, egg yolks, bread crumbs, salt, and a little stock in a mortar or food processor. When the paste is smooth, start adding the oil slowly, working it all the time. Add as much oil as it will take without breaking; then add stock to thin it to the desired consistency.

Makes 2½ cups

Sugar Cane Kebobs of Rabbit

ALLEN SUSSER, Chef Allen's,
North Miami Beach, FL

"Rabbit was one of my first—what I thought to be then—'exotic' meats that I not only had an opportunity to cook, but to taste. It was my first year as an apprentice at Le Bristol in Paris. In my first few days in Paris, I spied many rabbits hanging, skinned in the market butcher shops. Then my day came—twenty whole rabbits arrived at the back door of the kitchen. I knew the time had come to learn about rabbit. I had to skin, butcher, marinate, and roast them for a banquet party that night for the Interior Ministers. From disgust to delight in a day's hard work, I found rabbit to be wonderful and wholesome. As the dignitaries dined on the prime cuts, the cuisiniers all dined on rabbit stew—and we all enjoyed the rabbits with great pleasure."

> 3 tablespoons ground allspice
>
> 1 teaspoon ground cinnamon
>
> ½ teaspoon ground nutmeg
>
> 1 tablespoon ground coriander
>
> 4 scallions, chopped
>
> 2 tablespoons chopped garlic
>
> 1 teaspoon tamarind pulp
>
> 1 cup red wine
>
> ¼ cup olive oil
>
> 1 teaspoon salt
>
> 1 teaspoon chopped Scotch Bonnet pepper
>
> 1 pound rabbit loin

> 30 pieces sugar cane sticks (see Note)
>
> 4 cups Red Bean Ragout (recipe follows)
>
> ¼ bunch cilantro

To prepare the rabbit, combine the allspice, cinnamon, nutmeg, coriander, scallion, garlic, tamarind, red wine, 2 tablespoons of the olive oil, salt, and scotch bonnet. Clean and trim the rabbit loin. Cut each loin into 1½-inch-thick medallions. Marinate with the seasoning in a ceramic bowl for 2 hours.

To prepare the kebobs, skewer each rabbit medallion with a sugar cane stick. Move the rabbit to the center of the cane kebob.

To cook the kebobs, heat a small heavy-bottomed sauté pan until red hot. Remove it from the stovetop and place four to five kebobs in the pan at a time. They will sear and smoke immediately. Return the pan to medium heat and sear the rabbit kebobs for almost a minute. Turn them over and cook the other side for another minute. Remove from the heat and keep warm while continuing to cook the remaining rabbit.

To serve, warm the red bean ragout and divide it among the plates. Serve five kebobs on each plate. Garnish with a sprig of cilantro.

Note: The sugar cane adds a unique raw sweetness to the tropical preparations of the intense flavors of foie gras. To make the sugar cane sticks, cut the sugar cane into 3-inch lengths. Trim the bark from the cane and cut into lengths about 1 inch long by ¼ inch wide.

Red Bean Ragout

Spice paste

1 teaspoon grated ginger

1 teaspoon oregano leaf

½ teaspoon thyme leaf

½ teaspoon cumin

½ teaspoon cracked black pepper

1½ teaspoons coarse salt

2 teaspoons minced garlic

2 tablespoons olive oil

2 cups red beans, soaked

6 ounces pancetta, chopped

1 medium Anaheim chile, seeded and diced

1 medium tomato, seeded and diced

1 medium onion, diced

1 cup calabaza, cut in 1-inch cubes

3 tablespoons lime juice, fresh squeezed

2 tablespoons fresh chopped cilantro

To prepare the spice paste, combine the ginger, oregano, thyme, black pepper, cumin, salt, garlic, and oil in a small bowl.

Cook the beans in fresh cold water. When they begin to boil, lower the heat to a simmer and cook for 1½ hours.

To prepare the vegetables, cook the pancetta in a sauté pan over medium heat for 3 to 4 minutes, then stir in the spice paste, cooking slowly until aromatic. Add the onion, Anaheim chile, and tomato, continuing to cook for 5 minutes.

Add the vegetables and calabaza to the beans. Bring back to a simmer and continue to cook for 25 minutes. Finish the beans with the lime juice and fresh cilantro to serve.

Serves 6

5. Getting In
STARTING AT THE BOTTOM

I spent a month in France cooking for customers' dogs. On Sundays, I might cook for thirty or thirty-five dogs in one day. I'd make them fillet—either raw or cooked—and veal, fish, potatoes.

JEAN-GEORGES VONGERICHTEN

I feared I wouldn't even have a shot at ever becoming a successful chef because I hadn't gotten my start cooking in a three-star restaurant at the age of fourteen. I was surprised and pleased to learn that this was not the case for most of the chefs we interviewed, either.

Dieter Schorner, who went on to be named one of America's two best pastry chefs by *Time* magazine, got his start salting pretzels. James Beard Award–winning Miami chef Allen Susser got his start selling hot dogs at a Playland amusement park. Chez Panisse alumni Mark Miller and Judy Rodgers both got their start in ice-cream parlors—Miller at Friendly's, and Rodgers at Dairy Queen. Clearly, humble beginnings do not preclude great success.

This chapter tracks the process of what aspiring chefs go through in order to line up their first job, and what their work life is like when they're first starting out.

First jobs are an important learning experience. Not the least of the lessons to be learned includes developing the right attitude. Great success is often not the result of doing only one thing right. More frequently, it is a matter of getting all the minute details right, every time. No job—from sweeping floors to washing dishes to polishing doorknobs—should be considered beneath a cook. As Hiroyoshi Sone points out, "You need to know how to do something yourself in order to teach someone else how to do it."

In years past, just working in a kitchen—in any job—was seen as being in a position of servitude and thus "at the bottom." In France, Georges Perrier's mother was a doctor and his father a jeweler, and neither took well to the idea that young Georges wanted to become a chef. Perrier recalls, "When I told my father, he screamed bloody murder." Patrick O'Connell remembers, "People would say things like 'You're working in a restaurant? What's a bright person like you doing in restaurants?' When the father of Chris Schlesinger used to mention that his son was attending cooking school at The Culinary Institute of America, Schlesinger says people expressed their condolences that he "wasn't smart enough to get admitted to college." Susan Regis recalls how upset her mother was when she chose to work in a kitchen full-time. "She would say something along the lines of 'My Skidmore daughter is *not* going to go work in a kitchen. What would I tell the ladies at the club?'" Regis herself struggled with misconceptions and negative connotations about restaurant work: "In college, I'd studied women's literature, and should have realized that women have been the pillars of cooking in the world. My interest makes sense in that context."

Since then, leading chefs have gained celebrity status and, to the uninitiated, being in the kitchen of a top restaurant as a cook has the illusion of glamour. In reality, however, the people who cook your dinner likely arrive at the restaurant by 1 P.M., or perhaps even earlier. Their day begins by hunting for equipment like containers and cutting boards; squeezing into a tight place to work; roasting bones and vegetables to make sauces; reducing stocks; assembling their mise en place—all the ingredients that go into every dish they'll make that night; and preparing the ingredients (such as slicing and portioning vegetables). One cook may also spend thirty minutes making "family meal" for the kitchen and dining room staffs—anything from soup to pasta to marinated grilled pork chops. The people who cook your lunch probably get in around 7 A.M. and, in addition to the previous scenario, might also receive, inspect, weigh, and store produce, meat, fish, poultry, and specialty items; check to see that key equipment is working (and call in a repair order if it is not); and perhaps answer the phones until a manager comes in.

It's hard to understand what working as a cook is like until you spend your first week in a professional kitchen. The work is physically hard—a bag of sugar or flour can weigh twenty-five or fifty pounds. A pot is heavy to start with—then try adding vegetables, forty pounds of bones, and water. Even with the help

Chefs' First Food-Related Jobs

Rick Bayless	family restaurant
Lissa Doumani	dishwasher
Larry Forgione	family catering company
Joyce Goldstein	own cooking school
Emeril Lagasse	washing pots and pans at a bakery
Edna Lewis	cooking at Cafe Nicholson
Mark Miller	Friendly's Ice Cream
Mary Sue Milliken	working in a bakery
Patrick O'Connell	cooking frozen hamburgers at a carry-out
Judy Rodgers	Dairy Queen
Chris Schlesinger	dishwasher
Dieter Schorner	pretzel salter
Lydia Shire	making salads at Maison Robert
Hiroyoshi Sone	dishwasher
Allen Susser	selling hot dogs at an amusement park
Barbara Tropp	China Moon Cafe
Charlie Trotter	The Ground Round
Norman Van Aken	busboy at a Holiday Inn
Alice Waters	Chez Panisse
Jasper White	bar on the New Jersey shore

of another person, it's hard to lift or move. At the end of the week, the hand that holds your knife is callused and fatigued, and if you were not careful, your lower back might be sore. A week is often five or six days, eight to twelve hours a day. The end of the work day, if you work the dinner shift, may not come until 11 P.M. or midnight. In terms of what it takes to work in a kitchen, Mark Miller says, "Physical abilities come first, personality is second, and I would say cooking skills are third down my list."

Your time at work varies from relatively calm to frenetic. If you get in early to replenish your supply of mise en place, it can be smooth. "Frenetic" occurs when your preparation was insufficient to deal with a barrage of orders, either all at once in a single "hit," or unrelentingly over the course of a busy night. The pressure is not only the result of the sheer volume of meals that must be produced, but also from the overseeing chef, as well as self-imposed pressure to make everything perfectly. In the midst of your chaos a critic or a VIP may come in, requiring special attention, which can back things up and add additional pressure. On top of this, imagine the occasional burn or cut sustained in mid-shift. A burn makes its presence known every time you grab a pan from the back of the stove, or reach into the oven. You're aware of a cut every time you bang your finger or take a pinch of salt without thinking.

The scenarios described do not necessarily take place amid ideal conditions, either. A restaurant kitchen is a very different place from its dining room, and the more formal the restaurant, the starker the contrast between the two. Walking into a restaurant kitchen in the middle of service can be like walking into Dante's Inferno at the height of heat and frenzy. You might work in front of six blazing burners during the dinner rush, and ovens are typically turned on to 500 degrees. On the other hand, a pastry cook may occasionally try to escape the heat to finish off a delicate dessert, like chocolate truffles, by working with a coat on and an apron wrapped around it in the walk-in refrigerator. And every kitchen has its own individual temperament. While there are some kitchens in which no one is allowed to raise his voice or use profanity, there are also many kitchens in which yelling is a daily occurrence.

"Temperamental Chefs"

So what kind of person does it take to handle this pressured scenario? Research on the types of temperaments attracted to various careers gives some indication as to the personalities disproportionately drawn to the cooking profession. Keep in mind that there are, of course, many examples of successful chefs who don't fit the "typical" profile. As Elizabeth Terry points out, "This is a field with a tremendous tolerance for individual differences. There's amazing flexibility and space for creativity." Still, "you either have something for this business, or you don't," says Chris Schlesinger. "You have to love feeling pressure, working the line. That hollow feeling in the pit of your stomach has to be something that motivates you. We had a cook walk off the line last Saturday night who couldn't handle it. Other people tolerate it but don't like it. And other people laugh at it. They're the ones who love it."

People who are attracted to cooking on the line (not necessarily those who become chef/owners, where extroversion predominates) tend to be introverts, people who are energized by spending time alone, who tend to listen more than they talk. This is not so surprising, considering that while teamwork is essential to a well-run kitchen, most of the work a cook performs is done at his or her own station, independently. "I like to cook by myself—I had to learn how to be a team player," admits Elizabeth Terry.

People drawn toward cooking also tend to be intuitive, creatively oriented people who trust their own instincts, and value imagination and innovation. They also like to learn new skills, because good cooking draws on creativity and is a constant learning process. "Chefs are born possessing certain balances of the left and right brains, allowing them to master both technical and creative skills," says Jimmy Schmidt. "While a chef is not born knowing how to sauté, for example, technique and discipline are developed through attending school, working, watching, and experimenting. All of one's experiences are added to a mental resource file, which actually helps make the creative idea appear."

They also tend to like living spontaneously, and enjoy adapting to new situations. This is crucial to good cooking, as cooks often develop daily specials in order to take advantage of the ingredients that are in peak condition that day and use their creativity to come up with new and better ways of serving them. "Being a good cook has nothing to do with rote," echoes Joyce Goldstein. However, unlike artists, for whom the concept of time is relatively unimportant, Dieter Schorner sees chefs as "industrial artists who have a very, very rigid time schedule. When somebody orders a wedding cake for three hundred people for a certain day, it has to be ready. You can't say when they come to pick it up, 'No, no, it will be ready tomorrow or the next day—I didn't feel inspired to make it today.' It is great discipline you need to achieve these things."

Developing a thick skin is imperative. There will always be someone around with more knowledge and experience than you, and how their lessons are communicated to you will vary. The key is to associate feedback—whether in the form of constructive criticism as to how a dish you're making could be improved, or high-decibel screaming about what a so-and-so you are for being so ignorant to do something the way you just did it—with becoming a better cook. The criticism may hurt you, but it should never break you. As pastry chef Albert Kumin advises, "It's most important when you're starting out that you learn to accept correction professionally. If the chef complains, then it means something is not right. Accept it—don't take it personally."

Traci Des Jardins recalls coming of age as a chef in the 1980s when yelling was almost *de rigeur* in professional kitchens, especially French kitchens. "In my early years, cooks produced because of intimidation from the chef," she explains. "They worked because they were afraid as opposed to their own personal motivation. I was brought up in kitchens where you got screamed at and told you were an idiot. It wasn't motivating, but was definitely intimidating. In fact, at one point, *I* was in that school of management. However, I decided that I didn't want to be like that as a person, and that I would rather motivate my cooks than scare them, so I changed my management style. If I lose my cool now, I call it 'regressing.'"

It takes more than excellent cooking skills to propel a chef up the ladder. "Because you're a good and skilled cook doesn't make you a chef, even if you've got a palate and can make a menu," Alice Waters points out. "You need to be wonderful with people, and you need to be a manager. You need to be able

Sandy D'Amato: A Lesson in Job-Hunting Persistence

Sandy D'Amato recalls an annual tradition at The Culinary Institute of America—the showing of a movie called "The French Lunch"—as a magical inspiration. "It was about a day at La Caravelle restaurant in New York City," he recalls. "They would show the setup of the dining room, the cooks preparing their mise en place, the rush, and then the post-service breakdown. To me, that was magic. So the first place I applied for a job in New York was La Caravelle.

"I went there every week. Every week the chef would greet me and say, 'We have nothing this week, but come back next week,' which I did. In the meantime, I got a job working banquets at the Waldorf-Astoria [Hotel]. Unfortunately, I was making only eighty-five dollars a week. So, I still had to get another job and I still wanted to work in a French kitchen—which was also unfortunate, as it was the 1970s and there were not many Americans working in French kitchens.

"I eventually asked my chef from school for a letter of introduction for a job interview with Clement Grangerier, then the chef of Le Pavillon. However, by the time I went to meet him, he had already left the job. So, while on my still-weekly visit to La Caravelle, I asked the chef about Grangerier and showed him the letter of introduction. Well, he was so impressed with the letter that he sent me right over to Lutèce to talk to André Soltner. That letter changed everything.

"While André Soltner didn't have a position, he sent me to Jean-Jacques Rachou at La Vendue, who was the only chef in New York that hired Americans because he thought they worked hard and cheap. I explained that I was not looking for a job, but an apprenticeship. He thought something might work out, but unfortunately it didn't.

"Rachou sent me to talk to his friend Roland Chenus, the former saucier and poissonier at Le Pavillon, with whom I eventually landed my apprenticeship. I was the first American he had ever hired, at this small French bistro with a large clientele from the French Consulate. I worked sauté in a little corner where we never washed our pans; we just wiped them out. We would cook about a hundred and fifty meals with just the two of us on the line and a butcher in back who would help us set up.

"We made kidneys, *tête de veau,* brains, and tripe, which was great because other bistros were already cutting back on these classics. The chef had impeccable technique, and I learned a great deal. He could make a sauce or a classic fish *quenelle* that would blow your mind! I 'turned' buckets and buckets of potatoes, so now every potato I prep automatically has seven sides!"

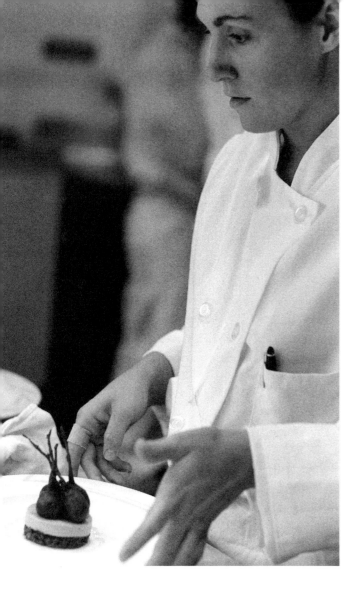

to evaluate how people can work together, how to get the best out of them, and how to inspire them. You must know when to push and when to pull back. You must also serve as a bridge in relating the food to the public, because the whole thing is not just about being a chef in the kitchen, it's about feeding people. You have to have a real nurturing side, at least to be a chef [at Chez Panisse]—I want someone who feels strongly and cares deeply about who's out there in the dining room." Mark Miller agrees. "Most people in food are generous. You have to take care of people. You have to give. It's not about accumulating—it's a different kind of personality."

In addition, different kitchens require different skills. "Unless you have an artistic temperament, you'd never make it in our kitchen," says Rick Bayless. "In some environments, they might prefer that you not be artistically inclined. But it's a must for us. I'll ask new hires what they like to do in their time off. I don't want to hear, 'I like to Rollerblade' or some other innocuous thing—I want to hear that they write poetry or paint or something else that taps creativity. I want people to have an artistic life away from the restaurant because it will feed what they do here.

"For example, when I ask for a more elegant balance on the plate, I want them to understand what I mean. I want them to say, 'Yes, it does look a little clunky.' I will have a cook make a dish and then have him or her sit down at the table and eat the whole thing. Cooks will always come back with suggestions about where to move the salad or that there is too much of something on the plate. They understand, because they are predisposed to understand," Bayless explains.

Increasingly, a commitment to the community and the environment is an important part of the shared values of working in leading restaurants. "If you are going to make it in our kitchen, you have to be interested in these things because we talk about them so much," says Bayless. "In fact, part of a person's review here is based on what steps they have taken in that direction. Our reviews are holistic; we base them on how cooks produce food technically, how motivational they are to the staff, how they have helped us work toward our mission, and how they have developed in the community."

The best chefs are sensualists who are given to wretched excess.

JOYCE GOLDSTEIN

Kitchen Options

Every kitchen is different. Many factors determine what working in a particular kitchen will be like, such as the number of cooks; the style of food (classical French versus casual barbecue); the type of restaurant (major hotel dining room versus small independent restaurant); and the geographic location (both regional and urban versus rural).

A small kitchen may consist of one to three cooks and a dishwasher. Its advantages include the necessity of taking on more responsibility, which provides a cook with broader exposure. However, a cook may not see as wide a variety of food. A large kitchen may save cooks from doing all of their own prep work while serving a larger number of meals—you might be involved in serving hundreds of entrees during lunch or dinner.

Working in a hotel probably provides the widest sheer variety of experiences. Through exposure to banquets, breakfasts, lunches, dinners, room service, and baking, there are ample opportunities to learn. Typically, hotel kitchens are the biggest and most formally structured of all kitchens. Another possible advantage of working in a hotel is travel; it's possible for executive or consulting chefs to travel or transfer nationally or internationally within leading chains. Hotels typically pay a notch above what restaurants do, and offer benefits to employees. Many are also unionized.

Catering, like hotel work, can offer tremendous variety, and demands unusual flexibility. "Catering is like a circus," muses Daniel Boulud. "You take all your equipment and food and when you arrive, you literally have to build a kitchen. It takes a lot of preparation, because if you forget something, it

can be a three-hour drive back to the restaurant. To perform in a place where you have never performed before, you need to have a 'warrior chef' attitude—wherever you go, you simply have to make it work! My biggest claim to fame as a caterer was serving fifteen hundred people in fifteen minutes: Under a tent with no kitchen, I served stuffed squab with *foie gras*, porcini mushrooms, and truffles on a bed of spinach with braised turnips. I had eighty chefs working with me, and it all went out hot!"

Chefs who have opened restaurants in small cities or towns or in the countryside agree on one thing: It's difficult to find good help. For those looking to break into the business, there's less competition to battle in convincing a chef to take you on and train you. This presents an opportunity for talented and ambitious cooks in these areas, because with dedication, interest, and self-motivation you'll find you can become indispensable quickly. However, there are also likely to be fewer great restaurants to approach. Urban areas offer more restaurants, including some of regional, national, or even international renown. Having name restaurants on your resume opens up more options when it's time to relocate to another restaurant or another city. Large cities offer the greatest concentration of restaurants and, therefore, potential job opportunities, representing the widest range of cuisines and types of restaurants. Also, other learning opportunities abound, as leading chefs from across the country often travel to major cities for special events or book tours. Working in a top restaurant, however, doesn't necessarily mean receiving top pay. Because working at a top restaurant is considered a learning experience and a career stepping stone, there is often an inverse relationship between pay levels and the status of the restaurant. You must consider this trade-off as an investment in your education.

Given countless options, how should you decide where to pursue a job? To pastry chef Albert Kumin, the answer is simple: "If you're interested in opening up a pastry shop, then you should start your career in the pastry shop field. If you're interested in restaurants, you should choose a restaurant of the type you feel comfortable in. For myself, not to be snobby or anything like that, I always had the ambition to work in fancy-type hotels and restaurants. When I was young, I always looked for the right job, even if it meant making less money. It's still important today to make the right moves."

Allen Susser agrees. Susser spent two years at Le Cirque (NYC) earning five dollars an hour, which represented a step backward in terms of what he had been earning previously. Still, he found the sacrifice worthwhile. "The important thing to me was to be around the right type of restaurant, the right type of food, and the right type of chef who would be able to teach me—that's where the value was. It didn't matter what I started out doing. I had a nice bachelor's degree from FIU, and I thought that even after four years of school, it was more important to still learn rather than to look for dollars," he says. "That's really where I think today's students are way off base—most of them, when they graduate, are looking for dollars instead of looking to be in the right place to learn for a few more years."

Alfred Portale stresses how important it is to choose first jobs carefully: "You really need to make the right choices in terms of your career. Once you start, it's critical that you get the right experience. Don't get off track and start working at some kind of crappy restaurant. Set your sights on the best, and try to get yourself the best experiences. I'm a product of all my different experiences. I see so many people who needed the money or went for the title or for various other bad reasons got into a series of kind of 'mid-restaurants' and now they're trapped. They can't come out. When you're starting out early, it's good to get a lot of varied experience. But as you mature, and you grow as a cook, you should commit to a place for a minimum of a year. It's better to see one-year stints at several restaurants than someone who's worked for four years at one."

Judy Rodgers cautions that people sometimes choose restaurants for the wrong reasons. "People get very wrapped up in working in a prestigious restaurant, as opposed to choosing a restaurant and getting a job where they're actually going to learn something," she says. "Just when a restaurant chef becomes very famous is about the worst time to go there. That's when they have the least time for you, and they already have their close coterie already wrapped around them who aren't going anywhere, and they don't really have time to teach people anything." Rodgers believes cooks can learn more from people who are either up-and-coming, or who take a lot of pride in their work but are not necessarily well known. "They're not as busy all the time, so they get to take more care with things. When my cooks are moving on after three years with me and ask me, 'Where should I work?' I tell them, 'You don't need to work at Chez Panisse. Work someplace where you can work closely with the chef, if that's what you're interested in.'"

Writing Your Resume

So, how do you go about landing a job? The first step is to write your resume.

The goal of a resume is to convey your experience, enthusiasm, and a positive attitude. After listing any prior restaurant jobs—and this applies especially if you're new to the business and need to stretch a little to fill a whole page—think beyond to other previous work or study that could increase your value to a restaurant. Play up experiences that have augmented your overall food knowledge. Did you ever work on a farm? Sell produce at a stand? Pack meat? I spent a summer canning salmon and salmon roe in Alaska, which taught me a love and respect for salmon. Mentioning this experience on my resume has prompted many interesting discussions with chefs I've interviewed with, and sometimes made me stand out in their memories. Don't hesitate to sell skills which might have been acquired in a previous career, where there is some degree of applicability. I was surprised that a former bank teller I met who was looking for a job in pastry didn't think it relevant to point out her math skills!

Also list your educational experience. Mention culinary classes you have taken and with whom, so that an employer knows about your specific food interests (e.g., pastry, garde manger, etc.). Even if you didn't graduate from a cooking school, mention any classes or seminars you've attended to demonstrate your genuine interest in food and in expanding your knowledge.

Landing an Interview

Do your homework. Drop by the restaurant to take a look at a copy of the menu. Read reviews that have appeared on the restaurant in local newspapers or city magazines (*Chicago, New York*) or even national magazines such as *Gourmet*. While "dressing up" isn't necessary, you should make an effort to look neat and presentable. Use the restaurant's level of formality to gauge how formally or casually to dress. (I'll never forget the look on the host's face at Le Cirque when I dropped off a resume wearing a black leather motorcycle jacket. I also learned to find out whether there is a separate kitchen entrance.) Find out as much about the chef's background as you can and, finally, do some self-examination: What are you seeking to learn from the chef? What do you hope to bring to the restaurant, to be shaped under the chef's vision? Why have you chosen this particular restaurant?

Try to drop off your resume when the chef is at the restaurant. Call ahead to find out the best time for you to stop by and the best time to catch the chef in. If the chef is unavailable when you arrive to drop off your resume, ask when the best time might be to try to call the chef to follow up. (Make sure to ask for the kitchen telephone number, which is often different from the reservations line.) Getting through to a chef can take the perseverance of a sled dog in the Iditarod. I wish this were an exaggeration. From the moment they first walk through the door, chefs have purveyors calling and people requesting donations or their participation in charity events, in addition to all the usual and unexpected demands of running a restaurant. It may take time.

Typically, the best time to catch a chef is between lunch and dinner service, but not always. That's why you must be politely aggressive about finding out his or her particular schedule.

"The trick to getting a job in a top restaurant is to not take no for an answer," coaches Mario Batali. "It may mean that you work free for six months, but in the scope of a thirty-year career, six months is nothing. I worked for free in Italy for three years. It was the most riveting, rich, and intensely personal experience and that is what has made my food what it is today.

"I have a cook from Texas who ate here and then sent me her resume every week for months until I called her up and offered her a job," he laughs.

"The way you are going to get where you want to be is to find someone whose cooking style and operation is something you love and want to strive for," says Batali. "Then watch, find out how they do it, and take notes."

The Job Application at Al Forno

At Al Forno in Providence, Rhode Island, applicants are handed a five-page questionnaire to complete before being considered for a job. The first page is biographical; the other three pages ask for answers to such questions as:

"What is crème brûlée?"

"What is radicchio?"

"Who is Alice Waters?"

"Who was James Beard?"

"What is blanching?"

"What is grilling?"

"What is the proper way to open wine?"

"Where have you traveled?"

"What food magazines do you read?"

Making the Cut

Barbara Tropp was frank about what she looked for in applicants, echoing what other leading chefs had to say on the topic: "The people whose applications we look at first are the people who've worked in restaurants that are like ours: Anne [Rosenzweig], Lydia [Shire], Jasper [White] can all send me somebody. If we can find someone who fits a New American–cook mold, in terms of passion and curiosity and emphasis on freshness, that works better for us than someone who has trained in a Chinese or an Asian restaurant [who may have cooked with MSG or canned water chestnuts]. As an example, someone who's done a year at Postrio [Wolfgang Puck's restaurant a few doors down the block] can come here because they're wanting a smaller environment. We know that their training has been impeccable, that they have learned to taste, that they have learned to cook, that the emphasis isn't on garnishes, isn't on ego—it's about the food."

What's most important in an interview is your attitude. You will typically be asked about your responsibilities at your last job, including how many covers (the number of meals served) you did each shift. You might be asked how you liked the chef you worked for and why you are changing jobs. Or what books you are currently reading, and what kinds of food you like to eat on your day off. Or maybe what you cook for yourself.

After finishing his apprenticeship and his mandatory year of military service in France, Jacques Torres was looking for a job with a friend, walking past the biggest, grandest-looking hotel in Nice, the Hotel Negresco. The friend laid a ten-dollar bet as to whether Jacques had the nerve to go in to apply for a job. After an interview in personnel, Jacques found himself face-to-face with Chef Jacques Maximin in the kitchen office, telling him he was unemployed. "The chef said to me, 'Listen, I have twenty-five guys here, and I don't do any sentiment. If you are good, you stay, and if you are no good, you go.' I said fine. He said, 'Come back in an hour with a jacket and pants.' I went outside and told my friend that I just got hired, went out to buy a jacket and pants, and went back and started working an hour later. I stayed at that hotel for eight years."

> **You have to be so earnestly devoted that if you were any more devoted it would be perverse, and any less, it would not be enough.**
>
> CHARLIE TROTTER

The chef will be listening for your attitude toward food and toward your work: whether you speak with passion about ingredients and your work or whether you're blasé, whether you talk first about the schedule you want before you talk about the food. Cooking is about food, not schedules.

André Soltner never hesitated when he said he looks for "good spirit, and willingness to learn—from there on, I can go anywhere. I don't need a chef who comes in who thinks he is Escoffier. Or Paul Bocuse. I do that myself," he jokes. "I don't ask them too much," he continues. "I look at them. I try to get the feeling that they want it. That's about all."

"I always choose attitude over experience," says the largely self-taught Charlie Trotter. "It's a judgment call, but you base it on talking to somebody. People give me resumes, and I think, 'What am I supposed to do with this?' I hate resumes. I've never had a resume in my life. I want you to tell me what you're all about, I want you to tell me what you're made of. I want you to tell me: Why cooking? Why in the world do you like to do this?"

Understanding the types of people that haven't succeeded in their kitchens in the past helps chefs know what to watch out for. "Often I see the most technically capable and talented people, the naturals, fail miserably in the field due to their interpersonal skills. This is what we look for most in hiring people: that they're not in any way going to be a prima donna," says Patrick O'Connell. "We spend a lot of time interviewing them about their previous work experiences. 'Did you like your boss? Did you like the restaurant?' Every time they say a negative thing, like 'That manager was such an idiot,' is a strong point against them.

"We feel that people develop and create a pattern throughout life, and if they've had a negative experience at a restaurant, it's as much their fault as it is the restaurant's. They chose it—they should have chosen better. Why would you choose a disorganized mess to go and work for? It reflects as poorly on them as it does the restaurant. So we try to find people who reflect a classic illustration: 'I loved my previous employer and would still be there, but they went bankrupt, and I stayed there one month after all my

> **To get hired into an entry-level position, it is not so much what you can do that is important. But you have to know the basics, be a quick learner, and be able to retain information. I can only explain things to someone so many times.** EMILY LUCHETTI

What the Top Chefs Ask in Job Interviews

It is never about your resume. It is all about your connection to food. So when I ask someone what they like to eat and why, I want to find out whether they have a connection to their body. I want to hear them say, "Today it was so hot out that I just had a cold piece of ripe fruit," or "I had some pot pie at a friend's house that had a crust that was as flaky as my mom's." CHRIS BIANCO

Where have you traveled? (Alice Waters)

What did your grandmother cook for you? (Alice Waters)

What do you cook for yourself? (Alice Waters)

What do you like to eat, and why? (Chris Bianco)

If you couldn't be a cook, what would you be? (Emily Luchetti)

What do you want to do with your life? (Norman Van Aken)

What are your five- and ten-year goals? (Norman Van Aken)

What do you think of waiters? (Norman Van Aken)

What books have you been reading lately? (Lydia Shire)

What do you think your strengths are? (Lydia Shire)

How many cookbooks do you have, and which are your favorites? (Mark Miller)

Tell me about a food experience from your childhood. (Mark Miller)

If you say you're interested in the Southwest, I'll ask, "Have you been to Latin America or South America? What books have you read about Latin America? How much history about Latin America do you know? How many friends of yours are Spanish?" If I hear "no, no, no, no," I say, "You don't even know what it is—how can you possibly be interested in it? How can you possibly be interested in something that you don't know anything about?" MARK MILLER

Craig Shelton on Training Yourself for Excellence

"The first thing I notice about a cook is his or her posture. Body language is 97 percent of all communication, and far more reliable than words. I notice the look in someone's eyes. I listen for the sincerity in their voice. What you know or don't know is not as important as what you believe in and what makes you tick.

"I tell my cooks that it is their own responsibility to educate themselves. When you go to college, the professor does not sit next to you and read you the book. As a cook, you have to read everything and eat everywhere on your own: That is your part of the deal. If you do that, then we can have a dialogue. If you haven't done any work on your own, it is just going to be a one-sided conversation.

"I will do that for a time, but I expect people to take responsibility for their own intellectual formation. No one can teach you to cook; you teach yourself. If I was going to learn aikido, it would do me no good to only go to class and never practice at home. My growth would be very slow. On the other hand, if I only practiced and never went to the dojo to study with a sensei and get the reinforcement of practice, that would also be very slow going.

"To grow as a cook is a 'ratcheting process,' in that you do some vigorous intellectual work [e.g., reading, dining out] for a time, and then some practical work, such as hands-on cooking with guidance and feedback from your chef [and the cycle is repeated]. You always want to come into the kitchen with new stimuli and to test what you have seen and learned. It is not enough to see a technique; you must make it your own.

"You want to be asking yourself, 'What is the protein structure of this dish? Why does gentle heat improve the flavor, while intense heat always ruins it? How can I apply that?'

"At the Ryland Inn, we say in our kitchen that if your nose is more than four inches away from the food as you cook it and plate it, you are losing 80 percent of the information you need to do your job. If you are too far back, you can't see it all or smell it all.

"You can learn a hell of a lot by cooking the same dish a thousand times, as long you approach it each time with a theory of how to improve it. Eventually, pursuing true depth of understanding this way will translate into the way you touch everything that comes in front of you when you cook."

paychecks bounced to do what I could to help them, and it was only after the fifth check bounced and I couldn't pay my rent, or else I would still be there.' Wow! That person has the capacity to be a devoted, loyal, trusting person who could be a really strong asset to the root synergy that you're trying to build. The applicant has got to learn to play the role of the interviewer, to put themselves into the head of the employer, either the chef that they're going to be hired by or the restaurant proprietor."

An important way to convey your interest is by expressing an understanding of the goals of the restaurant or the chef you're trying to impress. Larry Forgione says, "The first thing I ask anyone [in an interview] is 'Why do you want to work at An American Place?' Our starting pay rate is always less than the market rate, so that sort of shows me that you want to work here—and not just come here because I'm paying the same thing that everyone else is paying. But after you've been here, then we move you quickly up to the average New York rate. We don't take advantage of people; we just use it as a ploy to see if you're really interested in working here." Forgione wants to know that you've heard of An American Place and understand its influence. "I want to see that you want to be part of that movement to better American cooking or the image of American cooking, that some day you would like to go back to where you came from and open a little American restaurant, or something like that."

To be successful, it's important to have mastered the art of "kitchen speak." Nancy Silverton admits she looks for people with at least a basic kitchen vocabulary, either from cooking school or from extensive reading. "That way, if someone says, 'My sauce is breaking—hand me that whisk!' we're not likely to have the response from someone new on the job be 'What's a whisk?'"

It's fine to have high ambitions, even when you're starting out at the bottom. However, sheer ambition can prove fatal without the proper addition of humility and respect. Gordon Hamersley laments, "I'm amazed and shocked at the attitude of some of the people who come in to apply for work, who want my job and want me to pay them more than I pay myself."

Sandy D'Amato points out that ultimately, it all comes down to your attitude. "If you come in with your mind already made up, then you're not open to learning. And the most important question I'm trying

> **Young people today don't want to work too hard. I don't think they are that serious. They can't understand that if you want to accomplish something and improve on yourself, you've got to stick to it. You can't just go home, put your books down, and go out and have a good time. It's serious work. If it requires you to stay there all night to get it under control, you have to do that. You don't walk away.**
>
> EDNA LEWIS

to answer is 'Does this person want to learn?' I don't want this to just be a step toward whatever you're going to do next. And, ultimately, I'm looking to hire people that I like. I've made the mistake of hiring on skill only, and learned that that doesn't work out."

"When I interview someone, I never ask, 'How do you make a bouillabaisse or clarify a stock'?," says Marcel Desaulniers. "If someone had asked me one of those questions in an interview, I probably would have thrown up! All a question like that does is freak people out. So, all I do is try to gauge whether someone is a nice person, and then put them to work. It is a very unsophisticated system of hiring: You really don't know what you're getting until they work."

Trailing

If the interview goes well, it is indeed common to be asked to "trail" (work for free) in a restaurant for a few shifts to see if the chemistry works—for both the restaurant and you. While being asked to work without pay may sound strange, it's actually a very good system. After a single shift, you may find that you'd really rather work in a larger or smaller restaurant, or that the food being cooked is not a style you're interested in. In any case, you have an opportunity to preview what it would be like to work at the restaurant.

Alfred Portale years ago replaced Daniel Boulud as sous chef of the Polo at the Westbury Hotel in New York after returning from France. "I made a crucial mistake there that I've never repeated," admits Portale. "I didn't work an evening in the kitchen before accepting the position. I knew the first day that I'd made a mistake, once I walked into the kitchen." Portale believes it's important for a cook changing restaurants to get to know the food, the cooks, the chef, and the standards. "As a result, every single person who has ever worked at Gotham has always trailed first. How else can you make a decision whether you want to work with these people? You come in, you work in the kitchen, you meet the cooks, you talk to them, ask questions, see the food, see the condition of the walk-in, the quality of the products, understand the pace, understand the job."

These lessons came hard learned. "I didn't last there," says Portale, who was fired after four months at the Polo. "It wasn't a good fit between me and the chef."

There are certain guidelines for trailing in a kitchen that you should keep in mind. When you are trailing, you are there to watch, help, and learn. The best thing to do is talk to the cook you will be following to find out the best way you can be of help. And understand that when it gets busy, often the best thing you can do is step back and let them cook. The customers always come first—not your training.

Ask the cook if you can learn a dish that you can do for the shift, so that you can demonstrate your technique and your ability to learn quickly. As you learn one dish perfectly, ask for another. The whole time you should be watching all the stations' dishes. You do not want to be intrusive, nor do you want to appear comatose. Be humble and respectful of your teacher, and remember that you are in their territory. Help where you can, and often. While preparing mise en place and during slow times you can ask questions about the food. But talking too much, bragging about your prior experience, or bad-mouthing other restaurants will not win you any respect.

Depending on the size and stature of the restaurant, you may only get a few minutes to speak with the chef. Think in advance about what you would say to maximize that opportunity. Be complimentary about specific things you admire in the restaurant, be brief, and don't waste the chef's time.

By the last day of trailing, you should know most of the station and be able to work during some of the milder rushes of business without much problem or correction. You will not be expected to know anything perfectly or by heart.

Since you are working for free during the period you are trailing, you typically are not asked to work the whole shift. If you are told to leave before the shift is over, feel comfortable about leaving. On the second or third shift you work, you should help the person who is teaching you to clean their station, and you should leave when they leave.

"When we watch people who are trailing, we're not just looking at their skills but to see whether they want to jump in and do something," says Sandy D'Amato. "I don't want someone who just sits back and watches, but nor do I want someone who is so crazy that they'll burn out in three months."

Emily Luchetti insists that there is much a chef can learn about a potential hire from watching them cook for only ten minutes. "You can see if they know how to whisk or use a knife, and you can see how they move around a kitchen," she points out. "That is so important for us, and it's just as important for the prospective employee—because they can see in about the same amount of time if the kitchen is right for them."

> I was yelled at plenty, but the blessing for me was that, since I didn't understand French, I never knew how berated I was. Every time, I would just look up and say, *"Oui, chef!"*
>
> SANFORD D'AMATO

Choosing Your Path: The Line vs. Pastry vs. Baking

At a certain point in your career, it is important to ask yourself, "Am I a sweet, savory, or baking person?" AMY SCHERBER

It's important that every aspiring chef develop a broad-based knowledge of food, from the hot line to pastry and baking.

"Every chef should know how to cook both sweet and savory dishes," maintains Babbo pastry chef Gina DePalma. "Pastry chefs need to understand the mechanics of an entire kitchen, just as chefs need to understand how bread and desserts are going to fit into their menus."

Gaining such breadth of experience may naturally lead you to prefer, and to make a decision to pursue, one path over another. "At Stars, I worked every station in the kitchen, working my way up to lunch sous chef," recalls Farallon pastry chef Emily Luchetti. "In my heart, and eventually my head, I realized that I was losing interest in savory food."

Even if you decide to specialize in desserts, having experience on the line can make you a better pastry chef by ensuring your focus on flavor. "Too often, certain pastry chefs emphasize how a dessert looks rather than how it tastes. I've heard too many pastry chefs say things like 'I'm going to

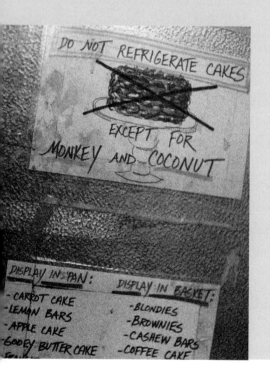

make something round that will have a tuile on it, which I'll sit on its side before adding a sugar stick that will come out at a right angle, in a pool of raspberry coulis because I want red on the plate,'" DePalma laments. "In contrast, like a line cook, I start the process by thinking about whatever it is I want to cook. A cook will get a piece of fish in and think, 'Now, am I going to grill, sauté, or poach it?' Likewise, if I want to use dates, I'll ask myself, 'What kind of heat am I going to apply to these dates?'"

Emily Luchetti agrees. "Because of my background [working the line], for me cooking is all about flavor and texture," she says. "Presentation is the last thing I think about."

The decision to pursue a particular path versus another should be based on an understanding of its demands, as well as its fit with your own personality and interests.

Working the line—cooking at the sauté or grill stations— is known for demanding speed, stamina, and skill at multi-tasking. Cooks must prepare their stations for service, and then fill orders quickly and skillfully as they come in.

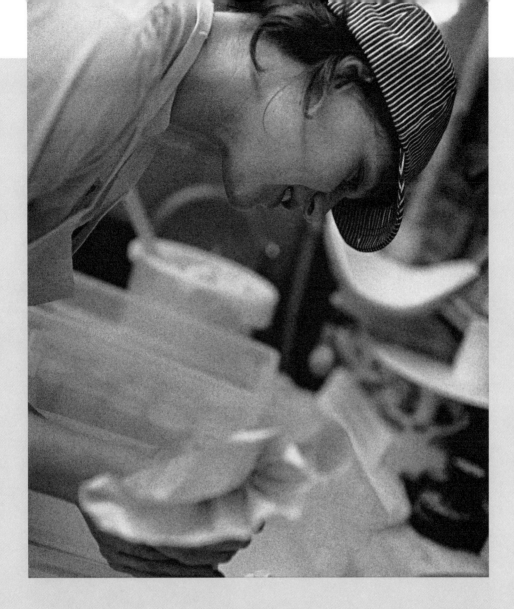

"They need to be of strong mind and body, and to be able to tolerate the heat of the flat top surging on their faces," says DePalma. "Yet they also need to be able to think sharp under pressure, while working at high speed."

Pastry work—because the majority of it is done in advance, with only plating and garnishing done to order—is seen as less frenetic. "I find it funny that whenever I am in the weeds and line cooks come over to give me a hand, they get fed up right away," DePalma laughs. "Pastry is much more thoughtful and, to some, more tedious than blasting out prep for service."

The thoughtfulness required of pastry work is a function of the range of variables at work in baking. "If you 'turn' a bunch of carrots so they are all the same size, and cook them in a pot of water with a pinch of sugar and salt, they will come out pretty much the same way every time. However, you can make a cake the exact same way day in and day out and it will come out differently," DePalma explains. "So, you will have to analyze what happened: Was it humid, which affected the flour? Did the eggs have more yolk, or white, than usual? Once you get to that point as a chef, your trained eye will serve you well no matter what you are cooking."

"Part of the appeal of pastry has to do with how my brain is wired and how I like to organize myself," Emily Luchetti explains. "I like to go in with a huge list of things to do, and then plow through the list and get it all done. When you work the hot line, you prepare your mise en place and wait for the hit to come. You don't know whether you are going to have four orders of scallops or forty, so you have no control over your day. With pastry, you don't know positively what orders will come in, but regardless, the bulk of your work is already done. I liked that level of control a lot better."

In baking, the dough itself sets the pace—literally. "The dough has its own time, and you can't force it," observes New York baker Amy Scherber. Given that one can't rush science, that tends to be a very slow pace at times. In addition, one's very lifestyle as a baker—from when the alarm rings to when one is able to sleep—revolves around the dough's preparation and baking.

As your preferences become apparent to you as a cook, they will help you to choose among these paths. "I found I liked working with recipes, because I felt a certain safety in knowing that something would work, yet that there were elements I could tweak. I find that allows me to channel my thoughts and energy better," says Emily Luchetti. "When I worked in the savory kitchen, it provided so many choices that I found it paralyzing. Working within the parameters of a more limited palette of ingredients, such as fruit, nuts, chocolate, and a few other things, I found that I could be more creative."

Amy Scherber says there is definitely a difference between a bread person and a pastry person. "Bread is technical, but pastry is more exact. Bread has a more spontaneous nature. I loved working in pastry but bread called to me more," she says. "In France, the bread people had their own world and these big balls of dough, and the pastry people would be eating all this sugar and getting wound up. They would both give each other a hard time: The pastry person was 'a sugar hound' and the bread person was 'Mr. Natural.'

"In bread baking, we break the process down to *mixing, shaping,* and *baking,* with mixing being the most technical, and thus the last thing a person will learn. We start people out shaping loafs, from 11 A.M. to 8 P.M. for six months, to get the feel of bread. That is followed by the going onto the night shift, from nine-thirty P.M. to five A.M., when we bake and score the loafs. This is the end of the process, which is my favorite part: You are deciding whether the dough is ready to bake, scoring it, and then making sure that it is perfectly browned. Mixing, the shift that starts at five A.M., requires a great deal of skill. You need to be able to look into a bowl and know 'Is the dough mixed enough or too much? Is it too warm or too cool? Too dry or too wet?' It is like being a saucier and taking a taste of something and knowing exactly what it needs. This takes a great deal of practice. Most people will work with bread for three years before they get to that stage."

Following Up

The restaurant may bring other cooks in to try out if they are actively seeking to fill a position, so you will need to follow up. By now, you know when to call the chef. Communicate how much you got out of the experience and what you liked about the food. Then cross your tongs and hope for an offer.

If you are not made an offer, be courteous and ask for feedback. In some markets and at certain times, there can be a lot of talented and experienced people competing for the same position, so don't assume an offer wasn't forthcoming because you made a mistake. Chefs tend to know one another, so it pays to inquire whether the chef knows of anyone else who may be looking for cooks. Always be gracious and thank them for their time and the opportunity to work in their kitchen. Never burn any bridges unnecessarily—there is a lot of turnover in kitchens, with cooks changing jobs every year or two in many cases. Maybe you'll even get a call back the next day with an offer when the chef's first choice decides to accept a job at another restaurant!

Structure of a Kitchen

The teamwork environment necessary in a kitchen starts with understanding the positions in a kitchen and how they interrelate. Every kitchen is different. The sidebar on pages 150-151 describes typical positions in a medium-sized restaurant kitchen. Large or small, a kitchen staff is a team and every member of the team is important and should be treated with the same respect.

A classical French restaurant is likely to be structured somewhat differently, more closely along the lines of the French "brigade" system originally developed by Escoffier. The stations may be referred to as the sauté, or fish, station; broiler/grill, or meat, station; vegetable station; pantry and hors d'oeuvre; and pastry/desserts. There is also likely to be a saucier responsible for making all sauces, which is an esteemed position.

The emphasis on continuous learning in this profession carries over to the kitchen, where advancement depends upon mastering the techniques and dishes of one station before moving on to the next. It makes sense to consider how to get the most out of your experience in a restaurant, and how to use your experiences to help you advance through your career as a cook.

Getting a Good Start

To start out on the right foot in a new job, you want to be the first person to arrive for your shift every day. If you are not set up on time, you will feel like an amateur and look disorganized. This will not put you in the frame of mind you need to perform at your best.

A cook starting out needs to proactively make the most of on-the-job learning. Identify a mentor who is willing to teach you and give you feedback on how you're progressing. Keep a notebook of kitchen essentials, such as lists and diagrams of mise en place, recipes and steps for executing each dish. Establish a daily plan that you can execute the same way every day. A good cook always has a pen and pad handy for a prep list and a diagram of the setup of his or her station, which will change with menu changes. Arrange the ingredients at your station in accordance with the steps necessary to assemble each dish. Establish your daily schedule; you'll want to do the same job at approximately the same time every day, so you'll know when you're running behind (or "in the weeds," in restaurant slang).

Jean Banchet emphasizes the importance of learning discipline: "You must be on time, you must be clean, you must write in a journal every day what you do. Write down everything you see."

Your goal is to be standing in front of a clean station when service starts. Heaven help the cook who hasn't prepared enough food for service. Sometimes, however, no matter how well you prepare, your station may take the bulk of orders, and you will find yourself low on or out of food. If you have done everything properly to prepare, your fellow workers will jump in to help you if they can. Even the chef may help out with sympathy.

Every kitchen has its own division of responsibilities. There is nothing wrong with wanting to take on extra work and to help co-workers, but never lose sight of why you were hired: to work your own station and fulfill your own duties. It looks bad and hurts the restaurant if you take on too much too soon

Before going to sleep at night, without fail, Carême (1783–1833) was said to have written and drawn in a journal all he had learned and done during the day in the kitchen. Escoffier (1846–1935) said, "One way in which I save fresh ideas is by the agency of a notebook in which I paste cuttings from the papers, description and circumstances, and actual happenings, that impress me as suggestive of a new recipe, or a fresh way of presenting a dish—always a happy thought."

The Positions of a Kitchen

Dishwasher Dishwashers wash not only dishes, but pots, pans, and cooking utensils. They are often responsible for maintaining the floors, cleaning and organizing storerooms, and taking care of garbage. They may also put away deliveries and do light prep work in the kitchen. When you're cooking on the line and need a favor, they're sometimes the only ones around who can free themselves to help, for example, by running to the walk-in for needed items. In the restaurants where I've worked, dishwashers butchered quail, opened oysters, and washed greens. They are invaluable and treated with much respect.

Prep Cook In many ways, prep cooks are the backbone of a restaurant. They serve to perform labor-intensive small tasks (such as chopping vegetables for mire poix, peeling garlic, cleaning salad greens), saving the more experienced cooks' valuable time. They may sometimes butcher less-expensive cuts of meat, clean racks of lamb, or strain stocks.

Pastry Assistant Sometimes the assistant sets up and plates desserts during service. A pastry assistant also helps the pastry chef in a number of other ways. This position requires speed and delicate hands, especially when the restaurant is trying to turn (make room for new parties at) tables during the eight P.M. mid-dinner service rush.

Garde Manger This station is most often responsible for hot and cold appetizers, such as salads, and desserts. Although garde manger is often considered a starting position in a kitchen because there is typically less technique needed for the food, its importance should not be discounted. The plates that come from this station are responsible for a customer's all-important first and last impressions of a meal.

Hot Line The cooks on the hot line produce the entrees, typically at two or more stations, including sauté and grill, described below. The hot line requires a cook to have experience with the delicate cooking temperatures of meat and fish. Often, cooks on the hot line are required to prepare their own sauces and to create daily specials. These cooks typically work with the most expensive ingredients used in the restaurant, which adds to the pressure of not overcooking or burning the food.

Sauté Cook This person sautés entrees on top of the stove and may or may not finish them in the oven.

Grill Cook This person grills meat, fish, or vegetables, while preparing side dishes on the stove.

Vegetable Cook This person works on the hot line in conjunction with the grill and sauté postions, and puts up the side dishes that are served with the entrees.

Rounds Cook This person holds what is often considered to be the most challenging position in the kitchen—that of filling in for each of the other stations on the particular cook's day off.

Sous Chef The sous chef assists the chef in running the kitchen. In cases where the chef is also the owner, the sous chef may hold primary responsibility for managing the kitchen while the chef manages the restaurant as a whole. There may be more than one sous chef in larger restaurants (for example, a day sous chef and a night sous chef). Again, the job varies from restaurant to restaurant. However, sous chefs typically work with the most expensive ingredients and may portion meat or fish. They often order food and supplies, train the staff, inspect work, answer questions, and may also expedite during service. (The expeditor calls out the orders as they come into the kitchen.) When they expedite, it is their job to taste the food and to see that it all goes out perfectly, as the chefs envisioned. They are responsible for the pacing of the food to the table. A sous chef typically has some of the longest hours of any cook in the restaurant, and may also fill in for sick or injured employees.

Pastry Chef In a medium-sized restaurant, the pastry chef may bake breads for the restaurant, as well as prepare custards, ice cream, sorbets, cakes, and candies. Pastry is far different from line cooking: A pastry chef typically works independently, and starts the day early in order to be finished by the time lunch service begins. The work involves a wide variety of cooking and baking techniques as well as a greater knowledge of culinary math and sciences, not to mention patience. In pastry, the distinction is made between the production person and the service person, with the former actually preparing the components of a dessert and the latter plating desserts during service and perhaps making garnishes such as sauces, compotes, or tuiles.

Chef The chef is responsible for hiring, firing, overseeing cooking and cleaning, and managing all aspects of the daily operation of the kitchen. They're typically the ones to make the call to bring in a repair person to fix the broken refrigerator or clogged drain. They write the menus. They set the tone of the kitchen. They also cook. And, typically, they receive the press mentions and, hopefully, the accolades. By the end of the next chapter, you should know how you can eventually work your way into their shoes (or clogs).

before you have mastered your duties. Recognize when you're too comfortable in a station and need to move to another station (or another restaurant).

Susan Feniger and Mary Sue Milliken describe their stint at Le Perroquet in Chicago, where the two met, as "the best education we could have ever gotten. The restaurant was run with food costs of about 25 percent, serving dishes like vegetable mousses with two scallops." The two also recall learning about the time-honored principle of not wasting anything in a kitchen, through examples such as saving and clarifying duck and chicken fat for use in sautéing on the line, a process which also imparts more flavor in cooking.

It's important to take on any task that is assigned to you, and to master it. Doing so will establish your reputation for professionalism. "One of the biggest problems with some pastry cooks is the attitude of 'I don't want to plate desserts—I only want to do production,'" observes Emily Luchetti. "They think plating is boring or that it is entry-level work. They don't see it as crucial because there is no actual cooking involved. However, all my cooks start in that position, and every cook at some point during the week will plate desserts."

Gina DePalma is confounded by the same observation. "What is going on in cooking schools today, in that many new cooks don't want to crack eggs or peel apples, and feel insulted when they are asked to do it?" she asks. "I have been cracking eggs and peeling fruit for desserts for fifteen years! What's the big deal?

"What this says to me is that there are people entering the business who are not suited for it. You have to be driven to work really hard, really fast, and be detail oriented as well as able to multi-task. You have to have a tough skin be able to take criticism. Many cooks just can't do it," she laments.

"I criticize my cooks every day. I used to get corrected by people who weren't nearly as nice as me! I would bite my lip, or go into the dry storage area to cry, or wait until I got home to cry. My friends and family will vouch for this! Then the next day I would come in even more determined not to screw up or to make the same mistakes again.

"If you do something wrong, of course I'm going to correct you. But you can't take it personally, throw a fit, be grouchy all day or get so emotional that it interferes with your work," DePalma says. "That unfortunately happens all the time."

In addition to developing a thick skin, Joyce Goldstein advises beginning cooks: "Make yourself invaluable. Pay attention. And taste, taste, taste."

Maximizing Your Learning

Many chefs were able to steepen their learning curves during their early years in the kitchen by how they spent their time outside of work. Some worked second jobs that exposed them to another aspect of cooking. Others were voracious readers who complemented their on-the-job practical learning with the more theoretical and technical explanations to be found in culinary books.

After graduating from the CIA, Marcel Desaulniers cooked in a private dining room on Wall Street. "The job was only seven hours a day, Monday through Friday, which allowed me to work other jobs on nights and weekends. I would work everywhere from Yankee Stadium to The Metropolitan Opera to a small French restaurant. In a short period of time, I got a really wide variety of experiences."

Desaulniers recommends that cooks pursue every possible chance to learn. "A cook should look for opportunities outside the kitchen, doing different kinds of work still related to food. Helping out at a catering company will teach you a great deal," he says. "Unfortunately, many young cooks at the end of their shift only want to go to bed. Granted, it does depend on the job and the cook—I know that there are a lot of times I send my cooks home too tired to do anything else!"

Such outside opportunities are dictated somewhat by geography. "Your opportunities to learn do depend on where you live, to some degree," Desaulniers admits. "If you are a young cook and moving to a place that is not a food mecca, and your job doesn't work out, you are stuck. That is where big cities offer a lot. You see a lot of top cooks coming out of New York, Chicago, and San Francisco because those cities offer a lot of exposure that you could not get in Uxbridge, Massachusetts, where I grew up. On the other hand, you can't mortgage away your future on jobs that pay well but don't push your skills. If you don't take into account the big picture, you'll end up selling yourself short."

> You can work in a different restaurant every year, but what does that mean? Is it two thousand hours a year, or is it four thousand hours a year? Do you work forty hours and then go to the bar, or do you work forty hours and then go home and read? You can work in six different restaurants that are very well known and be exposed to new things, but how much are you absorbing? While you're cooking, are you talking about the football game, or about the acid balance of the sauce and what kind of wines are going with the dish? You can enrich your environment while you're working, and continue to build your mental capacity. JIMMY SCHMIDT

As You Advance

When you have mastered your own station, start learning the station next to yours, so you can jump in to help when you're not busy and the other cook needs a hand. This will benefit both the restaurant and your career. It increases your value to the kitchen, and it clearly makes you a better cook because you are learning twice as fast.

After several months spent mastering the responsibilities of your station, start looking at the other stations in the restaurant to see where you would like to work next. Most often, a person will stay at a particular station for a year, but obviously there are exceptions to the rule. If you work at several stations around the kitchen, you will get the maximum exposure to the restaurant's food. When you've mastered your station to the point that you're always set up on time, and you can run specials successfully and smoothly, it may be time to change positions. You want to be challenged, so that you don't fall into cooking by rote. When you find yourself reaching this point, speak with the sous chef or chef about the possibility of changing stations.

In the restaurant business, there's always something more to learn. Tired of Italian? Move to a restaurant that cooks Spanish food. Similarly, you can also move to a larger or smaller restaurant, a more formal or more casual restaurant. You will never learn everything in a restaurant, but when you've moved nearly as far along the learning curve as you can, you can start thinking about moving on. Although there are no hard and fast rules, this generally happens after a year or two at a restaurant. After gaining a few years of basic experience, you may also decide to change restaurants for more opportunity. For example, at your current restaurant there may be others higher on the list than you to move into a sous chef's position.

As you advance in your career as a cook, you will largely be "moving through the kitchen," spending time in many of the positions of a kitchen. Finding your way through the profession means establishing a very personal agenda. Michael Foley says, "The only way I think you can be happy with the routine of 'chop, slice, and dice' is if you set up a program of goals for yourself. I don't care what trade you're in—you have to set goals. The goals have to be related to the industry, such as learning as much as you can about fish or meat. You should set up a program to learn as much as you can about your trade. Then you should learn as much as you can about operations, how to work a station properly. Always put your goals into a time frame. Don't say, 'I want to be a chef in five years.' Rather, say, 'I would like to learn how to cut fish and meat' and realize that that alone is going to take you five years."

I went through three phases at every job I've ever held: 1) Damn, I hate this, because I am out of my comfort zone. 2) Hey, I am going to be accepted, and I am going to learn. And 3) Damn, I don't want to leave!

MARCUS SAMUELSSON

Lissa Doumani remembers a colleague at Spago who would start every morning by boning two cases of chicken. "I finally said to him, 'Lord, Kazuto, you've got to quit boning chicken! How can you do that?' He said something that made a great impression on me, which was that each time he does one, he tries to do it better than the last one. There's always something you can improve on. Somehow, you can try to make it more perfect. And as long as you always do that, it's not monotonous, because you're always trying to better yourself."

There is a lack of glamour to certain moments in this business—the time spent doing dishes, sweeping, or mopping tend not to be highlighted in restaurant reviews, chef profiles, or cooking school catalogs. I still remember hosing down the floor at the East Coast Grill one Sunday night at eleven-thirty p.m., thinking about all my friends who were asleep at that moment, and how the restaurant life was definitely not "normal." But what makes it all worthwhile is looking beyond specific chores to the overall sense of accomplishment: the satisfaction you feel over the few dishes you put up over the course of the night that you knew were done perfectly, the fun of having spent the day with a group of like-minded people, and the amazement of how fast the time flew when you were engaged in doing something you love.

I don't really have any horror stories to tell about being a woman in a man's profession. While working [in her first job as a cook], every three or four weeks I'd open my paycheck and I'd have another ten-cent pay increase. I started at $2.62 an hour—then it would be $2.72, then $2.82. . . . LYDIA SHIRE

Baked Beans

SUSAN REGIS, Upstairs on the Park, Cambridge, MA

"Baked beans were often synonymous with blustery Saturday nights growing up in New Hampshire, an hour north of Boston. Unable to resist them hot, I would scald my tongue more often than not . . . ah, but relief was not too far off, as I loved them cold the next day just as well . . . a slightly modernized version equally intoxicating as those memories. . . ."

½ pound kidney beans

½ pound Great Northern beans

½ pound cannelinni beans

3 medium Spanish onions

1 carrot, chopped in ½-inch cubes

½ pound smoked bacon (Shaler & Weber)

Olive oil

8 garlic cloves, chopped

¼ cup toasted cumin seeds

3 jalapeño peppers, chopped

8 ripe plum tomatoes (cut into medium-sized dice)

One 8-ounce can crushed red tomatoes

½ cup maple syrup

½ cup brown sugar

½ cup cider vinegar

2 bay leaves

Zest of 1 orange

2 tablespoons black peppercorns, crushed, plus sprigs for garnish

1 bunch cilantro, chopped

8 pounds country or meaty pork ribs, cut into double-thick pieces (2 ribs each)

Salt and pepper

Soak the beans overnight, rinse, and set aside.

In a heavy-bottomed large stockpot, sauté the onions, carrot, and bacon over low heat for 10 minutes in olive oil. Add 2 garlic cloves, half the cumin seeds, and 2 jalapeños and cook an additional few minutes. Add the beans, both tomatoes, maple syrup, brown sugar, vinegar, bay leaves, orange zest, and a tablespoon of the crushed black pepper. Cover the beans with 8 cups cold water and add half of the chopped cilantro. Cover and bring to a slow simmer.

Meanwhile, rub or toss the pork ribs with a tablespoon of the toasted cumin seeds, the remaining cilantro, 1 chopped jalapeño, and 6 slivered garlic cloves, sautéed lightly in olive oil. Sprinkle with a tablespoon of the crushed black pepper. Marinate for 2 hours.

Salt and pepper the ribs and then sauté them in 2 tablespoons olive oil in a heavy skillet till brown on both sides. Remove.

When the beans have simmered for about 1½ hours, check the liquid amount, making sure it is ample. If necessary, add more liquid. Add the ribs and cook till the beans and ribs are tender. Season with salt and pepper and 1 to 2 tablespoons cider vinegar, according to taste. Serve the beans with a portion of the ribs. Garnish with sprigs of fresh cilantro.

Serves 8

Tripe Stew with Spaghettini

HIROYOSHI SONE, Terra, St. Helena, CA

"I used to hate tripe. Now it's my favorite. This dish has been on my menu at Terra for five years. The first restaurant I worked for was a great Italian restaurant in Tokyo. I was a dishwasher and a prep cook. Once a week, the chef gave me tripe to clean. It took about forty-five minutes, and the smell was so strong I couldn't stand it! But I thought, 'Some day I'm gonna be a chef—and somebody's gonna clean tripe for me!' I learned so many things from this chef—of course, how to clean tripe, but also how to cook the tripe. Thank you, chef!"

1 cup rice wine vinegar
2 pounds honeycomb tripe
1 celery stalk
1 thyme sprig
3 bay leaves
1 tablespoon black peppercorns

Put a gallon of water, the vinegar, and tripe in a large stockpot. Bring to a boil. Skim. Add the rest of the ingredients and simmer for 30 to 45 minutes until the tripe is tender. Drain. Cut the tripe into rectangles ½ by 2 inches.

Sauce

1 carrot, diced
1 onion, diced
1 celery stalk, diced
3 garlic cloves, chopped
1 teaspoon red pepper flakes
Olive oil
1 tablespoon fennel seeds
1 tablespoon cumin powder
1 cup white wine
3 cups tomato puree
2 cups chicken stock
Salt and pepper
1½ pounds spaghettini
½ cup Parmesan cheese, grated
2 tablespoons chopped basil
2 tablespoon chopped parsley

In a large saucepan, sauté the carrot, onion, celery, garlic, and red pepper flakes in olive oil until the vegetables turn light brown. Add the fennel seeds, cumin, and white wine. Reduce the wine by half. Add the tomato puree, chicken stock, and cooked tripe. Bring to a boil. Skim. Salt, pepper, and cover with parchment paper. Bake at 350°F for about 30 minutes.

Cook the spaghettini in salted water. Drain. Toss with the tripe sauce and Parmesan cheese, basil, and parsley.

Serves 6

Grandma's Honey Cookies

GINA DEPALMA, Babbo, New York, NY

"Since my grandmother's death, the lore surrounding these cookies has taken on epic pro-
portions in my family. Around the holidays, either
my mother or my aunt makes them with varying
results. It appears that each one of them has a different recipe and each insists that the other's is
the wrong one. It would be just like my Nonni, a
bit of an enigma herself, to pass on a different
recipe to each of her daughters.

"One year, I managed to look at both recipes and
through some trial and error came up with the
following, which I think perfectly captures the flavor of Nonnie's honey cookies, but with a softer
texture that I prefer. Store them in an airtight plastic container, with a bit of apple peel for complete
authenticity."

> 1¼ cups unbleached, all-purpose flour
> ½ teaspoon salt
> 1 teaspoon baking powder
> 1 egg
> ½ cup honey
> 2 tablespoons olive oil
> ½ ounce melted butter
> Honey Icing (recipe follows)

Preheat the oven to 325°F.

In a small bowl, whisk the flour, salt, and baking
powder together.

In another bowl, whisk together the egg and
honey. Add the olive oil and melted butter and
whisk thoroughly to combine.

Add the dry ingredients to the wet.

Drop the dough by small spoonfuls onto greased
cookie sheets, at least 1 inch apart. Bake until the
cookies are golden brown and firm to the touch.
Cool the cookies on the cookie sheet for 5
minutes, then remove to wire racks to cool
completely.

Glaze the cookies with the icing, allow the icing to
dry, and store the cookies in an airtight container.

Honey Icing

> 1 cup confectioners' sugar, sifted
> 1 tablespoon honey
> A few drops of milk

Whisk the sugar and honey until smooth. Add the
milk to reach the desired consistency. If you are
not using the icing immediately, cover with plastic wrap or store in an airtight container so it
won't dry out.

Makes about 2½ dozen cookies

Garlic Soup

SUSAN SPICER, Bayona,
New Orleans, LA

"This is one of the first recipes I developed on my own when I first started cooking. It was inspired by an old boyfriend of mine who used to spend a lot of time in Mexico and would come back talking about *sopa de ajo*. I researched lots of different versions and came up with this one. It has been my single most popular menu item for a long time and I still love it. My dishwashers used to have to peel all the garlic—now it comes peeled in gallons! Quite a breakthrough!"

2 pounds onions, roughly chopped (about 4 cups)

2 cups chopped garlic

2 tablespoons olive oil

2 tablespoons butter

1½ quarts chicken stock

1 tablespoon fresh or 1 teaspoon dried thyme leaves

½ loaf stale French bread, in chunks

1 pint half-and-half or cream

Bouquet garni (parsley, bay leaf, and thyme) tied together with butchers' or cotton string

Salt and pepper

Sauté the onions and garlic in olive oil and butter, stirring frequently, over low to medium heat until a deep golden color is reached, about 30 minutes. Add the chicken stock, thyme, bouquet garni, and bread. Simmer for 15 to 20 minutes. Remove the bouquet garni. Puree in a blender.

Strain through a medium strainer. Heat and add the half-and-half. Add salt and pepper to taste. The soup is better the second day, as it mellows out overnight.

Serves 8

Banana Blueberry Quickbread

AMY SCHERBER, Amy's Bread,
New York, NY

"Long before I became a professional baker, I loved baking for friends and family. One friend liked my baking so much that she recommended me for a job as private cook for a family. To my surprise, I was hired and had to create a repertoire of breakfast, lunch, and dinner menus. A clear favorite for breakfast was my quickbread, and I came up with new ones every week. I started with a base of liquid and dry ingredients, then changed the flour or fruit to make each one unique. To this day, the banana blueberry is one of our most popular bakery treats."

8 eggs, lightly beaten

1⅓ cups vegetable oil

2 cups milk

3 cups old-fashioned oats

6 cups unbleached all-purpose flour

2 cups sugar

2 tablespoons plus 1 teaspoon baking powder

½ teaspoon baking soda

2 teaspoons salt

4 cups coarsely mashed ripe bananas (not pureed)

4 cups fresh blueberries

Preheat the oven to 350°F.

In a large bowl, combine the eggs, oil, and a cup of the milk with a whisk.

Pour the remaining cup of milk over the oats and allow to soak for 5 minutes.

Combine the remaining dry ingredients. Pour the liquid ingredients into the dry and stir until par-tially moistened, then add the oat mixture and bananas. Gently fold together until nearly mixed, add the blueberries, and fold a few more times until all the ingredients are just moistened.

Pour the batter evenly into three oiled 9 by 5-inch loaf pans. Bake for 55 to 60 minutes, or until a toothpick comes out clean when poked in the middle of the loaf.

Let the loaves cool in pan for 5 minutes, then tip out of the pan and place on a wire rack until completely cooled. This quickbread tastes great when freshly baked, or keeps well for up to 5 days, wrapped tightly in plastic film and stored in the refrigerator. It also freezes well if wrapped in foil.

Makes 3 loaves

6. Developing as a Cook
THE NEXT LEVEL

If it does take ten or fifteen years for you to learn this profession, don't think you're stupid. You need time and dedication. Be patient. Don't take the elevator—take the stairs. **MICHEL RICHARD**

Once a cook has developed basic kitchen skills and good work habits (which is much easier to say than it is to do), further development takes place over a period of years through work at higher and higher levels, ideally under the watchful eye of a skilled chef. You build speed. You develop a larger repertoire of skills. You refine your techniques. You learn to grasp and translate the chef's idea of a dish more easily. You're more comfortable using new or exotic ingredients and better able to apply familiar techniques to working with them. You are able to develop more sophisticated specials. You begin to learn your own preferences in cooking, and to develop a sense of your own style as a cook—even while you're cooking someone else's cuisine.

I'm critical when the press comes out with stories about chefs at twenty-two or twenty-three. That's not because of jealousy, don't get me wrong, but because I don't think it's good to have these "wunderkinds." Even if they have talent, they lack the techniques, and you need both to be a "star" chef. These are the chefs about whom, ten years later, people ask, "Where are they?"

ANDRÉ SOLTNER

As you grow as a cook, the way you think—or care—about a particular dish will also evolve. A prep cook cares that the vegetables are sliced uniformly. A line cook cares that they're cooked through. A sous chef cares whether they're seasoned properly. And the chef cares not only whether the other cooks are doing everything right, but whether the customer will find the dishes delicious enough to come back and order them again.

Therefore, the key to advancement is to make yourself invaluable to a restaurant, which can be accomplished in two ways: through your cooking skills and through your management skills. The best cook doesn't always advance the fastest if he or she can't work with other cooks and command their respect.

Even after Alfred Portale had developed a solid cooking background, he recognized his need to develop management skills. He recalls, "I was always frustrated as a cook when I felt that I had the most efficient way of doing something and the guy working next to me didn't think so and wouldn't listen to me. Just because you have the title of sous chef or chef doesn't necessarily mean that people will follow you. You must learn how to motivate them and inspire them."

Earning the Title of Chef

Jasper White believes in planning a career. "I think it's realistic to want to be a sous chef after five to seven years, and to be a chef in ten years," he says. "Once a year, you should reevaluate where you've been and where you're going, and whether you're moving toward those goals."

When you've mastered being a sous chef and you have developed both a strong voice for your own food and a thorough knowledge of how a kitchen is run, you may be ready to become a chef. Chefs have made that transition in several ways. You may fall into an opportunity to do so, or you may seek one out.

However, even if an offer to become a chef is forthcoming, it doesn't necessarily mean it's the right time. After graduating from The Culinary Institute of America and spending sixteen months working at a French restaurant in Nashville, Edward Brown jumped at the opportunity to become the chef of a new restaurant in town. He recalls, "While they were thrilled with what I was doing, I wasn't learning anything new"—a chef's worst nightmare. "I realized I hadn't done the right thing."

Soon after, he received a call from a former classmate who was about to start working with Christian Delouvrier at The Maurice (NYC). Invited to join them, Brown says, "I left my job and my girlfriend, and was in Manhattan in ten days" to go back to working the line—and continuing his on-the-job education.

Charles Palmer also recognized his need to keep developing his cuisine out of the spotlight. He made a stint as chef of the Waccabuc Country Club part of his career plan at the age of twenty-one, explaining, "I had plenty of money to work with, and I was able to develop my own style of cooking while not having to worry about being reviewed." Two years later Palmer was asked to replace Larry Forgione at The River Cafe (NYC) when Forgione left to open An American Place (NYC).

Sometimes chefs played a hand in creating their own luck by doing their jobs to the best of their abilities. Anne Rosenzweig got her break when she was working as the pastry chef and brunch chef at Vanessa. While the restaurant itself received only a lukewarm review, Vanessa's brunch and desserts received raves, and Rosenzweig was tapped to become the restaurant's chef. Nobu Matsuhisa was twenty-three years old and working as a sushi chef in Japan when he was approached by a customer who was a Peruvian businessman. "There was a big concentration of Japanese in Peru, and he invited me to come and open a restaurant with him," says Matsuhisa. Recalling his fascination with his father's world travels, and knowing of Peru's abundance of fresh seafood, Matsuhisa agreed.

Emeril Lagasse recalls reading and conducting research in 1981 to find out "who was trying to make things happen in food," and hearing a lot about Ella and Dick Brennan. "A year later a friend told me that they were looking for a young American chef for their restaurant in New Orleans, Commander's Palace. Paul [Prudhomme] had been gone six or eight months and had opened

> Great cooks are going to find their level—it doesn't matter what their background is. They're going to succeed. Chefs are going to notice them—the drive, the fanaticism, all the things that to me make a great cook are very noticeable. Any good chefs worth their salt are going to notice talent when they see it, and are going to cultivate that talent.
>
> JASPER WHITE

Winning Moves: One Pastry Chef's Career

I was working at Le Chantilly with Dieter Schorner, and it was from him that I learned everything there was to know about desserts. I would work with him on my days off and every Saturday. Beyond being brilliant, he is a great teacher. On Saturdays, he would apologize because he didn't have anything new to show me. I would comment that [at school] I used to pay for the privilege of making the same things over and over again! SANDY D'AMATO

How does a long, successful career progress? Step by step, as evidenced by the career moves of pastry chef Dieter Schorner:

Age	Location	Position
14	Germany	Salted pretzels
17	Switzerland	Studied Swiss pastry; learned chocolates and confections
21	Germany	Worked in one of the country's finest pastry shops where he made 140 different types of chocolate
24	Sweden	Worked in the country's oldest pastry shop, which was the sole supplier to Sweden's royalty
25	Worldwide	Cooked on a Swedish-American cruise ship through the Caribbean and around the world, where he made ice carvings of bears, cats, eagles, and doves
27	England	After he was offered pastry jobs at both the Plaza-Athénée in Paris and the Savoy Hotel in London, he flipped a coin to make his decision to go to London, where he met his greatest mentor, executive chef Silvano Trompetto
32	Boston, MA, and Washington, DC	Worked with Sonesta Hotels in both locations, and opened a pastry shop at the Watergate

Worked as pastry chef in the following restaurants:

Age	Location	Position
32	New York, NY	L'Etoile at the Sherry-Netherland Hotel
34		La Seine, started by the son of the founder of Tour d'Argent in Paris, where he was the only non-French employee in the kitchen
36		La Côte Basque, and would moonlight in the evenings as a pastry chef for Elysée, where he worked alongside Jacques Pépin
40		Le Périgord Park
42		Le Chantilly
45		Le Cirque
49		Café Fledermaus
50		Tavern on the Green
51	Washington, DC	Opened The Potomac
52		Opened Patisserie Café Didier
60	New York, NY	Named Chairman of the Pastry Department at the French Culinary Institute
62		Sold Patisserie Café Didier
63	Hyde Park, NY	Appointed Associate Professor at The Culinary Institute of America
64		Honored with CIA Faculty of the Year Award; earned Certification as a Hospitality Educator and Diploma as a Master Baker

K-Paul's. I spoke to Ella weekly or biweekly over about four months—about people, about philosophies and passions. Finally, she said she'd like for me to come down for a long weekend. As she walked me through the kitchen, she asked me, 'So, what do you think of all this great food?' I told her, 'It reminds me a lot of my mom's.' So, as Ella tells the story, it was in the first ten minutes that the connection started." Lagasse was named chef of Commander's Palace in 1982.

Running a Kitchen

The business of owning a restaurant will be addressed in Chapter 7. But chefs should always feel a sense of ownership, whether or not they actually have a piece of the business. After all, they are ultimately responsible for ensuring that the kitchen runs smoothly—from developing menus, to hiring and training the staff, to controlling food and labor costs. A chef must also manage the support systems that enable a kitchen to function, from ordering products and supplies and ensuring their quality, cost, and timely delivery; to contracting out the cleaning of the kitchen after hours to provide extra attention to floors, walls, stoves, ventilation systems, etc.; to making certain the kitchen adheres to all safety and sanitation requirements. Finally, a chef must coordinate with the owners and the management of the dining room, the "front of the house," to ensure that customers are served well.

A chef must implement management systems that will allow the restaurant to operate smoothly and successfully and to minimize mishaps. "But it's a give and take," points out Edward Brown. "When you take the time to look at your systems, you give up something somewhere else. Maybe you could have been a little more creative that day or invented a new dish, but instead you made yourself more money. The goal is to achieve a balance in your week or your month. Both are imperative."

Like the old saying "It's easy to sculpt an elephant from a block of wood—simply carve away anything that doesn't look like an elephant," the secret to successful systems is changing or eliminating any systems that aren't successful. George Germon and Johanne Killeen made the radical decision to eliminate the sauté position altogether in their kitchen at Al Forno because of the "frenzies" it produced. That helped further define their style of cooking: "Now, everything is either roasted or grilled," Killeen says.

Al Forno, which makes everything from scratch to order, had to institute unique systems in its kitchen in order to be able to do so. For example, after deciding that "there's nothing like the taste of fresh ice cream, just as you turn off the motor," Germon and Killeen decided never to serve it any other way.

They invested in multiple ice-cream makers so the restaurant could serve only made-to-order ice cream for dessert. Killeen hated the taste of tarts that had been baked and left to sit before serving, and so such desserts were also made to order. Mashed potatoes are hand-mashed to order: "Amber, the woman who mashes them, has forearms like Popeye." Even lamb, which in most restaurants is cooked off partially before dinner service, is cooked completely to order at Al Forno. "At home, we never cook off lamb and

Defining the Goal: Creating a Mission Statement

One way that chefs are able to ensure that their crews are able to clearly understand and work toward their vision is through creating and articulating a mission statement for the restaurant. A well-written statement can lead the entire staff toward the same end point. When shared with customers, it can even create a stronger understanding of what is being communicated on the plate, through the restaurant, and in the community as a whole, adding value to the customer experience.

At L'Etoile in Madison, Wisconsin, Odessa Piper has led the restaurant through two decades using two mission statements. "The first is that 'We believe sustainability is achieved when all our relations prosper.' Some of the finest foods are raised in our own backyard. We want to thank our customers for appreciating these efforts and supporting these patient arts. To me, this is a mission statement of gratitude as well as a pretty ambitious goal.

"On the bottom of our menu, we say, 'For the benefit of all concerned, we use local naturally-grown foods whenever feasible.' We have to say that because we don't use exclusively organic foods or local foods, because that is not possible for us and because we don't want to. Our mission is to honor 'spirit of place,' which might include celebrating great vineyards on the Mosel [the German wine region], great peach orchards in Michigan, or the places where fresh shad is running. They all reflect 'spirit of place,' which we are happy to observe here in Madison."

At The Ryland Inn in Whitehouse, New Jersey, Craig Shelton ensures that his restaurant's mission statement is something that is discussed not only in monthly staff meetings, but every day in staff conversations. "The four credos of our mission statement are 1) integrity, 2) accountability, 3) passion for excellence, and 4) kindness," Shelton explains.

"We tell our crew that all the rules of the Ryland Inn are circumscribed in those four things, and that you know in your own heart whether you are in violation of them or not. The reason for a company is to bring you more life, and not make you a slave to a business. Our objective is to make everyone a better person based on values that are good for humanity—not just to prepare a great plate of food. Either we all grow, or we all stagnate.

"One of the most beautiful reasons to become a chef is to control all the elements of what you hear, touch, smell, and look at. You get to design your own little perfect world! We have even created an art gallery at The Ryland Inn that celebrates the New Hope School of Impressionism, which was a very important art movement. What is special to us is that it was created only twenty miles away.

"With all the artistic elements of dining and food, I have a little trouble with describing food as art. If a meaningful definition of art is that it is intended to create an array of emotions that the artist had in mind, that is all well and good—however, in cuisine, basically the only legitimate emotion you want to create is joy or happiness.

"My job with my team at work is no different from my job at home with my children, which is to help build their self-esteem, and then their self-discipline. With those two things, a person can achieve all their dreams in life.

"Restaurants are traditionally 'islands of misfit toys.' Unfortunately, most people's self-esteem was shattered somewhere within the socialization process. Everyone is damaged to a degree, and that is what we have to address. The Ryland Inn has taken young kids who have had addiction problems and helped to turn them around.

"Our goal is to work on the whole person—including self-esteem and inner values—and getting a person to embrace them, then to see that person flourish and grow. I get incredible joy out of creating beautiful food, but I get even more joy from helping another human being come into their own power. That's what makes me jump out of bed in the morning.

"In a big city four-star restaurant, there is typically one cook for four seats and one waiter for three seats. We have to work with one cook for thirty-five seats and one waiter for up to twelve at a peak crisis level—which means my crew is asked to produce three to four times as much as other crews. If I only focused on technique with my crew, I would never make it. We have to focus on inner *and* outer work.

"We spend a lot of time in one-on-one sessions with our team, coaching and mentoring each person. We help them with their goals, which they will write out as affirmations to keep in their wallet or pocket.

"If a manager has a problem, it is a problem for everyone. We all own it. The key that we work on is to make sure that the environment is a safe one in which to have a problem. Problems are a natural part of the process: As people go over one hurdle, it follows that another one will naturally appear if you are working in a healthy direction. If you have an environment that hides problems instead, it is stunting growth."

> I used to yell at people when they made mistakes, but I realized that in essence it took their experience away from them of actually making that mistake and learning from the mistake. Now, I'm more relaxed about it. One thing I learned at the Ritz-Carlton is that it's very good to empower your line employees—empower them to do what you do every day.
>
> **GARY DANKO**

let it sit for hours. Why should we do that in our restaurant?" Al Forno's special high-heat ovens do allow the advantage of some shortening of cooking time. By now, the restaurant has the whole process down to a science; every dish has its own staging time, cooking time, and plating and delivery time. Perhaps not surprisingly, every cook also carries around his or her own timer.

Such precision doesn't come without a price: Al Forno's twenty cooks make for an enormous payroll. "But every person is absolutely necessary," Germon and Killeen insist. Do customers appreciate the difference? "They know that things taste better, but they don't necessarily know why."

Learning where and how to cut costs, without sacrificing quality, is something that has to be analyzed at the very smallest levels. "The cumulative results add up exponentially," says Edward Brown. "I started with limes. At the last restaurant I was with, I bought two cases of limes, every single day, and we used them all. When people see what's there, they use what's there. But one day, I decided to cut back a case a couple days a week. I never heard a word from the bartenders, nobody was ever out of limes, and it worked. A case of limes is six dollars, which saved us twelve dollars a week, or forty-eight dollars a month, or hundreds of dollars a year—just because I decided I could cut out two cases of limes a week. Then I looked at the lemons, then the oranges, then the snapper and the swordfish, and things that are in the seven-to-eight-dollars-a-pound range. When you look at every little thing—like a lime, or a bag of onions, or a case of celery—then by the time you get to the intensity of five pounds of beef or ten pounds of fish, you are so tight and so closely controlled that you are saving every penny that is possible."

How does Brown communicate his cost-cutting mind-set to his kitchen staff? "I let it be very apparent to people what I'm doing. You need to produce data and use it," he says. "I don't hide in my office and calculate food costs. I do it out front. People see that it's on my mind, so it's going to be on their minds. And if it's on their minds, then they're going to be my agents out there, doing what they can in their own small way."

Alfred Portale has also learned a thing or two about managing others since his early days as a cook. He notes, "The only way to teach people and to inspire them is through example. That's the very basis of the way I have approached training people in our kitchens. You want them to work super hard?

Daniel Boulud, Chef-Restaurateur

One Philosophy, Three Executive Chefs

While Daniel Boulud is widely seen as the standard-bearer for culinary excellence among his peers nationally (and even internationally), he in turn invests his reputation in three very talented executive chefs: Alex Lee of Restaurant Daniel, Andrew Carmellini of Café Boulud, and Jean-François Bruel of DB Bistro Moderne. All were nominated for 2002 James Beard Awards: Lee and Carmellini as Best Chef: New York; and Bruel as Rising Star Chef.

I have had great talent come through my kitchens, and in fact my chefs were all nominated for James Beard Awards in 2002. I was very proud, but I was worried that people would think it was a setup! But I know they definitely succeeded because of their talent. I can't imagine that ever happening again, but I will always make sure my chefs have the best support around them so it is at least possible.

What I look for in a *chef de cuisine* is talent, creativity, and managerial skills. They also need to know that this is a business: I would never let a chef, no matter how much talent he has, run a business at a loss.

My chefs have to be able to lead, attract talent, be creative, and be spontaneous—because they need to get themselves out of any situation correctly and with taste! I suppose I want to be able to see something of myself in them. And I believe that all chefs must have a "fire" that drives them to do their best.

There are chefs who have great names but don't cook very much. Then there are young chefs who are building names for themselves and cooking very hard over their stoves. The latter is the case with my three chefs: they cook every day.

You have to be right next to them working super hard. You can't tell people what to do or how to cut something or how to plate something—you have to show them, over and over again.

"I'm terrified of putting up something into the window that's not perfect, or dropping something onto the floor and not bending over to pick it up. That terrifies me. If I allow myself to do that then, as a perfectionist, as a professional, I'm finished. But worst of all is if somebody else sees me and says to himself, 'Look, the chef put up that terrible-looking thing' or 'If he doesn't care, why should I?' If you catch yourself cutting a corner or taking a shortcut or doing something that you know is wrong or trying to pass something off that isn't perfect, it's like an addiction. You've got to stop it immediately."

Setting the Standard

As the head of a kitchen, the chef sets its standards. His or her expectations about everything, from punctuality to cleanliness to precision, dictate standards to the rest of the kitchen. In addition to serving as a role model, some of this is done explicitly. One of the other most important roles of a chef is that of a teacher. Gordon Hamersley says, "You teach people to do exactly what, if you had time, you'd do yourself."

Emeril Lagasse met with his staff daily for thirty minutes before lunch and dinner, and sometimes went to great lengths to teach them about the ingredients used in the kitchen: "We'd talk about food, wine, the customer, and service. A couple weeks ago, I flew a whole palm tree in and, for three days, we did a seminar for the staff on how the palm tree is dissected and what parts of it make hearts of palm, then how the process is to cure it to make edible hearts of palm, and then actually serving the hearts of palm to the guest. We once spent two days in seminars on about fifteen types of exotic and wild mushroom varieties." He also mandated his staff's attendance at three wine classes a month.

Other chefs agree that hosting tastings for the kitchen staff is a way for everyone to learn. "Do tastings at the restaurant, whether it's olive oils or anchovies or whatever. That needs to be a continuing thing," says Bradley Ogden. "You should never be satisfied with what you've got—always try to reach for something better."

Amy Scherber sees creating a perfect French baguette as the ultimate test for a baker. "A baguette is composed of four ingredients—flour, water, yeast, and salt—and it is made in every country in the world. Some are dreadful, and some are great. Beyond the usual basics, you might have a great starter, a bread that's shaped by hand, a different kind of flour, and so on. However, technique is the ultimate measure. I know that on certain days, due to factors such as the weather, it is not possible to make a perfect baguette. However, I still check my baguettes every day."

To ensure that she continues to maintain a standard of excellence, Scherber will meticulously research her competition. "I will go to various bakeries in New York, buying loaves of bread to bring back to the shop. Then, I will analyze various aspects of each loaf. First, I'll look at the outside color, the scoring, the size, and the proofing to see if the bread has risen properly. Next, I will slice it

> Mr. [Joe] Baum is one of the best tasters I ever saw. What unbelievably talented taste he had and still has today. To please him was like having to please a king. I liked to work with him because he was really fussy—honest and fussy. He's one of the bosses that I enjoyed the best.
>
> ALBERT KUMIN

lengthwise and look at the color and the size of the holes. If the holes are tight, that means it was made by machine. You want to see large and irregular holes, because that means it was started by a more unusual starter. Third, I'll smell the bread, to see if I can identify a toasty and milky aroma, which is almost popcorn-like or toasted hazelnut-like. Finally, I'll taste the bread, and note the texture of the crumb, which might range from chewy to airy. It is through analyzing food at this level of detail that you can make important distinctions to be able to improve your final product."

All chefs must learn how the ingredients they're working with should feel and smell and taste. Are the avocados at their peak? Is the fish still fresh? Is the cream that was good last night still good? They must also learn how to judge prepared and stored food, such as soup, to make sure it's still good the next day. If the taste is off, they must learn to analyze whether it is a result of one of the ingredients having gone bad or improper storage or some other factor, and take proper steps to correct the problem.

A Matter of Taste

Jean-Georges Vongerichten observes, "A lot of young people think that cooking is just art and painting. They forget that the main thing is flavor. We have a lot of young people that come in and want to do 'art,' and I say, 'If you want to skip your apprenticing, go downtown and open a gallery for somebody else. But if you are going to be a cook, you're going to have to learn how to season first.'" This includes teaching your cooks how to taste.

Alice Waters says that because so many people make decisions about how things happen at Chez Panisse, she spends time working with them to learn to really taste in a very critical way. "It's a matter of teaching cooks how to get the whole view of what's happening in the restaurant, how to see a menu, how to be critical about the ingredients we're using. Most people have taken shortcuts along the way and have not been exposed to such a range of flavors, tastes, and ingredients. A lot of places it's taken for granted that the ingredients worked with are of good quality, and many people probably haven't been the ones tasting five or ten different olive oils and asked to make a decision about why they like one over another."

A crucial part of the evolution of a cook involves developing the ability to taste. While this may seem basic, a surprising number of leading chefs know cooks who don't taste the food as they cook it. "I tell cooks they have no business being a cook if they're not willing to taste," says Susan Spicer. Joyce Goldstein agrees: "It's the difference between someone who's an artist with food and someone who's just

Mark Miller on Tasting

You have to think about food every single time you put something in your mouth. And it's not just particular foods like caviar, Burgundies, and Bordeaux. It's all food. We only pay a lot of attention to those things that eventually gain status. But every single food has more than one flavor. Even an apple is not appley; it has a dimension of a little bitter, a little citrus, and a little bit of this or that.

You learn to experience food. Most people cannot do that. They have this value system that certain foods are more valuable and other foods are less valuable. It's the same problem I had teaching art—people saw Western art as more valuable than primitive art. I had to say that it wasn't a class about form, but a class about understanding process—where art reflects status, function, ritual, class, identity, religious ties, historical context, scientific thinking. The same is true for food.

Many people cannot think about food. If I ask, "What is going on in this dish?" I hear, "What do you mean what's going on in this dish?" What I mean is what is the tomato doing? What is the onion doing? Where are the acids, the sugars, the flavors, the tones?

If I give people a chile (and I do this all the time in culinary classes) and ask them to tell me what it tastes like without telling me it's hot, after ten or fifteen minutes, one guy will say, "I think licorice." Finally! We go from unsure to licorice, then to tobacco, then to plum, cherry, smoke.

You begin to recognize that no one's ever been taught. There isn't a palate class. For instance, if I asked students how many types of tastes there are in your mouth, I'd bet 100 percent of them would say four. Basically, you get "sweet" and "salty" always. Then they'll say "bitter" and "sour." They never say bitter and sour first.

In Chinese there are five: there's also "hot." In Southeast Asia, there's also "aromatic." There's also "pungent"—something like fish paste, which is not sour or bitter, but it's sour, bitter, sweet, and salty. Do they teach these things? No. So consequently, people don't use aromatics. They don't use pungents. They don't use hot. They learn to think that they are lower on the evolutionary scale of taste.

Don't forget—language is the psychological way of reinforcing the phenomenal object. It's basically organization in the phenomenological world. That's what language is. Listen to people speak.

I would like to teach graduate-level composition. The way I teach is that I say there are these base tones, like garlic and smoky tones. We have mid-palate range, which are fruits and vegetables. We have high tones, which are lemon and chiles. These combined create chords.

We'd look at cuisine: Italian cuisine, French cuisine, Chinese cuisine. It is very biased and prejudiced that they make you make stocks for three or four days, and then they have you make curry by pulling a can off the shelf. This reinforces the idea that we have this great French tradition, and that the Indian tradition is really nothing—it's just really simple and not really worth anything. Do you actually

make curry from scratch, from twenty-five different ingredients, and teach how it's made in [various regions of Asia], and that you can control acids, aromatics, and pungency?

Ethnic foods are like ethnic art, where people say, "Well, it's not as beautiful." And I say, 'Well, the form is not as finished; however, the intent is expression versus form." We discuss food at the same level as we discuss art. Are we creating finished form in order to have a certain vision, a quantitative vision, of the food experience, which cuts us off from the real physical and expressive experience in food?

We'd look at chords. We'd look at cultural chords. We learn in order to play well. Chords can be very complex. Then we throw in acids and create rhythm. People say, "rhythm?" Well, yeah, how fast are the flavors? Can we slow them down or speed them up? But people don't get this. What I usually do is take a boom box and play a Guns N' Roses tape. I say, "This is what happens when you cook a recipe; these are all the notes. Now watch what happens with the equalizer system when I pull out the mid-range. You get all the notes playing, but it is distorted now. You get more bass and more treble proportional to the mid-range. It doesn't sound the same. Then watch what happens when I put up the treble and take the bass out. Food is a combination of chords, and we control these chords by our bass notes."

To me Introductory 1A would be, "Okay, everybody, let's start describing"—because language is thought, and thought is language. There is too much preaching and not enough thinking. The processes are very important. It isn't really important that someone actually knows any recipes. It's more important that they actually understand the recipe. I mean, Beethoven did his last three symphonies when he was deaf. I can actually look at recipes—most good chefs can—and conceptualize all the players, and you can drop some in and take some out, but you understand food and the food experience and cooking as a process. That's what creates great cooks.

intellectual with food. There are some chefs who, when you look at their menus, you know that they just play with ideas and put them together, and that they haven't eaten it."

Learning to taste analytically is quite different from tasting to enjoy. Anyone is able to identify whether they find the taste of a dish pleasing or not. The experienced cook can analyze the particular combinations of flavors—of both ingredients and seasonings—that make a dish "right." Jean-Georges Vongerichten believes "the most difficult thing in the business is to convey your tastes to somebody else, to make sure they come out the same way. The women I've had in the kitchen season the way I want better than the men. I can't explain it. Many times, I take young people in the kitchen that want to learn, and the women pick it up right away. The guys get it, but it takes a month for some to season the way I season."

Some chefs believe that better training is able to impart such judgment. "The old training model is simply to scream, 'Too much salt!' and to intimidate the cook, which doesn't really serve anyone," observes Craig Shelton. "The purpose of salt is to bring out flavor, but what does that really mean? I've found that it helps to actually explain salt to my cooks in terms of the science of it. For example, salt gets a bland starch molecule to become sweeter, such as in the case of a carrot—or cuts long protein molecules into short amino acids that have lots of flavor, such as in the case of a steak. As you cook, you should add salt little by little, tasting as you go along, until your tongue starts to salivate. When you hit that moment, you are exactly on the mark. I have found empirically that this method is a thousand times more reliable than telling someone to salt until they taste it. So, I get my cooks to pay attention to and heed their palates throughout the day and night.

"I also remind cooks that their palates will fatigue during the night," Shelton adds. "I have worked in top restaurants where plates start getting sent back to the kitchen around nine P.M., when cooks' palates would start to fatigue. The complaints would be both ways, too salty or not salted enough. Here, we can go six months without a plate coming back with a salt problem."

Alfred Portale also finds himself teaching his cooks how to taste. "We have a wild mushroom ravioli in a mushroom broth, with white truffle oil and chervil—it's marvelous. The mushroom broth is critical. It's different every day, and the cooks have to adjust it. They make a stock in the morning, and then the cook at night needs to taste it and make the adjustments. Maybe it needs an infusion of fresh mushrooms. Maybe it needs to be reduced a little bit. Maybe it's perfect. But you have to taste it and adjust it," he says. "If I come in at eight o'clock and I decide to plate a ravioli and I taste it and it's too light—there's no reason for that! The only time I get upset is when someone's done something he or she knows is wrong and serves it anyway."

Because tasting and seasoning are more subjective than objective, it's difficult to teach through a set of rigid rules. "I really try not to be too dogmatic," says Judy Rodgers. "The food I do is hardly ever from recipes. The menu is written every day, and we nurse food along, and at six o'clock I taste it and maybe change it. What I try to teach people is 'I'm doing this because it makes the food taste good today. This is what I think tastes good, and I am the person whose palate you have to mimic.' I help my cooks try to glean that."

Rodgers writes the menus for Zuni Café along with explicit directions as to how she would like to see everything done, yet she still tries to encourage her cooks to develop and use their own intuition and judgment when it comes to cooking. "Occasionally I'll write something in a note that says, 'Do this, this,

You can teach yourself the techniques of any cooking from a book—there's really not all that much to it. If you're dogged and scientifically minded or academically obsessive, you can learn the techniques of a cuisine. But you can never learn the flavors without eating, without tasting. BARBARA TROPP

and this for the soup, and when you get it this far, look out the window and see what the weather is and decide what the soup wants to be,'" she says. "I mean decide if it wanted to be pureed, decide if the potatoes are so good that you don't want to break them down anymore, decide if it needs extra fat because of the weather. My cooks have been there with me for six years, tasting food nightly. They know what I want."

Edna Lewis agrees that it's important in cooking to leave room for inspiration. "It's a creative process," she says. "Things just hit you that you weren't even thinking about. You start cooking something, and the herbs you were going to put in will lead you to something else, and you end up with something tasting better than you would have thought."

There are other reasons to allow the freedom to make adjustments. Jimmy Schmidt points out, "Sometimes people say, 'This is the way I always cook salmon—I don't know why it doesn't taste good now.' But it's impossible to have two pieces of salmon that are identical. Not every piece of fish will cook the same way—one piece will be lighter or heavier in texture, another piece will be cut thicker or thinner. The heat level in the pan will be different. The natural level of sodium within the fish will be different. You're dealing with an infinite number of variables. You must constantly think while you cook. It's like constantly running a computer program inside your head to account for all these different factors and how they'll affect your cooking."

One of the first aspects of seasoning a cook typically learns is how to salt food. If you can't season with salt, you can't move on to seasoning with saffron or any other herb or spice that's even more subtle or complex. Almost everyone has grown up eating salt, and it's a recognizable flavor. However, often the differences in taste among iodized, kosher, and sea salt need to be taught, and often chefs have their own preferences. "Even if someone's been cooking for five years, when you come to my kitchen you learn how to use salt the first day," says Gordon Hamersley. "When I went to work for Lydia [Shire], she taught me how to use salt the first day—and I was the sous chef! She taught me how to sprinkle it so that it evenly coats whatever you're salting."

There's even something to be learned about pepper. "As far as I'm concerned, you should only use pepper out of a peppermill," says Edward Brown. "Anything but freshly ground pepper tastes like dead, flat heat. What we want from pepper is not heat, it's flavor." Chefs also express different preferences for acidity, such as in their preferred ratio of oil to vinegar in a simple vinaigrette (perhaps ranging from 3:1 to 5:1) or in tasting a soup or a sauce and noting that "it needs a little lemon." At China Moon Cafe (San Francisco), the late Barbara Tropp emphasized, "What we do here is about big flavors—acids, heat—so it's quite dramatic. What you're talking about here is taking chile and sugar and working them together so that the heat becomes very full-flavored and very enlarged. Or you're working with citrus and salt so that the quality of the acid becomes vibrant rather than merely sharp." In pastry, there is also a range of preferences in the use of sweeteners, even in yeast. It is only by spending the time to taste critically that you will enhance your ability to discern increasingly subtle differences. In tasting you will also come to recognize textures: when or whether they're right, and how a particular effect was created.

At the highest levels, the tasting process involves tasting empathetically, and learning to ask yourself: Is this the taste the chef is going after? Is this the taste the customer will enjoy? As Jimmy Schmidt points out, "How a dish tastes to a cook is different from how it tastes to a customer. Cooks don't sit down and eat a whole dish of food—we just take one little taste. The sauce may seem great on your finger or on a spoon, but it may be very bland, for example, when paired with whatever it's saucing."

Learning taste distinctions through critical analysis and filing that knowledge away for future reference is one element of what is commonly referred to by leading chefs as "taste memory." Successful chefs have the ability to call up taste memories—to actually taste in their mind the exact flavor of something they tasted previously, even years ago—with the ease of punching buttons on a jukebox.

Creating a Dish

Tower describes the process of using inspiration in creating or re-creating a dish: "You must ask yourself, 'How can I do a modern version—without losing any of the things that made me love it in the first place, and without having ten slaves in the kitchen for four days?' Having tasted the best version, the real version, you work to be able to find your way back—through technique, through what's financially possible—to get the taste that you want to preserve."

Composing a dish is an advanced art. Jimmy Schmidt describes the ideal dish this way: "Being able to make a dish so that it changes and has a lot of components, so that as you're eating it you get different flavor combinations—[that] keeps a dish alive on the palate. For example, we do crispy seared

salmon triangles in a rimmed soufflé with roasted shallot and charred ravioli, tossed in burnt butter with a saffron- and ginger-infused vegetable broth splashed on it, topped with fried scallions and ginger. In each bite, it's impossible to get the same amount of ravioli, fish, scallion, ginger, and broth—so you get different flavors throughout."

Nancy Silverton uses remarkably similar terms to describe her ideal dessert. "It's one that keeps your interest from the first bite through the last. It can start with temperature: as a really hot dessert cools, its texture changes, causing contrasts in textures."

In combining flavors and textures into a finished dish, perhaps one of the most important things you learn as a cook is what to leave out. While leading chefs have the maturity to use multiple ingredients more successfully, inexperienced cooks often make a dish too complex, out of eagerness to display everything they know about color, texture, and presentation on a single plate. An experienced chef knows which items don't belong, and what will bring harmony to the plate. Susan Spicer notes, "Sometimes people don't have the experience, or the taste memory. They're inexperienced at putting things together and get carried away with ingredients for ingredients' sake." Norman Van Aken describes the process of maturation for a chef as "learning when not to hit certain notes. I listen to a guy like [guitarist Eric] Clapton play, and I remember him playing with Cream [his early band] all over the guitar, hitting every note known to man. That's an appropriate metaphor for what I felt that I was doing as a young cook. That restlessness, that curiosity, is a big part of being a young artist. Now, I'm choosing the notes a lot more, as opposed to just playing all of them."

The secret sometimes lies in simplicity. Jimmy Schmidt describes another equally impressive dish that relies on fewer ingredients and techniques: "We prepare some of the local fish very simply. Their flavors are so subtle that we try to accentuate them rather than add a lot of other ingredients that would tend to mask them. We use whole butter, which is very sweet, for sautéing. The flour is seasoned flour with a touch of paprika, which has a sweet pepper flavor to it. It's done at very high temperatures, which is crucial because the butter starts to develop a little bit of nuttiness, and you're able to seal the fish and capture as much of the moisture as possible. It also gives it a crisp outside while the flesh is very, very tender." And even Nancy Silverton admits, "I also like desserts that are studded with something in every bite, but still simple."

Even within dishes, the flavors of basic components can be altered through the application of various cooking techniques. Mark Militello says, "One of the things I worked very hard on was developing flavors. I learned things from all different cultures, and I learned some great things from Mark Miller and Rick Bayless, who related how they developed some of their flavors within their cuisine—whether through

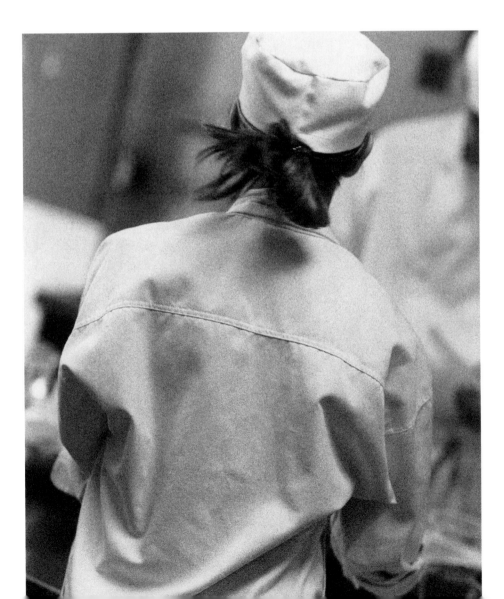

roasting or toasting or whatever. If you're working with an onion, why just work with a plain onion?—do a roast. Or if it's a tomato, taste the effect of blistering the skin. With spices, you can toast them to bring out the oils. We've learned to do some very different things that way."

Preferences about flavors within dishes vary. Using desserts as an example, Nancy Silverton explains, "There are certain basic flavors—chocolate, coffee, lemon—that people either love or hate. The secret is to make a dessert for people who love that flavor." Charles Palmer agrees. "I'm a big believer in concentration of flavors, so that if something's chocolate, it should be all chocolate," he says. "If it's a chocolate torte, it should have layers of chocolate genoise and chocolate mousse, maybe covered in chocolate ganache and wrapped with chocolate and served with chocolate sauces and maybe light and dark chocolate tuiles. Once you have the base, the rest of it is just fooling around."

Beyond "hitting the right notes" in the creation of individual dishes, there is also a certain rhythm to a harmonious menu. "The most beautiful dinner is not where you finish one course and then get hungry again, but one that flows from one course to another," says Dieter Schorner. Joyce Goldstein adds, "I know when I've eaten a good meal. I was at Frontera Grill the other night and I had a wonderful meal. Why? Because these people understand what they're doing with their flavors. We had a variety of different chiles, but not all of them were hot. The flavors were 'round.' There was a contrast in the menu that Rick [Bayless] had put together for us, and you went on a ride through this wonderful meal. Everything was in its own balance. He understood his vocabulary, and he knew when to put the right words in the right places. It read like a sentence or a paragraph or a poem."

In time, as part of a process spanning many years, cooks may develop these advanced abilities which allow them to, in the words of Jasper White, "not just move the pans around over heat, but to impose their will on the food"—that is, to orchestrate exactly how the food they are cooking will look and smell and taste.

> **While walking by his cooks who were making tiramisù, Jeremiah Tower stuck a finger in the bowl and tasted it. "Stop!" he yelled. Once stabilized with whipped cream, the creation became Stars' Fantasy Cream, one of the restaurant's specialty desserts.**

> **You could make a list of all the capital sins why cooks should be shot: too many ingredients, discordant flavors, things that sound okay but really are flat, trendiness for the sake of trendiness, not understanding the real essence of the ingredients but using them like a Band-Aid . . . JOYCE GOLDSTEIN**

Extra-Sensory Perception

An experienced chef's greatness is often evidenced by his or her development of a "sixth sense" when it comes to cooking, and many of the chefs we interviewed alluded to this ability in some regard. Over time, they have developed the ability to cook at a more intuitive level, for lack of a better description. Susan Spicer describes how, as a chef, she's developed acute powers of sensory perception: "I've really developed my eyes so that I can look at something three feet away and say 'that needs rinsing off,' or 'that doesn't look fresh to me.' I know when someone puts something in a sauté pan and it doesn't make a noise that the pan wasn't hot enough. I listen when someone is chopping an onion and it's going 'crunch,' and I know without looking that that person needs to sharpen their knife. I listen when I'm making a sauce in a blender, and I know if the sauce has broken by the sound. I smell everything out of habit, to make sure it's right. This is what you have to do."

Jeremiah Tower recalls a friend in the perfume business who claimed she could "smell" fragrances in her head. He believes the same is true for chefs and tasting. "When you write a recipe, you can taste it in your mind," he says. Daniel Boulud agrees: "Many recipes are written by chefs before the dishes are ever made, because they're created in your mind. Your senses give you the combinations."

Patrick O'Connell insists, "I don't actually have to eat food anymore. I do eat and I do taste, but I swear I can review the taste of it—without actually tasting it—by the visual. I can tell the age of the person who made a dish, the number of years of experience they have in the kitchen and their IQ, and I can write you a short biography of them. A dish represents a distillation of a cook's entire being."

Keeping It Fresh

For the kitchen's "chief," there are no longer the immediate pressures of a raised voice to respond to, and a chef's greatest challenge lies in creating and acting upon self-imposed pressure to keep innovating. Lydia Shire says, "I'll be placing the food order and I'll find myself not looking for something interesting to bring in for specials. And right away I get a guilty feeling inside and I think, 'How can I expect my cooks to come in and get all excited over a special with me when I haven't done my part in going out and looking for something interesting to bring in here?' Of course I like all of this, but every once in a while you just need to push yourself."

The inspiration to experiment can come from various sources. Norman Van Aken says, "I remember getting jicama in at Sinclair's [in the 1980s], and my dishwashers Carlos and Ray asked, 'What are you doing with that?' I asked them, 'What do you do with this thing?' Pretty soon they were peeling it and putting cayenne and lime juice on it, and eating it as happy as can be. So I tried it and said, 'Yeah, that's great!' Their attitude, unfortunately like that of a lot of people from other countries, was that their food was déclassé—and I had to tell them that it wasn't. I might want to take part of the idea and create a bridge to something more familiar [to customers]. The term 'fusion,' to me, reflected my desire to harness both the rustic power of regional cuisine and the intellectual power of classical cuisine, and to put them together."

Jean-Georges Vongerichten "forces" his staff to eat at Jojo once a month: "So many people don't eat their own food. I never put a dish on the menu unless I eat it first."

When experimenting, how can you tell when it's "right"? According to Joyce Goldstein, "When you think of really gifted cooks and how they play with ingredients, you know that at a certain point it was in balance for them. When you're tasting anything, it's like a seesaw—it's going up and down and up and down and finally you get in balance and, hopefully, you stop. That doesn't mean that all the tastes are even. Sometimes you want something to be lemony, maybe more lemony than lemons, because something is super rich and you want to cut it, or you want the lemon to be the star. But it's really in balance. Or sometimes you want sneaky heat—heat that people don't realize they've had until five minutes later. Not bludgeon-you-to-death heat, when all of a sudden you can't taste any other flavors because it's just hot. There's a balance to that as well."

Part of what keeps things fresh is a constant inquisitiveness. "Loving to learn has to be your lifelong passion as a chef," Rick Bayless insists. "The desire to understand flavor is a lifelong endeavor. I still learn new flavors every day. While some may be flavors I have had before, every day I am able to understand their nuances better."

The best chefs never remain static, but continue to evolve their styles and preferences. Often this involves a paring down of one's cuisine to its very essence. Jean-Louis Palladin used the analogy of an artist. "Like a painter, a chef's style changes over time," he observed. "The ingredients you use change. There's more simplicity, less sophistication. It's more pure, with no artifice." Norman Van Aken believes that "the death of any artist is to be afraid, to stop taking chances. [Bob] Dylan proved that. The really great ones continue to shatter the mold they make. Picasso was like that. I think that what will cause the good ones to go on will be the ability to continue to break their own molds, and to listen, to learn, and to move upon these influences in an interesting way."

Fresh Fruit Gyoza

LISSA DOUMANI, Terra, St. Helena, CA

"This recipe is special to me because the first job I took as a head pastry chef after leaving Spago was at 385 North and, as any chef will tell you, your first time out is really scary. Well, just about a month after I got there, 385 North hosted the second annual pastry competition in Los Angeles. The year before, Spago had won a couple of awards, so I was nervous, being the host restaurant and in a friendly competition with my friends at Spago, plus all the other top restaurants in Los Angeles. I made this dish to compete in the fruit dessert category and, luckily for my honor, I won! Thank goodness things went well, or I probably would have quit!"

2 medium prunes

1 cup Armagnac

2 Bosc pears

2 tablespoons unsalted butter, plus 1 stick for clarifying

1 cup sugar

1 tablespoon cornstarch

1 cup water

1 package gyoza skins

1¼ cups orange-cinnamon crème anglais sauce for serving

Place the prunes in a small saucepan with the Armagnac and let simmer until the prunes have plumped up and absorbed most of the Armagnac. Set them aside to cool.

Core and peel the pears and then slice them into pieces about 1/16 inch thick. In a medium-sized sauté pan, melt 2 tablespoons of the butter and then add the pears and the sugar. Keep an eye on the pears, stirring often until they are a deep caramel color. Remove to a plate and let cool.

To assemble the dish, chop the prunes into medium-small pieces—this is difficult, since the prunes are sticky, but just keep at it. Then also chop the pears up into about the same-size pieces and mix the two together.

Mix together the cornstarch and the water to make a paste. Separate the gyoza skins and lay them out on a clean surface. (The package has about 50 skins and you will only be using 20, so just wrap the rest and freeze for later.) Place a small teaspoon of the filling in the center of each skin. Pick up the skin in one hand and with the other hand dip a finger into the cornstarch and run it around half of the gyoza skin edge, then fold the skin over, making a half circle and pinch together. A tight seal is important so that the filling doesn't leak out. Repeat this process with the remaining gyoza skins. As you finish each one, lay it out next to the others; do not stack.

Make some clarified butter to sauté the gyozas in. This is really easy. Just take a stick of unsalted butter and melt it in a saucepan and then set aside for a few minutes. When all the impurities have floated up to the top, use a spoon to skim them off.

In a medium-sized sauté pan with a lid, put 4 tablespoons of the clarified butter and heat. Test the temperature with a corner of one of the gyoza; it should just bubble when it touches the oil. Slip 5 of the gyozas into the pan and sauté on a high flame until the bottoms are light brown; you will brown only one side of the gyoza.

Carefully add 2 tablespoons of water to the pan and cover immediately. (You have to be fast, since the pan will steam and spatter.) Let the gyozas steam for a couple of minutes and then lift the lid. If the tops of the gyozas are translucent, leave the lid on and sauté for just a minute more to crisp on the bottom. Remove from the pan and keep warm. Repeat with the remaining 15 gyozas. Pour ¼ cup orange-cinnamon crème anglais sauce on each of five plates and place 4 gyozas crisp side up on each plate.

Makes 5 servings of 4 gyozas each

Rhubarb Pie

MARY SUE MILLIKEN, Border Grill, Santa Monica, CA

"Rhubarb has always been a favorite of mine. One of my earliest memories is of my mother, harried as housewives often were, handing me a small plastic glass of sugar and sending me out to the garden to eat rhubarb. Raw rhubarb is an acquired taste, but I love the ultra-sour and slightly bitter taste. This is an old-fashioned country pie at its best."

  12 ounces pie dough
  3 pounds rhubarb
  1½–2 cups granulated sugar to taste
  3 tablespoons tapioca
  2 cups streusel

Lightly butter a 10-inch pie plate.

On a generously floured board, roll the dough to a ⅛-inch thickness and line the pie plate, leaving about a ¼-inch overhang.

Pinch up the excess dough to form an upright fluted edge. Chill for about an hour.

Preheat the oven to 350°F. To prebake, line the dough with a sheet of parchment paper or aluminum foil and fill with weights, beans, or rice. Bake for 25 minutes, remove the paper and weights, and set aside. Prepare the filling.

Clean the rhubarb and cut the across width in ½-inch slices. Combine with the sugar in a large bowl. Let sit at room temperature for 15 minutes. Sprinkle on the tapioca, toss well, and let sit for an additional 15 minutes.

Pour the filling into the warm, prebaked pie shell and sprinkle the streusel over the top. Bake until the juices bubble, about 1 hour and 15 minutes. Set aside to cool on a rack before serving.

Serves 8 to 10

Galette de Crabe Le Bec-Fin

GEORGES PERRIER, Le Bec-Fin,
Philadelphia, PA

"I wanted to create a dish with crab because on a trip to Maryland one year, I had a crabcake and found it heavy. When I came back to Philadelphia, using the technique of Jean Banchet's mousses (who I think is the king of mousses because of their lightness), I came up with a different texture and binding, which gave me a perfect galette de crabe. Now I can taste this beautiful Maryland crab. Bon appetit!"

> 1 bunch scallions
>
> 1 pound jumbo lump crabmeat, picked over
>
> 14 ounces peeled and deveined large shrimp
>
> 2 whole eggs
>
> 1 pint heavy cream
>
> Salt and pepper
>
> 2 tablespoons Dijon mustard
>
> 1 tablespoon Tabasco sauce
>
> 1 tablespoon Worcestershire sauce
>
> vegetable oil

Cross-cut the green part of the scallion ⅛-inch thick and sweat in 1 tablespoon butter. Mix together with the crabmeat. Set aside.

Put the shrimp in the very cold bowl of a food processor. Process on high speed for a minute. Scrape down the sides of the bowl. Add the eggs. Process on high speed until the mixture is smooth and shiny (about 2 minutes). Scrape the bowl again. Slowly add the heavy cream while the machine is running. Scrape the bowl. Process one more time to make sure the cream is incorporated. Season with salt and pepper. Add the mustard, Tabasco, and Worcestershire; fold into the crabmeat mixture.

Sauté ¼-cup portions of the crabmeat mixture in oil in a nonstick pan over medium-high heat for about 2 minutes on each side.

Makes 10 generous portions

Dry Poached Pear with Port and Cassis Ice Cream

JIMMY SCHMIDT, The Rattlesnake Club,
Detroit, MI

"Having grown up on a farm and with wonderful fresh fruit, especially pears, that matured to perfection after being picked from the tree, I tried to capture that perfect pear 'essence' in cooked form. Thus, the idea of poaching the pear in a dry medium that added no additional flavors, as well as allowed no flavors to escape, gave birth to this technique. When I enjoy this dish, it brings back memories of the fall harvest with wonderful aromas of Thanksgiving in the air."

½ bottle Beringer Cabernet
Sauvignon port

1 cup sugar

3 tablespoons balsamic vinegar

One 3-pound box kosher salt

4 large Comice pears

2 tablespoons unsalted butter

½ cup dark brown sugar

2 cups cassis ice cream

4 mint sprigs

In a medium-sized saucepan, combine the port and sugar. Bring to a simmer over medium heat and cook until the liquid is reduced to 1 cup, about 15 minutes. Remove from the heat and allow to cool to room temperature. Stir in the balsamic vinegar.

Preheat the oven to 425°F.

Select a medium-sized ovenproof pot large enough to later accommodate all four pears. Fill the pot with all of the salt and place in the oven for an hour to thoroughly heat. Remove the pot from the oven. Carefully remove two-thirds of the salt to another pan. (Reminder: the salt is 425°F!!) Position the pears on the remaining salt so that they do not touch each other. Completely bury the pears in the salt you took out. Return the pot to the oven and cook the pears are until tender, about 15 minutes. Remove from the oven, and carefully remove the salt from around one pear; test the tenderness by inserting a skewer, taking care not to puncture the skin. Remove the salt from around the remaining pears. Transfer to a plate. Carefully brush any remaining salt from the pears. Allow to cool.

To glaze the pears, rub the four dry-poached pears lightly with butter to coat the skins. Rub the skins with the brown sugar, allowing the sugar to stick to the butter. Using tongs, hold the pear over an open burner or under the broiler to heat the sugar and caramelize it onto the skin of the pear. Allow to cool.

Spoon the port sauce onto the serving plates. Position the pears in the centers. Scoop equal portions of the ice cream and position next to the pears. Garnish with mint and serve.

Cooked in this manner, the pear is seared by the salt, causing the juices to be trapped in the pear. The salt must be hot or the pear will be salty. For the same reason, do not allow the pear to cool in the salt. A properly cooked pear will have no taste of the salt.

Serves 4

7. The Business of Cooking
OPERATING AND RUNNING A RESTAURANT

Just do it. Do it your own way. Break all the rules. And look for a niche—they're still out there. The problem, it seems, is that everybody is scrambling for the same niche instead of being who they are. **PATRICK O'CONNELL**

A restaurant is a living work of art—one which reflects the chef-owner's philosophies about everything from food and wine to aesthetics and hospitality. When a chef becomes a chef-restaurateur, his or her reputation rests not only on what is served on the plate, but on the very plate itself—not to mention the glasses, the flowers, the wait staff, the host, and every minute detail the customer, who is a guest of the restaurant for a few hours, might notice and discuss the next day with friends and co-workers.

Every word of criticism is taken personally because, at its best, one's restaurant is one's home. Nancy Silverton paraphrases London chef Marco Pierre White's sentiment as expressed in his cookbook *White Heat* on chefs' sensitivity to criticism: "If I came to your house for dinner late, criticized your furniture and your wife, and said your opinions were stupid, how would *you* feel?"

Sometimes the "restaurant as home" analogy is even literally true: Silverton and husband Mark Peel have lived with their children above their restaurant Campanile in Los Angeles, and Emeril Lagasse and his family used to live above Emeril's in New Orleans. Daniel Boulud lives with his family in a condominium just stories above Restaurant Daniel in New York City.

The primary difference lies in the bottom line, which is that running a restaurant is a business. "In addition to knowing how to cook, chefs today need financial and managerial skills in order to run a kitchen," says Mark Peel. "They need to know everything from what their food and labor costs are to how to take inventory. This isn't just a craft; it's a business."

Leading chefs manage to stay gracious with their customers while tending to food costs, restaurant critics, and other mostly behind-the-scenes concerns in order to keep their restaurants successful. The business and management practices of leading chefs are like special effects in movies—they make the impossible seem effortless.

Opening Lutèce: A Historical Perspective

André Soltner moved to New York City in 1961 to open Lutèce. "It was very, very difficult, for many reasons. Today, restaurants open and everybody goes to look because the media right away talks about it, so everybody goes to see. Then, it wasn't so. It was pretty quiet. Word got around by word of mouth, so there was no explosion. Today, we are looked at as a classic restaurant. But then, we were looked at as very avante-garde. We opened with high prices. We didn't believe in anything frozen, anything canned, which was not so thirty-four years ago. Because of that, we had much higher prices than our competition. When we opened, our prix fixe lunch was $8.50, and it was so much of a scandal in New York that we went down to $6.50. It was the talk of the city that there is a crazy guy who opens at $8.50." [In 1995, Lutèce's prix fixe lunch was $38.]

"We flew in fresh Dover sole. Nobody flew in fresh Dover sole, but every restaurant had Dover sole on the menu—it wasn't marked fresh or frozen. So we sold our sole for maybe $8, and some of our competition sold it for $4. We made less money than they did. Today, you try to sell frozen sole when everybody's educated enough to know the difference, and you go out of business. It was not easy. But we held on, and little by little, we had more business. The first two years, we were closer to bankruptcy than to success. But we held on, and it worked."

What's It Like?

Depending on who you ask, running a restaurant can be made to sound easy, requiring only good common sense.

"Opening a restaurant is like throwing a dinner party," says Jeremiah Tower. "We all do dinner parties. You start at the front door, where guests come in. Is the light on? Is the carpet dirty? You go into the bathroom: Is there toilet paper? Is there soap? Is the soap dish clean? In the dining room, are there flowers? Are the glasses polished? Before you even get to the food or the wine, you take care of those things."

Patrick O'Connell finds Tower's analogy apt. "I think the feeling that I like best is a sense of walking into somebody's private space, or their home. I find that very touching. The more a restaurant can evoke that, the more trust I have in it and the more forgiving I am."

Tower admits that in order to be successful as a chef-restaurateur, "it has to be central to your life—you must be attuned to it all the time. I'm always on duty. I can walk into a restaurant and immediately tell which lightbulbs are out." And O'Connell acknowledges, "It's hard. It's a balancing act to deal with banks, finances, payrolls, lawsuits, and still try to open your home every night and care about people. But it can be done."

How? "I think of every detail as being equally important," says O'Connell. "How are you going to enjoy the food if the lighting is off or the server is dumb or the flowers are dead? The whole experience has to be conscious, so the chef needs to emerge as the controlling influence from the kitchen and produce the entire production, keeping it all at the same level."

Managing so many intricate details requires that a chef-restaurateur juggle many different roles and responsibilities. Joyce Goldstein says, "You need people skills, management skills, and artistic skills. I wear seventeen different hats." After working sixteen hours a day doing everything from transcribing recipes to running staff meetings, "I might not have touched a mushroom," Goldstein admits. "I feel guilty all the time, but I'm too valuable to peel onions."

Anne Rosenzweig concurs. "While many aspire to owning a restaurant, most don't have any business experience or any idea of how hard it really is," she says. "You become a businessperson first, dealing with bankers, accountants, bookkeepers, lawyers. You're also responsible for the front of the restaurant—training, dressing, feeding the wait staff. You have to develop your wine list, and be

> **If I overhear a chef say, "It is hard to find good people" or "If I want something done right, I have to do it myself," that person is usually the source of all their problems. That chef is not entrepreneurial.**
>
> CRAIG SHELTON

A Day in the Life of a Chef-Owner: Mario Batali

6:30 A.M. I get up to fix our two boys breakfast. In the beginning, my boys would say "I don't want this or that," so I came up with a menu and said "Here are the choices." We call it "The Batali Boys' Breakfast Book," and we made it together from a piece of construction paper. Each beverage on the menu is served with a complimentary vitamin.

Today, Benno ordered poached egg with "dunkers," which is a three-minute egg that you cut the top off of, served with toast cut into sticks which you can then dip into the egg. This morning he requested the egg sunny side up instead of poached, so I had to remind him that there were no substitutions on the menu. But then I relented. My other son, Leo, wanted a side of bacon, a side of ham, and yogurt. He got around the requirement that you have to order an entree, but since he was having different types of protein I let him do it.

Tomorrow is my wife's birthday, so we'll have the traditional "Cowboy breakfast," where the boys put on their chaps, vests, and hats to make pancakes!

8:00 A.M. I take one of the boys to school and my wife takes the other. Then I come home to deal with ongoing construction work, despite our renovation being "done."

10:00 A.M. I go to the gym, where I work with a trainer and box three times a week.

11:30 A.M. I catch up with my wife at home.

11:45 A.M. I get to Babbo and meet with my assistant, where I find out everything I promised to do, then I curse myself. Then it is into the kitchen to check on orders and see how the morning people are doing.

I double-check the printing of the menu, which we print by 1 P.M. so that when the kitchen crew comes in around 2 P.M., they know what is happening. Then it is on to more meetings, calls, and tasks. Today I saw my agent for a moment. Then I wrote two blurbs for other people's books and did an interview [with us!].

3:00 P.M. I usually go into the kitchen, but today I am interviewing applicants to be my new assistant. They have to be capable of writing recipes and managing the thousand things I don't have time to watch over, as well as making a two-year commitment. In the first interview I'm very nice, but in the second I paint them a picture of the worst-case scenario, so that when a hard day hits, they can't say I didn't warn them.

3:30 P.M. I glance over the "V.C." list, which is our Valued Client list [of who is dining at the restaurant that evening]. We will figure out what table to seat them at and what special things we might do for them, like send a dessert or appetizer. That is all done before service. Tonight, my family is coming in and friends from my days at the Four Seasons.

4:30 P.M. I'll have a pre-service meeting with the whole staff, where we'll go over the menu and what is happening at the restaurant.

5:00 P.M. The doors open at Babbo.

5:30 P.M. My main job in the kitchen is to be "The Hammer of Consistency, Light, and Truth." I watch and work with the cooks throughout the day and night.

10:30 P.M. I will either go out for a bite or go home.

responsible for tasting and buying wines. You have to take care of everything. Young chefs don't have a clue—they don't understand that the focus is taken away from the kitchen."

Despite the challenges, chefs find many rewards in having a place of their own, from having an opportunity to take advantage of multiple talents to being their own boss and having relatively more control over their schedules. "Opening your own place is the best route to success," says Elizabeth Terry. "I've always wanted to succeed and to please, and I've never been good at taking orders."

Knowing When It's Time

Deciding when it's time to open a restaurant is sometimes a matter of personal comfort. For some chefs, having one's own restaurant by a certain age is a long-term goal. Gaining experience, a reputation, and perhaps even potential investors gives them the means to begin to realize this goal. Daniel Boulud recalls, "My goal was to have my own business by the time I reached forty. I didn't have the money myself to open my own restaurant, so I definitely had to rely on hard work in order to become attractive for someone to invest in."

For other chefs, deciding to open a place of their own is practically a forgone conclusion. Chris Schlesinger had worked in various kitchens before becoming sous chef at Boston's Park Plaza Hotel, where he was relieved to be fired after six months. Schlesinger knew he couldn't keep working places where he didn't care about the food. "It wasn't so much 'Gee, I can't wait till I have my own restaurant so I can do my own thing.' I just knew I wasn't going to tolerate working for other people—that was the main thing," he says. "I didn't have a choice."

For the most publicly successful chefs, who have garnered rave reviews for their employers, the decision is sometimes rooted in wanting to profit directly from the reputations they developed through their talent and hard work. Before he opened his first restaurant, Jean-Georges Vongerichten, who had earned the hotel restaurant Lafayette (NYC) four stars, says he twice offered the Lafayette to "do like Le Cirque and separate the restaurant from the hotel" by giving the hotel 10 percent of the restaurant's gross for rent. The hotel demurred, and Vongerichten left to launch his bistro Jo Jo.

Charlie Trotter personifies the fact that there's no single answer that's right for everyone. Before opening his own restaurant, Trotter had only three years of cooking experience, in more than forty different restaurants, and had never been a chef or even a sous chef. "I'd never held any position higher than a

line cook," Trotter admits. "On the one hand I thought, 'Should I spend another year cooking? Should I go to New York and cook?' You always can say, 'I need more knowledge. Do I know enough about pastry? Do I know enough about butchering? Do I know enough about this or that?' And the answer is always 'No, no, no.' But, on the other hand, do I know enough to make it go? And based on some of the [notable] restaurants that I was spending two days or two weeks in, saying, 'This is a monstrosity. I know I can do better than this,' I decided maybe I should go for it."

Getting Ready

You begin to prepare for the experience of opening your own restaurant the first day you step into a kitchen. An entire cooking career, whether three years or thirteen or even thirty, spent carefully observing and learning everything your employers have to teach is the best preparation for setting off on your own.

You might actively seek additional exposure to other aspects of the restaurant business, namely, in the front of the house. Jasper White, after having been sous chef at the restaurant at the Copley Plaza Hotel in Boston, spent a year running the Harvard Bookstore Cafe on Newbury Street—as its general manager, not its chef. "I didn't like it, but learned as much as I could. I kind of taught myself and really paid attention to the table service, running the business, processing credit cards. Because at this point I had a goal, which was to have my own restaurant. I knew at some point to grab that year, and that's where I grabbed it."

To expand his knowledge, Chris Schlesinger formed a restaurant study group with others, including his eventual partner Cary Wheaton, to figure out what would be involved in opening a restaurant. When the group actually found a space available in Cambridge's Inman Square and it was time to take the next step, Schlesinger says, "Everybody dropped out but Cary and me. Cary and I had no intention of really doing it—none at all. But we did it." The space eventually became the site of the East Coast Grill.

Despite the traditional notion that in real estate the most important factors are "location, location, location," Charlie Trotter set about looking for an out-of-the-mainstream site, inspired by New York City brownstone restaurants like Lutèce and La Tulipe. He recalls, "I liked the fact that they were very discreet and had no signage, in a neighborhood with dwellings on either side. I found [the site of Charlie Trotter's] after looking at about forty sites, from liquor storefronts to office building spaces. We have a residence on either side of us." Similarly, when Todd English was looking to open Olives, he says he knew Charlestown (just outside Boston) was a risk, but that he wanted to be in a neighborhood. "I remembered all the Ma-and-Pa joints off the beaten path from my travels in Italy," he says. Olives also became a destination restaurant.

Zarela Martinez looked at 150 restaurant sites in Manhattan before selecting the current site of Zarela, which she said cost her an estimated $200,000, including legal fees. She signed the deal in four days and opened the restaurant with less than $20,000 in working capital within ten days. "The restaurant was there, and I just put up ribbons and brought in arts and crafts from home to decorate," giving the restaurant its notably festive ambiance.

Restaurant design can make a great difference. "Wolfgang [Puck] wouldn't be Wolfgang without Barbara [Lazaroff]," says Nancy Silverton of Puck's interior designer wife. Silverton and husband, Mark Peel, were the first pastry chef and chef, respectively, of the original Spago in Los Angeles. "The initial plans were for a pizza place with sawdust on the floor and red checkered tablecloths. Barbara added the design element, and made it about more than just food," Silverton says.

Lydia Shire's aesthetic tastes were reflected in more than just the food at Biba (Boston): "I interviewed six architects, and when I decided on [noted New York restaurant designer] Adam Tihany, I told him the things that were important to me, and he just went from there. I knew I didn't want any black in this restaurant, and that I wanted lots of curves. I knew I wanted Kilim rugs. I took him to my house and I showed him the Kilim rugs that I have at home that I love. In the end, he let me pick out certain fabrics, and I picked out the tiles on the walls. I actually designed the whole wood-burning oven area—I drew it on paper and I knew that I wanted it round. It was a good match. I don't take any credit for the design here; I only take credit for giving Adam the direction he needed."

Not everyone is in a position to hire an architect or designer. The East Coast Grill "was just what we wanted to do. It was driven by how much money we had," says Chris Schlesinger. In his case, this proved to be fortuitous. "We were fortunate because what we wanted to do jibed with where the market was headed. We opened a couple of years before the grill trend really exploded, before the casualization [of restaurant decor and prices], before the health concerns. We were there and established when they all hit. We were in the right place at the right time."

Choosing a Partner Wisely

Mario Batali swears that the most important advice he can give someone opening a restaurant is to choose one's partner(s) very carefully. "Choose them like you are going to be married to them, because you are," he says. "Lay down your expectations as best you can: what you want and expect to do, and what you want and expect your partner to do.

"The eventual demise of my partnership at Po was that at a certain point the restaurant was running fine—and that was enough for my partner. However, my expectations included the constant evolution of not only the kitchen, but also of the front of the house: the beverage program, the meet-and-greet, the hospitality, and the follow-up. All this can become very mundane on a daily basis if you feel you are already very good at it. But if your own quenchless thirst for constant reevaluation is not going to be matched by somebody, it will eventually lead to a parting of the ways—which is exactly what happened," Batali explains.

In the three years after being hired as chef by Drew Nieporent (with whom she'd previously worked as sous chef at Montrachet in New York City), Traci Des Jardins said she never discussed a partnership stake in Rubicon. "It's hard for a restaurateur to divest enough of a percentage to a working chef to make it worthwhile. Once the structure is in place, no one wants to give up much equity," she explains.

"I was not looking to leave Rubicon. I had established a reputation and wanted to open my own place, but I didn't want to go out hat-in-hand looking for money," she says. "However, I got a call from a real estate agent wanting to know if I was interested in a particular space, which happened to be one I

drove by every day that I knew and loved. The real estate agent then got [San Francisco restaurateur] Pat Kuleto and me together. I knew Pat and his reputation and after we started talking, he offered me an equity position that I could not refuse.

"Pat's restaurants are all chef-driven, and each is a separate corporation. What we all have is one common partner: Pat," says Des Jardins. "It made a big difference to go into business with someone who had a track record and knew the business side of the restaurant business. He had credit and purveyors, and that made a huge difference in being established right out of the gate."

Preparing the Menu

While Charlie Trotter was having preparatory work by architects and designers done on his restaurant in Chicago, he began to cater dinner parties in people's homes, once or twice a week for eight months, where he tested the recipes he was developing for Charlie Trotter's menu. "One dinner led to another. There would always be a couple at the party who'd say, 'Oh, we owe people a dinner, this is perfect, would you come in two weeks and do a dinner?' I charged money, but just enough to cover the costs, and maybe a little more. I stayed very active doing that, and I was able to actually fine-tune many of the dishes that made it to the opening menus."

Trotter's catering business had additional benefits. He adds, "What I didn't know at the time was that the parties were also serving the purpose of forming a small groundswell of intimates. So when I finally opened, there were some four hundred people who had experienced my food, and were privy to this restaurant. A lot of clients had been willing to let me step up before the meal and say, 'I'm going to open this restaurant on the North Side, and have a location, and I haven't picked out the name yet, but I have several ideas—what do you think?' They felt like they were part of it. I didn't understand the importance of that then."

The hardest part of developing their opening menu for Terra, according to Lissa Doumani and Hiroyoshi Sone, was figuring out what constituted their cuisine. "It's very hard when you've been at a restaurant that's as well known as Spago—you assume that what you've been doing is Spago cuisine. You forget that it's yours, because you made it up, and it happened that you did it at Spago. If you do it outside of Spago and continue to do something in the same light, it's still your food. If you try to drop all of your

past to find out who you are, you're going to be put away or become
psychotic from it. Still, it took a while to get to that comfortable place
where we weren't worried about 'whose' food we were doing."

Many chefs have developed specialties on their menus
which have particular strategic advantages, such as memorability.
Frequently, the first things customers are served when they sit down in
a dining room are water—and a basket of bread. "No one in the city was
baking their own bread when Emeril's opened," says Emeril Lagasse,
which allowed him to develop this specialty. Lydia Shire featured naan
bread baked to order in Biba's tandoori oven, as well as a couple of
other types of freshly baked breads. She explains, "I've always loved Indian food, especially in London—I
love their breads. One thing I wanted was a great bread basket. I always thought that some of the bread
you get in restaurants is so matter-of-fact. I really wanted to have the best bread basket in Boston."

Despite growing concerns about cholesterol, Jean Joho features two cheese carts at Everest
(Chicago) and finds that 80 percent of his customers order cheese after their meal. "I've always loved
cheese," says Joho, who has become known for spotlighting American cheeses. Georges Perrier adds, "I
think the first course that you serve, the appetizer, is also very important, because I think it is what the customer is going to remember. And because it comes last, people tend to remember desserts. I have worked
very hard on that, and I have four full-time cooks in pastry, and four apprentices, sometimes. I'm not
ashamed to say that I think we have the best dessert cart in the country, and maybe in the world."

Friendly advice on preparing your menu can come from the least likely of sources. Sandy
D'Amato recalls that critic John Mariani first opened his eyes to the media disadvantages of having a menu
that changed daily. "He advised me to change only part of the menu, because diners liked having something they could count on when they come back. 'Plus,' he told me, 'I want to be able to write about your
pear and Rocquefort tart and for people to be able to come in and try it,'" D'Amato recalls. "Jacques Pépin
also gave me the same advice, advising me to have some things the restaurant could become famous for.
He also underscored the importance of having people talking about dishes that others must try.

"When I was changing the menu daily, I was often shooting from the hip, so the dishes were
always very good, but none were great. After these discussions, I modified the menu so that only half would
change." D'Amato reports proudly, "We now have three signature dishes: the pear and Rocquefort tart, our
Provençal fish soup, and tuna tartar with cumin wafers."

A Recipe for Success

A chef-restaurateur learns quickly that the success of a restaurant lies in much more than its food. Charlie Trotter says the most important lesson he learned from the time he spent in Europe was "that it's not just food. Food is an equal part of a little formula that encompasses ambiance, service, and a wine program. Food is only one of the four parts, and no one of those parts is greater than the other parts. In Europe, I saw the attention paid to all these little things and I realized there was so much more."

According to Emeril Lagasse, "When the customer calls to make a reservation, or pulls up to the valet—that's when the whole process starts. We work at that, we talk about that, we study that, and we have training sessions about that. We try to know just about every customer when they walk through the door. I have 'commandments' that must be followed in order to work in the front of the house here, including 'name recognition,' where an effort is made to greet customers by name; 'gang service,' where all entrees are served at the same time, like a ballet; and 'in-house marketing,' where we try to get personal—but not too personal—with our customers. Even waiters will drop customers notes. We even have an in-house computer system that allows us, when Mr. Kohlmeyer comes in to have his Beefeater martini, to have it there waiting for him before he even sits down.

"If it's raining outside, the valet knows instantly that the umbrella box and three 'Emeril's' umbrellas have to be out for use in escorting customers to and from their cars. We also have a special mat for the front door so that clients can wipe their shoes clean. They're greeted by name. They're escorted to their table. Somebody has to be at their table within thirty seconds of their being seated. We even have service signals on the table so that others know whether their cocktail order has been taken. It's a very, very detailed process from the moment the guest pulls up to the valet to the time the guest leaves and the valet or the front door says goodnight—hopefully by name."

The ambiance of a restaurant, from its design to the background music played, sets the stage, and is a critical part of a restaurant. Jean Joho believes that while food is certainly important, "the reason people go to a restaurant is to enjoy themselves. It's not a church. You must make people feel welcome, relax, and enjoy the experience. Your goal is to get the customer to come back."

> **If people don't walk out of the dining room saying, "This is the best meal I've ever had," then you've sort of failed your mission. We're a special occasion restaurant, so it's very important to accomplish that.**
> GARY DANKO

Is the Customer Always Right?

Does making customers feel welcome always involve giving them exactly what they want? The issue of how far a chef-restaurateur will go to please a customer is an intensely personal one.

"My whole life—well, the last forty-five years of it—I gave my blood for the customers," says André Soltner. It goes without saying that some chef-restaurateurs believe strongly that satisfying customers is what being in this business is all about. "[César] Ritz said eighty years ago, 'The customer is king,'" says Soltner. "And that still has to apply to our work, if you're in the restaurant business."

Michel Richard agrees. "You must learn to please customers. You have to love them, you have to respect them," he says. "I have more respect for customers than they have for themselves. I don't try to impress them. I want them to enjoy, to discover new things. They have no idea how much we try to extend our hearts, how much we try to give to them."

Hiroyoshi Sone and Lissa Doumani credit their experience at Spago as chef and pastry chef, respectively, with teaching them the importance of always pleasing the customer. "Wolfgang [Puck] will do anything for a customer," says Sone. Doumani adds, "There's a customer at Spago who always wanted Beef Wellington, and he did that for him. There was another customer who had to have Häagen-Dazs ice cream, coconut haystack cookies, and Tab. At Terra, you can have anything you want, as long as we have the ingredients. Certainly the most important thing for the this day and age is giving customers what they want."

Emeril Lagasse believes it is critical for chef-restaurateurs to really pay attention to customer needs. "We constantly have our ear to the ground for what the customer wants, and what the customer's expectations are," he says. "That's most of the problem with other restaurants—they don't do that." Because it provides insights into what his customers are thinking, Janos Wilder believes that a negative letter from a customer is actually a favor. "I'll pull their orders from that night, I'll speak with the waiter and the cook," says Wilder. "Then I'll call a staff meeting and make sure everyone is giving a sincere effort."

Many chefs count on customer requests as a way of making sure they keep innovating. Jasper White says, "I listen to what people want, and I believe in making people happy. At Jasper's, I had many requests for vegetable plates, so I eventually put one on the menu, just so people didn't have to feel awkward if that's what they wanted." White also made an effort to balance heavier dishes with lighter ones, after hearing concerns from his customers. "Still, as a special occasion restaurant, I didn't feel a need to address everyday needs," says White. "I still used ingredients like veal stock, butter, and foie gras."

If a customer at Stars asked for anything, staff members were not allowed to say no. Jeremiah Tower kept a log book at Stars (San Francisco) with information on the specific preferences of his regular customers: "Every time two particular customers came in, waiting at their table were open packs of Pall Mall and Lucky Strike cigarettes, with an open matchbook." Tower speaks with admiration of the level of service of some of the great hotels of Europe. "At the Hassler in Rome, I could have called up the concierge at midnight and said 'I need a pair of rabbits,' and he would have said, 'Yes, of course, sir.' Not 'It'll take twenty-four hours' or 'Oh, my God, call back in the morning!' He would have just said, yes," enthuses Tower. "Just say yes. Then figure it out. Don't tell the customer your problems; they're simply not interested."

Does this mean Tower thinks the customer is always right? Not at all. "The customer is usually hardly ever right," he says. "I hate them for not trusting the restau-

rant. They should know why they're there." However, Tower has found his customers to be much more trusting over time. "At Chez Panisse, there was no choice on the menu. I was always going out to the dining room, and if I knew customers very well, I'd say, 'Isn't it about time you trusted me a little bit?' Sometimes I'd just go out and [making the motion of spearing food with a fork and moving it toward someone's mouth] say, 'Try it. Just try it. If you don't like it, I'll buy you dinner.' And they would try the veal kidneys. They'd never had wonderful veal kidneys before. And then they'd try the duck confit, the goat cheese, the mascarpone, the buffalo mozzarella, the walnut oil. In 1973 or 1974, no one had ever seen these ingredients before, and they didn't want to eat them. Americans are very, very conservative about food. But now, they're coming to trust a well-known restaurant or chef more, and they'll try it."

Alice Waters agrees. "I would like to persuade them to try things they might not eat otherwise, and I feel like I'm pretty persuasive. I like to think that we're helping them to moderate what they're eating, and showing them that you don't have to eat a twelve-ounce T-bone steak—you can enjoy just a couple of ounces of meat cooked quickly on the grill," she says. "But in case I'm not persuasive, I try to accommodate them. If I have the time, I'll really go to an extreme."

Patrick O'Connell on Customer Service

We have a mood indicator at the Inn at Little Washington: Every customer is given a mood rating when they walk in the door, from one to ten. The waiter needs to assess the mood of the party. This forces him not to treat them as a deuce [table of two] or a four-top [table of four], but to see them as human beings whose moods (whether they have anything to do with what we're doing or not) will ultimately affect the enjoyment of the experience. So it's the waiter's business whether they had a flat tire on the way or a marital dispute or anything. It also empowers him to change it, and that's the game.

So if the mood rating is below seven, it must be brought up to a nine by the dessert dupe [the kitchen's copy of the order]. Then if it's below six, it's put up on the blackboard by the kitchen: "Table 22, 5." And everybody who walks by that table lavishes warm vibrations, energy, and smiles, and makes every effort to turn it around. And it happens every single night. The first thing that everyone is instructed to do in our place is that whenever there is a problem or a complaint, smile. Give the person the complete reassurance that you've handled a thousand things a thousand times worse, and this is a piece of cake and no problem at all.

Because this mood indicator comes into the kitchen, the whole kitchen staff is alerted, and it's a real team effort on their part to bring somebody up or to change the experience. If need be, everything would be rushed to the critical or problem table, or some little extra thing would be sent. We use the phrase "pushing them over the edge," doing that extra thing, which is actually so easy, and it's so effortless—really, it's just caring. Usually I find that as soon as the cranky guest realizes that it actually matters to the staff whether or not they have a good time, it's crucial that they do. The customer turns around. Right away, it's a new experience for them that somebody cares.

Elisabeth Kübler-Ross—a fascinating woman—wrote a book called *On Death and Dying*. She realized that it is an experience which has identifiable, universal phases to it that everyone goes through, and that knowing them and chronicling them is helpful to people because it gives them a handle on the whole thing. So, I did it with "the five stages of dining," breaking the experience down into five distinct phases.

"The Five Stages of Dining"

1. **Anticipation:** For a great restaurant, this can begin two years or longer in advance, and people have little, yellow, faded clippings in their purse that they've carried around. They've always wanted to come. If nothing else, it starts in the car on the way there. They begin to think about what they might eat.

2. **Trepidation:** Then they hit the door. They open the door; the anticipation collides with what I call trepidation: kind of a primitive terror that the experience won't live up to their expectations or that reality

has intervened with the fantasy. Or that they should have worn the black dress instead of the red one. Or that the maître d' would be rude. It will evoke what I call "restaurant bruises" from the 90 million horrendous, awful experiences that they've had in other restaurants. And this is a very delicate kind of phase. At each phase, the waiter has a counter phase that he flips into to deal with this, so that we're in control.

3. **Inspection:** This is on the part of the diner. This happens after the second sip of the cocktail. They're in their seat and they still haven't looked around and eyed the room because they are too intimidated or too uptight. Only when they are given a drink are they really there. It's like an Irish wake, where the body of the person is brought out to prove that the person is dead. People aren't really where they are until they really experience it. So they are not conscious of being there, and they don't allow themselves to experience anything until maybe the second sip of the drink. Then you see them checking out the room. At the same time, if they see a flaw—a chipped glass, a dead flower—then they take a little nosedive down.

4. **Fulfillment or Ecstasy or Animal Satisfaction:** This doesn't take place until three-fourths of the way through the main course. They won't allow themselves to consider the experience a success until they have gotten to that place in the main course. Prior to that you'll hear them say, "Everything's been great—so far. Delicious—so far. But you haven't delivered yet, Sucker." They must be observed as experiencing a complete state of ecstasy at that point. At our establishment, they must use a superlative such as "fantastic," "wonderful," "incredible," or "amazing." I train the staff that "fine" means "awful." Do you think that somebody's going to pay $125 for a meal that's "okay," "very good," or "fine"? Absolutely not. This is supposed to be a superlative experience. If they don't use a superlative, then something's wrong. So get them something else. Do something. Move in. Don't accept "very good."

5. **Evaluation:** This begins when the check is picked up, the bottom line is examined, and the wife usually whispers, "How much was it?" and the husband says, "$236" and they smile. It was either worth it, or it wasn't worth it. And that evaluation continues for days later at the office when people say, "How was it? How much did it cost?"

As soon as you have one person on staff who is not plugged in, it doesn't work. You have to create a kind of energy field. I think that they expect people in the country [The Inn at Little Washington is an hour and a half from D.C., with no signs] to be sweet and innocent and kind and helpful and all of that. But I think it would be even more dramatic in a city, like New York, to have all warm, wonderful people who are genuine in providing such service.

Dieter Schorner remembers the time at La Côte Basque when Salvador Dali came in for dinner five nights in a single week. "He would order a whole plate of fried parsley for his entree. Yes, it tastes fantastic—but five days in a row for dinner? And he ordered the same thing for dessert every night: broiled grapefruit with honey." By comparison, Aristotle Onassis's tastes seem less exotic: "For lunch, he would always request minestrone soup and steak tartar, with vanilla ice cream and concentrated apricot puree for dessert."

Several chef-restaurateurs have made efforts, sometimes out of frustration, to educate their customers. When Raji Jallepalli first opened her restaurant, she recalled, "I used to have an impossible time getting people to eat medium-rare pork—they would send it back. I used to educate the waiters to tell them that 'the chef feels that the flavor is at a maximum the way it is. I want you to try it, and if you don't like it, we'll give you whatever you want.' Little by little, I changed their minds about these things."

Every chef must set his or her own limits in terms of striking a balance between the dual, and sometimes conflicting, roles of restaurateur and chef. While the restaurateur thinks that pleasing customers goes hand-in-hand with running a successful business and making money, the chef who feels a need to make a statement through the food that is served also feels the need to draw the line somewhere.

"I don't believe the customer is always right," says Johanne Killeen. "We try to make as many accommodations as possible. If we can make concessions and still make something really good, then we do it. But if somebody wants to eliminate ingredients from our dishes to the point that we think, 'This is not our cooking, this is not going to be good,' we just don't do it." Do customers ever leave? "Occasionally. As gently as we try to present this, some customers feel that it's not the way it should be, but it's a rare, rare thing." George Germon is even more emphatic. "People who go out should be going to experience what this particular restaurant does, and not alter it," he says. "If a person has dietary restrictions and other considerations, and wants to get out of the house, he should eat at home and go to the movies."

The one area chef-restaurateurs are in agreement that the customer is always wrong is customers' too-frequent practice of failing to cancel—or, worse yet, failing to show up for—their scheduled, and even confirmed, reservations. Nancy Silverton says, "We don't try to overbook the restaurant, but last Saturday we had eighty no-shows—and those were for reservations that had been confirmed by phone that day! So we do have to take this into account." Lydia Shire fumes, "We had forty no-shows tonight. That's so rude! I'm sure those people, if it were done to them in their businesses, would be furious."

The Power of the Press

If chefs have pet topics, this is definitely one of them. They can go on and on about restaurant critics, probably for as long as critics can go on and on about restaurants.

Admittedly, sometimes their comments have to do with their awe at their benefiting from the power of the press. Patrick O'Connell recalls, "Within weeks after we opened the restaurant, a gentleman diner asked to see me and introduced himself as a critic from the second biggest newspaper in Washington, which was then the *Evening-Star*. It was the neck-and-neck rival of the *Washington Post*. He said, 'I never do this, but I would like to introduce myself. I need to ask you if you really want me to write a review of your place.' I said, 'You know, it's taken us many years to get the door open, and we'd be quite delighted if you would like to say something about our existence.' He said, 'No, I have to ask this because what I'm going to say is going to change your life. You may have to hire someone just to answer the telephone after they read what I'm going to say, because I'm going to tell the truth: This is absolutely fantastic!' The idea of hiring somebody to answer the telephone was humorous because during the day, I answered at the stove on a long cord and took reservations, and at night Reinhardt [Lynch, O'Connell's partner] answered it from the front desk as he seated people." The adoring review—and dozens that followed—put The Inn at Little Washington on the map.

The majority of chef-restaurateurs' concerns, however, have to do with the flip side—the potentially destructive power of a single reviewer's negative, or even lukewarm, opinion of their restaurant. "Nobody has 'made it' in this business," observed the late Raji Jallepalli. " All restaurateurs subject themselves daily to critique from both consumers and the media."

Daniel Boulud articulates what he believes makes the difference between good and bad critics: "I think once you know the chef—what the chef's spirit is, what makes him happy and what business he's trying to attract—it's a good critique. But when you just have a checklist . . ."

It's precisely this attitude that bothers Mark Miller. "Food critics are worried about the same old check-off list: 'The lobster wasn't overcooked, and the plate was nice, and we got seated on time, and they had a good wine list. Oh, I think I'll give it three stars.'

Anne Rosenzweig recalls that Arcadia (NYC) was reviewed after being open only six weeks. "It was a two-star review that read like a three-star review." All plans of having Arcadia remain a "nice, neighborhood restaurant" were dashed: "It was two years before things slowed down at all."

It's like, how pretty can the toilet paper get?" says Miller. "Food critics are quantitative—what it costs, what it looks like. Real criticism is an ability to perceive more acutely a particular phenomenon by having knowledge beyond the ordinary. The critics don't respect us and are not creating respect for us as professionals. We really don't have anyone who writes about food the way that people write about drama or opera or dance. It's not taken seriously."

As a point of example, he says, "When reviewing modern dance performances, good dance critics don't write about the way people were dressed or what they paid for their ticket or how long the performance took. They write about the ability of the choreography to be in relation, or in counterpoint, to the music, how well the dancers performed, and the important significance of this dance in the history of dance. They try to educate the public about a particular form. They don't say that this was worth going to or how much it was worth. They educate you that if you should go to this dance, these are some of the things that should help you to understand what you are seeing.

"Similarly, great food has to be understood not by what it looks like initially, not by what it tastes like, not by what you paid for it. You have to understand it in terms of the human experience of food. Most critics don't understand the history of a particular chef—what he's done, where he's gone, what he's trying to do with his food. You never hear about this in food criticism," Miller says. "I think that if critics are going to write about restaurants, they should write about the totality of the restaurant experience. This includes how long the restaurant has been in operation. Is it fair to review a restaurant in the first month, just because your newspaper wants to get it out first? Well, is it fair to go down to an artist's studio and start reviewing the paintings he had before the show? Do you go to the theater previews and then start writing a review? This is what the food critics are doing, basically. But chefs and restaurateurs are afraid of the press. They don't want to say anything that's going to challenge anybody."

Odessa Piper has observed that a restaurant is only as good as "the eyes, heart, and intelligence of the person who is writing about you." She recalls, "In the 1980s, I was using the term 'sustainable' and a food writer from a large Midwestern newspaper asked if I could use a different word, stating that her readers wouldn't know what 'sustainable' meant. I immediately offered an easy def-

> The press intensifies what people expect of the food. Poor Alice Waters—she's had so much hype on her food that when some people make the pilgrimage to California to eat there, they're disappointed in the meal. Because it's so simple, they say, "It's no big deal." And I can understand what they're saying. I was blown away the other Saturday night at Chez Panisse, but I think I go in there with a higher level of education.
>
> GARY DANKO

Ushering in the New Age of the Kitchen: Patrick O'Connell

I use a lot of film analogies in our kitchen. I walk around with my hands in the shape of a box [which he illustrates with thumbs and forefingers touching] like the director or cameraman looks through and ask, "How would this look on the cover of *Food Arts*?"

We have a special table in the kitchen where guests may dine. Before the guests enter the kitchen, we have a formal lineup of the cooks. When the double doors to the kitchen open for the party, they are met by the cooks all in line and an altar boy in full regalia including the red cassock with an incense burner to lead them past the cooks to their table. It is amazing the impact that this has on the guest; they never forget that everyone in the kitchen was involved in their meal.

The kitchen and crew have to look sharp. We are always having people come through, whether guests or the press, and someone will inevitably pull out a camera or camcorder, so the camera analogy is good training for them. The cooks understand that the behind-the-scenes hard work contributes to the guests' enjoyment, and I take pride in instilling that understanding in the kids who come through here.

It is good for the industry to work to upgrade wherever we can. The behind-the-scenes experience is still too often ignored. When we built our new kitchen, people thought we were utterly crazy for creating something so overboard in ambiance that it was more beautiful than most restaurant dining rooms. What good would that do, they asked? Yet this kitchen reinforces the singularity of our guests' experience here every night; it makes them feel wonderful and reassured that nothing is off limits or hidden that they would not want to see.

The California wineries inspired me somewhat. You walk through them and see these gigantic spotless stainless steel vats, with floors that are absolutely immaculate. That is tremendously reassuring with regard to the product they are producing—you feel their pride, which in turn enhances your own experience.

In the restaurant business, we had a departure for a while glorifying the image of the chef as rock star. You saw the hair falling down the front of the face, cigarette dangling out of the mouth, filthy towel tucked into a bloody apron. There was an image that cooking is blood and guts, which was in reaction to the starched toque era of chefs. Now, hopefully, we are in a time were we can concoct a more reasonable image for diners and for our profession.

inition so that we could use the word. She stopped me, explaining she didn't have the room in the piece. That is the nightmare scenario, where someone has you in a niche and only wants to cut-and-paste you into that space.

"On the other hand, occasionally you'll find someone like Jonathan Gold of *Gourmet,* who is a very confident and competent writer who really does his research. He came from New York to L'Etoile [in Madison, Wisconsin] in the middle of winter, multiple times—spending time in the restaurant, visiting local farms, and even going out with my staff for drinks! My husband felt like it was the first piece that had actually 'seen' me. The ultimate compliment was the article's quote that 'Odessa Piper is Alice Waters' 'Alice Waters,'" Piper recalls.

When Piper won the James Beard Award as Best Chef: Midwest the same year that Gold's article in *Gourmet* hit, it made for her busiest year ever. "After more than twenty years of obscurity, it was overwhelming! I got all this very high-caliber attention and everyone began to call, asking me to do lectures, presentations, classes, and interviews.

"We get a lot of press and it *all* matters," she confirms. "We have been around so long that when the local papers review us, it doesn't have the same impact anymore. After all these years, people know us; we aren't 'new' news. However, we don't take for granted that these local papers still come to visit and still write positive things about us. It *always* matters."

Understanding the power of the press has led leading chef-restaurateurs to develop ways of trying to manage it. Patrick O'Connell says, "We do an exercise with our wait staff. They have to each take a well-known critic—from *The Washington Post, The New York Times, New York,* or elsewhere—and they have to write two reviews in the style of that critic: one on our restaurant, and one on another restaurant. It has to mimic that style, and in doing that, they get into the head of the reviewer. It's terribly instructive. They get into the vocabulary. They also see what a difficult job it is, encapsulating that experience so concisely.

"All the critics have different prejudices, from one extreme to another. So-and-so hates this, so-and-so loves this, whatever. Just be attuned to it, be alert to it. And as somebody said, 'They have a lot to do with our success. It's their job to remain anonymous, and it's our job to know who the hell they are.' And there's nothing wrong with that. That's an intelligent sort of business, to be able to sniff a critic. So I have all my staff trained to the extent that if they sniff a critic, they let me know right away. They write a 'C' on the check, and that means it's a critical table. So I call my staff over and check it out."

Throughout more than thirty years in the restaurant business, André Soltner seems to have developed a healthy philosophy concerning the press. "I never wanted to be number one, because there really is no number one," he says. "We were in the Zagat guide for five or six years as number one. Three years ago, we were number three. We're number six today. The press called me and said, 'How do you feel?' I said, 'I feel great! Look, thirty years ago, I was number one. Ten years ago, I was number one. Eight years ago, I was number one. Thirty years, and I'm number three! You don't think that's good?' The dream of most is to be in the top ten—and I'm number six after thirty years! I can cope with that. I can take it because I never thought I was number one."

Promotion

When business declined one winter for the first time ever, Rick Bayless responded by creating a newsletter to send out to a mailing list of his restaurants' customers. "It allows us to talk directly to our customers, and to let them know what we're all about," he says.

Janos Wilder sent announcements of the opening of Janos in Tucson to rented mailing lists of doctors and lawyers as well as members of local country clubs and museum societies. He also publishes a newsletter two or three times a year with information on the restaurant and special events. In addition, he has a response card on each guest check so that customers can indicate particular areas of interest, such as catering services or wine-maker dinners. Customized information on the topic indicated is mailed to the customer within twenty-four hours. In addition, a computerized database is maintained with this information so that Wilder can keep costs low by sending specialized mailings only to customers who have previously indicated an interest in the topic.

Raji Jallepalli had a list of customers to whom she faxed the menus for the special dinners she prepared on Sundays. "I also brought fifteen people at a time into the kitchen for cooking workshops like Toasting and Tempering of Spices; Creamless Sauces; Versatile Uses of Lentils; Fusion Beurre Blanc; Emulsions, Extractions, and Extensions; and Coulis Techniques, and everyone was served a three-course meal after the workshops." Jallepalli also organized special dinners to introduce new items to the menu at her restaurant, and held bimonthly wine tastings.

In this era, virtually every chef-restaurateur we spoke with sees it as crucial to have a presence on the Web. "You need it to be competitive, because it provides a place for people to find information about you and your locations quickly," explains Amy Scherber. "People are so visual and at their computers they are frustrated if they don't have access to you. You can offer your menu, the look of your store, a recipe, and a summary of your press mentions."

"Our Web site, though imperfect, is important," agrees Odessa Piper. "We put our wine list and cooking school information as well as menus."

It behooves chef-restaurateurs to wear the hat of marketer to keep their restaurants in the public eye, and to keep themselves and their clientele excited. Charlie Trotter sent letters to his best customers about his trip with Emeril Lagasse and their wives to France to visit leading restaurants and vineyards. In the mailing, he promised an extraordinary dinner two days after their return, incorporating dishes and wines inspired by their travels. (They faxed recipes and instructions to the Chicago staff on a daily basis during the trip.) "It's also a fun way for us to go and see these things, and do a dinner when we get back," Trotter says.

Leading chefs find themselves inundated with requests to participate in special events benefiting both good causes and, ostensibly, their own visibility through the resulting publicity. "A big part of being a chef is doing benefits—for cancer societies, cystic fibrosis, Meals on Wheels, S.O.S.," says Gary Danko. "It's a very interesting culture we live in now because this whole cooking thing has just sort of catapulted into these huge events for food and wine, and socializing is a big part of it."

Such out-of-restaurant demands can have chefs spending much of their time away from their restaurants promoting them, at benefits and other publicity events and meetings. While based in Los Angeles, Michel Richard described one week in his life as: "Monday in Vancouver, Wednesday and Thursday in New York City, Saturday in Santa Fe, Sunday morning in New York, and Sunday evening in Washington, D.C."

Participation can be not only time-consuming, but expensive, with some chefs estimating their out-of-pocket expenses in the thousands or tens of thousands of dollars—or more—a year. One chef who doesn't plan to participate, however, is Patrick O'Connell, for reasons other than the time and other expense involved. "I, for one, will never do those collective dinners for two hundred and fifty people, where you go into a strange kitchen and you make one of seven or eight or nine dishes, and you have no control whatsoever, and it goes out and you have no concept of how it's being presented," he says. "It's not what I do."

Still, many leading chefs appreciate the opportunity to get together with their peers—to compare notes on business, and to share ideas on food. "I enjoy the camaraderie, and learning what's happening outside my own kitchen," says Susan Spicer.

"It is critical to do events," says Amy Scherber. "If you are part of a community, it's your job to go out there and raise money for charity. You need to show that you care about more than just making money and being a businessperson. It also a way for the public to get to know you as a person and to be connected and involved with you. I want to be accessible but it is hard because we get asked for something every day. We get requests for food donations from schools, churches, and community and arts organizations. We had to set a budget for our annual participation, because it is so tough to say no."

Daniel Boulud concurs. "Charity is very important to us and we do a lot of it. It is the nature of a chef to be generous!" he explains. "Since we get approached a great deal, we are selective with what we choose, and then get really get behind those events.

"The difficult side of a charity event is that when they are requesting five hundred dollars or more a plate from the donor-guest, a chef feels that what they make had better be special! So it is very costly for the chef, very time-consuming and very disruptive for the restaurant. Some charities will offer to reimburse the chef and then 'forget,' so for a small restaurant, charity can be especially hard.

Mario Batali on Opening His First Restaurant for Less Than $50,000

We opened Po in New York City's Greenwich Village on May 27, 1993, for $41,000. The trick to opening a restaurant on that little money is finding a reasonable location—that is, a storefront with a stove and a hood—with no key money [a fee to the landlord].

The Location

Our location turned out to be brilliant luck: It was the only place I looked at. Rob Kaufelt of Murray's Cheese called and let my wife know about the spot because he knew she was looking to open a martini bar.

If you like the location and the people around the location, it gives you a much better chance to be good. I love Greenwich Village and wouldn't recommend that anyone open a place anywhere else! There is a freedom and tone of tacit rebellion, the area is arty, there are no tall buildings, and it is a city within a city.

The trade-off was that we didn't have a crushing business from Wall Street, so it took me two and half years to build a lunch business.

After Po, other restaurants popped up around it—which leads me to another tip: If you want to have a successful restaurant, build it next to one that is already doing well. If they are smart, they will know they can enjoy the scraps of your press, too. When the press wrote about Pearl Oyster Bar up the street, we always got mentioned. We weren't worried about competition because we were radically different restaurants.

The Equipment

In *The New York Times* every Sunday, they have a list of the unfortunate victims of bad restaurant management: the auctions of restaurants that have gone bankrupt. Although the auctions are well attended by guys from the Bowery [an area of New York where restaurant supply stores predominate], which is divided block-by-block by the chair guys, the table guys, etc., if you happen to be at the right place when the plate guy is not there, you can get a deal on plates! We didn't get a deal on everything but we did on most things. We bought our banquette at Po for twenty-five dollars. There was no one to bid against it, so when the auctioneer yelled, "Who will give me anything?" we yelled, "Twenty-five bucks." It ended up fitting to a T, which was pure luck. That kind of shopping radically lowered the cost of opening the restaurant.

You don't need the best slicer to open with; you need "a" slicer. We started with used refrigeration and that is always the first to go. Your refrigeration will break, so if you buy old stuff, you replace the compressors or hit them with some freon. You start with sub-par stuff, but then always have a list of things you would improve if you had an extra thirty thousand dollars. Then stick to that list as seamlessly as possible, to make sure that your restaurant's food, service, and quality aren't compromised.

There is never a day you would choose to pay two dollars if you didn't have to. Your budget will tell you what you can have. You have X for silverware and Y for plates, and nicer silver or plates doesn't necessarily mean your restaurant will be more successful at the beginning.

In light of the fact that all you want to do is get open, there is nothing that needs to be brand-new when opening your restaurant. Nothing.

The Crew

When we opened there was just me and the dishwasher who scooped gelato for desserts. After we got reviewed, I added a salad guy. We were a three-man crew for a year, six days a week. I would come in at 9 A.M. and leave at 2 A.M. My personal record was 159 covers, that was jamming at five-thirty and jamming at eleven! I am still one of the world's fastest line cooks!

I was smart in that I did tasting menus which work well for one cook, because you can serve a whole table using only one pan, versus seven pans. I also moved a tasting menu very fast. You could not have any choice and you had to have what I served. I would not do anything for customers! I wouldn't even do sauce on the side.

Eventually I added a lunch sous chef who would start things rolling, but I still worked the same hours, just not so hard at lunch.

The Food

The food is where you spend your cash. If you are doing Italian food, you assemble the very best ingredients you can—the best olive oil, sea salt, balsamic vinegar, and Parmesan cheese. You don't buy Canadian prosciutto; you buy prosciutto De Parma. Those ingredients alone will give you a restaurant that people will come back to.

Then it comes down to you. The inclination of the young cook is to put too much crap and ego on the plate, but if you make it simple and good, people will come in. Your individualism can be expressed in several things. You don't want to do the same stuff as everyone else, like penne with tomato sauce, linguine with clams, and grilled chicken with balsamic vinegar, though all those things can be done exquisitely. What will distinguish them is the way you treat them, price them, and market them. You need to understand that it does not necessarily have be the five-dollar Empire kosher chicken, it could be just a Perdue chicken if you understand your own alchemy.

My own alchemy? What I like about food is a certain caramelization of flavors with a pretty high level of acidity. There is a brightness to my food that is different than other cooks', and which I find refreshing.

That is something you learn as you go. I would say that my ideas about food have not changed in ten years. I think my food is a lot better now, although I was proud of Po in its day. Po was a sophomore effort and I would say that I'm now a junior.

"We are very fortunate that we have three restaurants, so I can afford it. Our budget for charity is $400,000 a year. We also have to be sensitive to how many times we can ask a customer to support our charities. However, as chefs we know that food is a big magnet for raising money and in the end there will always be charities and we will always be there helping."

Chefs as Cookbook Authors

The huge growth in the number of cookbooks published by chefs points to their increasing importance as marketing and communications tools.

"My first book came out when I was still at Po in 1997," recalls Mario Batali. "I don't have a strategy for how many books I want to do and when, because that would take the fun out of it. I actually like to work on my books on vacation, because it gives me something focused to do in the morning and I enjoy the process of writing.

"The beauty of the *Babbo Cookbook* was that we wrote down all of our recipes from day one, so it was just a matter of adding text. I would recommend to all cooks to document your recipes. Put them on a disk and let your family and friends around the country test them for you. By the time you get three years into your restaurant, you'll have a book."

Emily Luchetti recalls that when she first started writing cookbooks, it was for a new challenge. "Every cook you work with takes your recipes anyway, so I wanted to write my book before someone else did!" she only half-jokes. "Books are great for marketing, but there are so many out there at this point that, let's face it, no one needs another one. But to me books are like T-shirts: While people may not need another one, if it has a nice picture on it and fits well, people will buy it. Of course people buy books for the recipes, but you do need a great package.

"What makes books good for marketing is the way the media works: They are always looking for what's new. In recent articles on San Francisco in *Gourmet* and *The New York Times,* they didn't mention any restaurant that had been around more than two years. *Gourmet* did not mention Boulevard, Farallon, or Jardinière! While you wouldn't necessarily expect them to mention all three, certainly you'd expect mention of at least one of the top restaurants in San Francisco!

"The media, and audiences, want to know what is new, and books give the media something to write about that keeps your name out there. You ultimately have to fill seats in your restaurant and there are

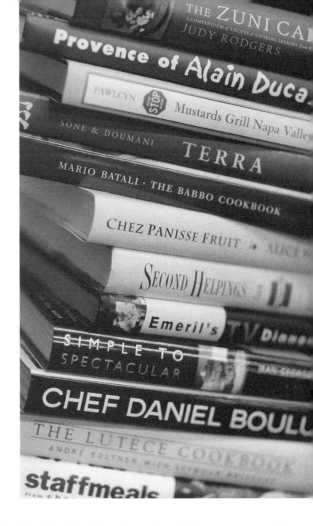

so many chefs and restaurants competing for that limited air time. You have to be out there and have a reason for it. We sell a lot of copies [of the *Farallon Cookbook*] at the restaurant. It is also great as a teaching tool; when we teach cooking classes we do recipes out of the book. We did a class in New York and a woman who was taking our class there made back-to-back reservations at our restaurant here. A book serves as documentation of what you are doing at your restaurant; it gets people excited for their next visit."

Marcel Desaulniers considers himself "lucky" that his book *Death by Chocolate* has been so successful that all his restaurant's press includes the line 'by the author of *Death by Chocolate*.' But behind his "luck" was the strength of his market research—not to mention his convictions. "After my first book, *The Trellis Cookbook*, my agent asked me what was next, and I told him *Death by Chocolate*. He and the publisher weren't crazy about the title. However, I stood by my guns and said that without this title, there is no book.

"The publisher wanted to call it *The Trellis Chocolate Cookbook* and fought me the whole way during the writing. The reason I was so confident was that I had been serving the Death by Chocolate dessert in my restaurant for almost ten years and I knew the selling power it had.

"Our waiters would tell every diner that tonight we had a dessert called Death by Chocolate and people would start getting excited from the time they sat down. The dessert itself is pretty formidable—it weighs in at a pound!—so when you see this seven-layer dessert going through the dining room, it gets attention. What makes the dessert work is that it defies the eye because it is so light, and though it has a fair amount of sugar it doesn't eat like a sweet confection.

"When we originally opened I wanted to put an emphasis on chocolate desserts, and it has almost become the 'tail that wags the dog' at the restaurant. We have people come here just for dessert. It is quite startling: We have had people come in with a party of six on a Saturday night and not want dinner, only dessert!"

Evolution of a Restaurant

A restaurant should never be static and unchanging; rather, it is a dynamic entity that continues to change and evolve over time. "We've all seen a lot of 'hot' restaurants that eventually fall into mediocrity," says Jimmy Schmidt. "They may not be doing anything differently than they did at their beginning, but they haven't evolved. If you and your staff aren't evolving, then your restaurant isn't evolving."

Nancy Silverton has observed that at Campanile "rather than make things easier as we go on, what we have done is take more things on." Whereas Mark Peel used to work the grill six nights a week, "Now I write all the special menus that are served in addition to our regular à la carte lunch and dinner menus," he reports. "For example, on Monday nights we create a menu that is served family style. On Wednesdays, the day of the Santa Monica farmers' market, we will shop for what is best, then create a very high-end special tasting menu based on the market. Because the menu is finished around 3 P.M., it is a high-wire act to pull it off! On Thursdays, we offer a special sandwich menu [featuring sandwiches since chronicled in *Nancy Silverton's Sandwich Book*]. These special menus are a challenge, but they help us develop because occasionally a dish from one of them will end up on our regular menu," Peel acknowledges.

Lissa Doumani likens owning a restaurant to being a parent. "In many ways, that's what it feels like to us. When we come back from being out of town, we drive by the restaurant to make sure that all the lights are off and it didn't burn down. You worry about it. You watch it grow. You look for your customers to say that it's better than it was the last time, because you want to know that you're growing."

In Doumani's terminology, Rick Bayless may be one of the most active "parents" out there: Not only have his restaurants evolved, but so have his cooks and community as a result of his "parenting." "Things really need to take on a life of their own, and we saw this with both our restaurants," says Bayless. "You can infuse them with all this life and energy but after a year they develop their own character. So you'd better think a great deal about how you get something started because it will refine its characteristics by itself.

"We are fifteen years old and the restaurants have taken on such a life of their own that *Chile Pepper* magazine calls us a 'Chicago-style of Mexican food.' I am thrilled because it affects everything down to mom-and-pop Mexican places here to do more traditional dishes.

"I've always told people that I won't say that we have truly become successful until we have staff go off and open their own

Your life and your career are two different things, but real success—not necessarily happiness—comes from fusing the two.

JEREMIAH TOWER

restaurants that are similar to ours but take it to another level. Then I'll know I have done a good job.

"One of our former sous chefs has two restaurants. He didn't know anything about cooking but learned his lessons well here. My former assistant Priscila Satkoff has Salpicon restaurant. Another restaurant has pointed out that the chef trained with Gino [Bayless's former sous chef], so that is yet another generation influenced by us. The other interesting thing we've seen is that some of our dishes are going out into the public domain and people are feeling comfortable enough to add their own spin to them."

Chefs need a vision to get their restaurants off the ground and to guide their necessary evolution. Their evolving vision is what keeps them fresh, educates their staff, and inspires their customers to keep coming back. Beyond that, Patrick O'Connell says, "I think it's important for the chef to make a connection with the guest in one form or another, not necessarily working the tables for compliments, but perhaps by putting a line on the menu expressing what they hope to do with the food, or what their inspiration is and where they're coming from. Or a thought for the day on a menu that changes frequently. Humor, I think, is a missing ingredient. I think there needs to be more fun and more humor—not forced, but natural humor—in terms of the dining room experience."

O'Connell believes we've yet to see the ultimate potential of the restaurant business actualize. "This business affords the opportunity to draw on every single talent that you have, but it's not viewed that way yet. It's viewed as more of a technical expertise or a trade, instead of the art form that it is," says O'Connell. "Nobody's pushing the outer limits, in terms of what it's really all about."

Many chefs and restaurateurs have gotten into making their own bread, which has made things harder because people who were my customers have become my competitors. However, they have already started to find it much harder and more costly than they ever imagined. AMY SCHERBER

Pasta from Hell

CHRIS SCHLESINGER, East Coast Grill, Cambridge, MA, and Back Eddy, Westport, MA

"Constantly challenged by my fire-eating customers to create hotter and hotter food, I decided to put a stop to it once and for all by developing a dish that would satisfy their desires and quiet their demands. A dish so hot that there was none hotter; so hot that never again would I have to take a ribbing from the heat freaks. This is it. Your heat source here is the Scotch Bonnet chile pepper, widely accepted as the hottest commercially cultivated chile pepper in the world. Many of my customers think this dish is just a bit too much, Kitchen Out of Control. But a handful of others, with sweat coming off the tops of their heads, eyes as big as saucers, bathed in satanic ecstasy, tell me that it's the best thing I've ever created. The truth lies somewhere in the middle, and in fact the heat of this dish can be controlled by using far fewer peppers without impairing the flavor of the dish. But . . . every once in a while, when the really hard case sits down and insists on something that has a 'real kick' to it, whip the full-bore Pasta from Hell on him. We're talking culinary respect here."

2 tablespoons olive oil

1 yellow onion, diced small

1 red bell pepper, diced small

2 bananas, sliced

¼ cup pineapple juice

Juice of 3 oranges

4 tablespoons lime juice (about 2 limes)

¼ cup chopped cilantro

3 to 4 tablespoons finely chopped fresh red or green hot chile peppers (Scotch Bonnet or Habanero are best) or 4 to 6 ounces Inner Beauty Hot Sauce

About 3 tablespoons grated Parmesan cheese

2 teaspoons unsalted butter

1 pound fettuccine

Salt and freshly cracked black pepper to taste

In a large saucepan, heat the oil and sauté the onion and red pepper in it, over medium heat, for about 4 minutes.

Add the bananas and pineapple and orange juice. Simmer over medium heat for 5 minutes, until the bananas are soft.

Remove from the heat, add the lime juice, cilantro, chile peppers or Inner Beauty sauce, and Parmesan cheese, and mix well.

Serves 4 as an appetizer

Whole Roast Artichoke with Aïoli

LYDIA SHIRE, Locke-Ober and Excelsior, Boston, MA

"These artichokes are the best! We have used them at Biba whole or in part—maybe cut a different way, but cooked with the same ingredients. My greatest 'food friend' from Rhode Island, Bob Fortunati, taught me how to cook this dish—it was his mother's recipe. I've sat with Bob for hours as he told me about how his family cured their own hams and olives, and made their own vinegars, and so on. Thank you, Bob!"

> 1½ cups capers
> 1½ cups parsley
> 1½ cups garlic
> 1½ cups anchovies
> Salt and pepper
> 3 cups olive oil
> 1 cup water
> 12 artichokes
> Basic garlic aïoli (such as Jeremiah Tower's recipe on page 119)

Preheat the oven to 375°F.

Blend the capers, parsley, garlic, anchovies, and salt and pepper to taste in a food processor. (Do not overprocess.) Bring the olive oil to a boil and add the caper mixture. Bring the water to a boil, and add the caper/olive oil mixture. Place the artichokes in a baking pan just big enough to hold them. Pour the mixture over the artichokes.

Cover with foil. Place in the oven and baste every 15 minutes so the caper/olive oil mixture goes down into the opening leaves. Bake for an hour until tender.

Serve with a little of the basting liquid and a spoonful of basic garlic aïoli.

Makes 12 artichokes

Pasta-in-the-Pink with Red Pepper Puree

GEORGE GERMON and JOHANNE KILLEEN, Al Forno, Providence, RI

"Shortly before we opened Al Forno in January 1980, we were hesitant and anxious. In an attempt to avoid facing the inevitable opening, the new responsibilities, and our mounting anxieties, we started thumbing through old issues of *Gourmet* magazine. In an article about Italy, we found a photograph that changed the course of our lives. We saw chiaroscuro, a casserole of what looked like baked pasta. The lighting was dim, the background smoky and mysterious. The only clear color in the photo was a flash of red that was probably tomato. The top of the casserole looked crusty and charred as if licked by the flames of a wood-fired oven. Our imaginations raced as we started conjuring up what the pasta tasted like. The image was so enticing that we could almost smell the aroma from the steam curling above it.

"We decided on the spot to change the format of our menu. That pasta was the kind of food we wanted to serve in our restaurant. That photograph evoked for us the new restaurant's possibilities. We began experimenting with baked pastas and adapted the flavors and textures that were familiar to us from our travels in Italy."

> 4 red bell peppers, charred and peeled
>
> ½ cup chopped canned tomatoes in heavy puree
>
> 2 cups heavy cream
>
> ½ cup freshly grated Pecorino Romano (1½ ounces)
>
> ½ cup coarsely shredded fontina (1½ ounces)
>
> 2 tablespoons ricotta
>
> 1½ teaspoons kosher salt
>
> 1 pound imported conchiglie rigate (pasta shells)
>
> 4 tablespoons (½ stick) unsalted butter

Preheat the oven to 500°F.

Bring 5 quarts of salted water to a boil in a stockpot.

Halve the peppers, remove the seeds, and puree them in a blender. You should have about 1 cup of puree.

In a large bowl, combine all the ingredients except the pasta shells and butter.

Parboil the pasta for 4 minutes. Drain and add to the ingredients in the bowl, tossing to combine.

Divide the pasta mixture among 6 to 8 individual, shallow, ceramic gratin dishes (1½- to 2-cup capacity). Dot with the butter and bake until bubbly and brown on top, 7 to 10 minutes.

Serves 6 to 8 as an appetizer

Variation: For a nice variation, add 2 Italian hot or sweet sausages that have been parboiled for 8 minutes, their skins removed, and coarsely chopped.

El Presidio Pan-Fried Chicken

JANOS WILDER, Janos and J-Bar, Tucson, AZ

"We were sitting around the picnic table one spring Sunday afternoon quite a few years ago, wondering what to cook for dinner. We really wanted hamburgers, but they were too high in cholesterol, particularly when made plump and juicy the way we like them. My wife, Rebecca, suggested making patties from chicken and seasoning them with chile and lime. We did, and they were great. Some years later, when a cook was stumped for a lunch special, I remembered our home barbecue, tweaked the recipe a bit with tomato, cilantro, and cheddar, breaded the patties and pan-fried them (no low-cholesterol treat, these morsels) and served them with calabacitas con queso, black beans, salsa fresca, and tomato beurre blanc sauce. They were an instant hit. Several years after that I was to appear on *Live with Regis and Kathie Lee*. At the last minute they selected El Presidio Pan-Fried Chicken for me to make with Regis. He ended up making quite a mess of himself in the process, and we had a terrific time on the show. The dish has now become a staple whenever we serve lunch."

"This dish is very much a blending of French techniques and Southwestern ingredients. Essentially a French mousse, but with chiles, cilantro, and cheddar providing the flavors of Tucson. I like to serve it with salsa fresca and black beans."

8 boneless, skinless chicken breasts

3 egg whites

2 Anaheim chiles, roasted, peeled, seeded, and finely diced

1½ cups grated cheddar cheese

3 tomatoes peeled, seeded, and diced small

6 scallions, finely diced

1½ tablespoons finely chopped fresh garlic

3 tablespoons roughly chopped fresh cilantro

¾ cup heavy cream

Salt and pepper

Breading

3 cups flour

1½ cups milk

3 eggs, beaten

4 cups coarse dry bread crumbs

Cut the breasts into chunks and quickly process in a food processor along with the egg whites. Do not puree; the chicken should be fairly coarse.

Fold in the chiles, cheese, tomato, scallions, garlic, cilantro, and cream. Season with salt and pepper to taste.

Shape the mixture into round patties about ½ inch thick.

Beat together the milk and eggs. Set out flour, milk and egg mixture, and bread crumbs in separate containers. Dust the patties with flour, then dip in the milk and egg mixture, then coat with bread crumbs, handling carefully so that the patties maintain their shape.

Preheat the oven to 350°F.

Heat ½ inch oil or shortening in a sauté pan. Add the patties and fry until golden brown, turning once. Finish in the oven for 7 minutes.

Serves 8

Frontera Grill's Chocolate Pecan Pie

RICK BAYLESS, Frontera Grill, Chicago, IL

"I am wild about pies and created this pie for Frontera Grill when we opened. It has never left the menu in over sixteen years!"

Crust

1½ cups (6¾ ounces) all-purpose flour (measured by scooping and leveling)

6 tablespoons (3 ounces) chilled unsalted butter, cut into ½-inch bits

3 tablespoons vegetable shortening or rich-tasting lard, chilled and cut into ½-inch bits

¾ teaspoon sugar

¼ teaspoon salt

1 egg yolk, beaten slightly

Filling

2 cups (about 6 ounces) pecan halves (make sure they're fresh and richly flavorful)

6 ounces semisweet or bittersweet chocolate

3 tablespoons all-purpose flour

¾ cup (6 ounces) unsalted butter, at room temperature

1 cup firmly packed dark brown sugar

5 large eggs, room temperature

¾ cup light brown corn syrup

¼ cup molasses

1½ tablespoons Kahlúa or brandy

2½ teaspoons pure vanilla extract

½ teaspoon salt

2 cups sweetened whipped cream flavored with Kahlúa for serving (recipe follows)

To make the dough, measure the flour, butter, and shortening or lard into a bowl or a food processor fitted with a metal blade. Quickly work the fats into the flour with a pastry blender or pulse the food processor until the flour looks a little damp (not powdery) but tiny bits of fat are still visible. If using the food processor, transfer the mixture to a bowl.

Mix together the sugar, salt, and 3 tablespoons ice water. Using a fork, little by little work the ice water mixture into the flour mixture. The dough will be in rough, rather stiff clumps; if there is unincorporated flour in the bottom of the bowl, sprinkle in a little more ice water and use the fork to work it together. Press the dough together into a flat disk, wrap in plastic, and refrigerate for at least an hour.

To prebake the crust, preheat the oven to 400°F. Lightly oil a 15-inch piece of foil and lay it oiled side down, into the crust (heavy-duty foil is too stiff to work here); press down to line the crust snugly. Fill with beans or pie weights and bake for about 15 minutes, until beginning to brown around the edges. Reduce the oven temperature to 350°F. Carefully remove the beans or weights and foil, return the crust to the oven and bake for 8 to 10 minutes more, until it is no longer moist. (If it bubbles at this point, gently press it down with the back of a spoon.) Brush the beaten egg yolk over the crust, then let it cool.

While the crust is cooling, spread the pecans on a baking sheet and toast at 350°F until fragrant, about 10 minutes. Cool, then break into small pieces and transfer to a large bowl. Chop the chocolate into rough, ½-inch pieces and add to the bowl, along with the flour. Stir until everything is well coated.

To make the filling, in a food processor or large bowl of an electric mixer, cream the butter and brown sugar until light and fluffy, about 3 minutes in the food processor and 5 in the mixer. With the machine still running, add the eggs one at a time, incorporating each completely before adding the next. Beat in the corn syrup, molasses, Kahlúa or brandy, vanilla, and salt.

Pour the filling over the chocolate and pecans and stir well to combine. Pour the mixture into the prebaked pie shell, set on the lower rack of the oven, and bake until a knife inserted into the center is withdrawn clean, about an hour. Cool completely on a wire rack.

Make the sweetened whipped cream.

Serve the pie at room temperature or slightly warm, topped with a dollop of Kahlúa-spiked, sweetened whipped cream.

Note: The pie can be made several days ahead, wrapped in plastic, and refrigerated. The pie also freezes well. Because the pie cuts easier when cool, I suggest making the pie ahead, refrigerating it, then slicing pieces for warming.

Makes one 10-inch pie

Sweetened Whipped Cream

Beat 1 cup cream until it holds luscious soft peaks, then whip in confectioners' sugar, vanilla, and Kahlúa to taste.

Two-Minute Calamari Sicilian Lifeguard Style

MARIO BATALI, Babbo, Esca, Lupa, and Otto, New York, NY

"This two-minute calamari recipe, along with my beef cheek ravioli, are two of the first recipes I created exclusively and without precedent for Babbo. Opening Babbo was one of the most exciting and nerve-wracking times of my life. It is all my cooking experiences pulled together. The restaurant is the best expression I could come up with to describe and share my feelings about Italy, New York City, food, and passion in the spring of 1998. That fact that people loved this dish and made it a signature of the restaurant is even more special."

Kosher salt

1 cup Israeli couscous

¼ cup extra-virgin olive oil

2 tablespoons pine nuts

2 tablespoons currants

1 tablespoon red pepper flakes

¼ cup capers

2 cups basic tomato sauce (recipe follows), or Molto Sugo Pomodoro Sauce (see Note)

1½ pounds cleaned calamari, tubes cut into ¼-inch rounds, tentacles halved

Freshly ground black pepper

3 scallions, thinly sliced

Bring 3 quarts of water to a boil and add a tablespoon of salt. Set up an ice bath nearby. Cook the couscous in the boiling water for 2 minutes, then drain and immediately plunge it into the ice bath. Once cooled, drain, remove, and set aside to dry on a plate.

In a 12- to 14-inch sauté pan, heat the oil until just smoking. Add the pine nuts, currants, and red pepper flakes and sauté until the nuts are just golden brown, about 2 minutes. Add the capers, tomato sauce, and couscous and bring to a boil. Add the calamari, stir to mix, and simmer for 2 to 3 minutes, or until the calamari is just cooked and completely opaque. Season with salt and pepper to taste, pour into a large bowl, sprinkle with scallions, and serve immediately.

Note: The basic tomato sauce can be replaced by Mario's Molto Sugo Pomodoro Sauce, available at Trader Joe's: www.traderjoes.com.

Serves 4

Basic Tomato Sauce

¼ cup extra-virgin olive oil

1 large onion, cut into ¼-inch dice

4 garlic cloves, thinly sliced

3 tablespoons chopped fresh thyme leaves, or 1 tablespoon dried

1 medium carrot, finely shredded

Two 28-ounce cans peeled whole tomatoes, crushed by hand and juices reserved

Kosher salt

In a 3-quart saucepan, heat the olive oil over medium heat. Add the onion and garlic and cook until soft and light golden brown, 8 to 10 minutes. Add the thyme and carrot and cook for 5 minutes more, until the carrot is quite soft. Add the tomatoes and juice and bring to a boil, stirring often. Lower the heat and simmer for 30 minutes, until as thick as hot cereal. Season with salt. This sauce holds for a week in the refrigerator or up to 6 months in the freezer.

Makes 4 cups

8. Travel, Eating, and Reading
LEARNING SOMETHING NEW EVERY DAY

Whatever you invest in yourself right now will come back to you a zillion times later. But you have to be willing to invest. You have to start spending your money on cookbooks and going to the best restaurants and traveling, for example, instead of blowing it on music CDs. I see too many cooks who stop thinking about food when their eight hours are done. **LYDIA SHIRE**

The best chefs, like the best restaurants, continue to evolve and grow. Nothing is stagnant; everything changes, either for the better or for the worse. If chefs are to change for the better, then their influences must be positive. There are three items that can provide nourishment and energy for positive change: the air you breathe, the food you eat, and the ideas you ponder. Travel can literally impart a breath of fresh air, as well as help give rise to a new perspective. Johanne Killeen and George Germon describe their experiences while traveling through Italy "like eating food for the first time." Eating new and different foods can nourish the spirit as well as the body. And reading can provide "food for thought," imparting new ideas or giving new depth to old ideas. Taken together, the combination of these influences can expand your real understanding of food.

Leading chefs never stop learning about food. This is the most important theme that our conversations drove home. They are always seeking out opportunities to learn more about food and to expand the way they think about food. Food becomes the lens through which they often see, experience, think about, and talk about the world. (Many even "pepper" their conversations with culinary terms—such as talking about putting things "on the back burner," letting ideas "simmer," etc.) Beyond the classroom and the kitchen, working chefs can find ample opportunities to increase their knowledge, primarily through travel, eating, and reading.

Chefs travel for vacation, but also to absorb culture and food. Their destination may be dictated by their desire to go to the source of a particular style of food. Eating out on their nights off is another way chefs keep up on what their colleagues are doing. On a Sunday or Monday night (chefs' most frequent nights off) you'll often find a chef "researching" a friend or colleague's restaurant over dinner. Many chefs have extensive cookbook collections of literally hundreds or even thousands of books, which they turn to for information or inspiration. Food rarely leaves their thoughts.

"I like to ski, and in the summer I play tennis. I may be doing something completely different [from cooking]. But I don't forget cooking during this time," admits André Soltner. "I think all the time about what I can do different, what I can do better. So I do that when I am on the ski lift, I do that when I sleep."

It's hard to describe the exact ways in which this knowledge manifests itself; the benefits accrue to the chef in a much more holistic manner than they do in any single, identifiable way, such as in improving technique or seasoning. Somehow, everything a chef has ever tasted, smelled, touched, seen, heard, read, or otherwise experienced is translated through the chef's hands and finds its way onto a plate. The greater these experiences, in both quality and quantity, the more the chef is able to bring to the kitchen. Aspiring chefs shouldn't stint on seeking out such experiences. Rather, you should view spending on travel, eating, and reading as an investment in yourself, your education, and your personal and professional development.

Jeremiah Tower observes that too many young Americans are raised on fast food, TV, and pop music. "It's frightening—they grow up with absolutely no other cultural heritage. They've never even wandered around the United States, let alone been to Europe. They know absolutely nothing about the richness of experience—

Cooking's not a secular thing. I've learned more about the history of the world because of my interest in cooking than I ever did in school. When I was writing Big Flavors of the Hot Sun, I learned about different lands, even the history of the Roman Empire, by researching the spice routes.

CHRIS SCHLESINGER

to have had some sort of experience that blew their mind, whether it was sliced tomatoes in Italy or having a plate of mussels on the ocean in Capri or whatever it is that just triggers them. This is a problem for an industry which relies on people's senses and the richness of their personalities. It's hard to do that on a corn dog."

Seeking out such experiences can be futile, however, if you're not awake to all the new impressions these experiences can bring. First, you must change yourself by changing your attitude toward the world, opening yourself to all the positive impressions it may bring. If you eat every meal at McDonald's on your first trip to Paris, you're not likely to grow and evolve. On the other hand, trying unfamiliar foods can help you grow. If you find a new food unpleasant, you can make a game out of trying to like it. For that matter, take a fresh taste of your favorite foods and try to dislike them. When you try to consciously understand the allure and distaste of various foods and experiences to you, real understanding follows.

Why Travel?

Travel has the potential to make the biggest impact on a person because of its all-encompassing nature. When you find yourself on street corners in other countries with unfamiliar languages and dialects and currencies, not to mention new sights and sounds and even new smells, it's almost impossible not to look at everything in a new way. Your immersion in a new and different environment causes you to rethink everything you might take for granted at home—from apparel to customs to food.

Sure, you're saying, travel sounds great—for those who've already hit the lottery. However, Mark Miller has little sympathy for aspiring chefs who claim they can't afford to travel anywhere. "You can get a charter flight for $398. If you did without a pair of sneakers, which cost $150, and a Walkman, you'd probably have the trip paid for. You can go to Costa Rica today for a dollar a day. You can go to Chile and live for a month on three or four hundred dollars," he argues. "I still travel extensively. I go to a new country every year, and am out of the country five to ten times a year, constantly challenging my palate." Nor does he have any sympathy for those who shy away from travel because of potential risks. "People worry 'If I travel, I'm going to get sick.' Well, I've had hepatitis twice. I've had dysentery several times. Life is dangerous. But you need to embrace it."

When chefs travel, they take special delight in absorbing the food and the culture of their destinations. The countries they choose to visit may be dictated by their desire to sample particular styles of food. Italy and, of course, France are both popular destinations for this reason. Many chefs love food first, and everything else second—and tend to plan their days accordingly. Susan Regis says she and Lydia Shire are ideal travel companions: "We love to do the same thing—shop and eat. That's it. Forget about the Sistine Chapel."

In his own early days as a cook, Patrick O'Connell would close his small restaurant every January in order to travel. "We'd go to the greatest restaurants in the world, and we'd spend every cent we had experiencing them," he recalls. "Sometimes we would have a letter of introduction, sometimes we wouldn't. It was [food writer] Bill Rice who wrote our first letters of introduction, to Paul Bocuse, Alain Chapel, and other chefs [in France], and they welcomed us and took us to the market and invited us to eat with their families. It blew us away that they were attuned to the purity of our motives."

A huge part of my education was dining in France. I had an aunt and uncle who were big foodies and would take me to Michelin two- and three-star restaurants. You can take in a lot by dining if you have a good foundation.

TRACI DES JARDINS

What's the Big Deal About France, Anyway?

France has historically been a destination that inspires rhapsodies among many aspiring chefs. Gordon Hamersley says, "I knew I'd never be at peace with myself until I'd cooked in France." He and his wife, Fiona, Hamersley's maître d', subsequently spent eighteen months traveling through France. "I wanted to live and breathe French food, not just French kitchens. So we ate and drank as much as possible, and traveled around the countryside and worked in various stops along the way. It taught me more about the French and the way they approach their food than just working in a three-star restaurant would have."

> When I was in France, I would save up all my money to eat at Paul Bocuse—then I would eat canned soup until I could afford another great meal and would go to Alain Chapel. In Italy, I would drink wine with lunch every day. And in Thailand, where the culture is about eating on the street, I learned all about chiles—and when to put rice in my mouth to cool off the heat from the chiles.
>
> **MARCUS SAMUELSSON**

While traveling in France after graduating from The Culinary Institute of America, Charles Palmer recalls, "I saw a much greater respect for food. After lunch, people would ask, 'What's for dinner?'" A family he stayed with had a seven-year-old son. When Palmer asked the boy who the President of France was, he didn't know. But when Palmer asked him who the greatest chef in France was, the answer came without hesitation: "Paul Bocuse."

Susanna Foo also ate her way through France. On a 1984 trip, she skipped breakfast and lunch and spent every night for nearly two weeks eating dinner in three-star restaurants. "I realized how refined, dedicated, and proud French chefs are," she says.

Chris Schlesinger argues that it's important that aspiring chefs travel wherever their desires take them. "Do whatever you want to do. Choose a place or a country based on whatever draws you there—the art, the people, a woman you met who lives there. You can learn about the food of that place. If you're eighteen and you've never been away from home and feel like going to Hawaii, go to Hawaii for a couple years. Or if you've always wanted to learn Italian, go to Italy," he advises. "Personalize your 'route' according to whatever you're into. It's not a matter of sitting down and analyzing 'what's best for my career'—that's putting the cart before the horse. It's a matter of saying, 'This is what I want to do, so I'm going to go do this.' A lot of times you'll incorporate that into wherever you end up. What it's about is having some sort of feeling and desire."

Rick Bayless followed his own passions to Mexico. "I'd always been interested in Mexican cooking, and I had the background to be able to do quite a bit of it, but I hadn't studied it in any kind of formal way," he recalls. "We worked hard for a couple of years, saved up all our money, put everything in storage, and just headed off. That was a very formative time in my life. We went to every state in Mexico. We cooked in both homes and restaurants. I'm very interested in street cooking and marketplace cooking, and so we really talked to people. That's a great place to learn, because they do all the cooking right in front of you. They'll tell you, 'I'm going to make my sausage in the morning. If you want to stop by, I'll show you how.'"

It was Anne Rosenzweig's love and study of ethnomusicology that led her to spend a year living in West Africa, Nepal, and Kenya. "I was welcomed into the community by being taught how to cook," she recalls. "Everything involved food—it was part of the religion. Most of the cultures were fairly poor, but the food was always delicious, made with only the simplest ingredients. I learned it takes real ability to make the simplest things taste wonderful." The influence on her as a chef was strong, but subtle. "People often asked me what they could find on Arcadia's menu that was similar to what I ate in Liberia," recalls Rosenzweig. "I have to admit that flying termites didn't quite make it on my menu."

Bradley Ogden took his first trip to Europe in 1985, as a guest of the Spanish government, with Alice Waters, Mark Miller, Lydia Shire, Ruth Reichl (now editor of *Gourmet*), and Colman Andrews (now editor of *Saveur*). Ogden recalls being impressed with the incredible markets, which he found "so clean. Each stall was hand-tiled." His memories of the trip were vivid and lasting: "I recall going into this one little

shop with Alice and Ruth in Barcelona, down this little alley. When you walked in, the only thing you could hear was this crackling noise. It turned out to be fresh roasted hazelnuts and almonds—there were two great big huge vats out of this olive wood-burning oven, and all you could smell was this incredible aroma throughout the store."

Jean-Georges Vongerichten spent time traveling through Asia while working in Bangkok, visiting Vietnam, Cambodia, Laos, and Malaysia. He subsequently opened restaurants in Singapore, Hong Kong, Japan, Portugal, Geneva, London, and Boston—his first stop in the United States. "I came for a weekend in New York. I went to the fish market, and other places I'd heard so much about. I went to Balducci's and I saw all the stuff and said, 'Wow! This is great!' I said, 'That's it. This is where I want to be.' I fit in right away."

Up to the point when Marcus Samuelsson left Sweden to work throughout Europe, he admits that he thought gourmet food was synonymous with French and other European food. "I never thought gourmet food could be had in Mexico or Brazil or Morocco or Thailand," he says. "At that point, Asian food was Chinese food and Mexican food was rice and beans. It was a very arrogant and naive point of view—which was very much a predominant point of view at that time in Michelin-starred kitchens.

"I hadn't realized there was a world of food out there. Every now and then, someone would bring in something like lemongrass, which we would look at and ask, 'What is this Chinese crap?' We didn't have a clue about how to work with it much less what was great about it!"

A transformational influence was a British chef with whom Samuelsson worked who had traveled a great deal throughout India and Southeast Asia. "He was the one who told me, 'You've got skills, but what you see here is not everything there is to see.' He would make real ethnic food for me, lining up three different curries—Chinese, Indian, and Thai—and ask me to describe the differences," Samuelsson recalls. "At that point I couldn't, but I fell in love with the flavors anyway. I knew that if I stuck by him and took his advice, something good would come out of it."

In fact, his chef's advice prompted Samuelsson at age twenty-one to take a job on a cruise ship, so that he could travel the world. "Every third day we would land in port and go to the market and shop. Before every port, I would be given a test: The chef would give me information about where we were going ten days before we got there. He would quiz me on what the food of the country was, and then when we got to port, we would go shopping and he would ask me what we should buy," he remembers.

"It was tough, but he really pushed me and prepared me for real life. It was hard because on a cruise ship you work double shifts every day, with no days off. But I used my downtime wisely, studying up on food and teaching myself French and German.

"The best thing about that year was that I actually discovered a whole new layer of passion for food," Samuelson marvels. "I became as passionate about the miso soup of Osaka and the seafood of Singapore as I was about the food of Europe."

> **Travel is key. You have to travel. You have to get bombarded. You have to put yourself into a new food context. You have to challenge that you know anything at all. You have to let go. Go to India. Go to Thailand. Go to China. Push yourself out there.**
>
> **MARK MILLER**

Learning Through Travel

Allen Susser found the change from cooking food to "living" food transformational. "I think there's some rich culture in food that gives you a sense of 'being' in cooking," he says. "There's so much within each culture, and how they treat food. You really have to see where food comes from, and the depth of the cultural beginnings to really understand food and get a great flavor for the food, to get it worked into your system. You have to live food, if you really want to be a chef."

Susan Regis agrees. "How can you make fresh pasta without knowing the roots of where it came from and how they do it, really? Travel brings an anthropological perspective. The food comes to mean more to you as a cook, and somehow that gets translated to the plate," says Regis. "While I'd never been to Italy before I met Lydia [Shire], now I've been three times. Travel is so crucial."

Bradley Ogden believes travel plays an important role in developing a palate. "If somebody tells you, 'Oh, I had the greatest French bread outside of Paris . . .,' you're able to have a basis of comparison to say, 'That wasn't the greatest French bread. I've had really great French bread right here in San Francisco from Acme Bread.'"

Cindy Pawlcyn encourages chefs to travel and eat all over America so that they can hone their palates. "How many people have eaten lobster in Maine or stone crab claws in Florida? How many have tasted the difference between barbecue in Kansas City versus Texas? You're born with a palate, but you need to develop and perfect it. You need to taste food, get it in your memory, and be able to draw on that taste memory when you next prepare something similar. And you need to learn to develop distinctions between similar things, to be able to taste the differences between a New Zealand lamb and a Napa Valley lamb, and learn how to use the products differently."

His New Orleans travel led Edward Brown to develop an appreciation of different ingredients, even Worcestershire sauce. "It's a totally misconceived item in the United States," says Brown. "It's a wonderful, sophisticated thing. It's not a crappy little condiment to be taken for granted, like yellow mustard—it's the salted broth extracted from cooking tamarind seeds."

It is not enough just to be able just to use a cooking term. If you are going to talk about something being al dente, is it the al dente of Naples, where it is really firm to the tooth and spaghetti just bends? Or is it the al dente of Torino, where pasta is much softer than in the rest of Italy? Each region has its own style. Young chefs need to understand those kinds of references so that they don't defame them.

CHRIS BIANCO

Travel abroad taught Alice Waters—and a legion of chefs who subsequently followed her lead—something about standards of freshness. "I really can't say enough about my first visit to France. I think that experience of tasting lots of different things, seeing how other cultures eat, how they do things, the way people shop, made such a difference," she says. "People were still cooking from their back gardens or from the farmers' market [in the 1960s], and I didn't know what it was that made that food so good. It took me a long time to figure out that that's what it was. It just tasted fantastic; you know, it was just a chicken, just a lettuce salad, but there was something about it. And then you'd start to put two and two together and it wasn't just a chicken—it was a chicken that was eating all the scraps from the backyard and was running around back there. It wasn't just salad—it was lettuce that they'd grown or they'd just gotten from the market.

"It was a real revelation to find what 'fresh' means. It means 'alive.' Even in salad, there's a life to a lettuce that is of that day. Every day it's kept in the refrigerator, it changes, it loses its life, it starts to get old. It's very different from when you go out there and pick it and eat it. France led me back to the garden."

Barbara Tropp recalled learning similar standards of freshness when she spent two years living with Chinese families in Taiwan in the late 1970s. "We shopped the market twice a day. Before I went to class, I shopped the market with the old man who headed our household—he was the gourmand—and the servant woman, and then after lunch we would again shop for dinner. I was part of an intriguing, very old-fashioned family where the husband was from Yangchow and there was an older wife who was from Beijing and a younger wife who was from Shanghai, so among the three of them they hit the epicurean epicenters of China. These were people who had grown up in imperial China—with those standards of eating they were all from well-off families—so that we shopped as if it was still the early nineteenth century. There were no refrigerators. You never bought a fish that wasn't alive. You never bought a vegetable that was more than eight hours out of the ground. All of what I later came to experience as so-called 'California cooking' to me was just everyday Chinese cooking as it had been done."

The effect of travel on Patrick O'Connell was no less than transformational. "After spending a year traveling, I had a whole different sense of the restaurant business, particularly in France. Food became art. I saw people crowded outside pastry shop windows, enraptured by the visual [elements]," he says. "So often I think that people aren't aiming high enough in the field, or they're imitating the imitators, instead of going to the source and always looking to the best."

> Travel for six to eight weeks. Go to the Greek Islands, go to northern Italy; go to the south of France. Spend two weeks in every area and really observe the culture. If you then happen to run into somebody that says, "Hey, I could use some help in the kitchen," you've already established some grounds.
>
> VICTOR GIELISSE

O'Connell's own early "search for the best" led him to experience culinary nirvana. "I had many peak food experiences. Marrakesh, for one. It was a breaking-through of all the piles of sandbags that our culture puts on you (mostly about sensuality, I think) in regard to food and its primal connection. It's very much blocked in middle-class suburban households. I think a peak food experience requires you to be a little out of control, so I would often find myself eating couscous in a tent or something in Marrakesh and experiencing something I had never experienced before. And the same in Paris, in Vietnamese restaurants or in little bistros, having brand-new sensations that I didn't dream existed."

Bradley Ogden's "greatest trip in the world" was an eating binge in New York City with noted restaurateur Joe Baum when Baum was working as a consultant to Ogden's Kansas City restaurant. "We went to forty places in two days," he recalls, rattling off a long list that included Balducci's, Dean & DeLuca, The Four Seasons, and Windows on the World. Particularly memorable was a dinner at The Coach House during a power blackout: "The restaurant was lit by candlelight, and all the cooking was done table side by the owner himself. There was just a table of four of us in the entire restaurant, including me and Joe Baum. I still remember everything, every detail: the black bean soup, the pepper steak, the crispy duck, and an incredible, incredible huckleberry tart for dessert, thickened with a blueberry and honey puree. I can still taste it. Those two days comprised the most enlightening experience."

Travel's Influence on Chefs' Food

Chefs' travel experiences are inevitably translated to the plate, either directly or indirectly. Observing new techniques and presentations can be as inspiring as the food itself. "When I travel, I look for pans that will make me think of a new dish that I want to make," says Lydia Shire. "For instance, I never forgot a little quail grill with a spit they brought to our table to turn quails on at a restaurant in Montreal. I went and had them made [for Biba]. They were outrageously expensive, but [in this business] you can't just sit and rest on your laurels. You've got to ask, 'What did I do this week that's special?' Travel can help by inspiring new ideas."

Jasper White contrasts what he gets out of traveling with how he sees it influencing his good friend Shire. White says, "When I travel and I taste something, I say, 'This is so good that it can't be dupli-cated on the other side of the ocean.' But with Lydia, it doesn't frighten her. She's driven to create a version that's better than anything anyone's ever tasted. It's a matter of personality. She's comfortable doing that, and I wouldn't be. So I don't try. I just feel comfortable with a little bit, here and there. I spent a month

Travel as Professional Development

Certain leading chefs, including Mario Batali and Rick Bayless, believe that travel is so important that they and their restaurants will make a financial commitment to making it happen for their staff.

"After cooks spend a year at my restaurant, I want them to go to Italy for a year," insists Mario Batali. "Three months is not enough. I'll send as many cooks as I can to Italy for as long as they can stay. I will split the cost of the ticket and their most expensive meal in the country. If they go for a year, I will guarantee a job when they return until they get their feet back on the ground again.

"I do that because I was lucky enough to do it myself, and know that these cooks need a little extra push to get them moving. I see a huge difference when they get back.

"After they spend time in Italy, they *really* understand seasonality. You can talk about seasonality, but until you can't get asparagus in August, some cooks will still use it. In Italy, it is simply not there, because the season for asparagus can be just four weeks and strawberries just five weeks. So, they come to understand how it should taste, and what it is to celebrate it.

"What they celebrate in Italy is the taste of the rain and the way the rain smells in the summer when their mom makes dinner. If my cook captures that Zen of Italian cooking by staying home on a rainy day and dealing with the lack of asparagus, then that cook is starting to understand what the essence of great food is. For a cook to see that is humbling and enriching at the same time. Understanding that is the key to understanding great Italian food."

Rick Bayless takes his entire staff to Mexico every year so that they can taste the authentic flavors of Mexican cooking.

"One of our servers describes our trips to Mexico like working five double shifts in a row!" laughs Bayless. "We take thirty-five people to Mexico, and it the most rewarding thing we do as well as the most difficult. We recently made our twelfth trip, and many crew members have been going with us for many years now.

"Over the years, the trips have changed because the crew is so much more knowledgeable and they have embraced the culture in an 'insider' way. What is remarkable is that these are not people who are Mexican—but some people have become so comfortable that they go there on their vacation. *I* don't go to Mexico on *my* vacation, because I need a break! However, it does make me happy to see them do it.

"We have our daily staff meeting before service, and someone different is responsible for it every day. Today, one of the servers showed her pictures of our recent trip and of a man we met who had a mescal still in Oaxaca. She spoke for fifteen minutes so passionately about this artisan mescal maker and how the experience affected her life. That is the reward, and that is why we continue to make the trip to Mexico year after year."

in China and everyone thought I would make everything Chinese when I came back. I do have a spring roll on my menu now, but it's all seafood inside—the classic combination of flounder and crab—and there's no julienne anything. That's as far as I go." Similarly, Mark Miller points out, "Design is about looking at something and understanding what someone else has created, and bringing that into one's own work: taking moo shu pork, for example, and translating it into a Southwest mode."

White also believes it's important for aspiring cooks to have the experience of tasting food at its source. "Chinese food—you cannot explain how good it is until you go to China. You can't taste it here; you have to go there to taste it," he says. "I believe the same thing is true of Italian food and French food. You really have to taste it there to truly understand it. I don't think it travels. I become introspective about food, and the traveling almost reinforces that introspectiveness. When I come back I say, 'I just want to be unique' and my way of being unique is to do uniquely New England food, using the ingredients that are here. I've matured. I'm not a young chef anymore. I've put in twenty years now, and I know what I like. And I keep growing, and learning, but in a different way."

Judy Rodgers first heard about Chez Panisse in Paris during her junior year of college abroad, and went to meet Alice Waters when she returned home in 1976: "She was the only person I knew in America who had any sense that 'a raspberry is not a raspberry is not a raspberry—you've got to get good ones!'"

Eating Your Heart Out

With the shrinking of our global village, you don't need to leave the United States in order to experience the foods of other countries. Nor do you need to cross the ocean to make a pilgrimage to a culinary mecca. You can find some of the world's greatest French food in the United States-based restaurants of the French chefs interviewed for this book. You'll also find some of the best Mexican food prepared by native Mexicans and even non-natives who've opened Mexican restaurants in the United States after extensive research and travel.

"Some of the Thai food at Bangkok Cuisine [an inexpensive Boston restaurant] is not that much different from what I ate in Bangkok. And it will cost you about ten thousand dollars less [than flying to

Michael Foley of Printer's Row (Chicago) recalls taking advantage of the rich ethnic diversity of the food in Washington, D.C., during his undergraduate days at Georgetown. "I loved D.C. It gave me a lot of background in ethnic food. There was a lot of authentic food in Washington at the time—it hadn't turned into what it is now, which is a real 'corporate' city—so you could have anything from Indian to Thai to Malaysian food to great French food, in very small restaurants."

Bangkok]," points out Lydia Shire. "If you don't have the money to travel, for a lot less you can buy good books and go to the best restaurants, and you're almost there."

By eating out on their nights off, chefs keep up with what their colleagues are doing in other restaurants, as well as remind themselves what it's like to be a customer. For the most part, when chefs eat out, they are driven to unlock the secrets of everything they eat. Sometimes, though, it's hard to enjoy a meal rather than critique it, because their perfectionistic mental checklists are always running.

"I try to relax when I go out to eat," admits Jimmy Schmidt. "I look at the overall experience. The dining experience is beyond just food—it's how the food plays on the plate, how it plays in the room, the aromas, and everything else that's happening are crucial to that whole experience. I look for what kind of pleasure it gives me. I may come across a new techniques or a different flavor, or a different combination, but I first look at it as a consumer. Then I break it down and say, 'Well, how did they do that? How did they get that flavor?' I like to see other people's food, not to get ideas that I take back, but to stimulate some other idea that falls within my range of cooking. That's the fun part. If you're a painter and you go out and see Stellas, that doesn't mean you go back and paint Stellas—you go back and do something else in your own range."

While it's almost a cliché for American chefs to get inspiration from traveling through Europe, some European chefs have likewise traveled through the United States. After leaving his job in the 1980s, Jean Joho took three weeks off to travel to New York, Los Angeles, and San Francisco. "While I was working, everybody had been talking about 'nouvelle American' cuisine, and I had no idea what they meant. I wanted to find out what they were talking about," admits Joho. "I ate at almost every major restaurant." He also spent a week in the kitchens of Chinois on Main and Stars, a professional courtesy often extended to chefs visiting from other cities. Joho advises, "When you go out to eat, see what you enjoy eating. You can change your style later on, but this gives you a direction for developing your own style of food."

Many of the chefs we interviewed could recount in minute detail entire meals they had eaten many years previously. Visiting Michelin-starred restaurants in France by himself, Charles Palmer found he was able to pay much more attention to the food. Palmer claims he can still recall "absolutely everything" about his restaurant visits, including lunch by himself on the terrace at Alain Chapel, starting with the house specialty Champagne cocktail: "Champagne with peach puree and cassis. I remember having little fried fish from the region as a first course. I had rolled, marinated salmon with salad wrapped inside it, like a roulade. I still remember the saddle of rabbit with caramelized garlic and beans, which, at the time, I thought was kind of strange. I was by myself, so the captain spent a lot of time speaking with me," Palmer recalls. "When I mentioned to him that I was working at Georges Blanc, they sent me about six desserts. At the time they were doing these little paired soufflés: one was chocolate and one was raspberry. I tried every dessert on the cart. The one I remember best was a pear napoleon: caramelized roasted pears layered between puff pastry, with a pear zabaglione or crème anglaise. Very simple, but just incredible tasting. I can still remember tasting that."

Jeremiah Tower described the memorable experience of eating a simple yet delicious white bean soup at Georges Blanc's namesake restaurant in France several years before. "I was amazed and thought, 'My God! How did he make that?' It was such an amazing thing. And then I realized it was half white-bean puree, but they were new crop dried white beans, or fresh white beans, which are extremely difficult to get here, and half crème fraîche, with a teaspoon of chopped black truffles sprinkled on top. You don't need to do much more than that. By tasting it, you could probably go back to your own kitchen and try it three or four times and probably get it. But it took me a while to figure out the quality of the crème fraîche and the new white beans, instead of the stuff we tend to get here, which I think is the second- or third-year rubbish that they export."

Aside from learning about food, learning about service and presentation is key for chefs. Tower recalls taking members of his staff to the Crillon in Paris for breakfast—at sixty dollars per person—as a "seminar" in service excellence. "Breakfast at the Crillon is a legend. We'd spend two hours analyzing everything

about the service at the table, down to how the butter is put on the plate. Once they'd stayed at the Crillon or the Ritz it all became clear; all my yelling and screaming and demanding suddenly made the point."

Tower is still befuddled over one aspect of the service he received one day at the Hassler in Rome. "We'd arrived, we were exhausted, and we asked the legendary concierge where we should eat. Once we got to the restaurant he'd recommended, I didn't like the look of it, so we ate at another restaurant close by. When we came back, there was a different concierge at the desk. As we walked in, he said, 'Good afternoon, Mr. Tower' and asked me how I'd enjoyed not the restaurant the concierge had recommended, but the one we'd actually eaten at! My general manager was blown away, and he asked, 'How did they do that?' and I said, 'Oh, I'll explain it later,' thinking, 'How did they do that?'"

Edna Lewis recalls how she learned about wine when she was cooking at Cafe Nicholson: "People brought their own wine. The customers would send me a glass of wine, and then I kept the bottles. I got to learn what good wine tasted like."

Eating out offers aspiring chefs the opportunity to meet people who share their passion for food. Years ago, Zarela Martinez and her mother decided to go on a culinary expedition to New Orleans. Their first stop was a local cooking school where, Martinez recalls with disdain, they made peanut soup out of canned chicken stock and peanut butter. She and her mother decided to instead eat at every great restaurant in the city and then try to duplicate what they'd eaten. The two were seated at K-Paul's near where chef Paul

Prudhomme was cooking, and Martinez's mother urged her to speak with him. "I told him about our experience at the cooking school, and he made me an offer," Martinez recalls. "He said he'd teach me Cajun food if I would teach him how to make Mexican food." Martinez and Prudhomme spent three or four days cooking together, becoming fast friends.

Even shopping for food and speaking with people in the markets can be educational. I enjoy wandering through farmers' markets, like the one at Union Square in Manhattan, and even little out-of-the-way specialty stores selling produce, spices, meats, and often unusual ingredients. Stopping by a meat market for flank steak and asking a question about the tripe that was prominently displayed, I was given an impromptu recipe for tripe from the Italian butcher who claimed it was one of his favorite dishes. When I was living in Boston, I used to love shopping in Chinatown and an Asian supermarket called Ming's, particularly after being taken on a tour by a coworker who knew a lot about Asian ingredients. Visiting in-laws in the middle of Illinois, I've even stumbled across little ethnic shops selling exotic cheeses and rices, as well as their own freshly baked breads. A little exploration—wherever you live—can yield new culinary discoveries.

Charlie Trotter recalls, "The first weekend I moved to San Francisco, I read the *San Francisco Chronicle* and it said, 'Sunday morning tour of Chinatown conducted by Barbara Tropp.' So after I'd been in the city four days, I went on a tour of Chinatown with Barbara Tropp. Right off the bat I had this unbelievable point of reference, and I was set for the next year and a half. I knew exactly where to go to get duck feet, I knew exactly where to go to get water chestnuts, I knew exactly where to go to get greens, bamboo shoots, lemongrass, fish, and squid. It was perfect. It set the tone."

Jasper White once worked with a husband and wife team in Seattle whose passion for food was contagious. "It's not like before there were famous chefs there weren't *great* chefs. This was a great classic chef from the old school—he knew the book inside out, and knew these wonderful dishes, stuff that would blow your mind. You would never see this today, it's so old-fashioned: Roast Pheasants with Sauerkraut and Champagne. He'd cook the sauerkraut with apples and ham hocks, and then roast the pheasants. On a big platter, he'd put the sauerkraut out with the pheasants all around it, and put a bottle of Champagne in the middle with the wire top off. The sauerkraut heated the Champagne, the cork flew out, and an eruption of Champagne doused all the food. Then he'd cut up the pheasants and you'd eat the sauerkraut and the pheasants with the rest of the Champagne."

Reading: Food for Thought

Reading offers chefs a way to make sure they are not cooking in a vacuum, but rather that they are informed about what has taken place in the past and inspired by what is being created in the present as detailed in cookbooks, books about food, and magazines. "As you try to figure out what direction you're moving in as a chef, it's helpful to read to discover what your colleagues are doing and what directions they're moving in," says Jean Joho. "Young professionals definitely have to buy books and magazines and do all they can to keep learning about food." I found that, since I never attended cooking school, I relied particularly heavily on books to supplement my on-the-job learning about food. Reading offered me a portable, convenient, and relatively low-cost way to learn.

The chefs we interviewed were not dispassionate about this topic. According to Alfred Portale, "It is singly the most important aspect of this career: reading, and studying, and being influenced. If you don't read, you're illiterate. You can't possibly succeed in this business unless you are well read and well prepared and you read everything. I used to just study constantly, constantly—reading, rereading, testing, thinking about it, contemplating, talking about it, experimenting."

Reading can broaden the repertoire of any aspiring chef. "In any place you're working, you're following through on pretty much one identifiable style of the chef you're working for, which by no means is the only way to do something," says Allen Susser. "By reading, you're seeing other techniques, other ways of doing things, other ways of adding different nuances to what you have, and the how's and why's. Reading cookbooks and reading industry and consumer magazines is really important."

While cooking at Chez Panisse, Judy Rodgers spent a summer house-sitting for Lindsey Shere [the pastry chef], who had an extraordinary cooking library. "Basically I went home every night from work and read a cookbook in order to learn, because I was definitely in over my head." Rodgers admits.

Many chefs went through periods of intensive reading during their early days in the business, representing almost a 'rite of

All of Joël Robuchon's books, which I read after I had worked with him, teach great technique. Robuchon opened my eyes to how great a man can be. He was very hard on his people because he believed in them. He saw the potential in everyone and never gave up on them or fired them. If someone left Robuchon's kitchen, it was because the cook gave up on himself and did not want the incredible training.

CRAIG SHELTON

passage' into the realm of becoming a serious professional. Norman Van Aken admits, "One of the cornerstone changes for me in my life was having someone say to me, 'Why don't you read cookbooks?' I had always considered myself well read, and so I asked, 'Like who?' He said, 'Like Beard—why don't you read James Beard?' And after work I went to a bookstore and picked up James Beard's *The Theory and Practice of Good Cooking.* I found it was a whole new way of looking at food, and it blew me away. It started to affect the way I was cooking at work, and I started spending all my money on cookbooks."

In his own early days as a cook, Charlie Trotter read incessantly about food and wine. "Everything I could get my hands on—every cookbook, every food history book. In San Francisco, I lived in a studio apartment with no furniture. I slept on the floor in a sleeping bag. For a year and a half, all I had was a light and maybe two hundred books and kitchen stuff," he recalls. "I really felt like there were so many people out there that seemed to know so much stuff, and I asked myself, 'How do I learn this stuff? What do I do? How do I get this information?' I learned you've just got to read and think about it."

Chefs' Top Recommended Books and/or Authors

Escoffier's *Le Guide Culinaire: The Complete Guide to the Art of Modern Cookery.* The first translation into English by H. L. Cracknell and R. J. Kaufman of this classic in its entirety (Hoboken, N.J.: John Wiley & Sons, 1997).

> When we were young chefs, we were almost forced by our chef to read Escoffier. To me, it's the basics. We should not forget these things. The danger is with trends, that the young chefs can follow the trends without knowing the classics. And when the trend changes, they are stuck. You need this basic training, and then you can do anything you wish. ANDRÉ SOLTNER

Larousse Gastronomique: The New American Edition of the World's Greatest Culinary Encyclopedia, edited by Jenifer Harvey Lang (N.Y.: Crown. 1988).

> [When first entering the profession], every night I would read heavy-duty stuff like Larousse. When you don't know about food, you look at something like Larousse and think that it's pretty bizarre that people thought about food like this. CHARLES PALMER

Mastering the Art of French Cooking, by Julia Child, Louisette Bertholle, and Simone Beck, vol. 1 (N.Y.: Alfred Knopf, 2001).

Irma S. Rombauer and Marion Rombauer Becker's *New Joy of Cooking* (N.Y.: Scribner's, 1997).

Elizabeth David's *Elizabeth David Classics* (N.Y.: Alfred Knopf, 1980).

James Beard's *American Cookery* (Boston: Little, Brown, 1980).

> Oh, I love James just to read. One of my favorite books of his has one chapter about Thanksgiving and another about Christmas. He tells about his childhood and why his mother liked crab and not lobster, and her plum pudding recipe. I mean, I could read that over and over and over and over. LYDIA SHIRE

Alice Waters's *Chez Panisse Menu Cookbook* (N.Y.: Random House, 1982).

Paula Wolfert's *World of Food* (N.Y.: HarperCollins, 1994) and other books.

Richard Olney's *Simple French Food* (N.Y.: Macmillan, 1974); and *French Menu Cookbook* (David R. Godine, 1970).

Craig Claiborne's *The New York Times Cookbook* (N.Y.: HarperCollins, 1990).

> That was my bible when I grew up. MARK MILLER

Ali-Bab, *The Ecyclopedia of Practical Gastronomy* (New York: McGraw-Hill, 1974).

The best book ever written. MICHEL RICHARD

Paul Bocuse's *Regional French Cooking* (N.Y.: Random House, 1977).

The Professional Chef, 7th edition. The Culinary Institute of America (N.Y.: John Wiley & Sons, 2002.)

Madeline Kamman's *The New Making of a Cook* (N.Y.: Morrow, 1997) and *In Madeleine's Kitchen: A Personal Interpretation of the Modern French Cuisine* (N.Y.: Macmillan, 1992).

Fernand Point's *Ma Gastronomie* (Paris: Flammarion, 1969).

It has really no recipes in it, but it has a lot of sayings and quotes. He's very fanatical about butter and about life, and about throwing people out of his restaurants when they lit up cigarettes. This was in the '50s that he did all this stuff. He was the man who trained Bocuse, the Troisgros brothers, Alain Chapel—they all came from Point. He's very inspiring and old-fashioned and funny. It's a wonderful book. It's probably out of print, so if you see it, grab it.
JASPER WHITE

Time-Life Books, *Foods of the World* (1968-70) and *American Cooking* (1970-71) series.

Harold McGee's *On Food and Cooking: The Science and Lore of the Kitchen* (N.Y.: Fireside, 1997).

Georges Blanc's *The Natural Cuisine of Georges Blanc* and *Ma Cuisine des Saisons* (N.Y.: Stewart Tabori Chang, 1987).

Simply French: Patricia Wells Presents the Cuisine of Joël Robuchon, Patricia Wells and Joël Robuchon (N.Y.: William Morrow, 1991).

The Auberge of the Flowering Hearth, Roy Andries De Groot (Hopewell, N.J.: Ecco Press, 1992).

I think everyone should have to read this the moment that they say they're interested in a culinary career, because it identifies the concept and the potential of a mystical, spiritual experience happening in relation to the dining experience. PATRICK O'CONNNELL

If you can't find a particular culinary book through your local bookstore, it's worth making a call to the experts at Kitchen Arts & Letters in New York City at (212) 876-5550 or The Cook's Library in Los Angeles at (323) 655-3141. In London, try Books for Cooks at www.booksforcooks.com.

Some of the Favorite Books of Pastry Chefs

Gina DePalma (Babbo, NYC)

The Cake Bible, by Rose Levy Beranbaum (N.Y.: William Morrow, 1988).

Rose! Rose! Rose! Rose broke everything down and demystified it. She explained the science and chemistry of baking. Her measurements are exact down to the grams in a teaspoon! With this one book, you can accomplish everything!

Chez Panisse Desserts, by Lindsey Shere (N.Y.: Random House, 1993).

She teaches seasonality and is very ingredient-driven.

Stars Desserts, by Emily Luchetti (N.Y.: HarperCollins, 1991) and Nancy Silverton's first book, *Desserts* (N.Y.: HarperCollins, 1991).

Both of these books are very accessible. I really like their palates and their stuff is great.

Emily Luchetti (Farallon, San Francisco)

A common question I ask my cooks is to name a few books they would take to a desert island—an island with a full kitchen for baking, of course! I would take these four: *International Dictionary of Desserts, Pastries, and Confections,* by Carol Bloom (N.Y.: Hearst Books, 1995). I love this book. It is not so much about recipes but rather ideas. It always spurs my creativity. *The Dessert Bible,* by Chris Kimball (Boston: Little, Brown, 2000). I like it because he is so anal and has patience that I don't have. When I read his work, I'll examine the first couple of paragraphs, then skip to the end to see which recipe worked. I always want to know the punchline, then I go back and read about the process. *The Joy of Cooking* (N.Y.: Scribner's, 1975) is great because it gives you what you need to know—then you can turn it upside down and make it your own. *Mastering the Art of French Cooking* by Julia Child (N.Y.: Knopf, 2001). It is a classic.

For my style of cooking, I look at the classics of Europe and America, then switch them around and make them my own. I also like to read really esoteric stuff like Jane Grigson's *Fruit Book* (N.Y.: Atheneum, 1982) or *The Food Chronology,* by James Trager (N.Y.: Henry Holt, 1997), *The Oxford Companion to Food,* by Alan Davidson (N.Y.: Oxford University Press, 1999), and for the really obscure, *The Book of Marmalade,* by Anne Wilson (Philadelphia: University of Pennsylvania Press, 2000).

I like books that put food in a historical context—I recently read *Wedding Cakes and Cultural History,* by Simon Charsley (N.Y.: Routledge, 1992).

I love going to Kitchen Arts & Letters [in New York City] and talking to [owner] Nach Waxman because he has tremendous knowledge. The other great place for culinary books is Books for Cooks in London. On my last visit, I found a terrific book called *Sorbets, Flummerys, and Fools.*

OATMEAL
RAISIN
COOKIES
$1.50

Larry Forgione says, "If you wanted to pursue what I pursued, I would recommend Waverly Root's *Gastronomy in America*, Evan Jones's book on American cooking, Beard's book on American cooking, the Time-Life series of regional American cookbooks (the old one, not the new one), the old White House cookbook, any of Mary Margaret McBride's cookbooks, and any books you can get your hands on that were printed before World War II that were compilations, like the Junior League cookbooks. That's how I got to know a lot about regional American cooking, through those types of books."

Anne Rosenzweig recalls that she would spend ten hours a day in the kitchen, and then go home and read books. "That was my academic training, that you always had to read. I think that helped speed up the process for me," she says. "I would come up with questions, and the next day I'd go into work to ask the chef, who was enamored of the fact that I was so studious. He'd order the ingredients I'd asked about, and then we'd work with it."

You can even discover a mentor through reading. Raji Jallepalli found her mentor in Jean-Louis Palladin through reading his cookbook: "I happened to see his cookbook, and found it one of the very rare, special cookbooks which inspired me a lot. Ordinarily, I don't read cookbooks and pick up the phone and call the chefs. But for some reason, the book was too magical, so I left a message for him," she recalled. "He called back, and I congratulated him on the book. He asked me what I did for a living, and I explained that I was a chef doing fusion cooking. He was impressed and said he'd come to Memphis. A couple of weeks later, I did a special dinner for him. He said I needed to be exposed, and invited me to come to his kitchen. I spent about a week there, and it was very helpful. It helped me to pick up some of the classical techniques, stocks, and plate presentations."

Larry Forgione recalls his treasured friendship with James Beard, who had an incredible library, as being a critical learning experience. In addition to reading Beard's books, "I would go up and sit and talk with him. He was himself a living encyclopedia. That's how I got all this information about the way things were and the way things should be. Other things, about the way foods grow, you don't find in cookbooks. You have to go and spend time in the farmers' market, or go and visit someone's farm. You don't have to go work on a farm for six months; you just have to understand the concepts behind it."

Jasper White credits Evan Jones's *American Cooking*—"a history of American food, with recipes"—with kindling his own interest in American cooking. "You have to remember 1976. I just got out of The Culinary Institute of America. [It] didn't have the American Bounty restaurant then; it was the diner and The Escoffier Room. There was nothing in between. So you'd aspire to learn French classics—that was the vision every chef had, and it wasn't that long ago. Everything's changed now, but back then it was all French. I bought Jones's book because of my interest in history, and read it and got a great sense of tradition and heritage in American food that I never got from The Culinary Institute of America, which might as well have been The Culinary Institute of France. I didn't go off on a binge, right away, but it grew inside me. That book kind of simmered on my shelf for years, and I'd pick it up from time to time. The recipes were fairly good, nothing real great, but the dishes were great: baked beans and Brunswick stew and chowders and all the great traditional American dishes. That book was one of the great ones."

Norman Van Aken describes the process he uses to get inspiration from his books: "I'll get pork tenderloin in the kitchen and wonder, 'How am I going to cook this tonight?' And I would have seven books out in front of me, flipping through them thinking, 'Pork tenderloin, pork tenderloin—oh, pork chops, I'd better read this.' I'll be in a Thai book, a French book, and an Italian book all at the same time. So I start cross-referencing all this material very, very eclectically, and informing myself of what to do."

Daniel Boulud skims cookbooks but doesn't read recipes: "A title might inspire the combination of two ingredients," he says. Alfred Portale agrees. "It's not really a literal thing where you look up a recipe and say 'Oh, I'll try that.' That almost never happens," he says. "Usually I read the index, in the back. Somehow, that starts to spark things. If I have 40 percent of the plate, or I have an idea, but I need the rest of the garnishes, then it might get a little more specific. But again, it's only an idea. I almost never take a recipe out of a cookbook."

Looking at pictures of visual presentations of food can help you begin to develop an aesthetic sense. "The more pictures you look at, the better," says Cindy Pawlcyn. "In time, you'll begin to develop a sense of what you like and don't like." Patrick O'Connell admits, "Because I'm such a visual person, all the early issues of *Gourmet* were very, very helpful. The mood was evoked—not the food itself, but the mood. The fantastic photography [by René

I'm mad about Italian food. I have a book by Carol Field called *Celebrating Italy.* They celebrate anything, but what I found was they celebrated lard! A day of celebration of lard?! I couldn't have agreed with her more! They also put pepper in their bread, weaving it through the dough, and they put cracklins in bread. Italians are mad for pork, and so are Southerners. A lot of Italian cooking is really like Southern cooking.
EDNA LEWIS

> **I was not inspired so much by books as by magazines. My mother and grandmother had every single copy of *Gourmet* magazine. When I went to visit *Gourmet*'s offices in New York, seeing all the covers brought back all these memories of food and childhood for me. Growing up in the Bronx, I never saw a field of lavender, or gravlax being made in Sweden, so *Gourmet* was it.**
>
> CHRIS BIANCO

Jacques, one of their renowned photographers] captured and said so much to me, that I can look at a picture, and everything starts clicking, clicking, clicking away," he says. "But my mind moves too fast now to read cookbooks any longer. So if I do, I just flip the pages very quickly, and scan the ingredients."

Many leading chefs have developed extensive personal libraries consisting of hundreds and even thousands of cookbooks and books about food, which they turn to for both information and inspiration. "I have well over six hundred cookbooks at home. I can't say I've read every one of them, but I've read more than four hundred of them, cover to cover," says Jasper White. "Many books and all books have served as an inspiration to me. I think the repetition of reading many books and seeing certain ingredients together time and time again has been a great teacher to me."

The same chefs, however, lament young cooks' lack of interest in reading about food and cooking, aside from glancing at an occasional magazine. "No one wants to borrow books anymore," observes Susan Feniger. Barbara Tropp also noted, "What kid coming out of cooking school reads? No one! I know I sound like an old fart, but people with backgrounds like Anne [Rosenzweig] and Alice [Waters] and Joyce [Goldstein] and Jeremiah [Tower] and Mark [Miller]—all of us were people who began to love cooking by reading, and who have a very philosophical bent to our cuisine."

To encourage his staff to read, Patrick O'Connell allowed each staff member to pick a favorite book, and also created a small library. What books does he recommend to his staff? "I think particularly when you're starting out, it's essential to use books that you totally trust to give you excellent results. Certainly, anything Craig Claiborne does is thoroughly tested and worked out. He even has a 'recommended cookbook library' in his autobiography (Craig Claiborne's *A Feast Made for Laughter: A Memoir with Recipes*), which I think is very helpful."

Part of growing as a cook involves opening yourself up to new worlds, new experiences, and new conceptions of what food can be. This may include savoring a meal in one of the world's best restaurants, if your previous culinary experiences are more humble. Or it might involve coming to appreciate the rich history and sublime flavors of a modest ethnic dish, simply cooked and seasoned, if you've had the privilege of being overexposed to expensive Western foods. Or it might be an unexpected combination of ingredients, discovered in a rare cookbook, which you would not have run across in a general cooking magazine, if that was your only food literature source. Travel, eating, and reading can provide the all-important sparks leading to new illuminations.

We ask our cooks, "How many cookbooks do you have?" and "What do you read after work?" If they say *Popular Mechanics,* we've got a problem. We tell them to read *Gourmet, Food & Wine,* and *Bon Appétit*—and that if they don't live and breathe this, they will stagnate. I'll be honest: When I was at cooking school I was reading James Bond novels. Reading was not emphasized; you would not have gotten a hernia carrying around the required books in those days. That has all changed for the better. I started reading cookbooks later, after cooking school, to direct myself.

MARCEL DESAULNIERS

Pollo en Escabeche (Pickled Chicken Salad in Aromatic Spices)

MARK MILLER, Coyote Cafe, Santa Fe, NM

"This is a dish that I created for the Coyote Cafe that represents the Spanish influences on Southwestern cuisine. Whenever I eat this dish it reminds me of my adventures on horseback in Spain in 1980. I traveled across the Andalusian countryside for ten days, passing through the white hill towns in the hot summer sun. The countryside was carpeted with sunflowers and dotted with black bulls. We would leave very early each morning while it was still cool out and ride until noon when the sun was at its peak. The days would reach into the low 100s.

"For lunch we would stop for two hours to rest the horses in the shade and take a meal in the old country inns that were stone cooled. On the sideboards there were cold dishes in refreshing sauces like this chicken in escabeche. These Spanish dishes were the prototype for all ceviches in the New World. We usually had pheasant or chicken and it was always served in brown terracotta dishes with crusty country bread and cool, refreshing wine on old wooden tables. I spent ten days on horseback from Arcos de la Frontera in central Spain to the beaches of the Atlantic. The best way to experience a country is to ride through it!

"Most Americans think of pickles as a vegetable garnish for sandwiches or burgers, but pickling in a spicy, aromatic brine (*en escabeche* in Spanish) was another essential method of preserving meat, fish, seafood, and vegetables in the days before refrigeration and canning. The pickling brine always contains salt as well as an acid in the form of vinegar or citrus juice, which chemically 'cooks' and preserves the ingredients. The technique has been used for centuries, especially in the Mediterranean region. You often see this method of 'cooking' used in the wonderful tapas dishes of Spain. The Spanish in turn brought this technique to the New World—one example of this transfer of culinary ideas is Latin American seafood ceviches. Ceviches use citrus juice to pickle fish and shellfish; citrus fruit was introduced in the Americas by the Spanish.

"This recipe makes a very refreshing salad for a hot summer day, and an ideal picnic or buffet item. It's important to make sure that the vegetables don't get overcooked in the pickling brine, or they run the risk of becoming too soggy. Note that the chicken should be marinated overnight. The pickled vegetables can be made up to one week ahead."

Marinade

2 teaspoons black peppercorns
½ teaspoon allspice berries
½ teaspoon cloves
½ teaspoon cumin seeds
4 teaspoons dried Mexican oregano
24 roasted garlic cloves, minced to a paste
Salt

2 tablespoons rice wine vinegar

Two 8-ounce boneless, skinless chicken breasts

Pickling Liquid

2 quarts rice wine vinegar

1 quart water

8 serrano chiles, thinly sliced into rings, with seeds

1 teaspoon dried thyme

2 teaspoons fennel seeds

1 tablespoon coriander seeds

1 teaspoon allspice berries

1 tablespoon star anise

1 cinnamon stick

2 cloves

1 cup sugar

1 cup packed fresh cilantro leaves

Vegetables

2 red bell peppers, seeded and cut into ¼-inch rings

2 yellow bell peppers, seeded and cut into ¼-inch rings

2 poblano chiles, seeded and cut into ¼-inch rings

6 garlic cloves

Salt

To Serve

8 ounces mixed baby greens, such as arugula, mizuna, frisée, mustard greens, red leaf lettuce (about 8 cups)

12 fresh cilantro sprigs for garnish

To prepare the marinade, grind the pepper, allspice, cloves, cumin, and oregano in a spice grinder or blender to a fine powder. Transfer to a mixing bowl, add the garlic, 1 teaspoon salt, and vinegar, and mix well.

Rub the chicken breasts with the marinade, cover with plastic wrap, and let sit overnight in the refrigerator.

To prepare the pickling liquid, place the vinegar, water, chiles, herbs, spices, and sugar in a saucepan and bring to a simmer. Reduce the liquid over medium-high heat by one-third. Remove from the heat, add the cilantro, and let steep for 20 minutes. Strain into a clean pan and return to a simmer.

Cook the vegetables in the pickling liquid until cooked, 8 to 10 minutes. Transfer to a bowl, cover with some of the pickling liquid, and allow to cool.

Meanwhile, preheat the oven to 325°F. Season the marinated chicken with salt to taste, place on a baking sheet or in an ovenproof dish, and roast for 8 to 10 minutes, until cooked through. Let cool and cut into thin strips.

To serve, place a bed of baby greens on each serving plate. Top with the pickled vegetables and arrange the sliced chicken at the side of the vegetables, on top of the greens.

Garnish with the cilantro sprigs.

Serves 4

Orchid's Tangy Cool Noodles

BARBARA TROPP (1948–2001)

"I learned to taste food—and also to become cheerfully obsessed by it—during two years in Taipei in the early 1970s, when I was a graduate student in Chinese poetry living in the very traditional homes of families from northern and central China. When I returned to the United States to continue graduate study, my chin hung down to my knees, so much did I miss the terrific food I'd eaten daily in Taiwan. To assuage my spirit, I taught myself to cook the food I'd loved, drawing on books, Chinese friends, and the fabulous taste memories I'd brought home.

"This Peking-style cold noodle dish was the first of my 'creations.' I mixed it up in the sink because I didn't have a bowl big enough! In Chinese fashion, I named it after myself, Precious Orchid being my very lyric Chinese name. In some ways, I think this first dish is probably the best dish I've ever made, so full is it of my love for Taiwan and the Chinese people who embraced me."

> 1 pound very thin (1/16 inch) fresh or frozen Chinese egg noodles
>
> 3½ tablespoons Japanese sesame oil
>
> 3½ tablespoons black soy sauce
>
> 1½ tablespoons balsamic vinegar
>
> 2 tablespoons sugar
>
> 2 teaspoons kosher salt
>
> ½ to 1 tablespoon hot chile oil
>
> ¼ cup green and white scallion rings, plus extra for garnish

Defrost the noodles, if frozen, and fluff well to separate the strands.

Cook the noodles in ample boiling water until al dente, swishing occasionally with chopsticks, 2 to 3 minutes for fresh noodles. Drain, rinse under cold running water to chill, then drain well.

Combine the seasonings in a large bowl. Add the drained cold noodles and toss well with your fingers to coat and separate each strand. Add the scallion rings and toss to mix. Taste, and adjust with a dash more sugar, if needed, to bring forth the heat.

Serve in bowls of a complementary color, garnished with a sprinkling of scallion.

For do-ahead cooks, seal and refrigerate the finished noodles for a day or even two before serving at room temperature. The flavors only enlarge as the noodles sit.

Serves 6 to 8

Spaghetti alla Carbonara

JOYCE GOLDSTEIN, formerly of Square One, San Francisco, CA

"Given our new 'cholesterol consciousness,' this is not the ideal pasta to eat every day, but it is my favorite. I spent the better part of a year in Rome eating this in innumerable trattorie, trying to find the best version. Now I eat it a few times a year and still find it delicious. It is difficult to get the perfect texture, and provides a constant challenge for the cook to not scramble the eggs or overcrisp the pancetta. But it is worth the effort."

¾ to 1 pound pancetta, cut in ¼-inch-thick slices

Salt

1 pound spaghetti

4 eggs

8 to 10 tablespoons grated Parmesan cheese or part pecorino and part Parmesan cheese

1 tablespoon freshly ground black pepper

2 tablespoons butter

2 tablespoons olive oil

Cut the pancetta into ¼-inch-wide pieces.

Bring a large kettle of water to a boil. Add a tablespoon of salt and drop in the pasta.

Combine the eggs, cheese, and pepper in a large serving bowl. Keep near the stove or atop a warming shelf.

While the pasta is cooking, heat the butter and oil in a large saucepan and add the diced pancetta. Cook, stirring occasionally, until bubbles appear in the pan. The pancetta will be cooked but not crisp. When the pasta is al dente, drain well and add to the bowl with the eggs and pancetta and most of the drippings. Toss very quickly to combine. The sauce should be a thick liquid. Serve at once. Pass additional cheese and pepper if desired.

Serves 4 as an entree, 8 as a pasta course

Crème Brûlée Napoleon with Hazelnut

MICHEL RICHARD, Citronelle, Washington, DC

"When I was sixteen, on vacation in Spain, I was madly in love with a local young maiden. We went on a date, to a restaurant, and we ate a crème Catalane, which was a kind of crème brûlée with anise flavor. After that, I had my first kiss. In the United States, we prefer the vanilla to the anise, and I added the crunch to the crème brûlée, with my pastry background, to constitute a napoleon. Both the silky texture of the cream and the crispy and crunchy texture of the thousand leaves complement each other very well. When I bite into the 'cake of love,' it reminds me of the Catalan adventure. Today, the Crème Brûlée Napoleon with Hazelnut still remains my favorite dessert as the Crème D'Amour.

"This was the most popular dessert at Citrus in Los Angeles. Its success does not come as a total surprise to me, for it is the ultimate napoleon. Made without flour, its crème brûlée filling is lighter and more refined than the pastry cream classically used. Studded with chopped caramelized hazelnuts, its phyllo dough layers are even crispier and crunchier than the puff pastry traditionally sandwiching the creamy interior. Unlike puff pastry, phyllo dough doesn't shrink. I've used a caramel sauce here, but the vanilla base of the filling lends itself to any flavoring or fruit accompaniment. This spectacular dessert offers an advantage to the home cook as well in that it does not require a *Grande Diplome de Patisserie* to execute. Though its multiple components may make it appear complicated, steps are simple to achieve. Everything except assembling the layers can be completed in advance.

"The crème brûlée, caramel sauce, and hazelnut-sugar mixture can be prepared two days in advance and refrigerated. The phyllo dough squares can be baked at any time during the day dessert is to be served. Assemble the napoleons just before presenting."

> **1 cup hazelnuts**
> **¾ cup sugar**
> **8 sheets phyllo dough (defrosted overnight in refrigerator, if frozen)**
> **8 tablespoons (1 stick) unsalted butter, melted**
> **About ½ cup confectioners' sugar**
> **Crème Brûlée (recipe follows)**
> **Caramel sauce (page 265)**

Preheat the oven to 350°F. Place the hazelnuts on a small baking sheet and toast until brown, about 15 minutes. Rub the nuts in a sieve or towel to husk. Grind the nuts coarsely with the sugar in a food processor, pulsing on and off. (The nuts can be prepared ahead, transferred to an airtight container, and set aside at room temperature.)

Preheat the oven to 300°F. Line two large baking sheets with parchment paper. Remove the phyllo from the package and unroll. Remove one sheet and cover the remaining phyllo with plastic and a damp towel. Brush the sheet with melted butter and sprinkle generously with the hazelnut mixture.

Top with a second sheet of phyllo, pressing to seal. Brush with butter and sprinkle with the nut mixture. Repeat with the third and fourth sheet.

Using a ruler as a guide, trim the edges with a knife or pastry wheel to form a 12 by 16-inch rectangle. Cut the pastry into three strips lengthwise and four strips crosswise, forming twelve 4-inch squares. Transfer the squares to the prepared baking sheets in a single layer, using a large spatula. Bake for 10 minutes, or until brown.

Make and bake twelve additional 4-inch squares, using four sheets of phyllo and the remaining butter and nut mixture. Rewrap the remaining phyllo and refrigerate or freeze for another use.

Preheat the broiler. Place as many phyllo squares as will fit under the broiler at one time on a baking sheet. Sieve confectioners' sugar generously over the squares and broil several inches below the heat source until golden brown, about a minute, watching carefully. Transfer to wire racks in a single layer. Repeat with the remaining squares. (The squares may be set aside for several hours, if prepared ahead.)

To serve, divide the crème brûlée among sixteen pastry squares, nut side up, spreading evenly. Make eight napoleons by stacking two crème brûlée-filled squares and topping with an unfilled square, nut side up. Place the napoleons in the centers of eight large plates. Reheat the caramel sauce and ladle around the napoleons. Serve immediately.

Notes: Phyllo dough is less brittle and less likely to tear if it has not been frozen. Though harder to find, unfrozen phyllo dough can often be purchased at a

Middle Eastern market. When working with phyllo dough, keep unused pieces wrapped in plastic and covered with a damp towel so they don't dry out.

Prepare half of the phyllo squares using half of the phyllo dough, melted butter, and the nut mixture and bake. Prepare the remaining phyllo squares with the remaining ingredients while the first half is baking.

Makes 8 napoleons

Crème Brûlée

½ cup milk

2 cups heavy cream

½ cup sugar

1 or 2 vanilla beans, slit lengthwise

9 room-temperature egg yolks, blended with fork

Place the milk, cream, and sugar in a heavy, medium saucepan. Scrape the seeds from the vanilla beans into the milk mixture. Add the beans and bring to a boil over medium-high heat. Remove from the heat and let the beans steep for at least an hour or until the mixture cools to room temperature. Discard the beans (or wash, dry, and reserve for another use).

Preheat the oven to 300°F. Place a 9 by 13-inch baking dish in a larger baking pan. Pour enough water into the larger pan to come three-quarters of the way up the sides of the baking dish. Remove the baking dish and place the baking pan with water in the oven to preheat.

Whisk the egg yolks into the cooled custard mixture. Strain through a fine sieve into a baking dish.

Place the dish in a baking pan with water and bake until the custard is set and a knife inserted into the center comes out dry, 45 minutes to 1 hour. Remove the baking dish from the water bath. Cool, then cover and refrigerate until 15 minutes before assembling the napoleons. (The crème brûlée can be prepared two days ahead.)

Adjust the heat so the water in the water bath does not go above a gentle simmer. If the water boils, the custard can curdle.

Makes about 2 cups

Caramel Sauce

1½ cups sugar

1¼ cups heavy cream

Place the sugar in a heavy medium saucepan. Cover with water and cook over low heat until the sugar dissolves, swirling the pan occasionally. Increase the heat and boil until the sugar caramelizes and turns a deep mahogany brown, watching carefully so it doesn't burn. Stand back to avoid being splattered and gradually pour in the cream. Simmer the sauce, stirring occasionally, until the caramel dissolves and the sauce is smooth and thick, about 3 minutes. Cool, then cover and refrigerate. (The sauce can be prepared two days ahead.)

To serve, stir over medium heat until melted and warm, thinning with additional cream or milk as desired. (The sauce can also be served cold. Thin with additional cream or milk.)

Makes about 1¾ cups

Omelette with Bacon and Croutons

JUDY RODGERS, Zuni Cafe,
San Francisco, CA

"I spent a lucky year in France with the Troisgros family in 1973. Some of my fondest memories are of homey suppers I shared with Madeleine Troisgros Serraille (la soeur) and her family, while the famous frères were stirring up sorrel sauce back at the restaurant where I lived. She often made a huge, satisfying omelette for dinner and this was one of my favorites."

Cut 4 slices of bacon into ½-inch-wide bands and set aside.

Tear some stale Tuscan-style bread into mouthful-sized wads, toss with virgin olive oil whisked with a little bit of Dijon mustard, and season with sea salt. Toast until just golden on the edges, but tender in the middle. Toss with lots of freshly cracked pepper.

Crack 9 very fresh eggs into a deep bowl and beat with a whisk about 30 strokes. Add 9 tiny pinches of salt and beat a few more strokes. Do not overbeat; the eggs do not need to be perfectly homogeneous.

Heat a large, steel omelette pan and render the bacon until it is just beginning to color. Add approximately 1½ tablespoons unsalted butter and raise the heat. When the butter is just starting to foam, whisk the eggs once and pour over. I prefer my omelettes rolled, so I slide the cooked egg to the far edge of the pan as I go. When about half of the eggs are set, drop in the warm toasted croutons, and continue sliding the cooked eggs forward, enveloping the croutons as you go. The bacon will end up dispersed throughout the omelette, rather than bunched up in the middle. Once the omelette is completely "rolled" tip the pan forward to brown the eggs slightly. Tip onto a warm platter, and serve instantly. Madeleine would always serve a salad of dandelions or other bitter greens afterward, to be eaten on the same plate to mix with the remains of the omelette.

Serves 4

Winter Vegetable Couscous with Ras El Hanout

GORDON HAMERSLEY, Hamersley's Bistro,
Boston, MA

"I'll never forget the first time I ate couscous in Paris. I went with a friend who lived there and he told me all about the North African influence in French cooking. We sat in this tiny place filled with unfamiliar smells and demolished this platter of couscous, vegetables, and lamb. The next day I went to the North African market to buy the spice mixture ras el hanout to bring back with me to America. The customs man checked it out with interest, too! Ever since, I've always included North African flavors in my conception of bistro cooking."

4 tablespoons olive oil for cooking the vegetables, plus 5 tablespoons

3 portobello mushrooms, cleaned and sliced

1 red onion, peeled and quartered

1 pint Brussels sprouts

1 celery root, peeled and cut into large chunks

2 purple-top turnips, peeled and quartered

6 large chunks rutabaga, peeled

2 leeks, cleaned and sliced

1 medium-sized cauliflower separated into chunks

1 teaspoon thyme and marjoram, mixed

Salt and cracked pepper

6 cups vegetable stock

5 cups couscous

1 tablespoon ras el hanout (a complex Moroccan spice blend that can contain dozens of spices; can be ordered from www.kalustyans.com or other specialty food store)

2 tablespoons lemon juice

1 tablespoon Dijon mustard

10 parsley leaves for garnish

In a pot large enough to hold the stew easily, heat the 4 tablespoons olive oil until hot but not smoking. Add the vegetables and herbs; stew them covered until they are about half cooked. Add

3 cups of the vegetable stock and continue cooking until the vegetables are cooked. They should be just tender. Season with salt and pepper to taste. At the end of the cooking the flavors of the vegetables should have blended together well, but each one should hold together and be distinct.

Meanwhile, cook the couscous.

Wash the couscous with water and add the ras el hanout and salt to taste. Try 1 or 2 teaspoons to start and see how it goes. Do not overpower the dish but add enough to get the taste and add character to the dish. Let it stand for about 20 minutes and then rub the couscous through your hands, separating the grains as you go.

To make the vegetable vinaigrette, reduce 2 cups of the vegetable stock over medium heat by three-quarters. Add the lemon juice and let cool. Add the mustard and then whisk in the 5 tablespoons olive oil. Season with salt and pepper to taste and reserve.

When ready to serve, make a well in the vegetable stew and put the couscous in the middle. Add a cup of vegetable stock to the pan and cover. Cook over medium heat until the couscous is heated through and the vegetables are hot.

To serve, slide the vegetables and couscous onto a warm platter and garnish with the parsley sprigs. Serve the vinaigrette on the side.

Serves 10 to 12

9. Persevering in the Face of Reality
THROUGH BAD TIMES AND GOOD

When you make as many mistakes as I've made, then you'll know as much as I know. **JACQUES TORRES**

In the days when I was a beginning cook, almost every mistake I made—from forgetting a pan of nuts that went from roasting to smoking in the oven, to nearly slicing off the tip of my finger on a meat slicer—caused me to question whether I was really cut out for this profession. I thought then that what made a great chef great was having never made a mistake. I wasn't alone.

Jackie Shen recalls crying constantly for the first six weeks she worked as an apprentice. "No one had ever yelled at me before," she says. "It was a real ego-deflator. I felt like a piece of dust. I thought I must be too dumb and couldn't hack it." Wayne Nish remembers, "One guy I worked for screamed at me so much I knew exactly how many fillings he had."

But mistakes are par for the course for a cook. "Perfection is not a word for this world," maintains Jean Joho. "It does not exist. Everybody makes mistakes. Anyone who says he never makes a mistake is a liar."

While the country's leading chefs possess the gift of being able to make the difficult seem effortless, this is a result of their years of experience—which includes making many, many mistakes. What led to their success was persevering in the face of reality or triumphing over difficulties, setbacks, or even out-and-out failures. Rather than being debilitating, to leading chefs these experiences represented just another (albeit painful) way for them to learn.

"Adverse situations are the best teachers. Learning by mistakes is one of the most profitable ways to do it—painful, but profitable—because you learn really quickly. You have to. You'll either learn how to do it or you won't be there," says Jimmy Schmidt. "There are many times when I questioned what the hell I was doing, why I was even in this business, because of the long hours, the relentlessness, the thankless jobs. But you have to have perseverance. No great gains occur by doing simple, easy things. It necessitates long, regular, steady, meticulous growth. Life isn't a hundred-yard dash. It's a long-distance race."

Gina DePalma sees as the key to a career as a chef overcoming adversity, again and again. "Making it through the first few years is the toughest. You make more money than folding shirts at the Gap, but not much," she admits. "I will tell cooks who want to come to New York and cook that 'You gotta have game,' because it is tough and there is so much you're up against every day. Just living on the pay is really tough until you get to a titled position. At one job, I grossed $425 a week and had to live in New York on that. Believe me, I ate a lot of Minute Rice and frozen peas!"

Larry Forgione believes, "You should always look at every experience, even the negative ones, as building this wealth of information. Just step out into the world and go forward."

Getting Their Feet Wet

When today's leading chefs were just starting out in their careers, they made their share of silly mistakes. Susan Regis recalls her embarrassment at not having the kitchen lingo down in her first cooking job at Seasons at the Bostonian Hotel. "I thought 'rare squab' was some kind of extinct bird," she remembers.

Bradley Ogden dropped out of The Culinary Institute of America after twelve months and went to work as a chef at a Holiday Inn. He remembers, "I was supposed to be making meatballs. I tried making them three times, and I couldn't get them to hold together into a ball shape. Finally, I asked someone who pointed out that meatballs were supposed to be formed when the meat was raw, not after it had already been cooked!"

When Ogden decided to return to The Culinary Institute of America four years later to complete his degree, it meant borrowing money from his in-laws and living in a self-described hole-in-the-wall apartment with his pregnant wife and child. It also meant working full-time while he finished his second year. "Being older and more mature made me extremely motivated," he admits. Upon graduation, he received the award given to the graduating student voted by professors as being most likely to succeed, not to mention numerous job offers.

On the drive out to the job he had accepted in Kansas City, Ogden had many of his treasured possessions, which were being moved, stolen in St. Louis. But he finally arrived, and moved his family into their home before his scheduled start date of September 15. He recalls that the night before he was to start, "A major flood hit Kansas City, wiping out the restaurant."

A philosophical Ogden admits, "Actually, it worked to my advantage. They gave me a job at another restaurant, paying me a good salary, working forty hours a week—which was the first time in my life I'd ever worked only forty hours a week. During that time, I got to work with all the corporate people, and work on all the opening menus and develop the dishes for the reopening in January."

Others' early jobs weren't always such a bed of roses. In one of the first kitchens where Anne Rosenzweig worked, she was hired by a chef who thought women didn't have the stamina for kitchen work. "He thought he would upset me so much that in two or three days I would leave in tears," she recalls. She, however, saw it as a challenge. "I thought it was kind of silly. Having done field work at nineteen and living on my own in a mud hut in Africa, some guy telling me I couldn't do something didn't mean a thing."

Co-workers sometimes had their own unique ways of welcoming cooks to a new kitchen. Mary Sue Milliken recalls that on her third day at a particular job, a co-worker offered her a sea urchin to try and, not wanting to seem unadventurous, she popped it into her mouth. "It was horrible—it hadn't even been washed, let alone cooked, and it was incredibly gritty," she remembers. "The guy was fired soon thereafter, for other reasons."

> I never really had a setback on the job. I had a much harder time getting used to the lifestyle in every new place: Where do I get my coffee? Where can I play soccer on Sundays? And where can I go for a great meal?
>
> **MARCUS SAMUELSSON**

Persevering in the Face of Reality **271**

Diversity in the Kitchen

In 1998, 58 percent of the employees in the restaurant industry were women, and almost 30 percent of all cooking school students were women. About 12 percent of those employed in the restaurant industry were African-Americans, and 16 percent were of Hispanic origin, which is the fastest-growing population in foodservice.

As the women chefs interviewed for this book exemplify, women are represented at the very forefront of cooking in this country. But women's place at other levels of the profession has gone through a real evolution. Women were not admitted to The Culinary Institute of America until 1970, whereas they now represent about one-third of the Institute's incoming students (and more than half of the students in its Baking and Pastry Arts program). In foodservice across the board women hold more positions than men, with nearly two-thirds being in supervisory positions.

As is true in every other type of organization in America, women are likely to find certain lines of work and employers within the profession more accepting than others. In particular, pastry work is associated with a somewhat less-pressured pace. As Rick Katz points out, "It's not as hectic as working the line because, in general, baking isn't tied to the service of a restaurant." Pastry chefs are typically the first cooks at work and often the first to leave at night, and have somewhat more predictable hours than line cooks. In addition, the work itself tends to offer pastry chefs more independence. Says Nancy Silverton, "I always liked having a small part of the kitchen that I could control myself."

As for employers who provide a fair environment for women, they're somewhat more difficult to predict. When Marcel Desaulniers was cooking in the 1960s, he'd never worked with a woman on the line, and only recalled them in the garde manger station. "Yet when we opened Trellis in 1980, my first sous chef was a woman," he recalls. "I went to the CIA to recruit cooks, and I was not looking for a woman chef—I was looking for talent. She stayed with us for the first three years and went through the same hell as I did every day. When we opened, we also had a woman on lead sauté and two other local women working the line.

"I didn't make these hiring decisions to be a trendsetter," Desaulniers points out. "I grew up with five sisters, so I never had any misconceptions about what a woman could or could not do. Now there are six women who compose our baking department, lots in the pantry, and a couple on the line. Gender is simply not an issue in our kitchen."

The restaurant business does not lend itself well to flexible work policies that might ease parental pressures for either men or women. As women still bear the majority of the responsibility for child rearing in most American families, however, this issue is likely to be of particular concern to them. A cook needs to cook when the restaurant's customers want to eat—period—whether that means breakfast at 7 A.M. or post-theater dinner at 11 P.M. The Women Chefs and Restaurateurs Association (see

Appendix B), spearheaded by the late Barbara Tropp, was formed in 1993 to address issues of concern to women in the profession.

Nationally known black chefs beyond Edna Lewis and Marcus Samuelsson are difficult to identify, although this is also changing. More African-Americans appear to be entering the profession, and are in fact being encouraged to do so by organizations such as The Culinary Institute of America's Black Culinarian Alumni Chapter, founded by Jason Wallace and Alex Askew. While their historical lack of representation at the higher levels of the profession is clear, their hesitancy to enter the profession has been lessening. It's only recently that the "chef-as-celebrity" phenomenon has brought acclaim to the profession. In years past, blacks might have become cooks because they had few other options open to them.

Edna Lewis comments, "I have noticed that there are a lot of blacks [who] are going to cooking school, male and female. And they get tucked away at the Marriotts. You never hear or see the daylight of them because they are not well known to chefs in the restaurants. In that way, you don't know how many black chefs there are. People who get recognition are people [who] work in restaurants. They are visible and, if the food is good, people find out who the chef is. But in hotels it's so impersonal and you have so many thousands of people to cook for—I don't think you have a chance to be known."

Some of the most difficult kitchens in the United States for minorities and women to break into and advance in have been those with a very traditional French attitude. However, a sign of our changing times echoes in the conviction of French-born chef Jean-Louis Palladin ten years ago that "a mixed kitchen is important to me. You need to have a mix. I have four women and three blacks in my kitchen." Norman Van Aken adds, "One of the interesting things that I've found is that it makes no difference if they're men or women or whatever—either they're tough as nails, or they're not."

Chefs are beginning to recognize the value of diversity and the creative energy that comes from having people of many different backgrounds working together. Cultural diversity brings obvious benefits to a kitchen, in terms of work habits, techniques, familiarity with various ingredients, and even styles of cooking, which has the potential to help everyone learn more.

Marcus Samuelsson observes that ultimately, cooking is a very fair playing field. "You can either do it, or you can't—and it doesn't matter if you are black, yellow, or green," he says. "I will always have a mixed kitchen, and I don't mean just black and white. I want Indians, Asians, South Americans—a large mix of cultures and sexes.

"Cooking is ultimately color-blind and gender-blind, because a chef can't afford to be prejudiced," says Samuelsson. "What it all gets down to is that at eight o'clock, we all need each other."

I don't think there's any discrimination. My son tells me that I just refuse to see it. I'm Mexican, a woman, short, and sometimes fat. But I believe that if you're fulfilling your talents, other people admire that and want to help you succeed.

ZARELA MARTINEZ

Murphy's Law often rules the day, especially on days when the stakes are particularly high. Replacing Charles Palmer as chef of the Waccabuc Country Club, Todd English made careful preparations for his first lunch serving the club's "grand dames." While the food was being served, English had to nurse both a cut finger and jangled nerves upon learning that he was fifteen lunches short. "We ended up figuring something out—you always do," he says, adding, "But maybe that's why I serve so much food at Olives."

Trying to meet customers' requests—at all hours—sometimes thwarted chefs' own perfectionistic standards. Dieter Schorner was the pastry chef at La Côte Basque when a customer came in one night asking for a soufflé at 11:30 P.M. "I had some mixture left [for a soufflé], but if it sits too long, the air goes out of [the beaten mixture]. Since it was so late the soufflé fell flat like a pancake the moment it was placed in front of the customer," he recalls.

Schorner said that instead of reprimanding him, the chef, who liked him, decided to have some fun. "When the manager on duty came back all upset to find out what had happened, the chef told him, 'Well, usually we have a pump in the kitchen to blow air into the soufflé, and the pump broke.' The manager shouted, 'Chef, I've told you, whatever you need, you get! Go out tomorrow and fix the pump!'"

It's hard to be inspired to excel when you can't stand the products you must work with. When Jean-Georges Vongerichten first traveled to Thailand to work, he found he hated many of the ingredients he tried. "The first time I tasted coriander, it tasted like soap," he says. "I thought it was inedible. I couldn't touch anything because everything was too spicy for me."

Vongerichten, who later opened the successful Thai-inspired restaurant Vong (NYC), also faced cross-cultural problems trying to manage other cooks as a consulting chef in Thailand. "Nothing was working," he recalls. "I was the only European in a restaurant with fifty employees and the cooks wouldn't listen to me. Someone finally had to explain to me that because the chef there was Thai, he was losing face and that I had to talk to the chef to have things done through him. But I didn't find this out for six months."

Given their hard work and frequent frustrations, sometimes chefs simply burn out. Alice Waters thinks that this seems to happen around the seven-year mark for most cooks. "It's very difficult to tell somebody that you can see that their focus is different from other people's in the kitchen and that they're not 100 percent here but clearly thinking about other things," she says. "It's important that they go off and see what it's like to work in other circumstances and to find out what their real passions are. I try to encourage people to move on and change. I'm a big believer in the sabbatical program. In an informal way, it does happen here. After seven or eight years, I just say, 'Get out of here, and go take a trip for six months, and see what you think when you get back.' Very often people come back and they're a lot better and it's great to have them return."

Some of the lessons that can only be learned over the years include trusting your gut instinct. Nancy Silverton and husband, Mark Peel, moved to New York City with the mission of revamping Maxwell's Plum, but left less than a year later. Silverton says, "It didn't work out, but we don't regret it. We learned that no matter how much money, press, and prestige is at stake, you must be in an environment that makes you happy." In fact, it was after this failed experience that the couple decided to take some time off to travel to Italy, which in turn inspired them to later open Campanile in Los Angeles.

Sometimes setbacks strike when they're least expected. Norman Van Aken recalls refusing to cook Bisquick shrimp at a restaurant where he was working. "I got fired," he admits. As chef of David Keh's restaurant Cafe Marimba (NYC), Zarela Martinez spent her days in the kitchen and her evenings working the door. She helped it become successful, and decided to celebrate by taking a six-week trip to Mexico, during which she was fired. The restaurant took a nosedive from there until she went back as executive chef to restore it to its old luster.

Being asked to move on can prompt realizations of changes one should have made on one's own. Emily Luchetti admits, "One of the reasons I switched to desserts was that Jeremiah Tower came to me when I was the lunch sous chef at Stars and said, 'It's not working out—we need to make a change.' I went home and looked in the mirror and said, 'Oh my God!' Then I looked a little longer and realized that he was right—I didn't really like working the line. I hadn't admitted to myself consciously that I wasn't doing that great a job.

"That is when the epiphany came. I asked myself, 'What do I like?' and the answer was 'desserts.' So that's where I went.

"The key is to be honest with yourself about your likes and dislikes," says Luchetti. "You are not going to succeed all the time. Everyone has something that doesn't work out in their life. You have to look at it in the mirror, wrestle with it, and move on. That is how you'll last in this business: by rolling over the bumps. Otherwise, you'll fade into oblivion."

A Woman's Perspective

I was the only woman at Bouley [a month after it opened], and it was total chaos because the restaurant was so new. I wanted to get onto the hot line but kept getting passed over by men. They continued to give the line jobs to cooks who had less experience than I did, so I felt very frustrated. The irony was that I was very organized and good at garde-manger, so they didn't want to have to replace me. I finally complained enough and got onto the fish station at lunch. I had to teach myself about fish, do all the purees, prepare two bus tubs of small containers of mise en place, set up my station, and prep the chef's station, all before 11:30 A.M. I was definitely in over my head, but I managed to rise to the challenge and I learned a great deal.
AMY SCHERBER

Being a woman may have actually been an opportunity for me. Because I was sort of an anomaly in the kitchen, people took notice of my perseverance and talent. I never thought about gender or being a woman in the kitchen—I just thought about cooking. Yes, some men have a problem having women in the kitchen. Yes, some women are too focused on the fact that they are women versus thinking of themselves as a member of the brigade. But it is only an issue if someone makes it an issue.   TRACI DES JARDINS

It's important to take responsibility for yourself and your career. I don't want to give the impression that there aren't people who have to work in difficult situations and can't always do something about it. That being said, my attitude has always been that if you are in an environment where you are not getting positive support, leave! You are not going to change the world overnight, so go find a place that is supportive and positive. If you are a woman and working for a jerk, you have to ask yourself, "Am I honing my skills? Am I getting more out of this than being demeaned?" If it gets to the point where his being demeaning is overriding what he is teaching you, then get out.   EMILY LUCHETTI

As a woman, you have to watch out for the mothering instinct. It is easy to fall into that trap. I had an African-American ex-con dishwasher, and sometimes after work when no other cooks were around, he would very respectfully say, "You have to be tougher on the crew—you are being too nice." And of course he was right! ODESSA PIPER

Bad Reviews

Restaurant reviews have also caused their share of ups and downs. Martinez recalls getting reviewed by Bryan Miller in *The New York Times* when she was chef of Cafe Marimba, and the huge letdown of receiving only one star. "I cried for three days. Then I sat down and wrote him a four-page letter about how I believed that the more talent you had, the greater the responsibility that accompanied it." In the letter, Martinez detailed the responsibility that she felt—and took—in sitting down with her waiters on a daily basis to explain each dish and each ingredient. She eventually won a two-star review from Miller.

While Mario Batali says he likes to shrug off most of the downpoints in his career with a beer and a laugh, one particular incident with a restaurant critic still makes him cringe. "I once sent Gael Greene [*New York* magazine's legendary restaurant critic] a plate of steamed mussels—and only then realized that the weird smell in the kitchen had been the mussels. The server put the plate in front of her, and she immediately said, 'Take them away!' That was a crushing moment. The waiter brought them back and I called the fish company and yelled at them, because I'd just gotten them in fresh that day. In hindsight, as it was the middle of June or July, I shouldn't have had them on the menu in the first place."

The mere thought of being reviewed can be, well, unsettling. Wayne Nish had just become the chef of La Colombe d'Or (NYC) when Bryan Miller walked in one night with an elderly couple. "By this time, I had already cooked for Miller [at The Quilted Giraffe and The Casual Quilted Giraffe] maybe sixteen, eighteen times, on separate occasions. I had been a senior member at The Quilted Giraffe, I was well trusted and was even allowed to make up my own stuff spontaneously for him during the review process." How did this excellent preparation prepare Nish for being reviewed once he was himself the chef? "I recognized him, and I went in the kitchen and threw up," Nish admits.

Miller returned for subsequent visits, tasting everything on the menu and even a few specials. Nish knew his review was imminent. "I figured if I was lucky, I'd get a good two-star review and I'd be really happy," he says. So it came as a total surprise to open the paper and find that Miller had given La Colombe d'Or not two but three stars. "I hadn't even been in the business for five years, and it was the first time a nonwhite-tablecloth restaurant had been given three stars."

> There's so much that can go wrong in a restaurant, and yet the standard we're judged by is "perfection."
>
> **GORDON HAMERSLEY**

How did Nish respond to receiving such an unprecedented, positive review? "I went into the kitchen to show the newspaper to the guys. The pressure was off, the relief came, and I turned around and threw up again."

Marcus Samuelsson: A Chef Who Happens to Be Black

"From day one, my [adoptive] father told me that because I was a person of color, I would run into people who would have an issue with it. By the time I was eighteen, I knew that to be true: How could people decide they didn't like me if they didn't even know me?

"In German and Dutch [kitchens], a lot of expressions even include the word 'nigger.' For example, they will use the term 'nigger' instead of dishwasher. What am I going to do—take on a sixty-year-old chef, in his world? If you are a person of color, you can have a war every day if you want. Or, you can overcome it and beat it.

"It is no different for a woman who works in a male-dominated world: You can't allow that negative energy to affect you. You have to develop a thick skin, better work habits, and better working relationships.

"The first time I saw any controversy regarding background was when I was working in France, and it was directed at Americans. The Americans couldn't handle it. Since they were young happening cooks in America and good enough to be sent to France, not to be given the time of day was more than they could deal with. They didn't have the key to know that in that moment, it was up to them. Every foreigner gets that treatment in France. Of course, white people don't think of themselves as foreigners in Europe, but they are. They weren't fair to me, either, but I just took it and channeled it to be better.

"I think being a minority actually helped me in France because I'd dealt with those attitudes from the time I was eight. By the time I was eighteen, I was stronger for it. Those twenty-two-year-old guys from Connecticut working in France had no idea how to deal with adversity.

"When Patrick Clark was alive, he was really the focus of African-American chefs because he was American. At first, I turned a lot of [publicity opportunities] down because I did not want to be pigeon-holed as a black chef. Now, I am more comfortable in my career and my ability. I am not known as a great black chef, but as a great chef who happens to be black."

Some chefs fairly credit a review with providing feedback that, while hard to accept, can point to areas that need improvement. Janos Wilder, who makes a practice of calling his staff together to discuss the contents of certain reviews, says that [former *New York Times* restaurant critic] Mimi Sheraton reviewed his and other restaurants in the Southwest immediately after he'd changed cooks: "She creamed us. Unfortunately it wasn't hard to believe that we had screwed up," Wilder admits. "Anything but a great review is bad."

Even a great review doesn't always ensure success. When Bryan Miller awarded Patrick Clark's restaurant Metro two stars, Clark was on top of the world. He had made a name for himself in New York City after successfully opening the Odeon in 1980 in Tribeca, then "a wasteland—there was nothing else in Tribeca," and later opening Cafe Luxembourg on the Upper West Side. So opening his own place in 1988 represented the culmination of a dream. He went all out, finding a great space on the Upper East Side and designing the kitchen and restaurant with noted restaurant designer Adam Tihany.

Then he learned that even a two-star review wasn't an ace in the hole. The downturn in the economy hit, and large monthly rent payments on the space started taking their toll. Metro closed in May 1990. Clark decided to take a month off. But a chef as talented as Clark doesn't stay down long, and he was soon tapped to run the kitchen at Bice in Los Angeles, where business was hurting. By the time he left to become chef of the Hay-Adams Hotel in Washington, D.C., he says the restaurant had tripled its weekly gross. Clark was eventually tapped to manage one of the top-grossing and highest-profile restaurants in America, New York's Tavern on the Green.

Money and Management

Some chefs had a hard time even getting the money to open their own places, despite their talent. While chef at Commander's Palace in New Orleans, Emeril Lagasse had a dream. "I lived across the street from this burned-out building in the warehouse district and I had this burning desire to turn it into my own restaurant," he says. But when he approached bank after bank about financing it, "I got turned down by every bank in the city."

Finally, Lagasse met up with the most conservative financial institution in the state, which believed in him and in the project. "They gave me the money in ten minutes." Still, he didn't have a lot of money and was unemployed for three and a half months while he spent sixteen to eighteen hours a day building every piece of the restaurant. So whatever became of the made-from-scratch restaurant in the burned-out building in the New Orleans warehouse district that most banks didn't believe in? For starters, Emeril's had an hour-and-forty-five-minute wait on opening night.

The shock of opening a restaurant is you find out that you thought you were doing everything only to find out you weren't. The biggest mistake chefs make is thinking that because they are great cooks it is enough to run a restaurant. It is not even close, it is barely a drop in the bucket!

SANFORD D'AMATO

A winter downturn in business forced Rick Bayless to rethink the way he ran Frontera Grill. "In a way, I was glad to have down months," he admits. "It made us take a look at cutting our fixed costs without cutting labor or food costs. We changed our laundry service, we changed our dishwashing system, and we cut telephone costs."

That frame of mind came in handy during the summer. Bayless landed a license for an outdoor café and, not wanting to hire people to staff it whom he would later have to lay off, he decided to pose his dilemma to his staff. He offered them the opportunity to earn extra pay for the extra work over the summer, which they accepted. "They worked hard, but they made a killing over four months," he says.

Knowing Your Market

Other lessons involve understanding your market when you venture into unknown territory. Cindy Pawlcyn and her then-partners opened two Fog City Diners in Japan in a joint venture with a Japanese company. Their idea was to copy the San Francisco restaurant exactly in terms of design, menu—everything.

Offering the San Francisco restaurant's identical menu just didn't make sense, Pawlcyn learned. "For example, the Japanese don't eat cheese, so I knew they wouldn't sell many quesadillas. What made it worse was that the cheese that the Japanese purveyors sold the restaurant was spoiled. "No one knew good cheese from bad because they never ate it—they just figured that it tasted bad because 'all cheese tastes bad,'" she laments.

"Only one of them is still going," admits Pawlcyn. "That one now serves Japanese food and plays country-western music." She learned the hard way that it's imperative to gear a restaurant to its particular location. "That's what we've always done here," she says, referring to Real Restaurants' success with their restaurants throughout the Bay Area.

When Work Impinges on Life

Norman Van Aken admits, "You almost have to be married to someone in this business if your marriage is going to succeed, because it's brutal. Otherwise, you can't share holidays, weekends, or other things that people think are normal."

I do think [the chef's lifestyle] is harder on women, although I think women are very important to have in the restaurant, so I'm torn to discourage them. It's a really hard pull with children, a really hard pull. It has been for me, even though I have Fanny [her daughter] around a lot; it's hard to be away when they're doing their homework and at dinnertime. My husband and I—he's in the restaurant business, too—have arranged it so I work Monday, Tuesday, and Wednesday and he takes care of Fanny, and then he goes to work and I take care of her Thursday, Friday, and Saturday. One night a week the baby-sitter takes care of her so that we can be together. That's all very nice if you can arrange a schedule that way, but most people can't do that. That's the luxury of being an owner. So I recommend being a chef-owner. **ALICE WATERS**

Amy Scherber's experience has been different. "Some couples can both work in the business together, but for others it is tougher," she admits. "When you're both in the business, you pretend you are not competing with each other—but in a way, you really are. I have seen the undoing when one person feels resentment when the other gets more attention. On the other hand, when you're in a relationship with someone who's not in the business, they need to realize that you need to be out at events socializing—and that staying out and doing an event is work!"

Susanna Foo admits that it was tough on her children to grow up in a restaurant family. "Sometimes I would ask them to come to the restaurant with me to eat, and they'd say, 'No! We never get to eat at home!'" she recalls. "I used to drag them to New York every Sunday. New York has such a variety of Chinese ingredients, and I wanted to see what was available for me to try. Now they just hate Chinatown in New York. They don't even like to go to New York. And they don't want to be in the restaurant business. But they do have good palates, and they like good food."

The Worst of Times . . .

Janos Wilder has no trouble recalling his single worst night in the restaurant business. "One busy night, in the middle of service, a customer knocked over one of two hand-thrown three-foot urns, filled with branches with sharp spines, from its pedestal. I couldn't leave the line, but I was told no one was hurt. Forty-

five minutes later, a busboy slipped bringing a load of dishes back into the kitchen, and wrenched his knee. Tickets were coming in, and again I couldn't leave the line. An hour later, a busboy in the kitchen backed up and put his foot into a boiling stockpot that had been set on the floor. He received major burns—I can't even describe his foot. Still, I couldn't get off the line for more than a minute because of all the dupes coming in. The stress, the feeling of being trapped and helpless was overwhelming." Wilder now primarily writes the menus and oversees the kitchen instead of working the line himself.

Sandy D'Amato faced a similarly harrowing night that he saw as a turning point in his career as a chef-restaurateur. "Up to this point, I'd had a vision of a restaurant where I would be going to the market every morning, making the four-hour round-trip drive to Chicago to pick up my fish, and baking my own bread—all while changing my menu daily. This vision in my head collided with the reality of having to *run* a restaurant.

"My wife, Angie, and I were living above the restaurant working sixteen- to eighteen-hour days, six days a week. One Friday when I had been working since early morning, one of our dishwashers didn't show up—so I was cooking *and* doing the dishes. I took some garbage downstairs only to have the bag break. When Angie ran across me at that exact moment, I looked at her and said, 'I don't know if I can do this. I know I thought I wanted all this, but I am in way over my head.'"

D'Amato credits his wife's encouraging response with restoring his confidence. "Angie looked at me and said, 'You just need some help—and we just got an application today.' At the beginning, a lot of people try to do too much. I couldn't go to the market every day. I found out that because of the size of my kitchen, I couldn't bake bread—it was so small that if I turned on the oven while the bread was rising, it would overproof." After learning to scale back, and to delegate, the D'Amatos went on to celebrate their restaurant's twentieth anniversary.

Winston Churchill's famous line: "Never give in, never give in, never, never, never, never in nothing, great or small, large or petty—never give in . . ." could be Nobu Matsuhisa's motto. He moved from his

> During the war, it was very complicated to work because of rationing. You had to do something with every scrap. It was challenging. We had little sugar. We had no wheat, and so we made bread out of potatoes. We even made almond paste out of potatoes— we pureed potatoes and added almond extract and a little sugar. The quality certainly wasn't much, but you had to be glad you had something to eat. **ALBERT KUMIN**

native Japan to Alaska to pursue his dream of opening his own restaurant, which took him six months to build. He was able to fly his family in from Japan to be with him once it opened. Less than two months later, they found little to celebrate on Thanksgiving—the restaurant had burned to the ground, taking Nobu's life savings and dreams with it.

Left with nothing, he borrowed money to get himself and his family back to Japan. A week later, he bought a one-way ticket to Los Angeles. He became a sushi chef and, seven months later, was able to fly his family out to live with him again. He developed his cooking style through stints at various Japanese restaurants before opening Matsuhisa, where, he says, "All my experiences came together, like condensing a nice sauce." The restaurant has been cited as the best Japanese restaurant in Los Angeles and perhaps in the United States.

. . . The Best of Times

"There are a lot of easier ways of making a living than this," states Charles Palmer. "It's only when you really look at it that it seems barbaric: You work in hot conditions, you work long hours, you get paid next to nothing. You cut your hands, you burn your hands. It's physically very bad for you: You breathe in smoke, you stand on your feet all day long, you sweat all the time. It's not pleasant—unless you love it. Then I think it's kind of neat."

Indeed. Despite the headaches, despite the heartaches, leading chefs have found enough rewards in this profession to keep them going until they again saw the light at the end of the tunnel.

"I always say that a slow day in a kitchen is still better than counting someone else's money wearing a suit," points out Mario Batali. "A great day in accounting doesn't come close to making thirty great dinners by yourself—even if you expected to do seventy. It is still great to be cooking. As long as you keep that in focus, that is how you get through the tough times."

"I'm as focused and as pumped up today as I was when I opened this place. This is all I think about. This is all I do. I wake up every day, and I can't wait to come over here," says Charlie Trotter. Raji Jallepalli agreed, "When everything is said and done, I don't think I've ever done anything that gave me this much satisfaction. There are times in the middle of the night that I get some ideas, and I can't wait to get up in the morning and go to the restaurant and get behind the stove to see how they work."

Norman Van Aken concurs. "This profession is not at all about being recognized. It has to be about the idea of the joy of discovery, of exchange, of seeing people smile after tasting your soup or your dessert."

The added pleasure for some chefs is almost certainly having discovered their love for more than just food in a kitchen. "Wolfgang Puck created our relationship," says Lissa Doumani of her alliance with husband and partner Hiroyoshi Sone. "He teased both of us relentlessly. When Hiro was at Spago in Tokyo, Wolfgang would call Tokyo and get Hiro on the phone and put me on the phone. Barbara [Lazaroff] came back from Tokyo once with a photograph of Hiro in his chef's whites holding a sign, with a message for me, to the camera. Finally, I asked Wolfgang if he'd hire Hiro if he moved to the United States, and he said yes. Wolfgang likes to stir things up."

Even in spite of the pressures that the all-consuming nature of this profession can have on family life, some chef-restaurateurs manage to find real benefits to this way of life. Elizabeth Terry's older daughter was seven when the family moved to Savannah to open Elizabeth on 37th, and for the first couple of years she voiced her wish that they could all "have their little house back." But a call from the same daughter years later—six weeks after she'd gone away to college in Montana—calmed any fears Terry might have had about the effect of growing up in a restaurant family. "She said, 'Mom, you really did it exactly right. I loved where I grew up, I loved my upbringing, I loved all the experiences and the excitement of living at the restaurant. It was really great.'"

Terry and her family found advantages in the atypical lifestyle: "Almost every night from the time she was thirteen until she went off to college, we would go out on the front porch [of the restaurant] after I finished cooking and she finished her homework, and we'd have a cappuccino or something, and we'd

> I burned out once in my career. I really just lost it and was ready to get out of the industry. What it basically comes down to is, do you love what you're doing? Do you love standing? Do you love chopping? And I do.
>
> GARY DANKO

> Success is difficult and presents lots of challenges. It wasn't like we opened the restaurant and were successful and didn't have problems. Even after thirteen years, every single day is like the first day you opened: There is a whole slew of new problems and problems you thought you solved that would never happen again. If you have absentee owners you don't see the problems. If you are here every night, you never stop catching things. NANCY SILVERTON

just sit. And I think because it was a restaurant and because it was after work, it was very neutral ground. We talked about all the things that parents say it's difficult to talk to children about. We never planned to talk about them, but we would just be there and saying goodnight to the last guests, and we'd just get into talking about sex and drugs and cigarettes and rock and roll and all those things just kind of came up in just the easiest way. There was something really magical about my being finished with work at ten-thirty at night. It was very, very nice for child rearing."

Other advantages included the ability to play a unique role in special events in their children's lives. Terry recalls fondly that "instead of doing a second seating, we had the whole high school class in for a sit-down dinner after graduation. I mean, nobody else could do that. We cooked for them, and the kids felt so grownup. It was so personal. This was just something that we could do, that we could give, and the emotional feedback from it was just extensive."

The roller-coaster ride of being in the restaurant business can generate cynicism on the part of a chef. "The more jaded you become—and I admit to being very jaded—the harder it is," admits Patrick O'Connell. But part of what makes it all worthwhile for him and other leading chefs is the undeniable, blissfully pleasurable moments in the profession—such as having the rare, moving food experience. O'Connell describes it as being "overcome by this distillation, this purity, this love that knocks you out—it hits you and then you just fall down flight after flight after flight of stairs because you are really craving that."

As a way to keep things in perspective on the toughest days you'll face in this business, Mario Batali strongly advises that you take the time to define your own taste by actually documenting what you love and why it is important to you. "Otherwise, you might forget these things when you open your own place," he says. "You need to remind yourself why you love doing this, and what excites you about it—and then remember that on a daily basis. I guarantee that after you open your own place, you will get so caught

The influences I always draw on include a guy who worked in a gas station who was one of those rare mechanics who could fix anything. Every day he would cook lunch for us, and I was always intrigued with his style of cooking. The things that he would cook would be phenomenal. And another was a guy named Whitney Dean, who was a black-hat chef I worked with at the University Club. He was from Barbados and had a French background. I got a lot from both of them, coming from two different points of view. I count them as my two biggest influences, besides my dad.

GEORGE GERMON

up being angry at your purveyors, or being pissed off at the customer who wanted to change your food, that it's vital to remember the joy of why you got into this in the first place.

"Write it down. Remind yourself what a joyous ride this can be and how much fun it is. Keeping that in focus is the most important thing you can do," he urges. "I still do this every day. I will lift my head up, look around, and say, 'Yeah. . . .' I am still in cooking for the reason I got in it for in the first place: the joys of cooking well, of making people happy, and of the table. That is what happens at our restaurants.

"There's a saying on our wall [in Italian]: 'At the table, you don't age.' That is the Italian belief," says Batali. "Time spent at the table is never taken away from the time you have on earth."

When you have the title of chef, some might expect you to know it all. I was at a cake supply store recently and signed up for their class on fondant. They were shocked: "You're Emily Luchetti—why are *you* taking this class?" I just said, "I have never done fondant and I am coming out of the closet!" No one should be afraid to admit that they don't know something.

EMILY LUCHETTI

Voodoo Beer-Steamed Shrimp with a West Indian Cocktail Salsa

NORMAN VAN AKEN, Norman's, Coral Gables, FL

"Bisquick recipes faded fast after those early 'daze' in Key West. The influence of islands south beckoned and changed my cooking dramatically. Here's my take on a simple dish perfect for the informal gathering of pals. Put a little salsa music on, too! With Tito or Celia going on in the background, you'll think the perspiration may be coming from their energy as much as it will be from the Scotch Bonnet peppers in my West Indian dipping salsa. It's New World—hot, hot, hot!

"Put the shrimp in a large bowl with some ice under them and serve the salsa on the side. Have an extra bowl for your guests to toss the shells (and bottlecaps and wine corks) into. Any beer can be used to steam the shrimp in. Just be sure the other three bottles in the six-pack are ones you will enjoy.

"If you want to steam more shrimp than this you can about double the amount of beer once before you would have to double everything else.

"With some simple boiled potatoes and corn on the cob, this can be turned into a nice summertime dinner. Another way to beat the heat is to serve with cold beer or tea."

1 tablespoon fennel seeds

1 tablespoon whole black peppercorns

1 tablespoon allspice berries

1 tablespoon mustard seeds

1 teaspoon cloves

2 tablespoons olive oil

1 medium red onion, peeled and roughly chopped

1 head garlic, cut in half crosswise

2 to 3 jalapeño chiles, stem discarded, chopped up roughly, seeds and all

2 bay leaves

Zest of 1 orange, all white pith scraped away

32 large, fresh, shell-on shrimp

Three 12-ounce bottles Blackened Voodoo Beer (or other)

1 recipe salsa (recipe follows)

Heat a large pot and add the fennel seeds, peppercorns, allspice berries, mustard seeds, and cloves. Allow them to toast by themselves for about 30 seconds and become fragrant.

Now add the olive oil. Allow the oil to warm and add the onion, garlic, chiles, bay leaves, orange zest, and the toasted spices. Stir completely. When the vegetables begin to get deeply glazed, add the beer and bring to a boil. Add the shrimp and return to a boil. Immediately lift a shrimp out at this point and check to see if it is done. If it is, remove the shrimp as quickly as possible and shock them in very icy water. As soon as they have stopped cooking and begin to feel cool, get them out of the icy water or you'll wash off the flavor of the beer, vegetables, and spices! Serve with the salsa.

Serves 4 to 6

Salsa

¾ cup ketchup

¼ cup chili sauce (such as Heinz)

2 Scotch Bonnet chiles, stem and seeds discarded, minced

3 garlic cloves, minced

½ cup red onion, minced

¼ cup roughly chopped cilantro leaves

Juice of 1 lime

¼ cup prepared horseradish

Salt and cracked black pepper to taste

¼ teaspoon Tabasco sauce

¼ teaspoon Worcestershire sauce

Mix all the ingredients together. Chill until needed.

Makes 1⅔ to 1¾ cups

Schenkli: A Swiss Carnival Delight

DIETER SCHORNER, The Culinary Institute of America, Hyde Park, NY

"Schenkli reminds me of my carefree youth where as a student in Basel, Switzerland, I, together with some friends, would go to the Carnival, which happens to be the biggest in all of Switzerland. Usually before going to the Carnival, we would first gather at a friend's house where we would wine and dine with schenkli.

Where schenkli, wine, laughter, and conversation abound, the world never looks rosier."

4 eggs

200 grams (about 1 cup) sugar

200 grams (about 1 cup) milk

Zest of 2 lemons

5 grams (about 1 tsp.) baking soda

100 grams (about ½ cup) butter, softened

750 grams (about 7½ cups) all-purpose flour

5 grams (about 1 tsp.) baking powder

Vegetable oil for frying

Cream the eggs and sugar. Add the zest. Dissolve the baking soda in the milk and add the soft butter. Add the flour and baking powder. Do not overwork.

Roll logs the thickness of a finger. Cut in 1½-inch slices and fry in hot vegetable oil to a hazelnut brown color. Drain the excess oil by placing the schenkli on a grill or paper towel. If desired, sprinkle with a little cinnamon sugar and sift with confectioners' sugar. With a glass of wine, you are in heaven!

Makes about 3 dozen

Shrimp with Cheese Grits and Country Ham

ELIZABETH TERRY, Elizabeth on 37th, Savannah, GA

"My husband, Michael, says this is his favorite dish of all the many I've created for Elizabeth on 37th because the flavors are bold. The dish is based on traditional Southern fare, so it is great comfort food. Finally, he loves creamy—as do I—and this dish is creamy."

The sauce

2 tablespoons butter

½ cup (4 ounces) country ham, minced

½ cup (4 ounces) shiitake mushrooms, stems removed (use for broth in another recipe)

½ cup minced onion

½ cup Madeira

2 tablespoons cornstarch

1 cup cold chicken broth

½ cup canned, diced tomatoes in juice, pureed

1 tablespoon minced fresh thyme

1 dash Tabasco sauce

Melt the butter in a skillet. Add the country ham and brown. Add the shiitake mushrooms and onion and continue to brown, stirring. Pour in the Madeira and simmer until it is nearly gone. Dissolve the cornstarch in the cold chicken broth and whisk into the ham and mushrooms. Bring to a boil, stirring. Add the rest of the ingredients and gently simmer for about 10 minutes to combine the flavors. Refrigerate.

The grits

1 cup grits

4 cups water

1 tablespoon minced garlic

¼ cup (2 ounces) grated sharp Cheddar cheese

Bring the water to a boil. Slowly stir in the grits and garlic. Simmer, stirring occasionally, until the grits are thick and soft. Add the grated cheese. Keep hot in a water bath, stirring occasionally. More water may be whisked into the grits if they become too thick.

The shrimp

2 tablespoons butter

1¼ pounds shrimp, peeled and deveined

¾ cup minced green bell pepper

½ cup minced parsley

In a large sauté pan, melt the butter. Add the shrimp and bell pepper over high heat until the shrimp begin to turn pink. Stir in the sauce and heat.

Divide the grits among six plates. Spoon over the shrimp and sauce, sprinkle with parsley, and serve.

Serves 6

Grandmothers' Chocolate Cake

EMILY LUCHETTI, Farallon,
San Francisco, CA

"I grew up on the frosting and Peter (my husband) grew up on the cake—hence the name. We serve it for most birthdays on both sides of the family. In addition, the more I bake, create, and eat chocolate desserts, the more I realize a good chocolate layer cake is the best chocolate dessert around."

Cake

1½ cups plus 1 tablespoon cocoa powder

1¼ cups boiling water

1½ cups cake flour

1½ cups plus 2 tablespoons all-purpose flour

1¼ teaspoons baking powder

1¼ teaspoons baking soda

5 ounces unsalted butter, softened

2¾ cups firmly packed brown sugar

3 large eggs

1¼ cups buttermilk

1¼ teaspoons vanilla extract

Frosting

4 ounces bittersweet chocolate

8 ounces unsweetened chocolate

8 ounces unsalted butter

3 cups confectioners' sugar

Pinch salt

2 teaspooons vanilla extract

To make the cake, preheat the oven to 350°F. Grease three 9-inch cake pans. Line the bottoms with parchment paper.

In a medium bowl, whisk together the cocoa powder and the boiling water until smooth. Cool to room temperature.

Sift together the cake flour, all-purpose flour, baking powder, and baking soda.

Cream the butter and brown sugar until light and fluffy. Add the eggs, one at a time, beating well after each addition.

Mix together the buttermilk and vanilla extract.

Stir in the dry ingredients alternately with the buttermilk. Stir in the reserved cocoa paste.

Divide the batter between the three pans, and bake the cakes until a skewer inserted in the middle comes out clean, about 25 minutes.

Cool the cakes. Unmold them by running a knife along the inside edge of the pans and inverting them. Carefully peel off the parchment paper.

To make the frosting, melt the chocolates and butter in a bowl over a double boiler. Cool to lukewarm.

Sift together the confectioners' sugar and salt into a large bowl. Combine the milk and vanilla extract. Whisk the milk into the confectioners' sugar. Stir in the melted chocolate, mixing until smooth.

If the frosting is too soft to spread, let sit for 15 minutes. Frost the cakes, making a three-layer cake.

Serves 10 to 12

Salmon Congee

SUSANNA FOO, Susanna Foo,
Philadelphia, PA

"Congee is a soup whose basic ingredient is rice, and it is a favorite breakfast dish in China, especially in the south. There are almost as many versions of congee as there are cities in China, with everyone offering a preferred version. Rice congee is often embellished with shredded chicken, seafood, beef, or fish. My husband's family enjoys their breakfast congee with eggs, sausages, or pickled mushrooms, while my family prepares congee with sweet potatoes, pumpkin, or mung beans. Texture can also vary. My grandmother, for example, insisted that the rice in congee should be firm, with each grain separate. If the cook was distracted and the rice became mushy, my grandmother would be quite upset. However, other people prefer a softer rice, with the liquid and solids blended together. When I was a child, rice congee was offered with scallion pancakes, or a dish of stir-fried vegetables and meat. I realized early on that congee offered a large canvas for culinary experimentation. Starting with basic congee, I added and subtracted ingredients until I came up with salmon congee. It's served as a soup course in my restaurant, but it can be a main dish at home—soup and fish in a bowl—that would need nothing more than another light course to make a complete meal. The salmon in this congee is thinly sliced and then marinated. It's gently cooked when hot soup is ladled over it. I find this the best way to prevent overcooked fish."

"Prepare the congee in a pot that's both deep and heavy. A sturdy soup pot will prevent the soup from boiling over and the rice from sticking."

¼ pound fillet of salmon, thinly sliced

¼ cup vodka

1 tablespoon soy sauce

5 tablespoons olive oil

1 tablespoon grated ginger

3 shallots, minced

1 celery stalk, finely chopped

1 jalapeño pepper, cored and seeded, finely chopped

½ cup rice

¼ pound shrimp, peeled and deveined, finely chopped

8 cups fish stock or chicken broth, homemade or canned

1 tablespoon rice wine vinegar

Salt and freshly ground pepper

¼ cup chopped coriander or basil leaves

Place the salmon in a shallow dish. Combine the vodka, soy sauce, and 2 tablespoons of the olive oil. Mix and pour over the salmon. Toss the salmon gently in the marinade and refrigerate for at least an hour.

In a large, heavy soup pot heat the remainder of the oil. Add the ginger, shallots, celery, and jalapeño pepper. Sauté, stirring, for 3 minutes.

Add the rice and shrimp to the vegetable mixture. Stir and add the stock or broth. Bring to a boil. Reduce the heat until liquid just simmers, and cover. Cook, stirring occasionally to make sure that the rice does not stick to the bottom of the pot. Remove from the heat when the rice is tender, about 1 hour and 15 minutes.

Stir the vinegar into the congee and season to taste with salt and pepper.

Divide the salmon with the marinade among six to eight soup bowls. Ladle the hot congee over the salmon and garnish with coriander or basil leaves.

Serves 6 to 8

Ginger Snap Cookies

MARCUS SAMUELSSON, Aquavit,
New York, NY

"This is the first recipe I remember making as a child. I made it with my grandmother, who was a professional cook and a great inspiration to me. The recipe evokes many memories; the smell and the flavor remind me of certain holidays, moods, and relationships. The associations are different depending on whether you enjoy it as a child or as an adult—whether you have the cookies with a glass of milk or a cup of coffee.

"Regardless of your age, however, these cookies are 'comfort food,' and are addictive. Whether you are young or old, they are a reward—something you deserve, and something you will climb up to the top of the shelf to get."

1½ pounds sugar
½ pound brown sugar
1½ pounds butter
3 eggs
2 cups molasses
½ tablespoon ground ginger
½ teaspoon cloves
½ teaspoon cardamom
1 teaspoon cinnamon
⅓ pound baking soda
1 teaspoon salt
3 pounds all-purpose flour
2 cups candied orange zest

With a paddle, cream the sugars and butter together until smooth and fluffy. Add the eggs and mix well, scraping the sides of the bowl. Add the molasses and mix well, again scraping the sides.

Sift all the dry ingredients together. Add to the bowl, mixing well. Stir in the orange zest.

Preheat oven to 325°F. Line a baking sheet with parchment paper. Using a medium-sized ice cream scoop, drop the dough onto the prepared baking sheet. The pan will fit 24 cookies (four across the short side and six across lengthwise).

Bake for 3 minutes, turn pan 180 degrees, and bake another 8 minutes, until the edges are set.

Let the cookies cool completely on the baking sheet or on a wire rack.

Makes about 8 dozen cookies

10. What's Next?
THE CHEF AS ALCHEMIST

Being a really good cook has to do with having a point of view.

ALICE WATERS

The chefs we interviewed are concerned with food beyond mere sustenance. They seem to realize cooking's potential for alchemy—the process of turning something common into something precious—that enables them to transform food from a mere physical experience into one which also affects the heart, mind, and spirit of the person to whom it is served. They appear to understand food as part of a total experience that has the potential to nurture, please, touch, awaken, move, even transport.

How did they develop this point of view? It was not the result of simply accumulating knowledge or memorizing facts. You could memorize every word of *Larousse Gastronomique*, and this alone would not help you develop your own point of view. Doing so only comes about through understanding and assimilating all you have ever learned and experienced.

These chefs shared how they've developed their own points of view through their lives, their education, and experience, as well as their day-to-day practice. Most importantly, it's also very clear how much time they've spent reflecting on the sensations, feelings, and thoughts brought about by their experiences. This has allowed them to develop their own visions of the way food should be cooked and served. Alice Waters's quotation that opened this chapter suggests the potential for an individual chef to have influence through his or her personal vision of what food can be.

The entire experience of cuisine begins with the will of the chef. The chef emerges as the director of an elaborate orchestra who directs the kitchen staff to create according to a specific vision. Without the chef's vision, nothing can happen. The chef's point of view serves as the driving force.

Chefs, having the power to affect and influence those who eat their food, also have a responsibility to ensure that their influences are positive ones. This entails understanding the factors that affect the outcome of their visions, including the ingredients that go into the dishes they create and the customers to whom they are served.

None of these factors exists in a vacuum; each affects the other. Even for the most talented of chefs, it is impossible to make the proverbial silk purse out of a sow's ear. The ingredients are critical; a dish is only as good as the ingredients that go into it. Yet what good is a perfect Valrhona chocolate soufflé if one's customer is allergic to chocolate? While artists may paint solely to express themselves, chefs must cook with the people who will eat their food always in mind.

Because both customers and ingredients play a critical role in the process, chefs have been driven to take steps to better understand their customers and their concerns and preferences, as well as take a stand on what they perceive as positive and negative influences on the ingredients with which they work.

The Influence of Customers

Customers change, and their changing needs and preferences must be acknowledged in some fashion.

Some of the biggest changes in restaurant customers are reflected in United States metamorphosing demographics. In the 1990s, the U.S. foreign-born population nearly doubled to 31 million, or 11 percent of the U.S. population. The Hispanic population has increased by more than 50 percent since 1990, compared to an increase of 13 percent for the population as a whole, making Hispanics the fastest-growing segment of the population. The corresponding rise of interest in their native cuisines should not come as a surprise, as it seemed to when it was widely publicized in the past decade that sales of U.S. salsa overtook those of ketchup.

While the U.S. Asian population has also grown significantly, coupled with the fact that more than 50 percent of the Asian population can be found in California, Hawaii, and New York and that 94 percent are concentrated in metropolitan areas, Asian (including Chinese, Indian, Japanese, Thai, and Vietnamese) influences on cuisine have been disproportionately strong. The confluence of the increasing availability of ingredients from those countries with the presence of trend-setting chefs (and media) in cities such as New York, San Francisco, and Los Angeles have served to influence the menus of existing restaurants as well as given birth to new upscale restaurants celebrating cuisines such as Indian (Tabla in New York City) and Vietnamese (Le Colonial in Chicago, San Francisco, and elsewhere).

With chefs' drive toward experimentation with the ingredients and techniques of other cultures, some might fear that certain cuisines will become unrecognizable from their authentic versions. However, many chefs believe there is a time and place for both authenticity as well as creative interpretations.

> **A lot of people are in love with the fact that they're going to have a microwave in the dashboard of their Chevrolet one day, so they can pop their Wendy's in there and reheat it, or something like that. That's part of the population. But a great percent of the population of our country is going to continue to make food, nutrition, health, the enjoyment of good wine, of good living, of exercise, and a balanced kind of harmonious life be the goals that they want for themselves and for their children.**
>
> **NORMAN VAN AKEN**

"In my own personal feeling, the only people who do non-American cooking with integrity are people who have lived in those cultures or traveled and eaten widely in those cultures," observed Barbara Tropp. "Some people are involved with authenticity or tradition, other people are involved with creativity. But they're very different things. For authenticity [in Chinese-style food], you might want to refer to what Cecelia Chang at The Mandarin used to do. People who are involved with tradition—that's me. People who are involved with creativity, with no hunger to be based in tradition—that's Wolfgang [Puck].

"There are brilliant culinary artists, like Wolfgang, who can appropriate flavors in a cuisine and, because of the excellence of their palates, can come up with something that's vibrant. It may bear no relation to that cuisine, but it's vibrant. It works on the tongue, but it may not work as any exemplar of what the real cuisine is about. It's interesting that there's that broad a spectrum. And as far as I'm concerned, if it tastes good, then who cares what it is? But they're very different sorts of things."

As chefs came to embrace all the ethnicities and ingredients around them, "fusion cuisine"—the melding together of the ingredients and/or techniques of more than one country—resulted. Raji Jallepalli was one of many chefs who observed the rise of fusion cuisine and described her own restaurant as "classical French cuisine incorporating Indian techniques and Indian spices. It's a marriage of Indian and French cuisines, which hadn't been tried anywhere else." Also seen as pushing the fusion movement forward have been restaurants such as Masa's in San Francisco (which melds Japanese and French), Chinois on Main (which melds Chinese and French), and Vong (which melds Thai and French).

Other changing concerns of consumers stem from the greater health-consciousness not to mention aging of the population, which are giving rise to new health worries and new eating habits. (This is compounded by the rise of ethnic populations that espouse the health-giving properties of certain foods, such as the Hispanic and Asian traditions of herbalism, or the Chinese observance of foods' yin-yang properties, which in turn raise concerns about ingredients' quality and efficacy.) This is spurring heart-healthy offerings from restaurants of the chefs we interviewed, ranging from spa cuisine to lighter techniques used when preparing dishes.

Some chefs admit they've changed their cooking practices in response to consumers. Alfred Portale recalls, "When I started at Gotham, it was butter, butter, and more butter. That was sort of the formula." Whether his cooks were preparing soup or a sauce, "I would tell them to 'puree it and add a ton of butter'—those were my instructions. We'd go through thirty-six pounds of butter every night on the line, just finishing sauces and stuff. But we rarely even sauté in butter anymore. We use light oil, canola oil to sauté. Even the vinaigrettes have lightened up dramatically in the last few years. A few years ago, everything was extra-virgin olive oil—you just loaded it up on everything. Not anymore. We're going for lighter oils, lighter flavors, cleaner flavors."

On the other hand, chefs point out that customers are not consistent in their health consciousness, particularly chefs at what might be considered "special occasion" restaurants. "They like to think they are, but basically I don't think so," says André Soltner. Despite all his customers' talk about cholesterol and other health concerns, those to whom he would offer a favorite regional dish—a potato pie with bacon and cream—always jumped in and enjoyed it, despite the cholesterol and calories. "Maybe they feel a little guilty afterward, but they shouldn't. We never, in good cooking, put in too much butter or too much cream. We put in just what it needs. Many chefs, especially thirty years ago, thought that the more butter or the more cream you put in, the better the dish. That's totally wrong, and I'm totally against that. My philosophy is that a healthy person can eat moderately of everything."

The rise in recent years of dual-income households, and the corresponding decline in time available for food preparation at home, has led to an increasing percentage—now a majority—of meals being eaten outside the home. Chefs have noted consumers' practice of making eating out less of a special occasion and more of a daily convenience. They are responding by expanding their cuisines through "downscaling" into more casual and accessible offerings and venues. Top-end restaurants have spawned lower-priced siblings, such as Restaurant Daniel's Café Boulud and db Bistro Moderne in New York City, as well as Citrus's Citronelles and Olives's Figs restaurants in locations across the country.

This expansion has also helped educate American palates in both a wide variety of cuisines and sophistication. True, the average American may still be learning to discern differences in food quality. Having lived through the 1980s and 1990s, however, when many customers developed a taste for new "gourmet" ingredients (a designation encompassing quality, freshness, and flavor), Americans as a whole have had their palates educated, and they have come to demand more from their food. This includes an insistence on learning more about exactly what they are putting into their bodies.

"Each day, in every town across the country, Americans are getting more and more sophisticated about food and cooking," observes Mario Batali. "In a way that makes things easier for us, yet it also means our standards have to be higher and higher every day."

Changing Ingredients

As ingredients change—sometimes because of different production processes that can change the character of the ingredients themselves—chefs cannot, and do not, remain unmoved by these changes. Certainly some chefs, and their customers who request them, appreciate the convenience of having softshell crabs or tomatoes available year-round, for example. Others, however, are very concerned about the safety and purity of the ingredients on the market, from foods sprayed with pesticides to genetically modified foods—not to mention the long-term availability of various types of produce or fish, for

> I love the fact that when I'm eating the food that we do here, I feel not only that I am in contact with a culture that I love—that of Mexico—but I'm in contact with all the growers that we buy from. I feel very strongly that I want to know the people who are raising everything—it just makes me feel good. I want to be able to have a sense of continuity from grower to cook to diner.
>
> RICK BAYLESS

example—and are both willing to make short-term changes themselves and to encourage others to do so in order to ensure long-term sustainability. These concerns are spurring chefs to take a more active role in selecting the ingredients that go into the food they serve their customers.

Through organizations such as Chefs Collaborative (www.chefscollaborative.org), leading chefs have been increasing their public support for sustainable cuisine by educating each other and teaching children about, and inspiring their customers to choose, clean, healthy foods. Many of the chefs we interviewed are taking up this cause by such means as building relationships with regional farmers and suppliers, and serving predominately organic ingredients, free-range poultry, and fresh local fish.

Alice Waters has added foragers to her staff who research new and better food sources. Rick Bayless has developed close relationships with his suppliers to ensure his ingredients' quality and freshness. Odessa Piper assigns the management of specific farm relationships to her cooks, as a means of increasing their knowledge of and connection to the ingredients with which they cook. These chefs' concerns reflect a growing trend across the country, which shows every sign of continuing.

"I love food and the miracles that we are afforded on earth," muses Chris Bianco. "Wild strawberries are a gift. If you are waiting for a miracle, look around: There is one every day. You can walk into a parking lot in New York City and find dandelion greens! Unfortunately, literally and figuratively, we are not looking down our own blocks enough as cooks. However, I am hopeful because every year we are seeing more regional ingredients being rediscovered and celebrated."

> Jimmy Schmidt cites the rising popularity of quinoa, a grain from South America that is 21 percent protein, as an example of "the modern diet for the twenty-first century, which is really a diet based on great foods that are enjoyable, that are available to feed the world's population, that supply all the nutritional bases—not only nutrition for health, but for the mind and soul—and that lead to lower incidence of chronic and long-term diseases.

The Right Wavelength

Chefs have the opportunity to put forth their own, very personal points of view, thereby making food their own—through cooking food they love and that is personally meaningful to them, while making a statement through their work and lives about what they want to support: local farmers, organic produce, regional varietals, free-range poultry and meats.

Being at the forefront of the culinary revolution also requires having the courage to "push the envelope" in new directions. In a sense, this is what happened in the 1970s and 1980s, when a group of new American chefs came into the restaurant business during an era when "good food" was synonymous with French food, and invented a whole new definition of what food could be and who could cook it. The 1980s and 1990s saw its own redefinition of "good food" with the rise of "FedEx chefs" who provided their clientele with "absolutely, positively" anything they wanted, whenever they wanted it—whether strawberries or tomatoes in January, or even Atlantic swordfish in the mid-1990s, when its popularity with consumers led to severe overfishing as well as its being temporarily placed on a list of endangered species.

But in the 1990s and through the turn of the new millennium, we are witnessing yet another period of redefining what is meant by "good food"—one that goes beyond nutrition and flavor to also encompass the attendant ecological, environmental, and social implications of our food choices. The catchphrase of this new movement is "sustainability," and its mission is to help chefs and customers alike understand the far-reaching impact of the decisions they make regarding food.

Central to this vision is helping people who care about good food think more broadly about ingredients' evolutionary process from farm

to table. Doing so leads naturally to the questions, Where does my food come from? How was it produced? What will it do to my body? How is this affecting the planet? And what's the best way to increase awareness of these issues among others?

Alice Waters of Chez Panisse has long held the torch for the importance of chefs' learning about the ingredients with which they work. "People say, 'I'm a trained cook—why do I have to wash the salad?' But in order to evaluate something properly, you really need to see it from the beginning," she explains. "Cooking is not just coming in on the tail end and giving something a sauce. It's about really trying to make distinctions about things, such as the different types of lettuce and which kinds you'd want to blend together to make a salad. It's about seeing the shapes of things whole, not after they've been prepped and all cut up into little pieces, because maybe you wouldn't have wanted to slice the potato—maybe you'd want to cut it lengthwise because it's so beautiful in its shape. It's things like that that get passed over when you don't start at the beginning."

It's the same reasoning that leads Chris Bianco to believe that it's imperative for aspiring cooks to get to know and have references to the seasons, to farmers, and to farmers' markets. "Getting to a farm is the most important thing a cook can do," he insists. "It goes back to the old line that 'Great wine starts in the vineyard.' The same is true for great food: You can't make a bad tomato taste good. A cook needs to experience that.

"Cooking is all about having references," says Bianco. "Say you had an apple tree that you were responsible for, and you had to prune it and water it. You'd watch it flower, then see those flowers eventually grow into apples over three months. How would that affect you? You would feel every windstorm that blew apples to the ground! You would learn that the ones left on the tree would be extra-sweet. If you got to make an apple pie at the end of the season after all your hard work, you'd forever look at apples, and apple pie, differently, because you'd have these incredible references. You would never again just take a couple of bites of an apple and toss the rest out your car window."

The experience of visiting Pizzeria Bianco is filled with references to the roots of Bianco's cuisine. Alongside the restaurant, you'll find a thin strip of earth planted with vegetables—an unusual sight in downtown Phoenix. Walking through the front door of the restaurant, you'll pass pots bursting with fresh herbs. The garden and potted herb plants reflect Bianco's philosophy of staying close to the earth, no matter where you are.

Charlie Trotter sees himself as having three-tiered goals for his work in the restaurant business: making an aesthetic contribution, a cultural contribution, and a social contribution.

"Having a garden is a chance for us to put our hands in some dirt," he explains. "It is a reference for myself—and hopefully for our customers—to walk by and see fresh lettuce growing. I hope that when they take a bite of their salads, they connect it to the earth and to the fresh beautiful leaves they just saw growing in it."

Bianco has noted that few people seem to have strong references to agriculture in downtown Phoenix. "When they see our restaurant garden, they will ask if we supply our restaurant with the garden—and I'll have to explain that we need four farmers to supply us," he laughs.

Craig Shelton is just as passionate about what his garden at The Ryland Inn in Whitehouse, New Jersey, brings to the cooks in his kitchen. "We have a great garden [which features 150 different herbs, 95 kinds of lettuce, 120 other vegetables, including 12 types of tomatoes, and two dozen types of fruit over its three acres], and it is incredible for my cooks to spend a year experiencing the seasons through it," he says. "They start to know viscerally when the asparagus is coming up.

Sustainable cuisine means nurturing that which nurtures us.

MICHAEL ROMANO

"All my cooks are required to spend time in the garden, but they love it," says Shelton. "Some will even come in on their days off just to work in the garden." He has seen his cooks take the idea of freshness to new heights as well: "I sometimes see cooks running out just before service to cut their herbs, and I have even seen them run out in the middle of service so they can serve something that's been just-picked from the garden!"

Odessa Piper's restaurant L'Etoile in Madison, Wisconsin, has become a destination workplace for some cooks because of what they're able to learn through having unusually close relationships with local farmers. "We'll send cooks out to Harmony Valley Farms to work on the farm, and sometimes even to work as the farm cook, before they come into our restaurant to cook," she says.

"I will assign line cooks areas of the menu where I want them to specialize, and they'll dedicate themselves to working with particular producers who supply us," Piper explains. "What this teaches cooks is that food is not just something you pick up the phone and order. Rather, it is a matter of responsibility and of relationship.

"Our kitchen staff is directly in touch with how small-scale agriculture works," she continues. "All our cooks will visit the farms, chat with the farmers over coffee, and get up from family meal at the restaurant when the order from their farm arrives to receive it. Our restaurant has gotten so specialized that my pastry chef does the fruit, while a garde-manger cook handles only herbs and the beautiful shoots that come in. Another cook specializes in the winter crop and putting it up, while yet another cook handles all the cheese."

Just as cooks learn the seasonality and lifespan of a vegetable, so too will they learn about meats and poultry. Most seem to have forgotten that chicken is a seasonal food. "Here, cooks may find out that the chickens are putting on weight slowly, which means we need to rethink chicken because they are not going to be ready when we need them," explains Piper. "They also know that our purveyors have such high standards that they won't supply us with anything before it is ready.

"Because chicken is seasonal, until recently we didn't serve it during winter. However, it is very hard not to have poultry on the menu from the guests' standpoint. So, working with our poultry farmer, we found a way to freeze chicken that kept it up to both our standards," says Piper. "This even helped the cooks, because they had to become so good that they could take a frozen chicken and make it taste as good as one in season! In fact, I don't 'graduate' cooks to preparing frozen chicken until they prove they can, so I first have them cook for a blind tasting by myself and the staff."

Traci Des Jardins takes an equally passionate view of the meat she serves at Jardinière in downtown San Francisco and at Acme Chop House next to San Francisco's baseball park. "We make a statement by using Niman Ranch meat [which is antibiotic- and hormone-free beef and pork; the livestock is humanely treated and fed only pure, natural feed]. We are also sourcing grass-fed beef from a cattle ranch in northern California, after conducting a blind tasting of the grass-fed beef next to the corn-fed beef and finding that we all liked the grass-fed beef better. While I am a big fan of Niman Ranch beef because of their standards and use them almost exclusively at Jardinière, it gets down to the fact that both meats have different things to offer. Grass-fed beef is just the right thing to do for the environment and the cow. Cows are meant to eat grass, but agriculture moved away from it because it was expensive.

What has changed a great deal since the advent of the Internet is our ability to communicate with all our farmers. That is the wave of the future. Many farmers either have Web sites or we are e-mailing each other constantly. The farmers are now educating customers on their Web sites. It is also a boon for the busy chef because I can get updates on crops and orders without having to stop in the middle of the day to make phone calls. It has become an incredibly efficient way to do business for both of us. ODESSA PIPER

Chefs Collaborative Statement of Principles

Preamble: We, the undersigned, acknowledging our leadership in the celebration of the pleasures of food, and recognizing the impact of food choices on our collective personal health, on the vitality of cultures, and on the integrity of the global environment, affirm the following principles:

1. Food is fundamental to life. It nourishes us in body and soul, and the sharing of food immeasurably enriches our sense of community.

2. Good, safe, wholesome food is a basic human right.

3. Society has the obligation to make good, pure food affordable and accessible to all.

4. Good food begins with unpolluted air, land, and water, environmentally sustainable farming and fishing, and humane animal husbandry.

5. Sound food choices emphasize locally grown, seasonally fresh, and whole or minimally processed ingredients.

6. Cultural and biological diversity is essential for the health of the planet and its inhabitants. Preserving and revitalizing sustainable food and agricultural traditions strengthen that diversity.

7. The healthy, traditional diets of many cultures offer abundant evidence that fruits, vegetables, beans, breads, and grains are the foundation of good diets.

8. As part of their education, our children deserve to be taught basic cooking skills and to learn the impact of their food choices on themselves, on their culture, and on their environment.

http://www.chefscollaborative.org

"We have found customers very receptive to the grass-fed meat, and we have a great source. My chef at Acme and I drove up to the ranch and inspected everything, including the slaughterhouse," she says. "The ranch pretty much prepares our meat to order, so we call three weeks in advance to get our meat slaughtered."

Des Jardins believes that chefs must come together to create a sustainable future. "We are not going to continue to have the resources that we have now if we don't pay attention to the impact of our actions," she warns. "Cooks need to be involved with organics and with how their food is harvested. And I want my son to be able to eat wild salmon, so I am very focused on the sustainable fishery movement. If we continue to buy farm-raised Atlantic salmon that is detrimental to the environment and the natural fish species, and if we continue to contaminate our oceans, eventually we are not going to have wild salmon.

"Chilean sea bass is another case in point: We have eaten it nearly into extinction. That is reprehensible—no cook should be buying that product. However, I still see it on the menus of chefs I respect, and I wish they wouldn't do it," she says. "As chefs and restaurateurs, we need to look all these issues, beyond the immediate consideration of 'What is the best product on the plate?'"

Des Jardins also believes that customers must be educated to be able to appreciate and demand the best ingredients, and to be willing to vote with their wallets. "At some point, our decisions will affect the consumer in terms of price point—and our businesses have to be sustainable as well," she points out. "The grass-fed beef we sell is insanely expensive—a fourteen-ounce New York steak is twenty-eight dollars—so to make it sustainable, the public will really have to get behind it. People complain about prices in restaurants all the time, but they don't realize how difficult and expensive it is to get that product to the plate. We don't have huge margins; fine dining restaurants just don't make that much money."

She sees the responsibility for education as falling on chefs as well as restaurant critics. "If critics were more aware, they might not be so cavalier about writing negative reviews or criticizing what they perceive as high prices. In fact," Des Jardins muses, "they could play a very important role in helping to educate the public about these things."

Expanding Their Reach

Chefs have long been fueling the research and development for the food industry. Their evolutionary drive to constantly innovate has resulted in a multitude of experiments with new—and old—cuisines, presentations, techniques, and ingredients. The most successful of these experiments—those which come to be embraced by customers and fellow chefs—achieve a broad influence: Think of flavored foams (Ferran Adrià), free-range chicken (Larry Forgione), gourmet pizza (Wolfgang Puck), and infused oils (Jean-Georges Vongerichten).

Increasingly, however, there is a revolution taking place in the media and the marketplace. Through their acute understanding of customers and ingredients, and their zealousness in communicating their philosophies to the market through every medium available to them—their restaurant menus, newsletters, and e-mail lists; their cookbooks; their media interviews; and, increasingly, their own TV shows, radio shows, and columns in the press—leading chefs are educating customers about food. In turn, the same chefs are providing products—from dishes at their restaurants to prepared foods with national distribution—to meet the market's growing demand for quality.

What are their motivations? It might sound naive to suggest that they're not entirely financial. After all, as Nancy Silverton points out, "It's difficult to make a great living in this business on just one restaurant." The economic realities of the restaurant business have led many of the most ambitious chefs to expand into multiple restaurants, either focused on one geographic area or, increasingly, across the country (including such meccas as Las Vegas) and around the world. This is the case with some of the most financially successful chefs such as Alain Ducasse, Todd English, Emeril Lagasse, Nobu Matsuhisa, Wolfgang Puck, and Jean-Georges Vongerichten, who have all been included on *Forbes* magazine's list of America's 100 highest-paid entertainers.

However, when it comes to considering new ventures, often other considerations play a role. "Our goal is to bring real flavors of Mexico to as broad an audience as possible," professes Rick Bayless. "In fact, our TV show was a three-year process from the idea stage to turning the camera on because I resisted doing it until I found the one that would allow me to shoot at least half the show on location in Mexico, because that is the inspiration for what we do.

"The TV show has brought us a whole new level of educated customers. When our TV viewers come in and see dishes that they consider unusual or exotic, they aren't making faces saying, 'We expected fajitas.'" Bayless adds, "It is great because they are open to new things—and while they might not know what those things are, they've come to trust us."

Mario Batali admits that his TV show *Molto Mario,* which began airing on the Food Network in 1995, was not the result of planning, but rather of pure luck. "I was at Citymeals on Wheels in 1994 and was approached by the director of program development for the Food Network. We had lunch and twelve weeks later I was doing my show."

Batali recommends that any chef who aspires to host his or her own TV show do the same: "Learn your craft first; any fame should be secondary. The reason my show works is because of my passion for my food and my historical perspective. These things made me interesting enough to put on TV. If you simply smile, wear expensive clothes, and chit-chat, eventually you're going to run out of things to talk about."

Bayless credits the success of his expanding empire to "organic growth." "People will ask what my 'five-year plan' is, and I just laugh," he says. "What is going to happen to us, what we are going to be involved in, and how we are going to grow are things I don't plan. Instead, I want to be open to what is presented to me and what is right for me in the moment. All the things we have grown into have worked out not because we sought them out as much as because we have been open to opportunity.

Rick Bayless Shares the Frontera Mission Statement

- To bring alive in the United States the best of Mexican dining by (1) educating ourselves and our customers about the breadth of great regional Mexican cuisine, and (2) adopting the generous, welcoming spirit of the country.

- To create a great restaurant by serving delicious food, skillfully prepared from the highest-quality ingredients and served to our guests with top-notch professionalism.

- To foster a respectful, profitable, engaging, and challenging workplace.

- To support the principles of sustainability of our planet by buying organically or naturally raised foods, working with local farmers, thoughtfully using (and reusing) resources and disposing of waste, to carry the principles of sustainability into our lives and those of our co-workers by developing realistic performance expectations.

"I never look around and say 'Chef Joe Schmo is doing X, Y, and Z—so I should, too.' Instead, I take into account three things: First, I look at what satisfies me, because if I am excited and passionate about something, it will flourish. If I am not excited, or feel like I 'should be doing it,' or have mixed feelings, the idea won't flourish.

"Second, I never start out on anything unless I believe we have the growth potential within the staff. Sometimes I need to take a leap of faith because I'm not sure the staff is up to the task, but I also realize they need to have a new opportunity to grow.

"And third, I look at how it fits into our overall mission. Sometimes I will get excited about something and try to make it fit. Then I will wake up at two in the morning and realize that, while it sounds fun, it ultimately doesn't jibe with our mission.

"We have a mission statement (see sidebar on p. 301), which is not just about food or Mexico or the environment. Rather, it weaves what we have learned from Mexico into our everyday lives—things like respect for traditions, generosity of spirit, and supporting sustainable agriculture. Our mission provides our foundation, so with every project we consider, we make sure it fits into that.

"We have decided not to have multiple restaurants [aside from Frontera Grill and Topolobampo, which are under the same roof] because I pour my life's blood into the staff here. That is the most satisfying thing I do. If I had multiple restaurants, that would be fractured to the point where I wouldn't get the satisfaction that I get now.

"Yet, like many chefs, I need creative outlets. I always have a writing project going on, which feeds back into the restaurants because our cookbooks create a great audience for us and the cuisine. For example, I'll take dishes from the restaurant and modify them for the home cook, which works out great because people will then come into the restaurant with a built-in appreciation for the food. They either want to see how we do it or they know how much goes into it so they appreciate all our work that much more."

Bayless describes launching his own line of Frontera Salsas as one of the hardest things he has ever done. "I didn't want people to think I was selling out," he admits. "So I had to find my comfort level in the realization that I am not selling salsa but rather that I am promoting the flavors of Mexico.

"It was a slow, difficult process because it took over a year to find someone who would cook the salsa just the way we wanted and because I wanted to make sure that our partner was a person I liked and wanted to spend time with. It was not just a business proposition to me. Our then-prospective partner would come in talking numbers, and I would look at him and say, 'Tell me about your wife' or 'What were your favorite meals as a kid?' He was ready to pull his hair out! But he has since come to appreciate the holistic nature of what we do."

Mario Batali has his own line of pasta sauces available exclusively through Trader Joe's. "The deal came about because they are very selective and only carry seven sauces versus thirty," he explains.

His experience was not dissimilar to Bayless's in his insistence on product quality. "They let me come down to the factory and watch them caramelize the onions exactly as they should be done. My problem with many prepared sauces is that there is a consistency issue. Also, you typically don't know how long they have been sitting on the shelves. We are using a 'just-in-time' system, where we make only what we need and store very little in inventory."

Why go to the trouble of dealing with all the related hassles? "Of course it's profitable," says Batali. "But the other reason to do a line of sauces is the satisfaction of knowing that you are providing someone with a good meal."

Are ever-expanding empires becoming *de rigeur* for the next generation of chefs? "In the end, I don't believe you have to have books or a TV show to be a successful chef or to have a successful restaurant," says Batali. "There are plenty of restaurants that don't have either, and they're still packed every night.

"Blue Ribbon restaurant [in Manhattan] jams! They are open four P.M. to 4 A.M., and they are full every time I walk in—and they don't have a book or a TV show," Batali attests. "What they have is good value: They fill your needs with an accessible menu, from exotic as you want to turkey burgers. They are as good a mold for a restaurant as you'll find."

Making It Your Own

The sheer volume of everything there is to know about food can be overwhelming and frightening—or inviting and exciting. "In 1470, to be a Renaissance man and to have read every book in existence was a possibility. By 1910, you couldn't have read every book, but you could have mastered something. However, in our lifetimes, there is no chance that you can know everything about anything," points out Mario Batali.

"That is the way food is. It can get more complicated, or simpler. Because there are so many options out there, it can be harder to find your own singular voice. But you don't find have to find your voice at twenty-one—you'll most likely find it years later," he explains.

"For that reason, I would advise aspiring chefs not to focus too early unless you are really sure about your interests," says Batali. "And if you decide that you are going to work with Italian food, understand that knowing one region is not enough. In Puglia, there is the food of northern, central, and southern Puglia. There is always more to learn."

> Pizza is "hot" now, but it is only a reflection of my life. Pizza is my medium; it is simple and humble. Most people's expectations for pizza are so low that I wanted to elevate something I love so much so that it would be respected.
>
> **CHRIS BIANCO**

"Because cuisine is so vast, you will never stop learning," echoes Rick Bayless. "The great cuisines are so rooted in their traditions and so solid that they will always be able to open themselves up to new twists. That's what keeps them alive."

Batali emphasizes that "going deep" doesn't just apply to mastering Italian or French or any other classic cuisine. "Your own journey may lead you to Morocco, Thailand, Shanghai, or even Erwin, Ohio, USA, to understand what makes the Ohio State Fair

Journey within. There lies truth.

CHARLIE TROTTER

Pickle the best pickle of the year," he says. "Nor does your journey have to be exotic: It might lead you to your own backyard and spark your inspiration for something you can personalize and love. That is what is going to make *me* want to eat your food."

Every American cook felt a greater sense of pride in the cuisine of our own backyards in 1994 when the White House finally hired an American chef to cook American food—after a long tradition of having a French chef with menus printed in French. "I think it was a sign that America was starting to mature," observed Mark Miller. "As long as we gave into this [French food being served in the White House], we kind of created a mold that says we were not good enough.

"Jungian psychology calls this the process of individuation—it isn't that you become better; it's that you become more aware of who you are and you realize the potential of your own self."

There is so much to celebrate in food: preserving our past, with the rich cultural heritage provided by authentic culinary traditions in our own backyards as well as around the globe; celebrating our present, with its increasing availability of a fascinating variety of dishes, ingredients, techniques; and forging our future, with the possibility presented by sustainable innovations to make food even more delicious.

You and I are creating the future of food and the profession with every dish we make, with every meal we serve. Having a point of view—or, becoming more aware of who we are as chefs and realizing the potential of ourselves within our cooking—will propel us to influence others through our cuisine. People will be affected and changed by it, one way or another. We must strive to make the influence of our food a positive one.

On this point, André Soltner, who has spent more years than any other chef we interviewed developing his unique point of view, leaves us with this advice: "If you give the ingredients what I call 'love,' you'll never fail. If you don't have that in your cooking, forget it. You can have all the techniques in the world, but you'll never become a great chef.

"I can teach techniques. And I can explain what I just explained. But I cannot teach it—I cannot teach the feeling.

"I know that when you cook, every time you cook, you must feel this feeling. If you can achieve this, you will not fail."

Gratin of Cardoon Francine

DANIEL BOULUD, Restaurant Daniel, New York, NY

"This is an adaptation of my grandmother's recipe served during the winter with roasted fowl. This Lyonnais dish is a Christmas tradition. The cardoon is a vegetable that looks like celery but tastes like artichokes and is popular in Southern France, Italy, and Greece."

> 1 tablespoon salt
>
> 3 bunches cardoon, outer leaves and ends trimmed, stalks sliced into 2-inch-long segments, each segment halved and stringy skin pulled off with a small paring knife (immediately plunge cardoon into 3 quarts water mixed with juice of 2 lemons to avoid browning)
>
> 1½ cups chicken stock
>
> 2 ounces fresh beef marrow, sliced
>
> 1½ tablespoons all-purpose flour
>
> Salt and freshly ground black pepper
>
> 1 cup Gruyère or Emmenthal cheese, freshly grated

Add the salt to the cardoon and lemony water, and bring to a boil in a large pot over high heat. Simmer the cardoon for 40 to 50 minutes or until tender. Drain well.

Preheat the oven to 425°F. Bring the chicken stock to a boil in a small pan. Place the marrow in a large pan and melt over medium heat. Add the flour and whisk for 3 to 5 minutes. Add the boiling chicken stock, stir, and cook for 5 minutes.

Add the cooked cardoon, salt and pepper to taste, and toss well.

Transfer to a buttered, shallow baking dish and sprinkle the top with grated cheese. Bake for 15 to 20 minutes, or until golden brown. Serve warm from the gratin dish.

Serves 4 to 6

Albóndigas Estilo Mama (Meatballs Like Mama Makes)

ZARELA MARTINEZ, Zarela, New York, NY

"This recipe calls to mind the *llaves* (outdoor water faucets) on the ranch, which were always surrounded with patches of *yerba buena*–"good herb," or mint. Whenever my mother made albóndigas, I would be sent out to pick some fresh for the soup. She always served it with freshly made corn tortillas, salsa casera (home-style sauce), and refried beans with asadero ('roasting' cheese; the nearest thing here would be mozzarella).

"Whenever my mother comes to visit, I always ask her to make me these albóndigas. I have tried to serve them at the restaurant, but people can't seem to get excited about meatball soup. Too bad–it's a fabulous soup. The meatballs freeze well, by the way, and reheat wonderfully."

7 garlic cloves

¼ cup masa harina

¼ cup warm water

1 pound lean ground beef, or ½ pound each lean ground pork and beef

¾ teaspoon salt, or to taste

Freshly ground black pepper

¼ cup lard or vegetable oil

1 tablespoon flour

2 quarts chicken stock

¼ cup chopped scallions, white and part of the green (about 4 medium scallions)

1 large ripe tomato, roasted, peeled, and chopped (or use ¼ cup tomato puree if good tomatoes are not available)

2 Anaheim or California long green chiles (or for hotter flavor, jalapeño chiles), roasted, peeled, and finely chopped

3 tablespoons finely chopped cilantro leaves

3 tablespoons finely chopped fresh mint leaves

Mince 3 of the garlic cloves. In a large bowl, combine the masa harina with the warm water. Add the ground meat, ½ teaspoon of the salt (optional), a generous grinding of black pepper, and one minced garlic clove. Mix these ingredients with your hands and shape into tiny balls, between the size of a large marble and a small walnut. (You should have 40 to 45 small meatballs.) Set aside.

In a small skillet, heat 2 tablespoons of the lard or vegetable oil over medium-high heat. Add a whole garlic clove. Let cook for 20 to 30 seconds to flavor the oil, pressing down with the back of a cooking spoon. Remove and discard the garlic.

Off the heat, add the flour to the hot fat and quickly stir to combine. Cook over medium heat, stirring constantly to smooth out lumps, until the mixture is golden (about a minute).

Meanwhile, have the stock heating in a large (at least 6-quart), deep saucepan or Dutch oven. Just before it boils, add a little hot stock to the browned flour mixture and whisk or stir to eliminate lumps. Pour the mixture into the hot stock and bring to a boil, whisking or stirring with a wooden spoon to keep from lumping. Reduce the heat to medium-low and simmer the stock, uncovered, for 5 minutes. It will thicken slightly. Season with a little salt and pepper, being careful not to overseason (the meatballs will add more salt).

To make a recaudo, in a large skillet, heat the remaining 2 tablespoons lard or vegetable oil over medium-high heat until very hot but not quite smoking. Add the chopped scallions, roasted tomato, roasted chiles, and remaining 2 garlic cloves minced, reduce the heat a little and sauté briskly for 2 minutes, stirring frequently. Add the sautéed mixture to the stock. Add the chopped cilantro and mint. Simmer uncovered for another 5 minutes. Add the meatballs. Let the stock return to a boil and simmer uncovered over low heat for 15 minutes. Correct the seasoning.

Serves 6 to 8 as a main dish

Potato Pie

ANDRÉ SOLTNER, formerly of Lutèce,
New York, NY

"As long as I can remember, my mother would make us potato pie. It was one of the dishes we would always ask for. This is a typical Alsatian recipe that was passed along to her from her aunt, 'Tante Louise.' Potato pie does not appear on Lutèce's menu—it is not the kind of cuisine we usually serve—but I will make it from time to time and offer it to some of my customers whom I know will enjoy it. It is delicious served with a salad for lunch."

Pastry

8 ounces (about 1¾ cups) all-purpose flour

¾ teaspoon salt

1 stick plus 1 tablespoon (9 tablespoons) unsalted butter, cut up

1 egg yolk, lightly beaten with enough ice water to make ¼ cup

Filling

1¼ pounds smooth-skinned Long Island or Maine potatoes, peeled and thinly sliced

¼ cup finely chopped parsley

Salt and freshly ground black pepper

5 ounces thick-sliced mild-smoked bacon, cut crosswise into ¼-inch strips

5 small hard-cooked eggs, peeled and thinly sliced

½ cup crème fraîche or heavy cream

Egg glaze

1 egg yolk beaten with 1 teaspoon water

Make the pastry: The day before you make the pie, mix the flour and salt in a bowl and rub in the butter with your fingertips until the mixture resembles coarse cornmeal. Make a well in the center, pour in the egg yolk beaten with water, and work with the fingers just until moistened. With one cupped hand, gather the mixture into a ball.

Quickly roll the dough out into a rectangle on a floured work surface. Fold in thirds, wrap in plastic, and refrigerate overnight.

When ready to assemble the pie, divide the dough into two equal parts. Roll one half into a round about 13 inches across, and fit into a 9-inch pie pan. (You can use a removable tart pan, if you prefer. If you do, be sure to make an upright, crimped edge that will permit the rim of the pan to be removed before serving.) Chill for 10 minutes.

Wash the sliced potatoes in cold water to remove excess starch; drain and pat the slices dry. Toss with the parsley, salt, and pepper. In a skillet, gently sauté the bacon for a minute or two, stirring until wilted and just browned on the edges. Drain.

Arrange a layer of overlapping slices of potato in the pastry shell. Cover with a layer of bacon and arrange the egg slices over the bacon. Top with the rest of the potato, overlapping the slices. Spread the crème fraîche over the potatoes. Roll the remaining pastry into a round large enough to cover the pie. Brush the edges of the lower crust with the egg glaze and cover the pie. Trim the edges, then crimp to seal well. Prick the top once or twice with a larding needle or the point of a knife. Refrigerator while you preheat the oven to 400°F.

Brush the top crust lightly with egg glaze. Bake the pie for 20 minutes on the middle shelf, then lower the oven heat to 350°F and bake for an hour longer. Lower the heat to 300°F and bake for 10 minutes longer.

Let the pie rest for 10 minutes before serving. Accompany with a green salad and a bottle of chilled Alsatian white wine.

Serves 6

Acorn Squash Risotto with Shallots, Sage, and Maple-Smoked Bacon

ALFRED PORTALE, Gotham Bar and Grill, New York, NY

"Holidays were very special in my house when I was growing up, in a close Italian family in Buffalo. My mother would prepare huge feasts for the family and our friends. Most of the dishes she prepared were American adaptations of the Italian specialties that her mother cooked for her family when she was young. One Thanksgiving a few years ago, I wanted to create a dish for my family that would capture the essence of Thanksgiving, much in the same way my mother created special dishes. I combined flavors—acorn squash, sage, and maple-smoked bacon—that are representative of the Thanksgiving meal and created a risotto dish. I found out recently that this dish is a traditional Venetian risotto served at an autumn holiday."

1 stick plus 1 tablespoon (9 tablespoons) butter

Salt and freshly ground pepper

1 large acorn squash

1 tablespoon brown sugar

2 ounces maple-smoked bacon, diced

1½ cups finely sliced shallots

1 pound Arborio rice

5 sage leaves

1 pinch fresh thyme

Up to 3 quarts rich turkey or chicken stock, kept at a simmer

2 tablespoons chopped parsley

Cut the squash into wedges. Peel and seed, then slice thin wedges crosswise to yield approximately 5 cups. Heat 4 tablespoons of the butter in a large saucepan. Add the squash and season with salt and pepper to taste. Sauté over medium heat until squash is nicely caramelized and very soft, about 15 minutes. Sprinkle with brown sugar and keep warm.

While the squash is cooking, in a large sauce pot sauté the bacon with a tablespoon of the butter until lightly browned. Add the shallots and cook for about 4 minutes. Add the rice, sage, and thyme. Stir until coated. Add the stock, 8 ounces at a time, stirring until the liquid is absorbed. Continue adding stock until the rice is cooked, approximately 15 to 18 minutes.

Stir in the sautéed squash and the remaining 4 tablespoons of butter.

Serve sprinkled with chopped parsley.

Serves 4

Butter Pecan Ice Cream

PATRICK O'CONNELL, The Inn at Little Washington, Washington, VA

"As a kid, I never believed that store-bought butter pecan ice cream really contained any butter, and the little chunks in it didn't really taste like pecan. I liked to think about the way it might have tasted in a perfect world. This recipe is a child's fantasy of how real butter pecan ice cream ought to taste."

¾ cup (1½ sticks) lightly salted butter
1½ cups pecans, halved
1 cup milk
2½ cups heavy cream
1 cup sugar
9 egg yolks

Melt the butter in a large skillet. Sauté the pecans until the butter browns.

Remove from the heat; strain the butter into a bowl and reserve. Cool to room temperature. Set pecans aside in another bowl.

In a heavy-bottomed saucepan, combine the milk, cream, and ½ cup sugar. Heat until just scalded; do not boil. Pour into a bowl and set aside.

In a large bowl, whisk together the egg yolks and the remaining ½ cup sugar until well blended.

Place the bowl over a pot of boiling water (or use a double-boiler), and whisk constantly. Heat until hot to the touch.

Slowly add the scalded milk mixture to the egg yolk mixture, whisking constantly until thoroughly mixed. Strain through a mesh strainer into the reserved butter, and whisk together.

Chill in the refrigerator. Freeze in an ice cream machine according to manufacturer's instructions. When the ice cream begins to stiffen, sprinkle in the reserved pecans and continue to churn until the nuts are evenly incorporated and the ice cream is thick.

Serves 8 to 10

Buckwheat Risotto with Wild Leeks and Goat Cheese

ANNE ROSENZWEIG, Inside, New York, NY

"This dish has two parts. Unless you grew up with Eastern European influences in your household or were a hippie, you would not necessarily know about kasha. Sometimes I like doing a playful version of a classic dish. Using orzo for risotto with these other ingredients makes a dish as creamy as risotto in a quarter of the time."

> 4 tablespoons unsalted sweet butter
> 1 cup chopped wild leeks
> 1 teaspoon chopped garlic
> 1 cup cooked buckwheat groats (kasha)
> 1 cup dry orzo
> 1½ cups rich chicken stock
> ½ cup crumbled goat cheese
> ½ cup chiffonade of Swiss chard
> 4 tablespoons chopped parsley
> 4 tablespoons chopped chives
> Salt and freshly ground pepper

Heat a medium saucepan over moderate heat. Add 2 tablespoons of the butter, let sizzle, and stir add the leeks and garlic, and cook, stirring, for 2 minutes. Add the buckwheat groats, orzo, and ½ cup of the stock and cook slowly until the stock is absorbed. Add the remaining stock in ¼-cup increments until all the stock is absorbed. The pasta should be al dente. Stir in the goat cheese, Swiss chard, parsley, chives, remaining 2 tablespoons butter, and salt and pepper to taste. The pasta should be creamy and luxuriant. Serve immediately.

Serves 4

Dad's Pan-Fried Spotted Brown Brook Trout with Fried Potatoes

BRADLEY OGDEN, The Lark Creek Inn, Larkspur, CA, and One Market Restaurant, San Francisco, CA

"I have been very fortunate over the years to have had many talented people share their expertise and love of food with me. Each one in some way has had an influence on the way I cook today. But there is one particular childhood memory that has stuck with me over the years. I was ten years old, living in Michigan, when my father took me alone on a fishing trip. As I was one of seven children, it was a real treat to have my dad alone for the day. We spent most of the day fishing for wild brown spotted trout out of an icy cold stream, fed from the melting winter snows. That night, my dad fried potatoes and onions seasoned with just a touch of salt and some freshly cracked pepper in a huge cast-iron skillet on an old potbelly stove.

In another cast-iron skillet, he fried the trout that had been dredged in lightly seasoned flour. Nothing has ever tasted as good. I can still remember the fresh taste of the food, the simple way Dad cooked it, and the fun we had. These qualities are the ones that I still try to integrate in my cooking style today."

Six 8- to 16-ounce fresh brook trout (depending on your catch)

2 tablespoons oil

½ cup flour, seasoned with kosher salt, freshly ground black pepper, and cayenne

3 to 4 tablespoons sweet butter

¼ cup chopped parsley

2 lemons, juiced

Fried potatoes (recipe follows)

Fillet the trout. Place a large cast-iron skillet over high heat. Add the oil. Lightly dredge the trout in the seasoned flour. When the oil is hot, place the fish carefully in the pan. Reduce the heat slightly. Add the butter.

Cook the trout on both sides until golden brown, 3 to 4 minutes. Remove and place on serving dishes and sprinkle with the parsley and lemon juice. Serve with the fried potatoes.

Serves 6

Fried Potatoes

3 large russet potatoes

3 tablespoons unsalted butter

1 small Spanish onion, peeled, quartered, and sliced ¼ inch thick

1 teaspoon freshly cracked black pepper

½ cup plus 1 tablespoon clarified butter or lard

Chopped chives, optional

Kosher salt

Rinse the potatoes and place in a 4-quart saucepan with salted water to cover. Bring to a boil over high heat and boil for 20 to 25 minutes until barely cooked through, leaving slightly underdone. Remove the potatoes immediately and cool at room temperature. When cool enough to handle, peel, cut into quarters length-wise, and slice ⅛ inch thick.

In a skillet over medium heat, melt a tablespoon of the unsalted butter. Add the onion and sauté until lightly caramelized, 2 to 3 minutes. Season with ½ teaspoon of the cracked black pepper and salt to taste. Remove from the pan immediately so as not to overcook. Set the onion aside to cool.

To cook the fries, use two large skillets so that the potatoes are not stacked. Add ¼ cup of the clarified butter to each skillet and place over high heat. When the butter starts to smoke, divide the potatoes and add half to each skillet. Cook on one side until golden brown and crisp.

Flip onto the other side and season with the remaining ½ teaspoon of pepper and salt to taste. Drain the excess fat from each pan, reduce the heat to low, and add half the onion to each pan. Sauté just to warm the onions through. Add 1 tablespoon unsalted butter, toss to mix, and serve immediately. Add the chives, if desired.

Serves 4 to 6

Appendices

Restaurant work is hard work. But you don't give up—you try to improve every day, even on the old things you do. It's a never-ending learning process. Even the same dish, every day it tastes different. Every day you find another angle to test.

EDNA LEWIS

APPENDIX A:

Selected Professional Cooking Schools in the United States and Abroad

United States

The Academy of Culinary Arts
Atlantic Community College

5100 Black Horse Pike
Mays Landing, NJ 08330
(609) 343-5000 or (800) 645-CHEF
http://www.atlantic.edu

Art Institute of Atlanta
School of Culinary Arts

6600 Peachtree Dunwoody Rd.
100 Embassy Row
Atlanta, GA 30328
(770) 394-8300
http://www.aii.edu

Art Institute of Fort Lauderdale

1799 SE 17th St.
Ft. Lauderdale, FL 33316
(770) 394-8300
http://www.aii.edu

Baltimore International Culinary College

17 Commerce St.
Baltimore, MD 21202
(410) 752-4710
http://www.bic.edu

Boston University
Seminars in the Culinary Arts
Boston University Metropolitan College

808 Commonwealth Ave.
Boston, MA 02215
(617) 353-9852
http://www.bu.edu/lifelong/seminars/

The California Culinary Academy

625 Polk St.
San Francisco, CA 94102
(415) 771-3500
http://www.baychef.com

California School of Culinary Arts

1416 El Centro St.
South Pasadena, CA 91030
(626) 403-8490
http://www.calchef.com

The Cambridge School of Culinary Arts

2020 Massachusetts Ave.
Cambridge, MA 02140
(617) 354-2020
http://www.cambridgeculinary.com

City College of San Francisco–Hotel &
Restaurant

50 Phelan Ave.
San Francisco, CA 94112
(415) 239-3152
http://www.ccsf.cc.us/hotelandrestaurant

Cook Street School of Fine Cooking

1937 Market St.
Denver, CO 80202
(303) 308-9300
http://www.cookstreet.com

The Cooking and Hospitality Institute of Chicago

361 W. Chestnut
Chicago, IL 60610
(312) 944-2725
http://www.chicnet.org

The Cooking School of Aspen

414 East Hyman Ave.
Aspen, CO 81611
(970) 920-1879 or (800) 603-6004
info@cookingschoolof aspen.com
http://www.cookingschoolofaspen.com

Cooking School of the Rockies

637 S. Broadway
Boulder, CO 80303
(303) 494-7988
csrockies@aol.com
http://www.cookingschoolrockies.com

The Culinary Institute of America

1946 Campus Dr.
Hyde Park, NY 12538
(800) CULINARY
http://www.ciachef.com

The Florida Culinary Institute

2400 Metrocentre Blvd.
West Palm Beach, FL 33407
(561) 842-8324
http://www.floridaculinary.com

The French Culinary Institute

462 Broadway
New York, NY 10013
(212) 219-8890
http://www.frenchculinary.com

Hiroko's Kitchen School of Japanese Cooking

25 W. 15th St.
New York, NY 10011
(212) 727-3085
hiroko@hirokoskitchen.com
http://www.hirokoskitchen.com

Indiana University of Pennsylvania

Culinary School
125 S. Gilpin St.
Punxsutawney, PA 15767
(800) 438-6424
http://www.iup.edu/cularts

Institute of Culinary Education

50 W. 23rd St.
New York, NY 10010
(800) 522-4610
http://iceculinary.com

International Culinary Academy

555 Grant St.
Pittsburgh, PA 15222
(800) 447-8324
http://www.icacademy.com

Johnson & Wales University

8 Abbott Park Place
Providence, RI 02903
(800) 342-5598
http://www.jwu.edu

Kendall College
The School of Culinary Arts

2408 Orrington Ave.
Evanston, IL 60201
(847) 866-1304
http://www.kendall.edu

L'Academie de Cuisine

16006 Industrial Dr.
Gaithersburg, MD 20877
(301) 670-8670
http://www.lacademie.com

La Varenne at The Greenbrier

White Sulphur Springs, WV 24986
(304) 536-1110 or (800) 228-5049
cookingschool@greenbrier.com
http://www.lavarenne.com

National Center for Hospitality Studies
Sullivan College

3101 Bardstown Rd.
Louisville, KY 40205
(502) 456-6505
http://www.sullivan.edu

The Natural Gourmet Cooking School

48 W. 21st St., 2nd Floor
New York, NY 10010
(212) 645-5170
http://www.naturalgourmetschool.com

New England Culinary Institute

250 Main St.
Montpelier, VT 05602
(802) 223-6324
http://www.neculinary.com

New Hampshire College
The Culinary Institute

2500 N. River Rd.
Manchester, NH 03106
(800) 642-4968
http://www.nhc.edu

New York City Technical College

300 Jay St.
Brooklyn, NY 11201
(718) 260-5630
http://www.nyctc.cuny.edu

New York Restaurant School

75 Varick St.
New York, NY 10013
(212) 226-5500
http://www.nyrs.baweb.com

Paul Smith's College

P. O. Box 265
Paul Smiths, NY 12970
(800) 421-2605
http://www.paulsmiths.edu

Pennsylvania College of Technology
School of Hospitality

One College Ave.
Williamsport, PA 17701
(800) 367-9222
http://www.pct.edu

Pennsylvania Culinary
School of Culinary Arts

717 Liberty Ave.
Pittsburgh, PA 15222
(800) 432-2433
http://www.paculinary.com

Pennsylvania Institute of Culinary Arts

717 Liberty Ave.
Pittsburgh, PA 15222
(412) 566-2444
http://www.paculinary.com

The Restaurant School

4207 Walnut St.
Philadelphia, PA 19104
(215) 222-4200
http://www.therestaurantschool.com

San Francisco Baking Institute

390 Swift Ave. #13
South San Francisco, CA 94080
(650) 589-5784
contact@sfbi.com
http://www.sfbi.com

Schoolcraft College

18600 Haggerty Rd.
Livonia, MI 48152
(734) 462-4423
http://www.schoolcraft.cc.mi.us

Scottsdale Culinary Institute

8100 E. Camelback Rd. #1001
Scottsdale, AZ 85251
(480) 990-3773
http://www.scichefs.com

Stratford College

7777 Leesburg Pike
Falls Church, VA 22043
(800) 444-0804
http://www.stratford.edu

Washburne Trade School
Chefs Training Program

3233 W. 31st St.
Chicago, IL 60623
(773) 579-6100

Western Culinary Institute

1201 Southwest 12th Ave. #100
Portland, OR 97205
(503) 223-2245
http://www.westernculinary.com

Abroad

Apicius—Lorenzo de' Medici Institute

Via Faenza 43
Florence, 50123 Italy
(39) 055287360
info@apicius.it
http://www.apicius.it

The Ballymaloe Cookery School

Shanagarry, County Cork
Midleton, Ireland
(353) 21-646785
enquiries@ballymaloe-cookery-school.ie
http//www.ballymaloe-cookery-school.ie

The Culinary Institute of Canada

4 Sydney St.
Charlottetown, PE C1A 1E9 Canada
(902) 894-6805
http://www.athi.pe.ca

Ecole Lenôtre

40 rue Pierre Curie, B.P. 6
787373 Plaisir Cedex France
(33) 1-30-8146-34
ecole@lenotre.fr

Escuela de Cocina Luis Irizar

#5, Bajo, San Sebastian
20003 Spain
(34) 943-431540
esc_cocina_irizar@facilnet.es

George Brown College of Applied Arts
& Technology
Hospitality/Tourism Centre

300 Adelaide St. E.
Toronto, Ontario M5A 1N1 Canada
(800) 263-8995
http://www.gbrownc.on.ca

La Varenne: Château du Feÿ

89300 Villecien, France
Phone 33-03-86-63-18-34
Fax 33-03-86-63-01-33
http://www.lavarenne.com

La Varenne in Burgundy, France

P. O. Box 25574
Washington, DC 20007
(800) 537-6486
http://www.lavarenne.com

L'Ecole des Chefs

P. O. Box 183
Birchrunville, PA 19421
(610) 469-2500
info@leschefs.com
http://www.leschefs.com

Arranges internships in the United States
and France with noted French chefs such as
Georges Blanc, Daniel Boulud, Alain Passard,
François Payard, Georges Perrier, Michel
Richard, Eric Ripert, Michel Rostang, Guy Savoy,
Troisgros, and Jean-Georges Vongerichten.

Le Cordon Bleu

114 Marylebone Lane
London WIM 6HH, England
(44) 20-7-935-3503
http://www.cordonbleu.net

Le Cordon Bleu

8 rue Leon Delhomme
75015 Paris, France
33-153-68-22-67 or 800-457-CHEF
http://www.cordonbleu.net

Lyons Culinary Arts and Hotel Management
School

Chateau du Vivier B.P. 25
69131 Lyon-Ecully Cedex France
33 (0) 4 72 18 02 20
info@each-lyon.com

APPENDIX B:

Leading Culinary Organizations

American Culinary Federation (ACF)

10 San Bartola Dr.
St. Augustine, FL 32086
(904) 824-4468
http://www.acfchefs.org

The 25,000-member American Culinary Federation, founded in 1929, is the professional organization representing U.S. cooks and chefs. The nonprofit ACF certifies cooks and chefs, offers culinary and pastry apprenticeship programs, and accredits postsecondary culinary and pastry programs. The ACF's honor society, the American Academy of Chefs, represents hundreds of top chefs in the nation. The ACF's official magazine, *The National Culinary Review,* focuses on food and cooking and is published for chefs around the world.

American Institute of Baking (AIB)

1213 Bakers Way
Manhattan, KS 66502
(412) 322-8275
http://www.aibonline.org
info@aibonline.org

The American Institute of Baking was established in 1919 to promote the cause of education in nutrition, the science and art of baking, bakery management, and the allied sciences. It is a nonprofit educational and research organization supported by the contributions of nearly 600 member companies in the baking and allied trades.

The American Institute of Wine & Food (AIWF)

304 W. Liberty St., Suite 201
Louisville, KY 40202
(502) 992-1022
http://www.aiwf.org
aiwf@hqtrs.com

The AIWF is a nonprofit educational organization promoting a broad exchange of information and ideas to benefit all who care about wine and food from chefs and restaurateurs to dedicated amateurs. The institute was founded in 1981 by Julia Child, Robert Mondavi, Richard Graff, and others to advance the understanding, appreciation, and quality of what we eat and drink. Through its programs and publications, members of the AIWF have the opportunity to meet and share their ideas with the most knowledgeable people in the industry, including leading chefs, restaurateurs, winemakers, journalists, and other leaders in the art of wine and fine cuisine.

American Vegan Society (AVS)

P. O. Box 369
Malaga, NJ 08328-0908
(856) 694-2887

The organization's mission is to help educate and be a support to people who wish to live without using animal products. Founded in 1960, they organize classes, have a newsletter, and provide other information regarding nutrition.

The Bread Bakers Guild of America (BBGA)

P. O. Box 22254
Pittsburgh, PA 15222
http://www.bbga.org
doughmaster@bbga.org

The Bread Bakers Guild of America is the only nonprofit organization in North America formed exclusively to provide education in the field of artisan baking and the production of high-quality bread products. The Guild offers seminars and other educational resources, and publishes a bimonthly newsletter. Membership is open to anyone with an interest in good bread, but its educational focus is on production methods and ingredients used by professional bakers.

Careers Through Culinary Arts Program (C-CAP)

250 W. 57th St., Suite 2015
New York, NY 10107
(212) 873-2434
http://www.ccapinc.org

Careers Through Culinary Arts Program (C-CAP) is a nonprofit organization offering a curriculum enrichment program designed for existing culinary programs in public high schools. C-CAP offers training for teachers, partners schools with industry mentors, arranges free supplies, sets kids up with internships and jobs, and gives the best of them scholarships to the country's top culinary schools.

Chefs Collaborative

441 Stuart St. #712
Boston, MA 02116
(617) 236-5200
http://www.chefnet.com/cc2000

Chefs Collaborative 2000 was founded in 1993, in conjunction with Oldways Preservation and Exchange Trust, following a symposium held in Hawaii entitled "Food Choices: 2000." This nationwide gathering of chefs organized itself to celebrate the pleasures of food, and to recognize the impact of food choices on public health, on the vitality of cultures, and on the integrity of the global environment. Integral to the members of the Chefs Collaborative 2000 was their belief in preserving the environment through sustainable agriculture; promoting the production and distribution of good, wholesome food to all; and educating for the future.

The Culinary Vegetable Institute

12304 Mudbrook Rd.
Milan, OH 44846
(800) 289-4644
http://www.culinaryvegetableinstitute.com

The Culinary Vegetable Institute provides the world's most innovative chefs with a place to share knowledge, experiment and discover techniques for growing and preparing the most flavorful varieties of vegetables in the world. The Institute is dedicated to the sharing of knowledge between chefs and farmers. Members of its Advisory Board include Daniel Boulud, Alain Ducasse, Thomas Keller, Charlie Trotter, Norman Van Aken, and Jean-Georges Vongerichten.

The International Council on Hotel, Restaurant, and Institutional Education (CHRIE)

1200 17th St., N.W.
Washington, DC 20036
(202) 331-5990
http://www.chrie.org

CHRIE was founded in 1946 as a nonprofit association for schools, colleges, and universities offering programs in hotel and restaurant management, foodservice management, and culinary arts. In recent years, International CHRIE has expanded and evolved into a marketplace for facilitating exchanges of information, ideas, research, and products and services related to education, training and resource development for the hospitality and tourism industry (food, lodging, recreation, and travel services). Serving as the hospitality and tourism education network, International CHRIE strives to unite educators, industry executives, and associations.

Earth Pledge Foundation

149 E. 38th St.
New York, NY 10016
(212) 573-6968
http://www.earthpledge.org

The Earth Pledge Foundation is a nonprofit communications company that produces projects with the private sector to advance the concept of sustainable development—our need to live and work in a prosperous and healthy environment. The Foundation's mission highlights the interconnectedness of art, architecture, technology, democracy, food, tourism, media, and the environment. Working with their partners, sponsors, and clients, Earth Pledge makes sustainability accessible through print, new media, special events, educational programs, community and public relations, marketing, and strategic planning. Its Web site http://www.farmtotable.org

aims to promote local farmers, environmental preservation, community connection, and cultural tradition, and offers a searchable database of sustainable products in New York along with recipes, online shopping, a dictionary, a listing of what's in season when, and other articles.

The Educational Foundation of the National Restaurant Association

175 West Jackson Blvd., Suite 1500
Chicago, IL 60604-2702
(800) 765-2122 or
(312) 715-1010
http://www.nraef.org

This Educational Foundation of the National Restaurant Association, a nonprofit organization founded in 1987, is the leading source of education, training, and career development for the foodservice industry. It focuses on upgrading professionalism in the foodservice industry by providing high-quality educational products and services for foodservice managers and others pursuing a career in the hospitality industry.

International Association of Culinary Professionals (IACP)

304 W. Liberty St. #201
Louisville, KY 40202
(502) 581-9786
http://www.iacp.com

The IACP is a not-for-profit professional society of individuals employed in, or providing services to, the culinary industry. IACP's mission is to be a resource and support system for food professionals, and to help its members achieve and sustain success at all levels of their careers through education, information, and peer contacts in an ethical, responsible, and professional climate. The association provides continuing education and professional development for its members, who are employed in the fields of communication or education, or in the preparation of food and drink. The current membership of 4,000 encompasses 35 countries and represents virtually every profession in the culinary universe: teachers, cooking school owners, caterers, writers, chefs, media cooking personalities, editors, publishers, food stylists, food photographers, restaurateurs, leaders of major food corporations, and vintners.

International Foodservice Executives Association (IFSEA)

3739 Mykonos Ct. #7, Suite 103
Boca Raton, FL 33487
(561) 998-7758
www.ifsea.org

The IFSEA is the foodservice industry's first trade association. Organized in 1901 as the International Stewards and Caterers, its members are worldwide with branches in Canada, Japan, Guam, Germany, Taiwan, and the United States. IFSEA is a professional organization dedicated to raising foodservice industry standards, educating members and future leaders, recognizing members' achievements, and serving the growing needs of the diverse, dynamic, multibillion-dollar-a-year market for food away from home.

The James Beard Foundation

167 W. 12th St.
New York, NY 10011
(212) 675-4984
http://www.jamesbeard.org

The James Beard Foundation was established as a charitable foundation in 1986 to keep alive the ideals and activities that made James Beard the acknowledged "Father of American Cooking." The Foundation fosters the appreciation and development of gastronomy by preserving and promulgating our culinary heritage, and by recognizing and promoting excellence in all aspects of the culinary arts. The Foundation is supported by benefactors, corporate donors, and a nationwide network of members, all of whom are kept informed of activities through the monthly newsletter, *News From The Beard House*. The newsletter details the events scheduled for the month; profiles chefs; and includes recipes, book reviews, articles by well-known writers, food and wine news from far-flung reporters, and a bit of gossip.

Les Dames d'Escoffier International

P. O. Box 4961
Louisville, KY 40204
(502) 456-1851
http://www.ldei.org

Les Dames d'Escoffier is a society of professional women of achievement with careers in food, wine, and other beverages, and the arts of the table. The purpose of the organization is to support and promote the understanding, appreciation, and knowledge of these professions in the tradition of Auguste Escoffier. Members are outstanding women with at least five years' professional experience who have distinguished themselves in gastronomy, oenology, and related fields. Active members include chefs, cooking school owners and teachers, food writers and editors, caterers, hotel executives, purveyors, administrators, and public relations specialists.

National Restaurant Association (NRA)

1200 17th St., NW
Washington, DC 20036
(202) 331-5900
http://www.restaurant.org
info@dineout.org

The NRA is the leading national trade association for the foodservice industry. Together with The Educational Foundation of the NRA, it works to protect, promote, and educate the rapidly growing industry. Since its founding in 1919, the NRA has worked to promote the ideals and interests of the foodservice industry, the employer of eight million individuals. To this end, the association provides members with a wide range of education, research, communications, convention, and government affairs services.

Oldways Preservation & Exchange Trust

266 Beacon St.
Boston, MA 02116
(617) 421-5500
http://www.oldwayspt.org
oldways@oldwayspt.org

Oldways Preservation & Exchange Trust, a nonprofit organization, was organized in 1988 by K. Dun Gifford, and began operating in mid-1990 when Nancy Harmon Jenkins and Greg Drescher joined it as co-founders and directors. The purpose of Oldways is to preserve the healthy, environmentally sustainable food and agricultural traditions of many cultures, and to make the lessons of these traditions more widely accessible. The mission at Oldways is to show the continuing significance of our agricultural, culinary, and dietary heritage—and show how the lessons of the past can be applied to address contemporary needs. Oldways brings together experts from all over the world to evaluate these traditions and define sustainable food choices, and on the basis of this information, to devise, organize, and administer educational programs that encourage sounder food choices.

Public Voice for Food & Health Policy

1001 Connecticut Ave., N.W., Suite 522
Washington, DC 20036
(202) 659-5930

Founded in 1982, Public Voice for Food and Health Policy is a national nonprofit research, education, and advocacy organization that promotes a safer, healthier, and more affordable food supply. Public Voice advances the interests of all consumers by fostering food and agricultural policies and practices that enhance public health and protect the environment. The organization's agenda focuses on the following food safety, nutrition, and sustainable agriculture objectives: seafood safety; healthy eating among children; nutrition labeling; sustainable agriculture; pesticide policy and international food standards; meat and poultry inspection systems; food security; commodity programs; and agricultural research and biotechnology.

Radcliffe Culinary Friends
Schlesinger Library at Radcliffe Institute

10 Garden St.
Cambridge, MA 02138
(617) 495-8647
www.radcliffe.edu/schles/friends

The goals of the Radcliffe Culinary Friends are to collect, catalog, and preserve a major collection of books and periodicals related to food; to make known these resources to all interested people; and to provide a forum for discussion about the history of food and the study of food in society. The Schlesinger Library Culinary Collection includes nearly 12,000 works in the fields of cookery, gastronomy, domestic management, the history of cooking, and related reference works. The books, which date from the sixteenth century to the present, represent the cuisines of all nations. They include many voluntary association cookbooks as well as classics of European and American cooking. The Radcliffe Culinary Friends also publish a newsletter, the *Radcliffe Culinary Times,* and sponsor special events.

Roundtable for Women in Foodservice (RWF)

1372 La Colina Dr.
Tustin, CA 92780
(714) 838-2749
http://www.rwf.org
national@rwf.org

The RWF is a nonprofit organization, established in 1982, dedicated to the promotion of the advancement and visibility of women throughout the foodservice industry. These goals are accomplished through educational seminars, mentoring, and networking. RWF provides members with a national directory and holds an annual conference in Chicago where Woman of the Year and Pacesetter awards are presented. RWF also presents student scholarships annually and provides a membership card, which entitles members to special benefits and discounts throughout the foodservice industry.

Slow Food

P. O. Box 1737
New York, NY 10021
(212) 988-5146
(877) SLOWFOOD
http://www.slowfoodusa.org

The Slow Food organization is dedicated to promoting and preserving the local traditions of cooking and products. Founded in 1986 with over 40,000 members in 35 countries, the members support local farmers and vintners and hold events educating the public on the benefits of artisanal products.

Sommelier Society of America

P. O. Box 1770, Madison Sq. Stn.
New York, NY , 10159
(212) 679-4190

The Sommelier Society of America is dedicated to wine education for both nonprofessionals and professionals. They offer a six-month course on wine education that requires no prior wine knowledge, as well as classes for furthering your education. They are part of the Association de le Sommellerie International. The Society has chapters in New York, Los Angeles, Atlanta, and Chicago.

Tasters Guild

1451 W. Cypress Creek Rd.
Suite #300-78
Ft. Lauderdale, FL 33309
(954) 928-2823
http://www.tastersguild.com

Established in 1987, Tasters Guild consists of over 78 chapters throughout the country that bring together consumers, wine and food establishments, and the wine and foodservice industry. Its objective is to promote the appreciation and responsible use of wine and food through education, specific tastings, special consumer benefits, and travel opportunities.

Women Chefs & Restaurateurs (WCR)

304 W. Liberty St., Suite 201
Louisville, KY 40202
Phone: (502) 581-0300
Fax: (502) 589-3602
wcr@hqtrs.com
http://www.chefnet.com/wcr.html

The mission of WCR is to promote the education and advancement of women in the restaurant industry and the betterment of the industry as a whole. Among its goals are to facilitate communication and exchange of ideas between members and to promote professional contacts; to provide educational opportunities for professional and personal development for women in all sectors of the restaurant industry; to create and expand professional and business opportunities for women working in or wishing to enter the restaurant industry; to provide support and foster an environment that ensures women equal access to the positions, power, and rewards offered by the restaurant industry; and to examine the issues of women in the workplace and to advocate the improvement of work environments in the restaurant industry.

World Association of Cooks Societies (WACS)

http://www.wacs2000.org

A global professional association founded in 1928 at the Sorbonne in Paris serving millions of chefs and cooks who live and work in more than 60 nations on five continents. (The American Culinary Federation is the representative organization for the United States.)

APPENDIX C:

Selected Culinary Media and Resources

Art Culinaire

40 Mills St.
Morristown, NJ 07960
(973) 993-5500
http://www.getartc.com

The Art of Eating

Box 242
Peacham, VT 05862
(800) 495-3944
http://www.artofeating.com

Beard House Monthly

The James Beard Foundation
6 W. 18th St., 10th Floor
New York, NY 10011
(212) 627-1111
http://www.jamesbeard.org

Bon Appétit

6300 Wilshire Blvd.
Los Angeles, CA 90036
(323) 965-3600
http://www.epicurious.com

Chef

20 N. Wacker Dr., Suite 3230
Chicago, IL 60606
(312) 849-2220
http://www.chefmagazine.com

Cooking Light

P. O. Box 1748
Birmingham, AL 35201
(205) 877-6000
http://www.cookinglight.com

Cook's Illustrated

17 Station St.
Brookline, MA 02445
(617) 232-1000

Fabulous Foods

http://www.fabulousfoods.com

Food Arts

387 Park Ave. South
New York, NY 10016
(212) 684-4224
http://www.foodarts.com

Food & Wine

1120 Avenue of the Americas
New York, NY 10036
(212) 382-5600
http://www.foodandwine.com

Global Gourmet

egg@globalgourmet.com
http://www.globalgourmet.com

Gourmet

4 Times Square
New York, NY 10036
(212) 286-2860
http://www.epicurious.com

Nation's Restaurant News

425 Park Ave.
New York, NY 10022
(212) 756-5000
http://www.nrn.com

Peterson's Culinary Schools

http://www.culinaryschools.com/

Peterson's, which publishes *Peterson's Culinary Schools,* a guide to U.S. and international professional cooking schools and apprenticeships, features detailed profiles of cooking schools on its Web site.

Restaurant Business

355 Park Ave. South, 3rd Floor
New York, NY 10010-1789
http://www.restaurantbiz.com

Restaurant Hospitality

1300 E. 9th St.
Cleveland, OH 44114
(216) 696-7000
http://subscribe.penton.com/rh/

Restaurants and Institutions

2000 Clearwater Dr.
Oak Brook, IL 60544-8809
(630) 288-8204
http://www.rimag.com

Saveur

304 Park Ave. South
New York, NY 10010
(212) 219-7400
http://www.saveurmag.com

ShawGuides

http://cookingcareer.shawguides.com and
http://www.chefjobs.com

ShawGuides, which publishes *The Guide to Cooking Schools,* features information about cooking schools (including tuition, number of students, specific programs offered, and faculty to student ratios) and jobs on its Web sites.

Williams-Sonoma Taste

15 East 32nd St., 8th Floor
New York, NY 10016
(212) 931-9800

Wine Enthusiast

103 Fairview Park Dr.
Elmsford, NY 10523
(914) 345-8463
http://www.winemag.com

Wine Spectator

387 Park Ave. South
New York, NY 10016
(212) 684-4224
http://www.winespectator.com

APPENDIX D:

Brief Biographies of Chefs Interviewed

Jean Banchet was the founding chef-owner of the legendary restaurant Le Français in Wheeling, Illinois. He was later chef-owner of Ciboulette in Atlanta. A native of France, he has worked in the kitchens of Fernand Point, Paul Bocuse, and the Troisgros brothers.

Mario Batali is chef-partner of Babbo, Esca, Lupa, and Otto restaurants as well as a partner in Italian Wine Merchants in New York City. He is the host of the televison show *Molto Mario* and the author of three cookbooks: *Mario Batali Simple Food, Mario Batali Holiday Food,* and *The Babbo Cookbook.* In 1998, Babbo won the James Beard Award as Best New Restaurant, and in 2002 Batali won as Best Chef: New York City. (http://www.babbonyc.com)

Rick Bayless is the chef-owner of Frontera Grill and Topolobompo, both in Chicago. He earned both undergraduate and graduate degrees in linguistics from the University of Michigan. In 1991, he won the James Beard Award as Best Chef: Midwest; in 1995 he won as Outstanding Chef; and in 1998 he was named Humanitarian of the Year. He is the author of *Authentic Mexican, Rick Bayless's Mexican Kitchen, Rick Bayless Mexico: One Plate at a Time* and is host of *Mexico: One Plate at a Time* aired on PBS. (http://www.fronterakitchens.com)

Chris Bianco is chef-owner of Pizzeria Bianco and Bar Bianco in Phoenix. He won the 2003 James Beard Award as Best Chef: Southwest. *The Arizona Republic* named Pizzeria Bianco "Best Italian Restaurant" in 1996 and "Best Pizza" in 2000. In 1999, Pizzeria Bianco was voted "Best Italian Food" by *Gourmet's* Readers Poll.

Daniel Boulud is the chef-owner of Restaurant Daniel (which holds four stars from *The New York Times*), Café Boulud, and db Bistro Moderne. In 1992, he won the James Beard Award as Best Chef: New York City, and in 1994, he won as Outstanding Chef. He is the author of *Cooking with Daniel Boulud, Daniel Boulud's Cafe Boulud Cookbook,* and *Chef Daniel Boulud: Cooking in New York City.* (http://www.danielnyc.com)

Edward Brown is the chef of The Sea Grill in New York City. He is a graduate of The Culinary Institute of America. He has worked at Lucas-Carton in Paris, and was previously the chef at Tropica and Judson Grill in New York City. He is the author of the *The Modern Seafood Cook.*

The late Patrick Clark, frequently cited as one of America's leading African-American chefs, was the executive chef of Tavern on the Green in New York City. In 1994, he won the James Beard Award as Best Chef: Mid-Atlantic. He graduated from the New York City Technical College and later apprenticed with Michel Guérard in France.

Sanford (Sandy) D'Amato is the chef-owner of Sanford and Coquette Cafe in Milwaukee. He won the James Beard Award for Best Chef: Midwest in 1996. His restaurant Sanford was chosen by *Esquire* as one of the Best New Restaurants in 1990 and has received the *Wine Spectator* Award of Distinction multiple times. Sandy was named one of America's Hot New Chefs by *Food & Wine* in 1985. (http://www.foodspot.com/sanford)

Gary Danko is the chef-owner of Gary Danko in San Francisco, which won the 2000 James Beard Award as Best New Restaurant in America. In 1995, he won as Best Chef: California when he served as chef of The Dining Room at The Ritz-Carlton in San Francisco. He is a graduate of The Culinary Institute of America, and also studied with the legendary Madeleine Kamman. He was also named one of America's Best New Chefs by *Food & Wine*. (http://www.garydanko.com)

Gina DePalma is the pastry chef of Babbo in New York City. In 2002 and 2003, she was nominated for the James Beard Award as America's Outstanding Pastry Chef. A graduate of Peter Kump's Cooking School (now ICE), she previously worked in pastry at Chanterelle and at Gramercy Tavern. (http://www.babbonyc.com)

Marcel Desaulniers is chef-partner of The Trellis in Williamsburg, Virginia. He is the only chef to have won James Beard Awards as both Best Chef: Mid-Atlantic (1993), and Outstanding Pastry Chef (1999). A graduate of the Culinary Institute of America, he has twice won James Beard Book Awards for his books *Death by Chocolate* and the *The Burger Meisters*. His most recent book is *Celebrate with Chocolate*. (http://www.thetrellis.com)

Traci Des Jardins is chef-partner of Jardinière in San Francisco. She was the executive chef of Rubicon in San Francisco and the opening chef de cuisine at Patina in Los Angeles. She won the James Beard Award as Rising Star Chef in 1995, and has subsequently been nominated multiple times as Best Chef: California. She previously worked with several culinary greats including Alain Ducasse, Alain Passard, and Michel and Pierre Troisgros. (http://www.jardiniere.com)

Lissa Doumani is pastry chef and co-owner, with **Hiroyoshi Sone,** of Terra in St. Helena, California. They are also co-authors of *Terra: Cooking from the Heart of Napa Valley*. They first met while working together at Spago, where they were pastry chef and chef, respectively. They were named two of America's Best New Chefs by *Food & Wine*. (http://www.terrarestaurant.com)

Todd English is the chef-owner of The Olives Group, which includes Olives and Figs restaurants across the United States, including the originals in Charlestown, Massachusetts; as well as in Aspen, Las Vegas, New York City, Washington, D.C., and Tokyo. In 1991, he won the James Beard Award as a Rising Star Chef and in 1994, as Best Chef: Northeast. (http://www.toddenglish.com)

Susan Feniger is the chef-partner, with Mary Sue Milliken, in the Border Grill in Santa Monica and Las Vegas. They also own Ciudad in Los Angeles. In 1985, they were inducted into the Who's Who of Food and Beverage in America. They are authors of many books., including *City Cuisine* and *Mesa Mexican: Bold Flavors from the Border, Coastal Mexico, and Beyond*. They have also hosted their own television show, *Too Hot Tamales*. (http://www.millikenandfeniger.com)

Susanna Foo is the chef-owner of Susanna Foo in Philadelphia. A former librarian from the University of Pittsburgh, she attended The Culinary Institute of America's continuing education division. In 1997, she won the James Beard Award as Best Chef: Mid-Atlantic. She is also the author of *Susanna Foo Chinese Cuisine: The Fabulous Flavors & Innovative Recipes of North America's Finest Chinese Cook*. (http://www.susannafoo.com)

Larry Forgione is the founding chef-owner of An American Place in New York City and The Beekman 1766 Tavern in Rhinebeck, New York, and is a founder of American Spoon Foods. In 1984, he was inducted into the Who's Who of Food and Beverage in America and in 1993, he won the James Beard Award as Outstanding Chef. He is the author of *An American Place,* and a graduate of The Culinary Institute of America.

George Germon is the chef-partner, with Johanne Killeen, of Al Forno in Providence, Rhode Island, and Cafe Louis in Boston. Al Forno was named one of the Distinguished Restaurants of North America in *Food & Wine*. In 1993, they jointly won the James Beard Award as Best Chefs: Northeast. They are co-authors of *Cucina Simpatica*. (http://www.alforno.com)

Victor Gielisse is the Dean of Culinary Arts, Baking and Pastry Studies at The Culinary Institute of America. He was formerly the chef-owner of Actuelle in Dallas. He is a Certified Master Chef, and in 1991, he was named The Culinary Institute of America's Chef of the Year. He is also the author of *Cuisine Actuelle*.

Joyce Goldstein is a consultant and writer, and was formerly the chef-owner of Square One in San Francisco. She won the 1994 James Beard Award as Best Chef: California. In 1985, she was inducted into the Who's Who of Food and Beverage in America. A graduate of Yale, she is the award-winning author of several books, including *The Mediterranean Kitchen, Back to Square One,* and *Kitchen Conversations*. She also writes a column for the *San Francisco Chronicle*.

Gordon Hamersley is the chef-owner of Hamersley's Bistro in Boston. In 1995, he won the James Beard Award as Best Chef: Northeast. Hamersley's Bistro has been voted to *Boston* magazine's Hall of Fame by the magazine's readers and is continually cited as one of Boston's top three restaurants by the Zagat Survey and the *Gourmet* reader's poll. He was also named one of America's Best New Chefs by *Food & Wine*. (http://www.hamersleysbistro.com)

The late Raji Jallepalli was the chef-owner of Restaurant Raji in Memphis, where she innovatively blended Indian flavors with French technique in her signature cuisine. A former medical technician, she was encouraged as a chef by her mentor, the late Jean-Louis Palladin. She also authored the cookbook *Raji Cuisine*.

Jean Joho is the chef-owner of Everest and Brasserie Jo in Chicago. He won the James Beard Award as Best Chef: Midwest in 1995, and was named one of America's Best New Chefs by *Food & Wine*. He previously worked with Paul Haeberlin at his Michelin three-star restaurant L'Auberge de l'Ill as well as at other two- and three-star restaurants throughout Europe. (http://www.brasseriejo.com)

Madeleine Kamman is the author of numerous cookbooks and books on food, including *The Making of a Cook, Dinner Against the Clock, When French Women Cook, In Madeleine's Kitchen, Madeleine Cooks,* and *Savoie.* In 1998, she was won a Lifetime Achievement Award from the James Beard Foundation in addition to its Cookbook of the Year Award for her revison of *The Making of a Cook*. In 1986, she was named to the Who's Who of Food and Beverage in America. She was the host of her own PBS cooking show *Madeleine Cooks,* and formerly ran cooking schools in New England as well as her own restaurant, Chez La Mère Madeleine.

Johanne Killeen is the chef-partner, with George Germon, of Al Forno in Providence, Rhode Island, and Cafe Louis in Boston. Al Forno was named one of the Distinguished Restaurants of North America in *Food & Wine*. In 1993, they were jointly named the Best Chefs: Northeast by The James Beard Foundation. They are co-authors of *Cucina Simpatica*. (http://www.alforno.com)

Albert Kumin heads the Green Mountain Chocolate Company in Vermont and has been cited as one of the two leading pastry chefs in the country by *Time* magazine. In 1992, he won the James Beard Award as Outstanding Pastry Chef, and was named to the Who's Who of Food and Beverage in America. He was the opening pastry chef of the legendary Four Seasons restaurant in New York City, and also served as pastry chef in the Carter White House. (http://greenmountainchocolate.com)

Emeril Lagasse is the chef-owner of Emeril's and Nola, both in New Orleans, as well as Emeril's New Orleans Fish House and Delmonico's in Las Vegas. He is the host of *Emeril Live!* on the the Food Network. In 1989, he was named to the Who's Who of Food and Beverage in America, and in 1991, he won the James Beard Award for Best Chef: Southeast. He has authored numerous cookbooks, and is a graduate of Johnson & Wales University. (http://www.emerils.com)

Edna Lewis is a consultant and writer considered a foremost authority on Southern cooking, and has authored numerous books. She has served as a consultant to many fine restaurants, including Gage & Tollner in Brooklyn, New York, and has been credited with reviving the art of Southern cooking. In 1984, she was inducted into the Who's Who of Food and Beverage in America.

Emily Luchetti is the executive pastry chef of Farallon restaurant in San Francisco. She is the author of *Stars Desserts* and *Four Star Desserts*, which was nominated for the James Beard Award in 1995. She is the former president of the Women Chefs and Restaurateurs association. Her many honors include being named one of America's "Top Ten Pastry Chefs" by *Chocolatier* magazine and being nominated multiple times for the James Beard Award as Outstanding Pastry Chef. (http://www.farallon-restaurant.com)

Zarela Martinez is the chef-owner of Zarela in New York City, which brings the flavors of her native Mexico to the United States. She is the author of *Food from My Heart: Cuisines of Mexico Remembered and Reimagined; The Food and Life of Oaxaca: Traditional Recipes from Mexico's Heart;* and *Zarela's Veracruz.* (http://www.zarela.com)

Nobu Matsuhisa is the chef-owner of Matsuhisa in Los Angeles, and of Nobu in Aspen, New York City, and London. He is the author of *Nobu: The Cookbook*. In 1995, Nobu won the James Beard Award as Best New Restaurant. He is a native of Japan, whose work as a chef has also taken him through Peru, Argentina, and Alaska. (http://www.nobumatsuhisa.com)

Mark Miller is the chef-owner of the Coyote Cafes in Santa Fe and Las Vegas. In 1996, he won the James Beard Award for Best Chef:

Southwest. In 1984, he was inducted into the Who's Who of Food and Beverage in America. He is the author of several books, including *Coyote Cafe: Foods from the Southwest;* he also produced the Great Chile Poster. He is an alumnus of Chez Panisse. (http://www.coyote-cafe.com)

Mary Sue Milliken is chef-partner, with **Susan Feniger,** in the Border Grill in Santa Monica and Las Vegas. They also own Ciudad in Los Angeles. In 1985, they were inducted into the Who's Who of Food and Beverage in America. They are co-authors of several books, including *City Cuisine* and *Mesa Mexican: Bold Flavors from the Border, Coastal Mexico, and Beyond.* They have also hosted their own television show, *Too Hot Tamales.* (http://www.millikenand-feniger.com)

Patrick O'Connell is the chef-owner of The Inn at Little Washington in Washington, Virginia. In 1992, he won the James Beard Award as Best Chef: Mid-Atlantic, and in 2001 as Outstanding Chef. In 1993, The Inn at Little Washington won the James Beard Award as Outstanding Restaurant and in 1997 for Outstanding Service. In 1984, he was inducted into the Who's Who of Food and Beverage in America. He is the author of *The Inn at Little Washington Cookbook.*

Bradley Ogden is the chef-owner of The Lark Creek Inn with locations throughout the Bay Area, and of One Market in San Francisco. He is a graduate of The Culinary Institute of America. In 1984, he was inducted into the

Who's Who of Food and Beverage in America and in 1993, he won the James Beard Award as Best Chef: California. (http://www.larkcreek.com)

The late Jean-Louis Palladin was the chef-owner of the celebrated restaurant Jean-Louis at the Watergate, and chef-owner of Palladin restaurants in Washington, D.C. and New York City. In 1991, he won the James Beard Award as Best Chef: Mid-Atlantic and in 1993, as Outstanding Chef of the Year. His oversized four-color cookbook *Jean-Louis: Cooking with the Seasons* was published in 1989, and set the bar for celebrity chef cookbooks to follow. In 1987, he was inducted into the Who's Who of Food and Beverage in America.

Charles Palmer is chef-owner of Aureole, Alva, Astra, and Metrazur in New York City. In 1997, he won the James Beard Award as Best Chef: New York City. He is the author of *Great American Food,* and a graduate of The Culinary Institute of America.

Cindy Pawlcyn is the chef-owner of Mustards Grill in Napa Valley, which she opened in 1983. In 1988, she was inducted into the Who's Who of Food and Beverage in America. She is the author of the *Fog City Diner Cookbook* and *Mustards Grill Napa Valley Cookbook.* She graduated from the University of Wisconsin at Stout in 1978 with a degree in hotel and restaurant management. (http://www.mustards grill.com)

Mark Peel is chef and co-owner, with his wife, pastry chef Nancy Silverton, of Campanile in Los Angeles, which won the 2001 James Beard Award for Outstanding Restaurant. They also co-own and operate LaBrea Bakery. Peel has been nominated several times for the James Beard Award as Best Chef: California. He co-authored two books with Nancy Silverton, including *The Food of Campanile* and *Mark Peel and Nancy Silverton at Home: Two Chefs Cook for Family and Friends.* (http://www.campanilerestaurant.com)

Georges Perrier is the chef-owner of Le Bec-Fin in Philadelphia. He won the 1998 James Beard Award as Best Chef: Mid-Atlantic. Le Bec-Fin was named one of the Distinguished Restaurants of North America in *Food & Wine* and has been called "the best in America" by food writer John Mariani. He is the author of *George Perrier: Le Bec-Fin Recipes.* (http://www.georgesperriergroup.com)

Odessa Piper is the chef-owner of L'Etoile in Madison, Wisconsin, which she opened in 1976. In 2001, she won the James Beard Award as Best Chef: Midwest. L'Etoile has also been cited as one of America's 50 Best Restaurants in *Gourmet.* (http://www.letoile-restaurant.com)

Alfred Portale is the chef-partner in Gotham Bar and Grill in New York City. In 1989, he was inducted into the Who's Who of Food and Beverage in America and in 1993, he won the James Beard Award as Best Chef: New York City. He is the author of two cookbooks, *Alfred Portale's Gotham Bar and Grill Cookbook* and *Alfred Portale's 12 Seasons Cookbook.* He graduated first in his class at The Culinary Institute of America. (http://www.gotham barandgrill.com)

Susan Regis is the executive chef of Upstairs on the Square in Cambridge. An alumna of Skidmore College, she worked closely with chef Lydia Shire for most of the past two decades, including the opening of Biba in Boston. In 1998, she won the James Beard Award as Best Chef: Northeast. (http://upstairsonthesquare.com)

Michel Richard is the chef-owner of Citronelle in Washington, D.C. and Santa Barbara, CA. In 1991, he was named to the Who's Who of Food and Beverage in America and in 1992, he won the James Beard Award as Best Chef: California while at Citrus in Los Angeles. (http://www.citronelledc.com)

Judy Rodgers is the chef-owner of Zuni Café in San Francisco. A graduate of Stanford University, she lived with the Troisgros family in France as an exchange student and later worked at Chez Panisse. She was inducted into the Who's Who of Food and Beverage in 1984. She won the James Beard Award as Best Chef: California in 2000, and in 2003, Zuni Café was named Outstanding Restaurant of the Year, and *The Zuni Café Cookbook* was named Cookbook of the Year.

Anne Rosenzweig is the executive chef-owner of Inside in New York City. She was formerly chef-owner of Arcadia and Lobster Club restaurants in New York City. Arcadia was named one of the Distinguished Restaurants of North America in *Food & Wine*. Rosenzweig, who has been nominated multiple times for the James Beard Award as Best Chef: New York City, was inducted into the Who's Who of Food and

Beverage in 1987, and is the author of *The Arcadia Seasonal Mural and Cookbook*.

Marcus Samuelsson is the executive chef-co-owner of Aquavit in New York City. In 1999, he won the James Beard Award as Rising Star Chef and in 2003, he was named Best Chef: New York. He takes pride in being the youngest chef to ever receive three stars from the *The New York Times*. He has spent time in many Michelin three-star kitchens, including that of Georges Blanc. In 2003, he published his first cookbook, *Aquavit*.

Amy Scherber is the baker and owner of Amy's Bread in New York City. In addition to baking for three retail shops, she provides bread to New York City's top restaurants. She serves on the board of both the Bread Bakers Guild and Women Chefs and Restaurateurs. In 1999 she was named New York Woman Business Owner of the Year by the National Association of Women Business Owners. She is also the author of *Amy's Bread*. (http://www.amysbread.com)

Chris Schlesinger is the chef-owner of the East Coast Grill and Raw Bar, in Cambridge, Massachusetts. He is also owner of the Back Eddy in Westport, Massachusetts. In 1996, he won the James Beard Award as Best Chef: Northeast. He has co-authored numerous cookbooks: *The Thrill of the Grill; Salsas, Sambals, Chutneys & Chowchows; Big Flavors of the Hot Sun, How to Cook Meat;* and *License to Grill*. He is a graduate of The Culinary Institute of America.

Jimmy Schmidt is the chef-owner of The Rattlesnake Club in Detroit. He studied with Madeleine Kamman at Modern Gourmet Cooking School in Boston. He was inducted into the Who's Who of Food and Beverage in 1984, and in 1993 he was named Best Chef: Midwest by The James Beard Foundation. (http://www.rattlesnakeclub.com)

Dieter Schorner is currently an associate professor at the Culinary Institute of America. He was previously the chef-owner of Patisserie Café Didier in Washington, D.C.'s Georgetown. Having served as pastry chef at some of the world's best restaurants, ranging from the Savoy Hotel in London to Le Cirque in New York City, he has been cited as one of America's two leading pastry chefs by *Time* magazine, and "possibly, next to Lenôtre, the most famous pastry chef in the world."

Craig Shelton is the executive chef-owner of the Ryland Inn in White House, New Jersey. He received the James Beard Award for Best Chef: Mid-Atlantic in 2000. He has worked in the esteemed kitchens of Ma Maison, La Côte Basque, Le Bernardin, L'Auberge de l'Ill, and Joel Robuchon. He served as chef de cuisine at Bouley, where he helped the restaurant earn four stars from *The New York Times*. (http://www.therylandinn.com)

Lydia Shire is the chef-owner of the venerable Boston landmark restaurant Locke-Ober and opened Excelsior in 2003. She was previously chef-owner of Biba and Pignoli in Boston. A graduate of London's Cordon Bleu cooking school, in 1984 she was inducted into the Who's Who of Food and Beverage in America. In 1992, she was named the Best Chef: Northeast by The James Beard Foundation.

Nancy Silverton is the pastry chef and co-owner, with husband, Mark Peel, of Campanile and La Brea Bakery in Los Angeles. She was named one of America's Best New Chefs by *Food & Wine*. In 1991, she was named the Pastry Chef of the Year by The James Beard Foundation and to the Who's Who of Food and Beverage in America. She is the author of several books, including *Nancy Silverton's Breads, Nancy Silverton's Pastries* and *Nancy Silverton's Sandwiches,* and co-author with Mark Peel of *The Food of Campanile* and *Mark Peel and Nancy Silverton Cook at Home.* (http://www.campanilerestaurant.com)

André Soltner is the former chef-owner of Lutèce in New York City. He is currently a dean at the French Culinary Institute in New York. In 1986, he was inducted into the Who's Who of Food and Beverage in America and in 1993, he was honored with a Lifetime Achievement Award by The James Beard Foundation. While he headed its kitchen, Lutèce was awarded numerous four-star reviews from *The New York Times.*

Hiroyoshi Sone is the chef and co-owner, with Lissa Doumani, of Terra in St. Helena, California. They are also co-authors of *Terra: Cooking from the Heart of Napa Valley.* They first met while working together at Spago, where they were chef and pastry chef, respectively. They were named two of America's Best New Chefs by *Food & Wine*. Sone won the 2003 James Beard Award as Best Chef: California. (http://www.terrarestaurant.com)

Susan Spicer is the chef-owner of Bayona and Herbsaint in New Orleans. She was named one of America's Best New Chefs by *Food & Wine* and in 1993, she was named Best Chef: Southeast by The James Beard Foundation. (http://www.bayona.com)

Allen Susser is the chef-owner of Chef Allen's in Miami. In 1994, he was named Best Chef: Southeast by The James Beard Foundation. He attended New York City Technical College and Florida International University, and worked in the kitchens of the Bristol Hotel in France and Le Cirque in New York City. (http://www.chefallens.com)

Elizabeth Terry is the founder of Elizabeth on 37th in Savannah, Georgia. The restaurant was named one of the Top 25 Restaurants in America by *Food & Wine*. She co-authored *Savannah Seasons: Food and Stories from Elizabeth on 37th*. (http://www.savannah-online.com/elizabeth)

Jacques Torres is the former pastry chef of Le Cirque and is now chef-owner of Jacques Torres Chocolate. Born in France, he was awarded the rank of Meilleur Ouvrier de France Patissier at the age of twenty-six, becoming one of the youngest French chefs to receive this honor. In 1994, he was named Pastry Chef of the Year by The James Beard Foundation. He

has authored two pastry books. (http://www.mrchocolate.com)

Jeremiah Tower is the former chef-owner of Stars and Stars Cafe in San Francisco. In 1984, he was inducted into the Who's Who of Food and Beverage in America, in 1993 was named Best Regional Chef by The James Beard Foundation, and in 1994 was named USA Chef of the Year by the Chefs in America Foundation, and elected to The Robb Report's prestigious Club 21. He is the author of *Jeremiah Tower Classics, Jeremiah Tower Cooks,* and *California Dish: What I Saw (and Cooked) at the American Culinary Revolution*.

The late **Barbara Tropp** was the chef-owner of China Moon Cafe in San Francisco. In 1989, she was inducted into the Who's Who of Food and Beverage in America. She authored *The Modern Art of Chinese Cooking* and *China Moon Cookbook*, and was the founder of the Women Chefs and Restaurateurs association.

Charlie Trotter is the chef-owner of Charlie Trotter's in Chicago, which won the James Beard Award for Outstanding Restaurant in 2000 and for Outstanding Wine Service in 1993. In 1992, he was named Best Chef: Midwest and Outstanding Chef in 1999 by The James Beard Foundation. He is the author of several books and was host of the TV show *Kitchen Sessions with Charlie Trotter*. He holds a degree in political science from the University of Wisconsin–Madison. (http://www.charlie trotters.com)

Norman Van Aken is the chef-owner of Norman's in Coral Gables, Florida. In 1997 he was named Best Chef: Southeast by The James Beard Foundation. He is the author of Norman Van Aken's *Feast of Sunlight: The Sumptuous Cuisine of Key West's Master Chef* and *Norman's New World Cuisine*. (http://www.normans.com)

Jean-Georges Vongerichten is the chef-owner of Jean Georges, Jo Jo, Mercer Kitchen, and 66, all in New York, and Vong (in multiple cities). He is also owner of Dune and Prime in Las Vegas. He won James Beard Awards as Best Chef: New York in 1996 and as Outstanding Chef in 1998. He has studied under such Michelin three-star chefs as Paul Bocuse, Paul Haeberlin, and Louis Outhier. While chef of the Lafayette in New York City, he earned a four-star review from the *New York Times*. He is the author of several books. (http://www.jean-georges.com)

Alice Waters is the legendary founding chef-owner of Chez Panisse and its Café in Berkeley, California. In 1984, she was inducted into the Who's Who of Food and Beverage in America and in 1987, she was one of two non-French chefs on the Gault et Millau Guide's list of the world's top ten chefs. In 1992, she was named Chef of the Year and in 1997 Humanitarian of the Year by The James Beard Foundation. She has also authored many books, including *Chez Panisse Menu Cookbook* and *Chez Panisse Vegetables*. (http://www.chezpanisse.com)

Jasper White is the chef-owner of Summer Shack in Cambridge, Massachusetts, and was the former chef-owner of Jasper's in Boston. A graduate of The Culinary Institute of America, in 1984 he was inducted into the Who's Who of Food and Beverage in America and in 1991, he was named the Best Chef: Northeast by The James Beard Foundation. He has written two books, *Jasper White's New England Cooking* and *Lobster at Home*. (http://www.summer-shackrestaurant.com)

Janos Wilder is the chef-owner of Janos and J Bar in Tucson, Arizona. He was awarded the 2002 James Beard Award for Best Chef: Southwest. His restaurant was named one of the Distinguished Restaurants of North America in *Food & Wine*, and has been praised by *Bon Appétit, Food Arts, Gourmet,* and *Travel & Leisure*. Janos has earned four stars from the Mobil Travel Guide annually since 1989. Wilder is the author of *Janos: Recipes and Tales from a Southwest Restaurant*. (http://www.janos.com)

INDEX

Kougelhopf (Joho), 54
K-Paul's, 15, 16, 168, 248–249
Kuleto, Pat, 203
Kumin, Albert
  apprenticeship of, 97
  biography, 342
  on chefs' personality, 128
  on perseverance in bad times, 284
  on starting out, 133
  on tasting, 174
Kump, Peter, 66

L

Lafayette, 198
Lagasse, Emeril, 17, 46, 75, 194, 216,
    310
  alma mater of, 70
  on apprenticing in Europe, 105, 109,
    111
  biography, 342
  on customer service, 206
  first job of, 125
  Kale Soup, Portuguese, 29–30
  menu specialty of, 204
  on success factors, 205
  as teacher, 174
  transition to chef, 165, 168
Lamb with Mint Sauce (Pawlcyn), 56
Larousse Gastronomique, 10, 76, 252
Lasser, Riad, 94
Lazaroff, Barbara, 200, 287
Learning
  chef as teacher, 174
  continuing, 82–83, 85–86, 314
  through eating out, 245–249
  from mistakes, 269–271, 274
  outside opportunities for, 153
  from past, 51
  through reading, 250–259
  self-education, 108, 140
  to taste, 174, 175–181
  through travel, 240, 242–243
Lee, Alex, 99, 173
Lenôtre, Gaston, 86, 99
Lewis, Edna

  on African American chefs, 273
  biography, 342–343
  on early influences, 41
  first job of, 125
  on Italian food, 257
  on starting out, 141
  on tasting and seasoning, 180
Line cooks, 127, 144–145, 164, 277
Location, in opening a restaurant, 200,
    218–219
Lucas, Dione, 10
Luchetti, Emily, 46
  apprenticeship of, 105
  biography, 343
  book recommendations of, 254
  Chocolate Cake, Grandmothers',
    293
  cookbooks of, 220–221, 254
  on cooking school graduates, 82
  on early influences, 41
  education and training of, 67, 69
  hiring criteria of, 139
  on pastry work, 147, 152
  on perseverance, 275, 277, 289
  on specialization decision, 144, 275
  on trailing, 143
  on women chefs, 277
Lutèce, 16, 105, 194

M

McGee, Harold, 104, 253
Madison, Deborah, 103
Making of a Cook, The (Kamman), 14,
    79, 102
Malgieri, Nick, 66
Management skills, 164
Management systems, 168–169,
    172–173
Mariani, John, 204
Marketing. See Promotion
Martinez, Zarela, 17, 102
  biography, 343
  early influences on, 44
  Meatballs Like Mama Makes,
    317–318

  on opening a restaurant, 200
  perseverance of, 274, 275
  on restaurant critics, 278
  on travel experience, 248–249
Mastering the Art of French Cooking
    (Child, Beck, and Bertholle), 12,
    41, 45, 252
Matsuhisa, Nobu, 17, 46, 310
  apprenticeship of, 101
  biography, 343
  early influences on, 48
  perseverance in bad times,
    284–285
  Sea Urchin Roe, Spinach-Wrapped,
    in Spicy Hollandaise, 30–31
  transition to chef, 165
Maximin, Jacques, 99, 137
Meat, grass-fed, 307–308
Media
  cookbook promotion, 220–221
  culinary, 257–258, 337–338
  television shows, chefs', 310–311
  See also Restaurant critics
Medici, Caterina de, 5
Menu, 203–204, 222, 223
Metro, 280
Michelin three-star restaurants,
    108–109
Militello, Mark, on composing a dish,
    183, 185
Miller, Bryan, 278, 280
Miller, Mark, 15, 17, 18, 102, 103, 183,
    238
  biography, 343
  book recommendations of, 252
  on chefs' personality, 128, 130
  Chicken Salad, Pickled, in Aromatic
    Spices, 260–261
  on early influences, 34, 35
  on ethnic cuisine, 300
  first job of, 123, 125
  hiring criteria of, 139
  on restaurant critics, 211–212
  on tasting, 176–177
  on travel experience, 236, 239, 245
  on White House chef, 316

Culinary Artistry (Wiley; $29.95 paperback; 448 pages; ISBN 0-471-28785-7). *Culinary Artistry* is the first book to examine the creative process of culinary composition as it explores the intersection of food, imagination and taste. Through interviews with more than thirty of America's leading chefs—including Rick Bayless, Daniel Boulud, Jean-Louis Palladin, Jeremiah Tower, Jean-Georges Vongerichten, and Alice Waters—the authors reveal what defines culinary artists, how and where they find their inspiration, and how they translate that vision to the plate.

In *Culinary Artistry* . . . Dornenburg and Page provide food and flavor pairings as a kind of stepping-stone for the recipe-dependent cook. . . . Their hope is that once you know the scales, you'll be able to compose a symphony.
MOLLY O'NEILL, *New York Times Magazine*

Andrew Dornenburg and Karen Page go where no culinary writers have gone before, exploring what inspires great chefs to create new flavor combinations, dishes, and menus. *International Cookbook Review*

Culinary Artistry receives honorable mention as one of the year's best culinary reference books. . . . [It] offers insights into creative cooking.
WILLIAM RICE, *Chicago Tribune*

Dining Out: Secrets from America's Leading Critics, Chefs, and Restaurateurs (Wiley; $29.95 paperback; 368 pages; ISBN 0-471-29277-X). *Dining Out* was a finalist for the two most prestigious awards in American culinary literature—the 1999 James Beard Book Award and the 1999 IACP/Julia Child Book Award—and was cited as one of the world's best culinary books of 1998 at the World Cookbook Fair held in Perigueux, France. It is the first book to demystify the clandestine process of restaurant criticism and to unlock the secrets of a great restaurant experience.

Fascinating. . . . Illuminating insights. *New York Times Book Review*

Anybody who has ever dreamed of joining a restaurant critic's inner circle will thoroughly enjoy this gossipy, insider's view. . . . Thanks to the unexpectedly dramatic lives of the characters involved, the pages buzz with often surprising tension, humor and emotion. *Publishers Weekly*, lead starred review

An intriguing foray into the secret and powerful world of restaurant criticism.
NANCY NOVOGROD, *Travel & Leisure*

Chef's Night Out (Wiley; $29.95 paperback; 368 pages; ISBN 0-471-36345-6). *Chef's Night Out* is a transcontinental journey through 28 major U.S. cities chronicling the most beloved eateries of 100 of America's leading chefs, from Mario Batali's ultimate spot for hot dogs in New York City to Nancy Silverton's favorite taco joint in Los Angeles. You'll learn why top chefs rush to eat at Bizou in San Francisco and Uglesich's in New Orleans (and what you shouldn't miss a taste of when you're there!). The book is also a guide to top chefs' own restaurants, as they share tips on what to order and how best to enjoy the experience.

Chef's Night Out is the #1 culinary book of the year.
CHERI SICARD, www.fabulousfoods.com

An indispensable restaurant guide for cross-country chowing. *Bon Appetit*

If you've ever wondered where the likes of Charlie Trotter or Paul Bartoletta go for a pleasant dining experience, tune in tonight as we welcome Andrew Dornenburg and Karen Page, authors of *Chef's Night Out.*
MILT ROSENBERG, "Extension 720" on WGN Radio

The New American Chef (Wiley; $29.95 hardcover; 448 pages; ISBN 0-471-36344-8). In this groundbreaking book that comprises a virtual international cooking school, Andrew Dornenburg and Karen Page interview a Who's Who of leading culinary authorities—from top chefs like Mario Batali and Rick Bayless to award-winning cookbook authors like Nina Simonds and Paula Wolfert—who share their insights into 10 influential cuisines and distill the essence of each cuisine into lessons that will make anyone a better cook—no matter what they're cooking.

Dornenburg and Page collaborate successfully once more, bringing together the international inspirations that today's chefs draw from in one handy volume . . . [A] deceptively thorough guide to the values, tastes and methods that form each cuisine.
Publishers Weekly

Preparing good food is an act of love, which comes through on every page of *The New American Chef*.
DR. ROBERT MULLER, Retired Assistant Secretary General of the United Nations and Nobel Peace Prize nominee

An invaluable reference.
PATRICK O'CONNELL, chef-owner, The Inn at Little Washington in Virginia

A groundbreaking work. . . . Fresh, vital, and immensely interesting.
MICHAEL ROMANO, chef-partner, Union Square Cafe in New York City

The New American Chef thoroughly demonstrates that the zeitgeist of modern cooking in this country has shifted to the various ethnic influences that make up our populace. This glorious work literally sings with the excitement of what is our own culinary make-up: diversity, passion, exuberance, intrigue, and spice. You will be well served if you study these pages!
CHARLIE TROTTER, chef-owner, Charlie Trotter's in Chicago